Repositioning the Missionary

Pacific Islands Monograph Series 24

Repositioning the Missionary

Rewriting the Histories of Colonialism, Native Catholicism, and Indigeneity in Guam

Vicente M. Diaz

CENTER FOR PACIFIC ISLANDS STUDIES

School of Pacific and Asian Studies

University of Hawai'i, Mānoa

UNIVERSITY OF HAWAI'I PRESS • Honolulu

Library of Congress Cataloging-in-Publication Data
Diaz, Vicente M. (Vicente Miguel)
   Repositioning the missionary : rewriting the histories of colonialism, native
Catholicism, and indigeneity in Guam / Vicente M. Diaz.
     p. cm. — (Pacific islands monograph series ; 24)
   Includes bibliographical references.
   ISBN 978-0-8248-3434-0 (cloth : alk. paper)
   ISBN 978-0-8248-3435-7 (pbk. : alk. paper)
   1. Catholic Church—Missions—Guam—History.   2. San Vitores, Diego
Luis de, 1627–1672.   3. Chamorro (Micronesian people)—Guam—
Religion.   4. Guam—Colonial influence.   I. Title.   II. Series: Pacific islands
monograph series ; no. 24.

   BV3680.G8D53 2010
   266'.296709032–dc22

                                        2010009970

⸙ Maps by Manoa Mapworks, Inc., and Cartographic Services, Research School of
⸙ Pacific and Asian Studies, The Australian National University.

Design by University of Hawai'i Press Design & Production Department
Printed by The Maple-Vail Book Manufacturing Group

This book is dedicated to you who seek socially just political futures from Native cultural pasts in that battlefield and promised land called academia.

Editor's Note

Pacific studies has advanced significantly in recent years with its emphasis on Islander agency, local voice, indigenous epistemologies, and ethnographic analysis. The field, however, continues to suffer from an intellectual isolation that tends toward provincialism, and an analytical framing that is too often binary. This characterization is especially true for histories and ethnographies of those islands labeled as Micronesian. Things will soon be changing if Vicente M Diaz's *Repositioning the Missionary: Rewriting the Histories of Colonialism, Native Catholicism, and Indigeneity in Guam* is any indication of the future direction of scholarship from the area.

Diaz demonstrates an acute awareness of the ways in which colonialism works through representational and narrative strategies. His ultimate concern is the cultural and historical study of indigenous identity construction. In this history of the efforts to canonize Fr Diego Luis de San Vitores, the late seventeenth century Spanish Jesuit priest who brought Catholicism to Guam, Diaz writes of an island people who engage in complex, layered, and sometimes conflicted ways with imperial entities and institutions. While hegemonic forces and their local agents press the case for the canonization of the martyred San Vitores by demonizing and silencing the natives who took his life, Diaz sees the Chamorros of Guam as reading a proliferation of meanings into the Spanish missionary's death. This proliferation of meanings makes possible the incorporation of Catholicism into Chamorro culture. For the historian, recognition of these multiple meanings necessitates a careful reconsideration of Matå'pang, the chiefly slayer of San Vitores, and of the histories gathered in support of the missionary's canonization. Diaz argues persuasively that the rewriting of colonial history entails an acknowledgment of the complex and messy ways that Natives engage systems of power to their advantage and their detriment. He sees these engagements as transforming both native cultures and foreign systems.

Repositioning the Missionary is a rich, innovative, deeply nuanced, and self-conscious study. Diaz's interdisciplinary approach uses history, anthropology, and literary criticism to promote the rediscovery and inclusion of indigenous forms of discursive analysis. This commitment to the foregrounding of indigenous forms of critical discourse is a distinctive feature of his work—one that allows him to establish communication with like-minded scholars across disciplinary and regional boundaries, and around such issues as culture, history, race, gender, sexuality, and spirituality. There is an intellectual honesty to Diaz's work that is compelling. While committed to the recovery of indigenous political agency, he does not shy way from the tensions, contradictions, and ruptures he finds in the local as well as colonial histories of San Vitores. Diaz is acutely attentive to the complexities and politics that surround accounts of the missionary's death. Impressive as well is his respectful analysis of the contestation and ambivalence on Guam that still surround the person of San Vitores. Diaz gets well beyond four centuries of presumption about the demise of Chamorro culture to show an island people actively and creatively engaged with forces that have sought to remake them. In short, Diaz has repositioned the missionary, in a manner that allows for the reemergence of a Chamorro cultural history.

An early reviewer of this work, Vicente Rafael of the University of Washington, commented on the joyfulness and play that infuse Diaz's writing, and on the seriousness of purpose that underlies it. He finds much to celebrate in this original and lucid work. The Pacific Islands Monograph Series joins in this celebration. We believe quite strongly that *Repositioning the Missionary* will prove a seminal study in the field of Pacific studies—one that promotes a long overdue, mutually enriching conversation with other historical and culture studies projects.

DAVID HANLON

Contents

Illustrations

Acknowledgments

ACKNOWLEDGMENTS in a book can be likened to the acts of humble recognition, expressions of joyful gratitude, practices of soulful meditation, and even delivery of hopeful petition that comprise that other vital discourse called prayer. The litany here, in no way a protestation of anything, begins properly with the Creator, and then the Blessed Mother, my patron saints and guardian angels, and finally, the ancestors and the spirits of the places covered in this book.

Onward to more temporal matters and to more human beings. I want to thank the following people who provided commentaries on earlier drafts of the whole manuscript: Lawrence Cunningham, Greg Dening, Christine DeLisle, Phil Deloria, Greg Dowd, David Hanlon, Robert Kiste, Rodrigue Lévesque, Lamont Lindstrom, Susan Najita, Vince Rafael, Dean Saranillio, and Teresia Teaiwa; and those who read specific chapters: June Howard, Gina Morantz Sanchez, Damon Salesa, and Amy Ku'uleialoha Stillman. Of this particular bunch, Cunningham, Hanlon, Deloria, Rafael, Stillman, and Teaiwa deserve special recognition: Hanlon's patience kept me in the game, while Deloria recognized the form of the final essential book in the penultimate manuscript. On the sidelines, Cunningham, Rafael, Stillman, and Teaiwa cheered, and pushed me, when needed.

Because of this book's provenance as a doctoral dissertation (at the History of Consciousness program at the University of California–Santa Cruz), I also must thank my mentors, James Clifford, Donna Haraway, Gary Lease, and Noel King, and of course former classmates, many of whom have become lifelong friends: Elena Tajima Creef, Vivek Dhareshwar, Ron Eglash, John Hartigan, Mary John, Yves Labissiere, Nancy Luna-Jimenez, Lata Mani, Ruth Frankenberg, Glen Mimura, Marita Sturken, Teresia Teaiwa, and Raul Villa.

I also cannot forget those who mentored me earlier, who first set me on my intellectual voyage of critical analyses. These include Professors Michael Shapiro, Manfred Henningson, Glenn Paige, and James Dator at the University of Hawai'i–Mānoa (UHM) Political Science Department; Tom Dinnell and Luciano Minerbi at the UHM Urban and Regional Planning Department; Joe Tobin, Pat Couvillon, Hidetoshi Kato, and Wimal Dissanayake at the East-West Center, and Diane "Metgot" Strong and Robert Sajnovsky at the University of Guam.

Most of the research occurred in bursts, over the past three decades, at the University of Guam Richard T Flores Micronesian Area Research Center. Former directors Don Rubinstein and Hiro Kurashina, and research faculty Marjorie Driver, Fr Tom McGrath, and Dirk Ballendorf were especially supportive. I am also grateful to Elaine Concepción, Lavonne Guerrero-Meno, Rose Hatfield, Lou Nededog, Carmen Quintanilla, John Sablan, Chilang Salvatore, Monique Storie, and Rose Tosco for their technical assistance.

In Guam, the list of those to thank is like a long procession, and I ask forgiveness if my memory fails me in recognizing a patron or two. My study relied heavily on interviews and conversations with the late Msgr Oscar Lujan Calvo, his sister Aunty Mag, Frank Agualo, Archbishop Anthony Apuron, Fr David Quitugua, Deacon Joseph Barcinas, Juan Borja Dueñas, Engracia "Acha" Dueñas Camacho, Maria "Tita" Leon Guerrero Mesa, Eduardo Siguenza, and John Benavente. Fr Juan Ledesma, SJ provided important perspective as the compiler of San Vitores's *Historico Positio*.

Dangkulo na si Yu'os ma'åse' to Robert A Underwood, Laura M T Souder, and Penelope Bordallo-Hofschneider, whose critical scholarship first inspired me. Thanks also to Guam's revered historians, the late "Doc" Pedro Sanchez and Rev Joaquin Sablan, and to Tony Palomo. I am especially indebted to the members, writers, and staff of the Guam Political Status Education Coordinating Commission (PSECC) with and for whom I had the pleasure of working. My years with the commission grounded and corrected my thinking about many things, and I thank former PSECC Director Katherine Aguon and Chairman Tony Palomo for their leadership. Joey Muñoz is responsible for bringing me on board.

At the University of Guam, where I taught Pacific history and Micronesian studies, I received solid support from administrators, fellow faculty, and students. President Wilfred Leon Guerrero hired me, and John Salas took care of me. Deans Remington Rose-Crossley, Culley Carson-Grefe, the late Joyce Camacho, Helen Whippy, Mary Spencer, and Jeff Barcinas always supported my research. My understanding of Guam and Chamorro culture, history, and politics was deepened by discussions with the following colleagues: Rosa Palomo, Benit Camacho Dungca, Jose Cruz, Marilyn Salas, Arlene Salas, Peter Onedera, Anne Hattori, Evelyn Flores, Lilli Iyechad, Joe Babauta, Rick Castro, Vivian Dames, Gerhardt Schwab, Nick Goetzfridt, Bill Wuerch, Becky Stephenson, Gary Heathcote, Jim Sellmann, Robert Rogers, Dick Wytenbach-Santos, Don Shuster, Don Platt, and the late Pete Patacsil. Former students in my history of Guam classes might recall some of this book's central claims. As graduate students in Micronesian studies, the following individuals gave feedback to portions of earlier chapters: Nicole Santos, Kayoko Kushima, Maria Yatar, Vince Diego, Betsy Kalau, and Kelly Marsh. I cannot recall the Mangilao years without thanking Joseph and

Tony Perez, Angel Petros, and Moses Francisco at the Robert F Kennedy
Library, and Rudy Villaverde, Joseph "Jojo" Perez, and A J Tiong at the
Computer Center.

In the wider community, both on and off the island, I want to acknowledge the intellectual support of Michael Perez, Faye Untalan, Miget Bevacqua, Ron Stade, Laurel Monnig, and Joakim Peter. On Guam, the following
individuals were also caring supporters: Bert Unpingco, Tony Lamorena,
the late Angel Santos, the late Ron Rivera, Judy Flores, Cecilia "Lee" Perez,
Chris Perez Howard, Debbie Quinata, John Benavente, Ed Benavente,
Michael Phillips, Leland Bettis, Manet Dueñas, Toni Ramirez, Hope Alvarez-Cristobal and Andy Cristobal, Ron Teehan, William Hernandez, Al
Lizama, José Garrido, Patty Garrido, Phil Alcon, Herman Crisostomo, Kim
and Simeon Kihleng, Martha Dueñas, Tez Perez, Dazdo Dueñas, Frank
Rabon, Leonard Iriarte, Eddie Alvarez, Howard Hemsing, Carl Alerta, and
Marc Pido.

In this book the outrigger canoe and seafaring are important analytic
motifs. The Chamorro canoe builders, Rob Limtiaco and Gary Guerrero,
jump-started me in the learning process and introduced me to master navigators in Polowat Atoll, Chuuk State, Federated States of Micronesia. *Kirisou
chapwur* to those who became my own mentors: the late Chief Manipy, the
late Sosthenis Emwalu, and my canoe house brothers-in-arms Celestino
Emwalu, Santiago Onopey, Mario Benito, and Mike Emwalu. In Guam, Man-
nas Ikea took over after Sosthe's untimely passing and continues to mentor
my fellow seafarers, including Joe Tuquero, Erwin Manibusan, Ward Kranz,
Ken Perez, Gus Cruz, and Tom and Anicia Taisipic of the Guam Traditional
Seafarers Society. I am especially grateful to Lawrence Cunningham and
Frank Cruz for their inspired and dedicated leadership, and all the mem-
bers, past and present, who had made my association with the canoe house
Sahyan Tasi Fachemwaan a foundation of my life and my scholarship.

At the University of Michigan's Program in American Culture (AC), I
want to thank my colleagues in Asian/Pacific Islander American Studies
(A/PIA)—a kind of canoe itself—beginning with its visionary and navi-
gator, Amy Stillman, and its intrepid crewmembers Susan Najita, Damon
Salesa, Scott Kurashige, Emily Lawsin, Phil Akutsu, Sarita See, and Matt
Briones. A/PIA is also, as my parents would say, my *barcada,* my principal
fellow travelers, and the reason I am in Michigan. Switching metaphors,
I want to thank my "comrades" in our sister ethnic studies units for their
solidarity: Nadine Naber, Evelyn Asultany, Andy Smith, Tiya Miles, Joseph
Gone, Maria Cotera, Larry LaFountain-Stokes, Tony Mora, Jesse Hoffnung-
Garskof, and Catherine Benamou. I have received nothing but enthusiastic support and encouragement from all my colleagues in the wider AC
community. Alan Wald, Phil Deloria, and Greg Dowd provided outstanding
guidance, and Carroll Smith-Rosenberg, June Howard, Julie Ellison, Sandra
Gunning, Penny Von Eschen, Magda Zaborawska, Matt Countryman, Jay

Cook, and Paul Andersen have been especially nurturing. Dick Meisler and Hap McCue have been the Ann Arbor equivalents of the Polowat master navigators whose experience and wisdom I consult. In the AC program, I also want to thank our staff, who have been amazing in their warmth and assistance. Linda Eggert first welcomed me to Michigan. Judy Gray, Tabby Rohn, Mary Freiman, and Marlene Moore continue to run things smoothly, with more of the same grace and style. Also at AC, I have had the pleasure of working with an outstanding group of doctoral students who have probably done more than anybody else to keep me on my toes. Among them I want to thank those who are pushing at the boundaries of Pacific Islands studies: Kealani Cook, John Low, Veronica Pasfield, Kiri Sailiata, Dean Saranillio, Lani Teves, and Lingling Zhou. Low and Pasfield, in particular, have broadened my knowledge of the first peoples of the US Great Lakes region. At the University of Michigan, Pacific Islands studies also receives rigorous treatment in the form of the Pacific Islands Workshop, founded by my A/PIA colleague Damon Salesa, and led by Stuart Kirsch, David Akin, Sela Panapasa, and the aforementioned Najita and Stillman. Pacific studies also has a very attentive and able librarian in Susan Go. These Pacific scholars have opened their homes to my family, but in this regard, my deepest appreciation goes to Kaafi and Sharon Tuinukuaafe and Damon and Jenny Salesa for the warmest (and most delicious) elements of that island-oriented hospitality.

My decision to publish this book in the Pacific Island Monograph Series was motivated by my admiration for the series and my intellectual and scholarly indebtedness to the University of Hawai'i–Mānoa (UHM). My biggest debts are to Robert Kiste, Geoff White, and David Hanlon for their stalwart support. Terence Wesley-Smith, Vilsoni Hereniko, Tisha Hickson, and Linley Chapman have been the best colleagues in a department to which I never formally belonged, the UH Center for Pacific Islands Studies (CPIS). For their heroics in the pre-production of this book, I thank CPIS Managing Editor Jan Rensel and her graduate assistant, Marata Tamaira. This book's copy editor, Jackie Doyle, ensured its readability and continued to safeguard academia's biggest secret: that even scholars make repeated typographical and other errors of grammar, diction, and exposition. *Si Yu'os ma'åse'* to Joe and Delores Taitano Quinata and James Viernes for correcting the Chamorro spellings.

I am also grateful to the following people who assisted me in finding photographs, including giving me permission to draw from their personal collections: Professors Lawrence Cunningham and Marita Sturken; Mr Bill Fliss of the John P Raynor, SJ, Library, Marquette University; Mr and Mrs David L Sablan (for permission to use his painting); Mrs Therese Carlos Santos; and Aunty Mag Calvo.

From my years as an undergraduate and graduate student at UH Mānoa, and through subsequent workshops, conferences, and meetings, I have gained the deepest appreciation and inspiration for 'Ō'iwi Maoli scholarship, particularly as it challenges mainstream academic and colonialist production of knowledge. At the UH Hawai'inuiakea School of Hawaiian Knowledge I acknowledge Haunani-Kay Trask, Lilikalā Kame'eleihiwa, Jonathan Kamakawiwo'ole Osorio, and the late Kanalu Terry Young. Across the UH campuses, Ty Kāwika Tengan, Daviana Pōmaika'i McGregor, Noenoe Silva, Hokulani Aikau, Noelani Arista, Leilani Basham, and Noelani Goodyear-Ka'opua have been important friends and allies.

Across the seas there are yet other friends and allies—new and old—whose constant encouragement, comfort, criticism, and love have kept me going. *Kalahngan* to J Kēhaulani Kauanui, Dan Taulapapa McMullin, Audra Simpson, Mishuana Goemann, Lisa Hall, David Wilkins, Dale Turner, Brendan Hokowhitu, Roger Maaka, Bobby Hill, Alice Somerville, Anna Christian, Katerina Teaiwa, April Henderson, Paul Spickard, Elizabeth Deloughrey, Virginia Dominguez, Jane Desmond, and Margaret Jolly.

I began this section by acknowledging the Creator, and spiritual and temporal friends and ancestors. I end it by recognizing my extended, virtual, and immediate *familia*. At the flanks are my *compadres* and *comadres:* John and Maryann Carr, Bubba and Clarissa Artero, Tony Diaz and Yvette DeLisle, Vince Muñoz and Alicia Limtiaco, Jesse (Sholing) and Julie Martinez Perez, Gerry Dacanay, Tony Sanchez, Willie Atoigue, Randall Sgambelluri, and Melissa Taitano. Here, too, are virtual family members: Keith and Juliann Camacho, Mark and Polly Paulino, Dan and Lizzie Guerrero, and Lawrence and Cheryl Cunningham. Closer in proximity, at one side, are my immediate and extended families, too numerous to name, but who are self-identified collectively as Todos los Diazes. Todos is led by Pappy and Mammy, better feared and loved in Guam as Judge Ramon V and *eskuelan påle'* teacher, Josefina C Diaz, respectively. At the other side are members of the Juan and Maria Taitano clan (Familian Lucas), especially the Duke and Maria DeLisle branch. A subbranch particularly important to me consists of Nicole DeLisle Dueñas, Elliot Marques, and Sol, who, like me, is kept in line from above and below, respectively, by Gabriela DeLisle Diaz and Eva Pilar Diaz. Christine Taitano DeLisle (who is Nikki, Gabby, and Eva's mother) also happens to be my partner, confidante, colleague, best friend, and most valued critic. Tina has helped me through this voyage more than any other person in any other place, and for her I reserve my deepest gratitude and eternal love.

Prologue

Hagåtña Bay, Guåhan, 1662

In a transaction that can already be considered customary by this time, Chamorros aboard outrigger canoes sail out to greet the Manila-bound *San Damian*. Seventeenth-century Jesuit historian Padre Francisco García explains that the Chamorros sought to "exchange fruits and other island products for iron, knives and other articles of metal" (Higgins 1936b, 10). Indeed, a lay minister would later observe, "Iron is an irresistible attraction to the islanders, more precious than gold or silver" (Ansaldo 1971, 16).

Customary, too, are European commemorations of perceived transgressions attached to such exchanges. The first and most notorious in this part of the world is credited to Fernão de Magalhães (Ferdinand Magellan), the famous Portuguese explorer who stumbled on these islands in 1521. It was Magellan who first christened the archipelago "Las Islas de los Ladrones" (Islands of Thieves), for the alleged theft of iron and a skiff, for which he burned to the ground the first village he encountered, slaughtering some of its inhabitants (Pigafetta 1969, 60). In the twentieth century, Filipino Jesuit historian Father Horacio de la Costa wrote with tongue in cheek that the infamous moniker might be attributed to the indigenous penchant to confuse "mine for thine" (1961, 455).

But in 1662 the *San Damian* carries someone who is different, even if he is to play a similar yet larger role than did Magellan in renaming and commemorating these islands with other (at least initially) nonindigenous sets of meanings.[1] With tears streaming down his face, and feeling things "impossible to express," Spanish Jesuit missionary Diego Luis de San Vitores is initially overwhelmed by what García depicts as "the poor, naked natives, who [lived] in the path of the Spanish Galleons, [but] never enjoyed the blessings of Christianity." For San Vitores, as for successive waves of commentators, this moment of incommunicability is an epiphany, surging within "as the ship drew nearer to the islands . . . like a celestial light" (Higgins 1936b, 10). García describes it as "a volcano, that God set burning in his heart" and for which the priest falls into an "ecstasy" (2004, 96).

1

San Vitores himself says he is "moved" by pity for these Natives (quoted in Lévesque 1995, 169). Sympathetic observers have agreed that these were but alternative ways of referring to one thing: the Holy Spirit's way of revealing providence, or the working of God's hand in all matters, especially as referred to in the scriptural passage, *Evangelizare pauperibus misi te* (I have sent you to make me known to the poor) (Matthew 11:5). More than three hundred years later, as we shall see, the Roman Catholic Church would also certify this immediate message to be both manifested in, and in firm control of, the particularities of San Vitores's life and death among the Chamorros. Then, too, we will examine the power—and the costs—of this particular interpretation of San Vitores's life and times. For the moment it is enough to know that in 1662 San Vitores continues aboard the *San Damian* for the Philippines, where he will distinguish himself in the story of the Jesuit mission. Before he leaves the Ladrones, however, San Vitores vows that he will return one day to establish a mission in these, he believes, misnamed islands.[2]

Vatican, Rome, 1985

In 1668 San Vitores did return to establish the Jesuit mission among the Chamorros, a mission that also effectively commenced Spain's colonial rule (until 1898) in the Micronesian region. In April 1672, however, San Vitores was killed by an angry *maga'låhi* (chief), Matå'pang, who was chief of the seaside village of Tomhom, Guam, because the priest persisted in baptizing the chief's infant daughter against the chief's explicit warnings. The priest's body was then dumped in the ocean and was never recovered.

In the late twentieth century, San Vitores returned, so to speak, a third time, and with a vengeance. In a pontifical Mass at Saint Peter's Cathedral attended by thousands of Spaniards and some two hundred Chamorro "pilgrims," Pope John Paul II beatified San Vitores and two other Spanish Jesuits.[3] "Blessed Diego," as we practicing Catholics under the Metropolitan Archdiocese of Agaña now get to call him, is well on the road to sainthood, insofar as the ritual and juridical process of beatification is the penultimate step toward full canonization or inclusion in the Catholic Church's registry of saints. Perhaps San Vitores is even farther along the road: cases of martyrdom (like the one argued on San Vitores's behalf) have historically constituted "the surest route to sainthood" (Woodward 1990, 51). As part of the Church's "highly rational and bureaucratic" process of canonization under its Sacred Congregation for the Causes of Saints, the pope's decision to beatify San Vitores was based on the Congregation's authenticating his death as a bona fide martyrdom and its credentializing the source documentation submitted by the Metropolitan Archdiocese of Agaña in the early 1980s in support of the Cause (Woodward 1990, 51). In "elevating" him to the ranks of the "blessed," the Church now recognizes San Vitores to be venerable, but only for the faithful under the jurisdiction of the Metropolitan Archdiocese of Agaña. Therefore, parishioners under this archdiocese may now look to San Vitores as a model for imitation and may seek his intercession (*PDN* 1985g, 20). If and when he is formally canonized, attaining an even higher elevation that would recognize his presence in "the full Glory" of God in heaven, San Vitores will enjoy universal recognition as a saint (Apuron 1991). For San Vitores to be declared a saint, his proponents *now* have to demonstrate with credible documentation the workings of a contemporary miracle that is attributed to his intercession (J Ledesma 1991). Until such time, recognition and veneration of his heroics are restricted to the Church in Micronesia, but most especially the Chamorro Catholics in the Marianas.

Ann Arbor, Michigan, 2007

Repositioning the Missionary labors through histories of Chamorro cultural politics, as they labor through Native Chamorro Catholicism, as it labors through the historic and contemporary effort to make a patron saint in the US colony of Guam. Here (or there) I navigate a sea of Vatican, Jesuit, local clergy, and lay—namely Native Chamorro—interests to canonize Blessed Diego, the Spanish Jesuit who established the Catholic mission in these islands in the seventeenth century. That canonization effort was first launched by San Vitores's companions shortly after his death at the hands of Matå'pang. The initial movement consisted of collecting sworn testimonies from individuals who knew him in his fields of ministry, beginning in the Marianas immediately after his death, then in the Philippines, Mexico, and Spain—the reverse of the geographic trajectory of San Vitores's ministry. These testimonies were gathered in juridical processes in each of these locations, and the documents were forwarded to the Congregation for the Causes of Saints in Rome for deliberation. It was, in fact, a singular effort to convince Rome of the authenticity of San Vitores's reputation as a holy man whose life and circumstances of death were also singularly committed to serving God, and whose ultimate purpose was to crown him with the Church's highest honor, that of sainthood. His companions consistently described these attributes of holiness and service to God as "modest" and "selfless." For various reasons the effort to canonize San Vitores had dissipated by 1700 only to be resurrected in Guam in the late 1960s and 1970s, under the leadership of Chamorro clergy with apparent popular support, and with technical assistance from Jesuits inside and outside Rome. Vatican officials were especially enthusiastic. Recognizing that the Cause originated in an indigenous church, Rome considered the movement an additional and compelling testament to the universal truths of Catholicism. Thus, and at a historical moment when most other Pacific Islanders were clamoring for decolonization, Guam Chamorro religious leaders and their flock were joined by the island's civic leaders to seek the Church's highest honors for the individual who has been most identified, rightly or wrongly, with the political and cultural subjugation of the Chamorros.

The primary purpose of this monograph is to answer the question, "Man, what's up with that?" Why, when the rest of colonized Oceania is trying to decolonize itself, are Guam's indigenous leaders and laity celebrating the island's most conspicuous colonial figure? Why, for heaven's sake, did Chamorro Archbishop Anthony S Apuron, Order of the Friars Minor Capuchin, the titular head of Guam's Roman Catholic community, travel to Spain in 2005 to apologize for San Vitores's death at the hands of Matå'pang back in 1672?[4] Heaven, it turns out, is an important part of the multiple answers. Temporal Chamorro concerns round out the rest.

Recounted in this way, the story of San Vitores (and Matå'pang) can also be recognized as an enduring and robust sign—or, we might even say, a "canoe," and a particularly *loaded* one, in the double sense of carrying capacity and multiple meanings. *This* canoe, I contend, carries much meaning about Chamorro political and cultural history in particular, and also has the capacity to complicate studies of indigeneity in general. By indigeneity, I mean the cultural, historical, and political condition of being indigenous or native to a place, and the analytical possibilities that such an ontology or mode of being offers critical scholarship and political movements. This book, then, is a cultural and historical study of indigeneity that considers the San Vitores and Matå'pang story as emblematic of Chamorro political and cultural history in Guam. More precisely, it examines the narrativization—the discursive or linguistic crafting or telling—of this political and cultural history, but with an eye, or ear, or whatever organ it takes, to revealing how colonialism works through representational practices, and to revealing which residual indigenous cultural and political meanings have not been allowed to circulate under an equally complex and enduring colonial legacy over the past four centuries.

This book is divided into three parts, each containing two chapters. Part One, "From Above: Working the Native," focuses exclusively on the narratological reconsolidation of official Roman Catholic Church viewpoints as staked in the historic (seventeenth-century) and contemporary (twenty-first-century) movements to canonize San Vitores, including the symbolic costs of these viewpoints for Native Chamorro cultural and political possibilities not in line with Church views. In chapters 1 and 2, I examine the theological and historiographical arguments, respectively, as postulated in *Historico Positio*, the official deposition submitted on behalf of the Cause. I argue that the terms used in making and certifying the case of San Vitores's death as an authentic martyrdom have been defined under a Roman Catholic discourse about martyrdom in particular and under an ideology of providential truth more generally. This overarching, indeed omnipotent and omnipresent, logic gives shape and form to the narrative and circumscribes the range of possible meanings allowed in relation to the San Vitores story in the Marianas. I argue further that the labor expended to demonstrate the credibility of the documentation and the veracity of the event mirrors the labor expended to make the theological case, and that their combination constitutes a discursive working on Native agencies to produce the saint in ways that mirror the more general social and political history of colonial subjugation by way of negative historical and cultural representations of Natives. Of the official imperatives examined in this part, we might say that through a determined discourse of martyrdom, the beatification of San Vitores "works" the Native to produce a saint, in efforts at reconsolidating official or canonical Roman Catholic viewpoints and hierarchies. Furthermore, this colonial operation helps us understand similar foreclosures in Guam's Native political and cultural pasts, presents, and futures.

Part Two, "From Below: Working the Saint," shifts attention and perspective to local, competing forms of Chamorro piety. If the effort to canonize San Vitores works the Native to produce the saint, Natives also rework the saint to negotiate new cultural and social canons for themselves, in ways that produce new meanings for their island. At the very least, Chamorro investments in San Vitores, through local legends, devotional rituals, and memorials and shrines, represent a proliferation of meanings and possibilities of and for Chamorro and Catholic cultural and political life. This explosion of meanings lies in stark contrast to the will to arrest or contain the possible meanings of San Vitores as witnessed in the first part of the book. Shifting grounds and perspectives, the chapters in this section call attention to differential Chamorro social, cultural, and political investments in Catholicism. Chapter 3 thus follows historic and contemporary stories and devotional practices centered on the exact spot in the seaside village of Tomhom, Guam, where San Vitores is believed to have been killed. The stories and practices at this spot render it an important portal through which we are permitted to see other cultural, political, and historical narratives typically overlooked by official Church rituals and practices. Chapter 4, "Traffic on the Mount," also locates itself in Tomhom, and concerns itself with the heightening and intensification of meanings as they battle for control over San Vitores's legacy among the Chamorros, or over Chamorro investments in San Vitores, for the cultural and political meanings pivot around who gets to occupy the subject position of the narrative. Though transnational and transcultural in character, the economic, political, and cultural stakes that are "staked" in Tomhom Bay also describe competing indigenous Chamorro histories of "localizing" ideas and practices that originate from beyond their shores. In addition to ventilating these competing narratives, I scrutinize their uses and abuses as modes of narrativizing Guam's cultural and political pasts and presents.

Part Three, "From Behind: Transgressive Histories," shifts a third time, from official and lay Roman and Chamorro Catholic viewpoints to my own critical project of rendering alternative portrayals of this book's central agents: San Vitores and Matå'pang. In chapter 5, "Disrobing the Man: A Second Peek," I foreground the problematic of San Vitores's image and self-awareness in order to critically examine formal properties of his ministry and his demeanor. This critical project is extended in chapter 6, "Kinship with Matå'pang." Treating Matå'pang as an important mediating sign in the San Vitores story, I draw out the symbolic kinship relations between the two by first calling attention to the gendered terms of Catholic kinship that San Vitores introduced among the Chamorros in the seventeenth century. Such terms are now deployed in the twenty-first-century move by Chamorro Catholics to canonize San Vitores and in contemporary Chamorro devotion to the Blessed Virgin Mary. But particularly because of Matå'pang's impor-tance in the telling of the San Vitores story, I return to key moments in their fateful encounter for narratological clues that might provide an alternative reading of Matå'pang and the meanings he is taken to exemplify. These I find in San Vitores and Matå'pang's final moments together in a canoe in Tomhom Bay. Ending the book as I began, I close this chapter and the book's analyses proper with a meditation on Matå'pang as vehicle—more specifically, as narratological canoe or vessel—for alternative meanings and stories staked on San Vitores's legacy.

In the introductory chapter, I return more fully to the issues at stake in this cultural and historical study. Here I want to offer two caveats that underwrite this monograph. The first is that my study of Chamorro Catholi-cism focuses specifically on the island of Guam and not, in the main, on the larger Marianas Archipelago. As with the ongoing colonial history, and with few exceptions (eg, K Camacho 2005), modern historiographies of the region have also severed the Chamorro people of Guam from those of the northern islands. I recognize nonetheless that, in the interest of specificity, my analytic decision to focus exclusively on Guam risks complicity in that colonial history.

Second, for much of this book's coverage I re-create key scenes set in "original" venues for both dramatic and analytic purposes. The interest in drama stems from what I take to be historical moments that are in and of themselves dramatic, the likes of whose value as performances for historio-graphical purposes in Pacific studies have best been treated by Greg Dening (1996). Simultaneously analytical and dramatic, the storytelling mode is also deployed to help provide a graphic impression of the matter and stakes at hand. Moreover, the analytical and theoretical interests also stem from a critical assumption that the facts of cultural and political history are always produced through tension between the formal properties of narrative acts and practices in the present on the one hand, and identifiable historical and political forces acting on them on the other. Furthermore, the crafting of such re-creations allows me to highlight, in storytelling mode, the tensions evident in the transhistorical and transcultural forces that I also see always at work in the production of "local" and "Native" discourses in addition to the reverse, that is, the profoundly local and Native influence over such ambulatory forces. The similarity between this freedom to move about in narrative and God's omnipresence through his omnipotence is not lost on me, but I prefer to liken it more properly to that historical convention of storytelling called "the novel," first seized on around the sixteenth or seventeenth century in Europe and since then utilized quite productively the world over. Though employing novel-like tactics, this book is not a novel, nor is it merely fiction. Nonetheless, it is specifically with this power and for these purposes that I present to the reader a conscious tactic of lacing into the re-creation bits of information and knowledge taken from historical and geographic settings long and far removed from the setting at hand. For the same reasons stated above, I also move freely between the past and present tense in my descriptions. Being in, or at least transiting in and out of, narrative or storytelling as a kind of epistemology is central to my project (Dhareshwar 1989).

Manila, 20 June 1665

In a letter to his superiors in which he pursues the topic of returning to establish a mission among the Ladrones, San Vitores provides this interpretation of the spectacle of canoes that had surrounded his Manila-bound ship three years earlier in Hagåtña Bay: "[The *indios*] came out to meet our vessels, tacitly to tell us the grave charges which will be made against us for leaving them in their blindness, we who come to bring the light to the Gentiles" (quoted in *Positio* 1981b, 279). In this passage, San Vitores plays on his superiors' conscience, of their duty to proselytize the heathen. The passage even reminds us of the role of missionary work in justifying and consolidating the Castilian empire. But perhaps unwittingly, as well, San Vitores's invocation of indigenous motives alludes to the presence of Chamorro desires for expanding their own horizons through exchanges with the other men aboard this ship. As San Vitores is the first European to formally establish a permanent presence when he returns in 1668, his legacy since then serves as a canoe, a vessel, from which we can view the political dimensions of Chamorro cultural continuity and construction as they wend their way through encroaching systems, systems that sought similarly to establish their own permanent presence in these still-misnamed islands.

Introduction

Ann Arbor, Michigan, July 2007

This book queries the multiple and competing cultural and political stakes—things potentially won, and lost—in the historic and contemporary effort to canonize the seventeenth-century founder of the glorious (or notorious) Spanish Catholic Church on Guam. Why have modern-day Chamorros revived the effort to canonize San Vitores? More pointedly, what does the effort tell us about highly political processes of indigenous cultural and identity construction and historical consciousness, particularly in highly colonized places like Guam? Does it express only the acculturative forces of colonialism—in particular, the tragic demise of indigenous society at the hands of foreign forces? Or might the movement also reflect the remarkable ability of Native culture to survive, even if by adopting or adapting to elements from beyond the island's shores? Should we lament or celebrate the Cause, and are these the only viable "positions" we can imagine in relation to it? These questions—and the frames of analysis used—derive from an intellectual and political genealogy forged at the intersection of several interdisciplinary fields, namely Pacific area studies, Native Pacific studies, and a composite form of cultural studies (formed in relation to postcolonial studies and feminist studies), especially as they have been "triangulated" into an emergent academic field called Native Pacific cultural studies.[1] Though there are by now many strands, the "field" of cultural studies in its most basic self-understanding posits cultural phenomena to be the central site of and for the articulation and rearticulation—the "cobbling together," as Stuart Hall has theorized—of structures of power as they interpellate or recruit groups of people by appealing to their social and cultural identities and practices.[2] Not phenomenally "given," as (once?) understood in anthropological definitions, however, the culture concept in cultural studies requires critical attention to how culture and identities are produced historically in relation to structures or discourses of power, such as capitalism, imperialism, or modern-state formations. For example, how are culture and identity produced through colonial discourses, including

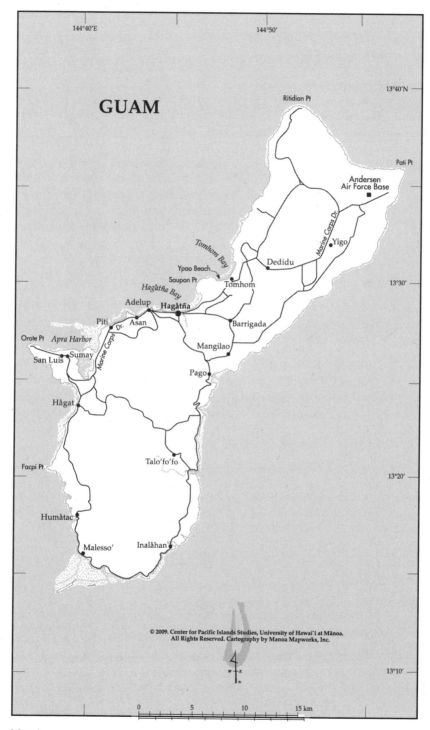

GUAM

Ritidian Pt

Pati Pt

13°40'N

Andersen
Air Force Base

Marine Corps Dr.

Yigo

Tomhom Bay

Dedidu

Ypao Beach
Saupon Pt
Tomhom

13°30'

Hagåtña Bay

Adelup

Hagåtña

Piti

Asan

Dr.

Barrigada

Orote Pt

Apra Harbor

Marine Corps

Mangilao

San Luis

Sumay

Pago

Hågat

Facpi Pt

Talo'fo'fo

13°20'

Humåtac

Malesso'

Inalåhan

© 2009. Center for Pacific Islands Studies, University of Hawai'i at Mānoa.
All Rights Reserved. Cartography by Manoa Mapworks, Inc.

13°10'

0   5   10   15 km

Map 1

"post" colonial discourses, or through new forms of oppression in the wake of anticolonial and nationalist achievements of political independence from Western or Asian powers?[3]

These questions are intensely personal for me. A Chamorro writer once described herself as being, like most Chamorros, "born and raised a Catholic at the same time that [she was] born and raised a Chamorro"; I too was born and raised a Catholic on Guam, despite the important fact that I am not indigenous Chamorro.[4] In fact, I grew up among indigenous Catholics whose islands continued to struggle against similar historical and political forces. Later in this introduction, I will return to my personal and intellectual stakes, and to a host of auxiliary questions and projects that are staked on this study; for now, I want to highlight the story of indigenous Catholicism on a heavily colonized island. First I give an overview of the island's political history, framed generally by the predicament of indigenous cultural survival through competing colonialisms. Next, I provide a shorter overview of the centrality of San Vitores's mission in this colonial legacy. Finally, I conclude with the other intellectual and political stakes in the Chamorro Catholic story, including the implications for critical scholarship forged in relation to Native Pacific studies, Pacific Area studies, and cultural studies.

Guam: "Where America's Day Begins"

Guam, or Guåhan in the vernacular, is the southernmost island in an archipelago renamed the "Marianas" by San Vitores in 1665 in honor of the Blessed Virgin Mary and the reigning monarch (and his benefactress), Queen Mariana de Austria (Driver 1972, 41). In his writings, San Vitores indicated he clearly felt that the Chamorros did not deserve the name Ladrones, though the archivist Rodrigue Lévesque surmised that his renaming of the islands "was a smart political move that won [Queen Mariana's] patronage for this new mission" (Lévesque 1995, 276; San Vitores quoted in Lévesque 1995, 63). As the largest and most populated island in the archipelago—and, significantly, because its presumably most powerful *maga'låhi*, or chief, Kepuha, first welcomed San Vitores and would later provide key military support for the missionaries—Guam, and its "principal" village, Hagåtña, would become the seat or capital of the Spanish outpost from 1668 to the end of Spain's rule in the Marianas in 1898, following the Spanish–American War with the United States. Since 1898, American colonial officials, and for a brief stint during World War II, Japanese colonial officials, would follow suit in keeping Hagåtña the island's capital (map 1). In the century and a half before San Vitores established the mission and a colonial station for the Crown in 1668, Guam (and the Mariana Islands) had been visited, sporadically at first, by European explorers and traders

(Barratt 1996). After Miguel Legazpi in 1565 formally claimed the island for Spain and launched the transpacific galleon trade that connected the Americas with Asia through the Philippines, ships and their cargo in the Marianas began to increase with relative regularity (Barratt 1996), despite galleon captains' and entrepreneurs' protestations over the numerous typhoons and the treacherous seas, and, in due time, their perception of the Natives as conniving and duplicitous in their (own) desire for iron and other goods.

The coincidence of Spain's desire to convert the so-called heathens and to establish a colonial outpost, both to protect the missionaries and to address Crown needs in the *imperio* (empire), is captured in the Spanish term *reducción* (reduction), referring to the evangelical and civilizing impulse, which also revealed the ideological and theological bases of the Crown's reason for existence: it was not for temporal secular motives but for God that the Crown justified and legitimized its existence (Del Valle 1972; Driver 1988; Velarde 1987). It would not be long before the combination of spiritual and political differences between Spaniards and Chamorros—and differences among Chamorros in addition to differences within the "Spanish" side—would also spell trouble for San Vitores and his companions. In fact, the start of the misnamed "Chamorro–Spanish War" (misnamed in that there were as many Chamorros killed among those who supported the padres as among those trying to oust them) is typically associated with San Vitores's bloody death at the hands of Maga'låhi Matå'pang in 1672. The war is foundational in canonical narratives of Guam's cultural and political past inasmuch as it is said to represent, tragically or heroically, the complete termination of indigenous life in favor of a subjugated, Hispanicized, peasantry.[5] Policies during this period included the relocation and socialization of converts into new communities, called *barrios*, first organized around a chapel and out of which grew parishes organized spiritually and socially around a church dedicated to a patron saint. In time, the parish's Catholic calendar also came to express indigenous cultural values and principles. An especially important transformation was the gradual displacement of the "traditional" social and political powers that Chamorro women enjoyed through a system of matrilineality (if not matriarchy), whereby an individual's title and access to resources were obtained through his or her maternal lineage. In such systems, the principal male figure of authority was one's mother's highest-ranking brother, and not one's mother's "husband." Moreover, children "belonged" to their mother's clan and not to that of their biological father. This system was challenged directly in the padres' efforts to institutionalize the sacrament of matrimony, which began a gradual if not insidious process of subordinating matrilineal relations beneath patrilineal, and eventually, patriarchal, social and political systems (Cunningham 1984, 1992, 2005; B Palomo 2000; PSECC 1996a; Rogers 1995, 75; Souder 1992, 54; Thompson 1941, 100). I return to this historical displacement in later chapters. Such changes were direct outcomes of numerous measures to ensure "constancy" or guard against converts' slipping back into paganism, and particularly aggressive campaigns to conquer "hostile" or "rebel" Chamorros. The result of the successful *reducciónes* of the Chamorros has, in the canonical narrative, led to results that have been received ambivalently, even in the eyes of observers who sympathize with the mission project: if the conversion of the Chamorros succeeded, it came at a great price. Between the drastic changes in lifestyle, military skirmishes, and, especially, diseases against which there were no immunities, the pre-mission Chamorro population for the entire archipelago collapsed from an estimated 100,000 individuals on the high end (Carano and Sanchez 1964), or 30,000 to 40,000 on the low end (Cunningham 1992; Hezel 1982), to fewer than 4,000 by 1700. The fact that the Jesuit effort in the Marianas constituted the first Christian mission in all of Oceania, and the reality of the tragic legacy, motivated anthropologist Douglas Oliver to issue his famous and problematic observation, "The rape of Oceania began with Guam" (1979, 334).

Guam's subsequent history and historiography is basically one of benign neglect and obscurity—the term "sleepy backwater" recurs in present-day popular and even academic press to describe Guam and the Marianas between the start of the eighteenth century and end of the nineteenth century, right up to the Spanish–American War of 1898. As a result of that war, the United States took Guam (it would later pay Spain), and Spain sold the northern islands, and its other Micronesian "possessions," to Germany (Farrell 1994). This ultimately racist characterization of the Marianas (as a sleepy backwater) is said to derive from the archipelago's geographic distance from Spain, or its supposed "remoteness" and "insularity" from any other center of social or economic significance, and its size, which was erroneously characterized as diminutive.[6] About thirty miles long and four miles wide at the waist of its footprint-shaped contour, Guam is actually the single largest landmass in all of Micronesia. The epithet also reflects the low regard colonial officials and visitors had for the indigenous people, whom they typically pathologized as semi-civilized, "mongrel" peasants.[7] Indeed, the Marianas, and Chamorro society, are typically depicted as sites of ruin and annihilation (Olive y García 1984, 3), stagnation (Sullivan 1957, 97), and amnesia (Russell 1998, 13). Alternatively, they are depicted as sites of the tragic "loss of innocence" (Rogers 1995, 4), where the typically miserable conditions were compounded by natural disasters (such as typhoons and earthquakes), and almost mitigated by an occasional reform-minded colonial governor, or by the sporadic visits of other European and American whalers and traders, especially in the nineteenth century.

Politically separated from their cousins on the northern islands, the Chamorros of Guam after 1898 had to live under a new colonial ruler in the United States and saw their island slowly transformed into a coaling station and US Navy military outpost. Where Chamorros (and resettled Carolinians) in the northern islands experienced sufficiently different histories under German, and later, Japanese, rule, the Chamorros of Guam were subject to what is stereotypically characterized as the benevolent rule of a paternal US Naval government, headed by a commander who doubled as a colonial governor, with a new one appointed every two years. From 1900 until the Japanese invasion and occupation of the island in December 1941, the navy's basic policy was to maintain a naval station and modernize (read: "Americanize"; see K Camacho 1998) the Chamorro populace through basic education and vocational training (Bevacqua 2004; R Underwood 1987); public-works projects such as road building (Diaz 1998); and health and sanitation (DeLisle 2001; Hattori 2004). Modernizing and civilizing, via Americanizing, effectively meant "the work of regeneration" (*Guam Newsletter* 1911a, 1). But until the outbreak of World War II, naval colonial officials were still lamenting that their efforts had not fully succeeded. Modernization and Americanization didn't have the traction that US officials thought they should, especially among the common folk, who seemed to prefer speaking the Chamorro language to speaking English, and who appeared more interested in their supposedly "sleepy" ways of subsistence farming, fishing, and hunting. The navy also repelled, or at least obstructed, and at times absorbed local elite agitation for political reform.[8] Moreover, the navy's process of Americanization did not include granting American citizenship (Bordallo Hofschneider 2001; Dames 2001), but rather consisted only of a benevolent and paternalistic effort to "modernize" the "mongrel."

But the "Americanization" of the Chamorros (and the quest for US citizenship) received a big boost from the Japanese. The Japanese invasion, and especially Chamorro memories of the brutal occupation, accomplished in less than three years what US Naval officials could not do in almost fifty, and what took the Spanish padres almost three centuries— that is, they fused the Chamorros to their colonial overseer, with religious zeal and cultural prescriptions of gratitude and loyalty. Indeed, the bloody American recapture of the island in 1944 was almost universally regarded by grateful Chamorros as an act of liberation, understood in religious terms of salvation and redemption.[9] Despite an oral and written archive of dissatisfaction, complaints, and outright refusal to comply when it came to the postwar military government's indiscriminate land grabs, Chamorros were deeply grateful, and thus were forged feelings of loyalty and kinship to "Uncle Sam" for "liberating" them from a Japanese occupation consistently remembered as cruel and brutal (K Camacho 2005; C T Perez 1996; Souder 1989). Yet again, despite these sentiments of loyalty and patriotism, members of the Guam "Congress," an advisory body that in fact had no legislative powers, staged a "walkout" during one of its sessions in 1949 to protest the absence of democratic rule and the tyranny of military governance (Hattori 1995). The wire services reporting this "revolt" in the very backyard of a country that espoused the principles of democracy and self-determination resulted in widespread national and international coverage. This, perhaps more than any other factor, led directly and quite rapidly to the passage of the Guam Organic Act of 1950, which established home rule; clarified and defined, for the first time, Guam's political status as an unincorporated territory (a status that limited the reach of the US Constitution in favor of congressional plenary powers); transferred executive oversight of the island to a civilian department (the US Department of the Interior); and, finally, conferred on Chamorros in particular a special, circumscribed, form of legislated US citizenship. Under American hegemony, the passage of the Organic Act is celebrated as a significant political milestone within a political teleology of gradual democratization (Skinner 1997). Other "milestones" include the 1962 lifting of the US military's requirement that everyone undergo security clearance for passage in and out of the island, and, in response to new rounds of local agitation by Guam's political leaders in the 1960s, the implementing of a succession of more federal laws that permitted Guam to send a nonvoting delegate to the US Congress and to hold gubernatorial elections beginning in 1970. Subsequent federal legislation, again in response to local Chamorro political clamoring, sought to resolve the issue of Guam's colonial status—an issue that still remains unresolved. These local and federal activities resulted in a series of political plebiscites (1976, 1982), a constitutional convention (1976) whose pro–United States constitution was defeated (1979), and a short-lived movement (1982–late 1990s) to change Guam's unincorporated-territory status to an enhanced commonwealth status that included provisions sympathetic to the specific cause of Chamorro (as opposed to "Guamanian") self-determination.[10] In the late 1990s, this movement was killed by "Bush-league politics," a local reference to former President George H W Bush and his administration's refusal to entertain Guam's wishes (Ada and Bettis 1996).

From the late 1960s to the late 1980s, Guam experienced one of the world's fastest rates of economic and social growth and transformation, owing principally to contemporaneous Asian development and especially to the wild success of a tourism industry that catered to Asians—primarily Japanese young adults—but also Korean and Taiwanese honeymooners and other youngsters, seeking fun, sun, sex, and duty-free shopping on American soil. Subsistence farming and fishing from the prewar days was replaced almost overnight by a cash-based, wage-earning consumer economy, while ancestral lands became real estate, and English was mastered at the expense of the Chamorro language, which soon lost status as the island's lingua franca. Following the 1980 census results, Chamorros for the first time found themselves totaling less than 50 percent of the island's resident population, although they remained the single largest "ethnic" group, followed by Filipinos, Asians, Caucasians, and other Pacific Islanders. In 1960 there were 34,762 Chamorros (52 percent) and 32,282 non-Chamorros (48 percent). In 1980 there were 47,845 Chamorros (45 percent) and 58,134

FIGURE 1. Felixberto C Flores was the first Chamorro to be ordained a bishop and, later, an archbishop in the Roman Catholic Church. Flores championed the effort to canonize San Vitores, and died one week after San Vitores's beatification in 1985, leading one observer to remark after his death that Guam now has a second "intercessor" in heaven. Photo courtesy of Dr Lawrence Cunningham.

non-Chamorros (55 percent). In 1990, there were 57,648 Chamorros (43 percent) and 75,504 non-Chamorros (57 percent) (Rogers 1995, 273). The 2000 census showed the continued downward spiraling of the proportion of Chamorros, with the Chamorro segment of the population dwindling to 37 percent.

It is an understatement to say that these demographics have been noted by Chamorros themselves.[11] As early as the 1970s, the more critical and outspoken had begun to openly question the narratives of loyalty and obedience to the United States, while the more militant began to articulate Chamorro social and cultural concerns about Guam's political status as a colony that had (and still has) yet to exercise the right to self-determination (Alvarez-Cristobal 1990; M P Perez 1997; Perez-Howard 1993; Rivera 1992; Souder and Underwood 1987). As mentioned, these sentiments informed a series of nonbinding plebiscites and political referenda in the late 1970s and 1980s that led directly to efforts to change Guam's political status to that of a commonwealth, a proposal that included measures such as the call for a future exercise of Chamorro self-determination (as opposed to self-determination for "Guam"); local (Government of Guam) control of immigration; and a "mutual consent" clause that prohibited Guam or the United States from taking unilateral actions (Ada and Bettis 1996; PSECC 1993a, 1993b, 1994, 1996b). This political clamoring was a direct response to what is generally understood to be the chaos of modernization, specifically as informed by liberal American values, including the opening up of the "floodgates" of immigration and Chamorro emigration (R Underwood 1985).

In this milieu, the island's Catholic Church hierarchy, now known as the Metropolitan Archdiocese of Agaña (composed of twenty-some parishes), stepped up its efforts to shepherd modern-day Guam and Chamorro culture through the turbulence. Said Archbishop Felixberto C Flores in 1974 (figure 1), "I am extremely concerned about the possible disappearance of our language and culture" (quoted in *Pacific Voice* 1974a, 1). The Chamorro Catholic force, augmented by a predominantly Catholic Filipino community (Diaz 1995a; de Viana 2004), can be viewed as the heir apparent, the spiritual, political, and cultural descendant of Padre Diego Luis de San Vitores.

The Mission in Guam's Historiography

As the founder of the Catholic mission in an archipelago whose inhabitants have the dubious distinction of being the first recipients of a Christian mission in the Pacific Islands, and thus having the longest experience of all Pacific Islanders of enduring the yoke of foreign domination, San Vitores occupies a privileged position in both the history of the Marianas and in the history of Christianity in the Pacific. The story of the Catholic mission figures so prominently in the general history of Guam that it prefigures, as I argue in this book, the range of narrative possibilities and limits of Guam's imagined cultural and political realities. As the late "Doc" Pedro Sanchez, coauthor of Guam's first modern general history, used to say, Catholicism in Guam is "more than just religion"—which is to say that it is also a political and cultural force in the lives of the Chamorros and other residents of Guam (Carano and Sanchez 1964; P Sanchez 1989, 416).

Despite continued characterizations of the island as remote and insular, Guam continues to be an important outpost for colonial excursions, for instance in the massive US military buildup for its global "war on terror" following 11 September 2001.[12] The island's cultural politics will continue to implicate global forces that since 1565 have established the island and region as important sites for their machinations. Indeed, Guam has been an important, if often overlooked or underappreciated, site of global forces, both Western (Spanish and Roman Catholic, followed by American) and Asian, notably Japanese imperial interests during World War II. Since the mid-1970s, Chinese, Taiwanese, and Korean businesses have also invested heavily in this piece of "American soil." As Ron Stade aptly demonstrated in his critical ethnography of Guam's cultural politics (1998), the island has long been subjected to larger "worlding" forces, such as those requiring a fundamental rethinking of the spatiality and valences that comprise the competing layers of "local" Chamorro cultural articulation. In Guam, one finds not the classic remoteness and insularity that is supposed to deliver the specificity and particularity of cultural alterity on which modern anthropology cuts its teeth; instead, one finds the complexity of creolized culture forged out of centuries of intercultural mixing as the principal form of indigenous social and cultural articulation.[13] In fact, Guam has been a particularly important crossroads for an assortment of multinational and multiethnic interests, all of which have left indelible imprints on the island's social, cultural, political, and natural topographies. Guam was an important stopover for the so-called Acapulco–Manila galleon runs between the Americas and Asia from the sixteenth century to the second decade of the nineteenth century. From the seventeenth to the twentieth centuries, Guam was a fertile field for missionizing, led first by a band of Jesuits actually composed of multinational and multiethnic individuals.[14] In the nineteenth century, Guam was an important watering hole for American and British whalers and traders. In the past four hundred years, Guam has become a new home for immigrant Filipinos, and since the end of World War II (and especially during and since the last quarter of the twentieth century), for citizens of the so-called Freely Associated States—the Federated States of Micronesia, Republic of Palau, and Republic of the Marshall Islands. These histories of "globalization" challenge conventional definitions of indigeneity based on presumptions about cultural purity and insularity, without losing important dimensions of indigenous political and cultural alterity or difference.[15]

Native Catholic Personal Spiritual Stakes

The discrepancy between the island's more cosmopolitan history and cultures and those described in canonical historiographies and cultural analyses motivates a second set of questions, which are staked on the story of San Vitores's canonization: How does a critical interrogation of this story, including the processes by which he has been canonized, raise alternative ways of understanding and narrating the cultural past, especially cultural processes like conversion, or even warfare? What do the multiple and competing meanings manifest in the movement to canonize San Vitores—indeed, the very meanings of San Vitores himself—tell us about the indigenous past and present? What do they tell us about indigeneity and about the epistemologies and traditions that have been forged in relation to it and its histories, including the histories of European and American colonialism and political and cultural subjugation? How might we begin to understand indigeneity (which might be defined as the historical condition of being indigenous to a specific region or place and claiming aboriginal status in it) as an indigenously oriented and driven product of complex and often extremely messy entanglements with nonindigenous peoples, places, ideas, and things? How do such histories offer specifically indigenous modes of narrating and analyzing political and cultural pasts and presents? How do these processes shape how we think and understand Native spaces and places? Much as devout missionaries were driven to faraway places to convert, or relocate, "lost souls," returning them to their "proper" place under God, people from these faraway places have sought to localize new ideas and practices (such as Christianity) within indigenous ways of life. In examining the official and popular stakes in the contemporary and historic effort to make San Vitores a saint for the Chamorros, I query the cultural and political stakes and thereby raise new questions about the history and historiography of mutual but unequal appropriations and displacements between Natives and Christianity in the Marianas. To understand the stakes in the effort to canonize San Vitores is to comprehend Spanish Catholic and Chamorro historical and cultural desires to convert—or to "contract," as Vicente Rafael has argued of Tagalogs (1993)—the foreign and dangerous into the familiar, the pleasurable, and the valuable. Indeed, the effort to canonize San Vitores involves the historical and political task of constructing, guarding, and transgressing the boundaries between the categories of indigeneity and exogeneity, the local and the global, and tradition and progress, among a host of other terms usually understood as mutually exclusive and logically or inherently oppositional. But the historical and contemporary effort to

canonize San Vitores can furnish us with the materiality to begin to imagine alternative forms of historical and cultural understanding and analyses
here in the islands, or there, wherever this book happens to finally wash up.
Through this study, I aim to share a sense of the complexity of what might
otherwise appear to be simple stories of local faith, or, alternatively, the sim-
plicity of complicated cultural and historical entanglements between local
and global forces.

Such a feeling of and for the simultaneously overdetermined and inde-
terminable cultural conditions as they transgress time and space runs
through the subject matter. The effort to canonize San Vitores fuses the
systematicity of hagiographic scholarship (devoted and devotional writings
about the lives of saints) within a highly formal juridical procedure in the
Vatican's Congregation of Saints, with a rich set of stories bellowing from
"below," that is, from a local, vernacular, observant Catholic community
on the island. For the hybrid nature of this process, and for the interest in
rewriting the cultural and political history of the Native Catholic Church
on Guam along more fluid grounds, I find myself also tacking between the
apparently systemic and the whimsical, the academic and the popular, the
theoretical and the descriptive. Thus, there is also something admittedly
transgressive and disruptive about my objective. Indeed, from the conviction that no single group of people, no one epoch, practice, theory, or
method, holds a monopoly over intellectual and critical sophistication and
commentary and access to truth, I hope to re-fuse these and other restrictive
distinctions as they are theorized and practiced in rituals such as historical
scholarship and cultural critique, and in things such as books. Moreover, I
am driven as much by a desire to be true, as it were, to the polymorphous
realities encountered here as by a desire to reach the equally diverse audience that comprises my personal, intellectual, and political communities
on Guam and far away. How does one write for an audience that ranges
from scholars and professional intellectuals on one side to friends in the
islands on the other side who never attended college, or that ranges equally
from Natives exquisitely literate and brilliant on wide-ranging topics, and
scholars remarkably ill-informed about matters Native? How does one write
for such a diverse range of readers who are nonetheless bound by their
refusals to abandon their respective claims to truth and reality? Tacking
back and forth between the seventeenth and twentieth centuries, between
the local tale and the global commentary, between the indigenous and the
exogenous reality, between theory and story, this study hopes to articulate—
to cobble together—the cultural and political weight of the historic attempt
to canonize San Vitores, in order to render a more nuanced understanding
of indigenous cultural and political traditions.

That the historic and contemporary effort to canonize San Vitores is led
by his spiritual kin also helps us understand the movement's political stakes
in particular, and the stakes that undergird larger efforts to build identity

and community on the basis of faith in general. Indeed, the current effort to canonize San Vitores constitutes one such virtual voyage of indigenous individual and collective self-fashioning, especially as these adhere to fundamental ideas about good and bad, right and wrong, true and false. The effort to make Blessed Diego a saint—to register his membership in an official list of Church heroes and heroines—involves a historical attempt by a deeply entrenched Roman Catholic Church (begun by Spanish Jesuits; followed later by Spanish, German, and American friars; and led now by religious and secular Chamorro clergy[16]) to galvanize a long-standing bond with the Chamorro people of Guam and the Marianas. But insinuated in the Native clergy's sponsorship and leadership is the latent interest of the faithful to rediscover and maintain, rather steadfastly, crucial aspects of what is commonly taken to be "traditional" Chamorro culture and identity. In what is locally referred to as *kostumbren Chamorro* (Chamorro custom or culture), Chamorro "tradition" features a *familia* system that finds expression in a wide variety of Spanish Catholic rituals such as the *nubena* (novena, or nine-day devotions), the *lisåyu* (rosary), and *fiestas* (feasts) honoring village patron saints (Crumrine 1982; Hinnebusch 1967; McGrath 1985, 5; Meagher 1967, 543; Souder 1987, 8). In celebrating the beatification of Blessed Diego, for instance, the late Most Reverend Felixberto C Flores, DD, the first Native Chamorro archbishop in the Roman Catholic Church, wrote:

[The beatification] brings to reality a dream the people of the Mariana Islands have prayed for. These islands . . . have retained many features of Spanish Catholicism. Fiestas in honor of our patron saints for each village, public processions, rosaries and novenas are all woven into our cultural traditions. All of these are a part of the legacy that Blessed Diego and his successors brought to us—the people of the islands they converted. Today the faith that Blessed Diego brought to the islands is embraced by virtually all the local population of the Marianas. (F Flores 1985, 1)

Although the late archbishop articulated the deep bond between Chamorro culture and Spanish Catholicism, it is crucial to bear in mind that not all have dreamt about or prayed for, much less embraced, the faith brought by Blessed Diego.[17] And, moreover, one must keep in mind that those who did embrace Catholicism did so under a range of political and social forces, coercive and noncoercive, in ways that force us to remember that the benefits, opportunities, and costs of conversion to Catholicism were not always the same, and were not always the same for everybody. While some Chamorros converted (and did so enthusiastically), others did not. Some profited; others lost out. We must also keep in mind that Chamorros did not necessarily view their conversion to Christianity and their Chamorro sense(s) of self as mutually exclusive. Still, following Flores above, we might view the effort to canonize San Vitores as emblematic of a historical intercourse between the indigenous Chamorro people and Spanish Catholicism, a deep bond that constitutes a significant part of the indigenous Chamorro bid for continuity and survival. If Native political and cultural continuity finds expression within the very intrusive systems typically viewed as hostile toward local tradition, the results can be surprising.

As unlikely as it may seem to supporters and detractors alike, the contemporary movement to canonize Blessed Diego has political and cultural kinship with an upstart Chamorro cultural nationalist movement for political self-determination and cultural stewardship. The movements are coconspirators. Whereas vocal supporters of the cause to canonize San Vitores tend to be conservative Catholics who also favor Guam's status as a US possession, and detractors regard San Vitores as the key symbol of foreign conquest and hostility, there is nonetheless, or all the more, something of a pious alliance between "traditional" Catholic views and a nascent Chamorro cultural and political nationalism in the face of common foes: liberalism and modernity.[18] In Guam these are synonymous with "America," which in turn is synonymous with the United States, and which in turn is stereotypically cast as the archenemy of traditional island Chamorro values and customs. At the same time, however, Chamorro Catholicism can also be understood as something of an heir apparent to the social and political regime instituted by San Vitores and company. This has included, as we shall see, an active suppression in the seventeenth century of Chamorro elements that resisted vigorously, for a time at least, the presence of the new order. These tensions are still evident in Guam today, particularly when Chamorro Catholic missionary impulses collide with Chamorro missionary impulses invested in other systems.

Missionary Impulses in Pacific Studies

In this intellectual and political milieu, which is not unlike that of other islands in the contemporary Pacific, any assertion that Chamorro (or any island) culture and tradition has been made or remade—the more contentious term is "invented"—deserves explanation.[19] Indeed, scholarly claims about the invention of island culture or tradition through colonial materiality have not been well received by Native Pacific scholars and activists (to put it mildly). Infamous, for instance, was the heated exchange between Hawaiian activist, scholar, and poet Haunani-Kay Trask (1991) and the late anthropologist Roger Keesing (1989, 1991).[20] Hovering nearby and entering the fray were other anthropologists and other Native and non-Native Pacific Islanders whose scholarly and heated exchanges raise the academic and political antes in Pacific cultural and historical critique.[21] In that particular exchange, Keesing bemoaned contemporary Pacific nationalism, lamenting the inauthenticity of these (more recent) invocations of culture and tradition in the service of the distinctive political agendas of metropolitan elite intellectuals and activists (1989). Trask responded that anthropologists are threatened by Native political expression and empowerment over issues of culture and identity. She asserted that such claims (about the inventedness of culture and tradition) are simply new forms of old-fashioned (academic) racism and colonialism in the islands (Trask 1991). Keesing, later rejoined by another anthropologist, Jocelyn Linnekin (1991b), protested that he was sympathetic to and boasted an honorable track record of champion-ing Native struggles, particularly those outside mainstream, metropolitan, and educated elite circles (Keesing 1991). Trask rebutted anthropologists' presumption of affiliation and solidarity with Native Islanders by invoking the joke about Tonto's reply to the Lone Ranger's anxious question when the two find themselves surrounded by restless Natives (Trask 1999, 123): "What do we do, Tonto?" asks the Lone Ranger. Tonto replies, "What do you mean *we*, white man?"

Islander activists and intellectuals have reacted vehemently against such critical claims by white, expatriate scholars, and have regarded their analy-ses of cultural invention as hostile denials of the legitimacy of indigenous cultural and historical agency, as disavowals of specifically Native claims to cultural decolonization, or as efforts to reconsolidate white, academic authority amid the historic proliferation of discourses about indigeneity (Diaz and Kauanui 2001; G White and Tengan 2001). On the other hand, nonindigenous Pacific scholars have lamented efforts or strategies to reg-ulate, curtail, or appropriate scholarly and academic inquiry for political or ideological purposes. For a variety of reasons, I choose not to dwell on the exchange, other than to suggest that it reveals the intensely contested nature of scholarship in the contemporary Pacific.

More important, these changes reveal the theoretical and political necessity of moving past the invention paradigm and replacing it, provi-sionally, with a framework that pays attention to the historical *articulations* of indigeneity. Drawing from the work of the British cultural studies scholar and activist Stuart Hall, Teresia Teaiwa (2001a, 2001b) and James Clifford (2001, 2003) have each demonstrated the usefulness of viewing Pacific subjectivities as articulated in relation to colonial, neocolonial, and post-colonial forces, but in ways that do not posit purity or authenticity, and, more importantly, do not sacrifice the essentially concrete and enduring indigenous determinations that often get lost or theorized away in other critically minded paradigms (Diaz 2006). One way to illustrate a theory of Native articulations is to historicize the processes of conversions to Christi-anity in terms of Native agencies whose investments in Christianity tactically invert and then displace canonical narratives. These articulations invert the story from "what outsiders do to Natives" to "what Natives do to outsiders" (Hanlon 2001) in ways that reverse and thus unsettle commonplace ideas of conversion as a one-way process (Rafael 1993). What get displaced in the unsettlement are prevailing historical, cultural, and political ideas about colonialism, Christianity, and indigeneity. What get unsettled, too, are the big ideas about history, culture, politics, and analyses themselves.

The Critique of Chamorro Catholicism

The ongoing history of Chamorro conversion to Catholicism signals the transformation and the multiplication of indigenous notions of personhood and community. Following Vicente Rafael's seminal study of early Tagalog conversion to Christianity in the Philippines (1993), Chamorro submission to Catholicism can be shown to be simultaneously a colonial process of rearticulating Spanish Catholic ideas and practices and circumscribing its colonizing reaches in socially layered ways—ways analogous to those by which Tagalogs rearticulated themselves through engagement with Christian doctrine and rituals. As part of the Church's effort to remain pertinent, if not strengthen its position, in places like Guam, the effort to canonize San Vitores can also be seen as an arduous indigenous journey to reconsolidate Chamorro culture and identity through Spanish Catholic doctrine and rituals. This journey continues into the twentieth and twenty-first centuries a legacy of colonial and counter-colonial practice, now rearticulated in relation to American (and Asian) patronage and influence in the region. The effort to canonize San Vitores expresses a longer and deeper Native history of invoking and honoring ethereal beings such as patron saints, especially Santa Marian Kamalen, the local Chamorro manifestation of the Blessed Virgin Mother, and participating in a host of other Church rituals and practices (Iyechad 2001; Jorgensen 1984; Poehlman 1979). As a powerful expression of traditional culture over the last three centuries, Chamorro investment in San Vitores also reflects contemporary anxieties over the nature and character of Guam's economic and social development, especially against what are perceived to be the debilitating effects of modern America on Chamorro society, most especially on family values.[22] But these self-conscious, "redemptive strategies" (as James Clifford has observed of such discursive and "spatial practices" employed in modern ethnographic writing and fieldwork [1988, 99; 1997]) are also subverted from within Native Chamorro investments in other intrusive systems. Nonetheless (or all the more) at stake in the effort to canonize San Vitores is the maintenance of the Catholic faith's privileged position in the makeup of Chamorro and Guam culture. Especially since the end of World War II, there has been a conspicuous articulation between Catholicism and Chamorro culture, a particular indigenous formation of local society that understands it to be the only real antidote to the social ills of modernity found in Guam's rapid economic and social growth. The making of a "San" Diego is underwritten by this formation.

Saints—as Chamorro Catholics and others believe—are spiritual beings in the presence of God. They are residents of heaven, of paradise, of a place not like earth but better, insofar as earth is filled with loss (Rafael 1993). Saints are individuals recognized by the Catholic Church to have been inspired properly by God. They lived lives of virtue, or died heroic deaths of martyrdom; that is, they gave their lives in the unselfish service of God and Church, gifts that Christ himself is taken to exemplify perfectly. Saints are heroes and heroines, powerful friends in God's presence. Their lives are seen as inspirational and exemplary, but their intercessory powers can also provide material and temporal favors and assistance for those who seek them, especially in moments of crises. Saints, we might say, reflect and refract earthly images and concerns.

Other "Saints": Genealogies as Histories

Born and raised on Guam, although not of indigenous Chamorro ancestry, I was named after both my grandfathers. Vicente Diaz and Miguel de la Concepción were Natives of the Philippines and of the Micronesian island of Pohnpei, respectively, and were converts to Catholicism in the late nineteenth and early twentieth centuries. Both converted to Catholicism, in their respective cultural and historical situations, for deep spiritual and temporal, even political, reasons. My maternal grandfather, Miguel, was one of the first Pohnpeians from Wone, in the chiefdom of Kitti, to convert to Catholicism at a time when, as David Hanlon recounted (1988, 186), the Catholic and Protestant missions were themselves the objects of intense political interest and opportunity by warring Pohnpeian factions. Miguel's mother, a member of the powerful Dipwinmen clan, was baptized Teresita.[23] In 1887 she left for the Philippines, a year ahead of her son, and died of an unknown illness before his arrival there. In the Philippines, Miguel was raised by the last of the Spanish Capuchins, though their plans for his religious vocation were thwarted when he fell in love and married my grandmother. Still, his devotion and loyalty to the last vestiges of Spanish Catholic rule in the Philippines were such that when he died he was allowed to be buried in the hooded cassock by which the *Capuchinos* are recognized worldwide.

Hailing from the Philippine province of Ilocos Sur but raised in the province of Zambales, my paternal grandfather, Vicente, was a self-educated man whose father, Hilario Diaz, was an *herbolario*, or folk healer, who tended to and idolized noted figures like José Rizal and other *ilustrados*, the cadre of liberal and "enlightened" men who "fathered" Philippine nationalism and political revolution (Rafael 1989). Like his father, Vicente also joined and quickly moved up the ranks of Philippine Masonry—"the archenemy of the Catholic Church" (Calvo 1991). Unlike his father, who as a *provin-*

ciano (someone from the province) did not have the means to receive a liberal education abroad, Vicente was able to parlay his self-education into advanced degrees and to become a school principal, and later, an executive assistant to the parade of American governors during the territorial period. As an adult, Lolo (grandfather) Vicente converted to Catholicism, because, family tradition has it, this was the only way that my grandmother would agree to marry him. Unlike Vicente, whose pedigree was provincial and *indio,* Lola (grandmother) Bibiana was a proud *mestiza,* which in our family tradition translates to a fierce self-suppression of one's indigenous heritage. But because Vicente was educated, and because he eventually rose in the ranks of the Catholic Church (in the Knights of Columbus), my grandmother always referred to him (with a wave of her hand) as different from the rest of the *indios* or *provincianos.* So pious became this particular *indio* that his daughter-in-law (my mother) described him as a veritable saint. Indeed, Vicente Diaz and Miguel de la Concepción bequeathed intense traditions of faith and piety to their respective sons and daughters, the likes of which would make their Spanish Catholic namesakes proud, even though neither of these men were Spanish and they became Catholic only later in life. For these reasons, my parents, uncles, and aunts passed on the faith to the next generation, whose upbringing in an increasingly Americanized Guam only intensified the faith's hold as antidote to the social ills on Guam.

I grew up, then, in this milieu: Catholic schools, lives of saints, and—ringing in my ears—the maxim that "a family that prays together, stays together." With prayers, too, came admonitions not to act like a *provinciano,* even as I grew up away from the Philippines. Today, a family that once prayed together struggles to stay together within a modern island context that exerts profound pressures and imposes challenges on traditionally tight-knit clan systems. Such developments tax a family with a staunch Catholic pedigree: six sisters named after the Blessed Virgin Mary, three brothers named after saints, a father who was among the first married men on Guam to be ordained a deacon in the Catholic Church, and who initiated and administered a Sunday-evening televised program, *The Family Rosary Hour,* for nearly two decades. My mother, now approaching her ninetieth birthday, continued to teach *eskuelan påle'* (padre's school, or catechism class) until she was in her seventies. If it is not surprising that the themes of Natives, converts, and saints would come to occupy privileged positions in my upbringing, it should also be understandable that they would comprise inextricable elements of my analytic, political, and intellectual project.

This project is also fundamentally transcultural: In Guam, where my parents relocated after the war, and where I was born and raised, I grew up among other families—Chamorros, Filipinos, other Micronesians—with similar histories and values. Because I was born and raised on Guam, and because of the similarities between my heritage and that of Chamorros, Chamorro grew to be a surrogate culture. Despite my appearance and accent, it often comes as a surprise to many people with whom I grew up that I am not Chamorro. But just as I do not identify myself as Chamorro, I also do not intend to make definitive claims of expertise in Chamorro culture and history. At the same time, I do not want to relinquish organic claims to the common and kindred history of indigenous political and cultural struggles in relationship to Spanish Catholicism and liberal Americanism that I see among Micronesians, Filipinos, and Chamorros.[24] How can this insider/outsider status and my own Asian Pacific Islander, and yes, American, Catholic genealogy "work" to access and understand Chamorro political and cultural history as articulated in Spanish Catholic and liberal American impositions? How can it assist me in comprehending the Spanish Catholic and liberal American histories of my own genealogies? Can Chamorro people (and other folks on Guam) learn as much from me as I have learned about myself through this study of their cultural history? For historical reasons, such as ease of travel to and from the island, immigration, and the infusion of American cultural ideas and institutions, my own histories, values, and beliefs—like those of my Chamorro neighbors, and, increasingly, other Filipino and Micronesian neighbors—have been challenged profoundly. Still a firm believer in saints and prayerful petition, I ask: What indigenous desires underwrite the effort to canonize San Vitores? What model of living and dying does he provide? But equally important: What cultural models of living and dying does the Catholic hegemony of that veneration—whether Roman or Chamorro Catholic—directly and indirectly preempt? In one sense, this study stems from a deeply personal desire to comprehend my own cultural and historical traditions by way of understanding other Islanders' interests in making a saint for themselves. One might say I am both a historical anthropologist and a kind of missionary, assigned to a particular "field" and reliant on specific archives, except that the latter are also my homes; but I am not an anthropologist, much less a priest, notwithstanding the intensity of my convictions about the history and cultures of Native struggles for self-determination.

Thick Veneers

A central objective of this study is to pursue the politics of indigenous articulation and historical narrativization. A secondary goal is to offer a fresh interpretation of cultural change and continuity in Chamorro political history. The literature on cultural change is immense. So, too, is the field of mission history. Yet there is also a venerable tradition of understanding Native Catholicism as folk or syncretic.[25] Often identified with so-called peasant classes or societies (I prefer the term "subaltern") in Central and South America, the Caribbean, Africa, and Melanesia, syncretism is generally regarded as a form of acculturation—Fernando Ortiz prefers the term "transculturation" to describe the two-way flow and impact—whose Native essence is accessed through a figural peeling away of a veneer of Western Christianity.[26] To describe transculturalisms such as Chamorro Catholicism in Guam, I coin the oxymoron "thick veneer." Thick veneer describes those cultures whose histories of interweaving (Flores's description of Chamorro culture and Spanish Catholicism) yield no clearly demarcated layers or boundaries of what is and is not Native, in analytic favor of attention to historical and cultural processes of simulation with(in) Christianity. Thick veneer religiosity and spirituality entail historical layerings of Native and non-Native realities that allow us to sense separation and difference, and profound cultural fusions that simultaneously befuddle any attempt at demarcation or disaggregation. The history of thick-veneer cultural production also allows us to witness what we might call the "ferocity of indigeneity." In the historical context of near genocide that characterized the Spanish–Chamorro Wars of 1671–1694, where radical alterity—radically different customs and practices that are nonetheless understood to be paganistic, infernal—could very well get you killed, those Chamorros who did not initially side with the Spaniards could survive only through eventual processes of simulation and identification. In this context, making the sign of the cross could have meant unburdening oneself of the priest and his soldiers. The sign of the cross literally meant the possibility of life in the here and now (eternal life, in this case, can be appreciated as a nice perk). Where fight and flight, confrontation and fugitivism, reached their strategic limits as oppositional modes of encounter and survival, those recalcitrant Chamorros made a tactical turnabout, and proceeded to embrace Catholicism as a practical if not more successful bid at survival than the resort to arms or feet. Describing a "great change" that overcame the Natives, Jesuit historian Father Charles LeGobien in 1700 equated the "docility" of the Natives with their "embrace" of Catholicism (1949, 125).[27]

In the late seventeenth and early eighteenth centuries, following if not illustrating the profound social changes that came in the wake of the Spanish–Chamorro Wars, we might say that the thickness of the veneer described the intensity of the subsequent interweaving of Christian and non-Christian values and practices. Recalcitrant Chamorros realized the need to relocate Native cultural and spiritual practices (especially those that were denigrated and demonized by the padres) to someplace safe, somewhere they could not be identified and finally destroyed. I think that Chamorros took these values and beliefs with them into the new residential and social sites that the conquistadors built specifically to relocate Natives in efforts of colonial management and surveillance. In Spanish, the term for the theocratic ideology was also the term for the administrative policy of relocation: *reducción*.[28] But the Spanish process of reducing Natives to Catholicism was simultaneously the Chamorro process of reproducing indigenous spirituality and values. In the barrios that became parishes, in the new Catholic calendar of rituals and practices, Chamorros found refuge within the Catholic Church. The refuge can also be seen as a virtual "inoculation" against the Church itself, as Rafael has demonstrated of Tagalog discourses of conversion (1993). This history is illustrated well in the ways that the physical structures of the parish churches, *conventos,* and missionary schools served as literal refuges in times of natural disasters like typhoons (which were understood in providential terms by Spaniard and Native alike) and not-so-natural disasters, like enemy invasions. However, from the seventeenth century to the present, the historical record is also replete with complaints by priests, colonial officials, and ignorant visitors of the superficiality—at best, the "inconstancy"—of the Native brand of Catholicism.[29] Writing in 1700, the French LeGobien observed, "There are Chamorros who embrace the Christian religion and submitted to the Spaniards. But many of them had done so for their interests . . . they wept in secret . . . and only awaited a favorable occasion to vent their hatred and resentment" (1949, 128).

My leading questions about conceptualization are accompanied by questions of approach and method: What narratives and practices can count as concrete evidence for these ideas? "Doc" Pedro Sanchez's evocation of Guam Catholicism as more than "just a religion" involved historiographical concerns: it is also "a major curator of the past" (1989, 416). If this is so, what better archive is there in Chamorro Catholicism than narratives and rituals of individual and collective piety and devotion? One example of the archival nature of Chamorro piety can be seen in stories of its intensity or, in reverse, its superficiality, as observed by visitors since the seventeenth century. For instance, Jacques Arago, a French Catholic member of the Freycinet scientific expedition to the Marianas in 1819, found among the Chamorro people a "wretched" condition in which "nine-tenths" of them had "been exterminated; and that religion, which ought to have established in them peace and happiness, [had] covered them with a funeral pall" (1971, 1:268). Instead of peace and happiness, Arago found among the living a kind of intense but corrupt piety, which led him to observe, "Nowhere, perhaps, is there so much and so little religion as at Guam" (1971, 1:248). Noting the ubiquity of Catholic figures and statuettes in almost every home, and the frequency of rosaries said throughout the course of a day, Arago exclaimed, "These scenes of devotion are affecting, and would be more so, if we did not know how easily these senseless people forget their religious duties as soon as the moments of prayer are at an end" (1971, 1:246). He was also astonished at the "prodigious numbers of processions and religious ceremonies" and noted that the local observance of Passion Week was celebrated with "superior pomp and greater impositions on the people, . . . here as they [were] at Manila, and at Manila as they [were] in Spain." The "superior pomp" led him to conclude, "There is no exaggeration, I assure you," in calling the festival of Easter "the day of scandal." To Arago, Catholicism on Guam was scandalous for its superficiality and its fanaticism: "The women bestow their favors for a rosary. The men do not blush to offer you a sister, or some other of their relations, and will immediately after prostrate themselves at the foot of the altar. In the churches the two sexes are separate; and if you see few girls without a veil, you also see few men gazing at them. In church the people behave like Christians; in the city, and in the country, like savages" (Arago 1971, 1:248–250).

What Arago saw as the corrupt forms of Catholicism on Guam in the early nineteenth century can themselves serve as portals into the political and cultural histories of Chamorro Catholic interweaving and simulation. Such moments of tension and contradiction in local Chamorro Catholicism—whether figured as tenuous or inconstant, excessive or fanatical—yield insight into dynamics of exchange and encounter between indigenous and exogenous systems, into processes of cultural continuity and discontinuity. Thick histories of simulation, or histories of interweaving, reveal themselves in narratives that describe the alleged superficiality of Catholicism among the Chamorro people on the one hand, or that describe excess—or what can also be called conversion with a vengeance—on the other. And on Guam such narratives play themselves out predominantly in the *familia* system, which is the currency (to recall Arago's horror on meeting men who would offer their sisters or some of their relations) of a contested, layered Chamorro Catholic system. Or, to put it another way, the *familia* system is the shifting ground on which faith and piety, and Chamorro cultural continuity, express themselves. This is why Catholicism is not just a religion on Guam, and why the Catholic Church and the Chamorro family have enjoyed such a deep intimacy since the seventeenth century. Outside the door, or peering into the interior of a woven Chamorro culture, I wonder how best to avoid the arrogance and the error of presumption that has informed Arago and all those other non-Chamorro voyeurs of Native cultural history.

Whatever the eventual verdict, the effort to canonize San Vitores is driven by a historic tension between the Catholic Church's desire to reconsolidate its privileged position in local concerns (through the vehicles of beings such as the Blessed Virgin Mary and saints), and indigenous Chamorro cultural and political self-determination. Thus, this hagiography-in-the-making is also holographic: seen one way, it is about the heroic triumph of a seventeenth-century Spanish Jesuit. From a different angle, the hero is the Chamorro who survives five hundred years of colonization. However, the holograph is also a prism, refracting light not only on possibilities that are explicitly preempted or negated but also on possibilities that just have not been commented on explicitly. In this study, I grope for different analytical positions from which we might cull alternative meanings of the San Vitores story, meanings that might especially reveal indigenous sensibilities that tend to be occluded by official or conventional perspectives and narratives. Speaking of positions, I need to account for the title of this book, its sections, some of its chapters—and much of its wordplay.

The term "missionary position" is a colloquial expression for conventional face-to-face sexual intercourse, typically connoting heterosexual normativeness, with the man "on top." Indeed, nonnormative sexual practice can also include the missionary position. One origin for the reference to missionaries has to do with their proselytizing among Native peoples who were consistently stereotyped as lascivious and often engaged in what the missionaries believed to be unnatural and immoral sexual practices, including homosexuality, incest, lewd cultural dances, and a multitude of other activities considered scandalous, abhorrent, and contrary to proper civilized and Christian behavior. Among the Chamorros, for instance, what San Vitores believed to have been socially sanctioned prostitution caused him much pain (*Positio* 1981b, 197). All these were and are seen as fundamentally sinful in Christian, not just Spanish Catholic, discourse. One joke, from Native circles, takes the phrase as merely descriptive of the preferred and unimaginative position for sexual intercourse as practiced by the missionaries with their wives (as attested to by Native eyewitnesses). Whatever the origins of the phrase, we can be certain that most people will immediately draw some kind of mental image in their heads about sexual acts or practices.[30] This, too, is the predominant image I have in mind, except that the image is also inextricably linked with ongoing histories of the exercise of power and authority—by narrative acts and practices—over what is normative and what is not, what is right and what is wrong, and what happens to those people who are considered abnormal and wrongheaded or living wrongfully, when those in the right can muster state or other forms of power to enforce their story lines.

From the title of this book and a cursory glance at its table of contents, the reader will quickly see similar allusions to sexuality, but in terms of the exercise of power and authority: Activities from "above" reference the making of official perspectives, especially as they presume to speak on behalf of the Almighty God "on high." Narratives from "below" mark the space of quotidian, rank-and-file perspectives and realities, especially as these are, in Native studies or cultural studies, presumed to be a better place from which to comprehend how power actually operates in society. In this sense, the imagery, narratives, and practices "from behind" can be seen as deliberately and provocatively transgressive. Though it brings immediately to mind that which is colloquially referred to nowadays as "doggie style," a style that needs no further description, the multiple sexual connotations with reference to power and morality attached to the image most certainly do. Whether it references hetero- or homosexual anal sex or bestiality, the image evokes unnatural, and for many, downright repulsive, behavior. In Christian discourse, these are not only unnatural but are morally reprehensible sins against God's proper designs for the human body. In this monograph, the referencing to narratives and practices "from behind" involves

matters that consciously do not adhere to prevailing viewpoints, and sensibilities that can be defined as transgressive of them.

Much as they might seem to represent a figurative "sticking it to the man
(from behind)," however, in this monograph the actual cultural and historical materials are not largely oppositional, despite the fact that they clearly
do not align themselves with prevailing binaries.[31] Indeed, the cultural
and historical materials and practices I follow in that section come in most
instances from devotional narratives, but I pull and examine their loose
threads closely for the competing cultural and political meanings they may
reveal. My use of such sexual metaphors, then, is precisely to foreground
issues of power and authority that are fundamental to the subject matter.
Thus, such apparently sexual metaphors and idioms are more than coy sexual innuendo or indulgent wordplay; I use these metaphors substantively,
in direct reference to varying positions of authority, and counter-positions
to that authority. But precisely because religious discourse is so deeply inter-
twined with sexuality, particularly with articulating its rules and regulations
and its self-understandings in terms of what is morally wrong and right
about sexual practices, it remains virtually impossible to study and engage,
in this case, Roman Catholicism, without also quickly rubbing up against
deep views about normative sexuality (Kennedy 2001; Maguire 2004).

The specific topics in Catholicism, if not within the wider history of
Christianity, are familiar and do not require elaboration here: privileging
degrees of sexual purity as virtuous, while seeing impurity as sinful, and
holding deep views of the body as a sacred temple of God, not to be des-
ecrated or profaned. Likewise, there is a long history of sanctioned normative heterosexuality, as raised, for example, in the supposed threat that
same-sex marriage poses to the Christian-based fundamentalist view of marriage and family; the sinfulness of homosexuality and other nonnormative
practices, including marriage of priests and adultery; and even proscrip-
tions against masturbation, insofar as the body as temple of God is holy and,
for men, the wastage of sperm is wastage of God's seed. Women's bodies, in
particular, have been important sites of and for the narrativization of Catholic virtuosity and sinfulness (Eve succumbing to temptation; the primacy
of the Blessed Virgin Mary as the supreme model for chastity and purity).[32]
These, alone, speak volumes about the deep ways that Church teachings
on good and bad are engendered and heavily sexualized. There are also
the sexual-like pleasures—bliss and ecstasies—that saturate much of San
Vitores's experiences with God and the Blessed Mother, and sweet innocent
children, including adult Chamorros. For example, part of a tool kit of conversion tactics he used, called the "mini-mission," consisted of hurling holy
maxims, called *ejaculaciónes*, at the hearts of the heathen. With such *ejaculaciónes* in particular, according to his hagiographer, Alberto Risco, such
mini-missions "allayed the throbbing eagerness" that San Vitores felt in his

desire "to plant the seed of the Gospel" (quoted in Calvo 1970, 65). The "throbbing eagerness" of course referred to the intensity of his piety, which at times is referred to as "ecstasies," as when experienced during apparitions and visitations or at the precise moment of his death. Such was the particular ecstasy when San Vitores first laid eyes on such "native men," or "wild savages," whose "naked, brown, and athletic builds" were also indications of just how "tame and tractable . . . trustful, yet shy" such Natives could be, and thus, just how "attractive they appeared" to San Vitores (Calvo 1970, 73). It was in the company of such pleasingly wild men that San Vitores experienced that bolt of light that called him to evangelize these islands in particular. But these highly sexualized narratives are also sensed in desires and pleasures directed toward San Vitores by many of his companions; certainly the companionship and "male bonding" describe a homoerotic relationship whose legitimacy of course is forged by way of opposing it to the illegitimacy of homosexual love.

Through all these sexual legacies, my continued referencing to positionality also involves a critique of space and an interest in the attendant and consequent spatial practices that come with narrativization. A critique of space is a critique of vantage point and of grounds. The politics and scholarship of grounds is also articulated in feminist calls for "situating" knowledge critically in the appropriate and specific historical and social "sites" of their production.[33] In Native Pacific studies, the premium is on indigenous orientations and perspectives, located canonically in the islands and on local, specifically Native, cultural and historical perspectives as the privileged vantage point.[34] Insofar as the Native Pacific has been and continues to be colonized, then, the Native position is also one from below, a subordinated or subaltern one, particularly in relation to other Native positions that are empowered by way of capitulating to, or aiding and abetting, colonial determinations and desires. The allusions to above, below, and even behind have to do then with the vantage points privileged in the writing of cultural and political histories. In this book, I switch-hit, so to speak, and try to "ground" myself in these different positions as I seek to comprehend their essential truths as narrativized in their respective sites, or their historical, cultural, and political situations.

Part One

From Above
Working the Native

Chapter 1

The Mission Positio

THERE IS A CURIOUS inversion or circularity in the report by the Historical Commission of the Sacred Congregation for the Causes of Saints that accompanies the official *Cause of Beatification of Ven. Diego Luis de San Vitores,* hereafter referred to as the *Positio* (1981b). In a summary of the centrality and the veracity of the terms of San Vitores's martyrdom, the Historical Commission chairman, Father Agostino Amore, first writes: "The human and spiritual figure of the Servant of God, as well as the circumstances of his death, *should stand out from the [supporting] documents*" (1981, 23). Two pages later, however, he asserts that "this *documentation aris[es] hard upon the martyrdom*" (emphasis added). Though the rest of the sentence describes the importance of a *fama martyrii,* or a "reputation for holiness" in the candidate's *life,* a reputation that must persist to the present, the slippage in the text from martyrdom verified in historical documentation, to historical documentation verified through the terms of martyrdom, betrays other important layers of contradiction found in the official Church rituals used to beatify San Vitores. Whether inadvertent or not, Amore's slip reveals a fundamental back-and-forth movement inherent in the particular question of the veracity and authenticity of "true martyrdom."[1] The veracity of the event, and its authenticity as martyrdom, requires ("should stand out from") authentic documentation. Yet the terms of a document's authenticity "arises hard upon" not just "true martyrdom" but also an ongoing *fama martyrii.*

This circularity, or self-referencing, corresponds to movement that occurs at other philosophical levels, as in the tacking back and forth between a piece of evidence and the truth or truths it is supposed to corroborate by virtue of a natural or objective correspondence that is assumed to exist between them. This kind of truth-claim relationship has been challenged enough in post-structuralist analytical paradigms that we can entertain the alternative, if troubling, idea that items taken as empirical evidence for some corresponding or underlying truth are themselves constituted in and by a language or discourse that relies on that truth-claim to furnish the terms needed for understanding the meanings of that item to begin with.

This is a kind of epistemological chicken-and-egg problem for which there is probably no solution other than to displace the regime of truth or sets of assumptions about truth that underlie the perspective. My critical assumption here is that truth in and of itself is not absolute, and that evidence to establish the essential and incontrovertible truth about a phenomenon is not self-evident but must be constituted in language—and language in broader historical discourses that establish the parameters for allowing us to define and make meaningful statements about the phenomenon in question, including other phenomena in opposition to and against which it is primarily distinguished and defined. Among other things, this state of affairs also requires us to acknowledge that at some fundamental level we really are trafficking in articles of faith. But I am also not simply being reductionist: historically, there are different discourses of faith, and the differences are real and they matter materially.

This circularity then is also self-referential, and it takes place in the *Positio* at two other levels. The first level is a narratological or storytelling structural level aimed principally at interpreting the psychological character and motives of the two principal players, San Vitores and his assassin, Maga'låhi (Chief) Matå'pang, in a drama whose principal burden is to establish the authenticity of San Vitores's death as a bona fide martyrdom. The second level is historiographical, involving the documentation used to prove the veracity of the event, and will be pursued in chapter 2.

This chapter concentrates on the first question, also defined in the *Positio* as the theological question or argument. The burden of this argument is to satisfy an established theological test in Roman Catholic discourse that requires that the assassination be "religious in character," meaning specifically that it concern God directly, on the parts of both the victim and his assassin. My primary argument in this chapter is that the terms used in making the argument have successfully been defined under a Roman Catholic discourse about martyrdom in particular, but also under a more general ideology of providential truth. This overarching, indeed omnipotent and omnipresent, logic gives shape and form to the range of possible meanings allowed in the Cause to beatify San Vitores. My secondary argument is that this discursive operation results in the elision or negation of real and imaginable Native Chamorro political and cultural meanings and possibilities, both historically and in the present, by delimiting or circumscribing the range of meanings. However, as I will show in the second and third parts of this book, such official imperatives have not been entirely successful in stamping out opposition or even in controlling the multiple and competing ways that meanings about Catholicism or about San Vitores or Matå'pang are reproduced by the Catholic community of Guam for its own political and cultural purposes. Still, for the official imperatives examined in this chapter we might say that through a determined discourse of martyrdom the beatification of San Vitores "works" the Native to produce a would-be saint in efforts at reconsolidating preferred, that is, official or canonical,

Roman Catholic viewpoints and hierarchies. Further, this colonial operation helps us understand similar foreclosures, both in Guam's Native past and in past narrations of that past that continue into the present and work to delimit our future political and cultural possibilities. Whereas in the introduction to this book I stressed that the effort to canonize San Vitores also encompasses indigenous bids for cultural continuity and expression, in this chapter I dwell only on official Vatican determinations and the symbolic costs for Chamorro and non-Chamorro political and cultural history in Guam.

Amore's curious inversion marks not just the peculiar ways by which San Vitores's death is reread but also how this rereading functions to reconsolidate the Catholic Church's (waning?) position in Chamorro society (and around the globe) in the late twentieth and early twenty-first centuries. To address this, and as a framing device, I first set the lens deep and wide by surveying briefly the general significance of saints and martyrs in Roman Catholic theology, with an eye toward examining the reciprocal relationship between them and the laity, including Church efforts to maintain control over the more unwieldy or excessive tendencies in popular piety and devotion to saints. Then I focus tightly on the theological argument about San Vitores's death as one of true martyrdom and consider critically how it requires and effectuates a negative figuration of Chamorro social and cultural agency in the way that it interprets Matå'pang's motives. In the *Positio*, the certification or authentication of San Vitores's martyrdom features the antics of Matå'pang as a kind of negative witness, although other Chamorros are trotted in either as accomplices or as important supporting characters, witnesses to the murder. How is this symbolic operation accomplished in the narrative *Positio*, and what are the costs of lionizing San Vitores and demonizing Matå'pang? Using the logic and fundamentals of providentialist thinking, and via its scripting of good over evil in imitation of Christ's passion, San Vitores's death at the hands of Matå'pang is also understood as a testimony to everlasting life with God. But what futures, other than hell or purgatory, are preempted by these symbolic maneuvers—especially for those still alive?

Of Saints and Martyrs

O God, You inflamed Your Servant, Blessed Diego of the Marianas, with zeal to spread Your name and love in the Marianas, even to water them with his blood. Deign to glorify them with him at Your altars and to grant us, through his intercession, the special favor we beg of you. (McGrath 1985, 91)

The official processes of beatification and canonization entail the framing of a candidate's life story in terms of an epic holy enough to merit inclusion in a special class of beings known as saints. With Christ as their head and supreme model, and through the workings of the Holy Spirit, these men and women are certified, through long and rigorous juridical processes of beatification and canonization, to have lived lives in the active service of God through Christ. Hence, they function both as exempla for popular behavior and as spiritual friends through whose intercession a petitioner may gain comfort for, or assistance in, some earthly matter.

The term "saint" is derived from the Latin *sanctus,* which, like its Greek and Hebrew cousins *hagias* and *qadosh,* refers to a state of sanctity or holiness (Attwater 1986). For the Roman Catholic Church, saints are individuals who are recognized to have lived lives of "heroic virtue" or to have suffered "true martyrdom" (O'Neill 1967, 852). Whether by "tradition," as, for instance, with the early Christian martyrs and Desert Fathers, or by formal canonization by the Vatican's Sacred Congregation for the Causes of Saints, they are believed to live in heaven under the "Queen of all Saints," Mary, the Blessed Mother of God (Thurston 1912). Saints also belong to a larger community outside heaven. The Apostles' Creed, recited during Mass, also commemorates Christ's male followers (the apostles) as part of a "communion" of saints comprising all practicing Catholics, who profess the creed. Belief in the communion of saints as professed in the Apostles' Creed thus reveals a self-referential element for mortals: the communion of saints pertains to heroes and heroines in heaven, and their reciprocal relationship with a union of the faithful on earth (Thurston 1912). This self-referencing recalls the circular movement between evidence (documentation) and truth (authenticity of martyrdom) as betrayed in Amore's slip in the opening of this chapter, or the way in which God's truth can be verified through documentation whose authenticity relies on faith in God's omnipotence and omnipresence through his agents and the evidence of the work they do, and as mediated by the Church.

Thus, in Roman Catholic tradition, the term "saint" refers both to particular individuals (saints in heaven) who are recognized to have led virtuous lives or to have died in the active service of God, and to a wider collective, the still-living faithful, who abide by the Church's teachings and subscribe to its beliefs. "Saint," in other words, refers not just to a person but also to a series of transactions between mortals and spirits, and between historical and political processes by which these sacred relations are sanctioned by the Catholic Church.

To understand the notion of sanctity, one must appreciate its relation not only to God the Almighty but also to "the faithful in general" as grounded in Scripture. (The ensuing discussion and citations are from O'Neill 1967, 852–853, unless noted otherwise.) In the Old Testament, for instance, God is prefigured as "the Holy One par-excellence." Holiness is "His proper name that expresses His apartness and awesome inaccessibility." However distant the Creator, the notion of his covenant with Israel nonetheless served both to identify a "chosen people" and to establish a manner by which to communicate with him. The chosen people could "share in His Holiness" to the extent that they "purified" themselves, worshipped him, and obeyed his laws. The prophets of the Old Testament "spiritualized" the desire to share in God's holiness by maintaining that such a sharing required his people to separate themselves "from the profane through renunciation of sin and [through] purity of conscience."[2]

In the New Testament, the "holy nation" is "the Church," and Jesus Christ is recognized as "the Holy One of Israel." The saints are the "faithful," those who, with a "dominant personal attitude," look to Christ for everlasting life. It is through "union with Christ" that the saints "share in the divine holiness," a union that is established by a "consecration of divine service . . . in love" and perfected through a "moral effort." O'Neill wrote, "The appeal that the chosen people should be holy (as God is holy) is a plea for personal moral goodness to which no limit is placed. This holiness leads to the vision of God and to bodily resurrection with Christ" (1967, 853).[3]

The scriptural idea of sanctity, then, has two primary emphases. The first is that "it is God through Christ who takes the initiative to communicating His holiness," and second, the "holiness of the creature consists primarily in [loving] service of God, i.e., worship and observance of divine law." These are known, in Roman Catholic theology, as the "beatific vision" and "the union of charity." And although these "supernatural gifts" and "theological virtues" are "perfected in the "New Covenant" of Christ, they do not "remove the fundamental obligations of the creature to his Creator." In spite of God's holiness, and in spite of the "supernatural gifts" he gives us, humans still have a "fundamental obligation" that emanates from the relationship between creature and Creator. God gives us our lives and we are indebted to him.[4] In my Catholic-school upbringing, this gift from God was also understood as temporary, as in this line of a favorite hymn ("Pilgrim's Song"): life is "but a temporary thing, only on loan while on earth." The point is not only that our lives are on loan from God, or that life is a gift, but also that we who profess the Catholic faith have an obligation to make good on the loan.

The beatification of San Vitores hinges on the authentication of his death as one of true martyrdom. In Catholic theology, the martyr is technically a "person who has given or exposed his life in testimony to the truth of the Christian Faith." In modern teachings, martyrdom involves providing testimony, or giving "witness"—providing evidence—with willingness to suffer and die for God enjoying a special place in the quality of that "testament" (F X Murphy 1967, 312). This is the main reason that Jesus Christ's life and passion are known in Christendom as "the New Testament." Suffering, and especially death, under specific conditions and qualifications, are said to testify to the "living truth of Christ" (Gilby 1967, 315).

The modern Catholic formulation of martyrdom, like other general Catholic precepts, has roots in Greco-Roman and Judaic terms and ideas about suffering and death as signs of truth. These earlier conceptions also prefigure and inform modern and secular concerns and methods for ascertaining truth and for certifying or edifying those who will get to be classified as the secular equivalents of "chosen peoples." In Judaism, for instance, a martyr was a pious individual whose effort or labor to resist evil "perfected" that person and made him or her eligible for edification.[5] In Greek Stoic thinking, the term "martyr" concerned philosophical modes of learning and teaching. In this sense, a martyr was a philosopher who not only taught with words but also "confirmed the truth of his message by deeds," referring particularly to those who showed "indifference to the movements of passion, worldly experience, and even death." These ideas were refined and formulated by the early Church fathers. Clement taught that it was the apostles' "endurance" of suffering that proved their martyrdom, although in time that "stoic" sense of suffering endured by Christ's apostles was reworked in Christendom to be viewed finally as a "result of their faith rather than as a sign of its truth." Ignatius of Antioch introduced the idea of the "shedding of one's blood as a testimony to the truth of Christ as God." It was also he who introduced and favored the Greek terms and ideas for "discipleship" and "imitator" over the idea of bearing "witness," for he considered the martyr to be "the one who perfectly imitated Christ in his suffering and death." Ignatius also emphasized "bodily suffering" as an "antidote" to heretical teachings that denied that "Christ had a real body." Bodily suffering, henceforth, would play in Christendom, or at least in the Roman Catholic Church, a crucial function in maintaining a belief in Christ as Man–God, a contested and contentious theme over which major religions and Christian sects often went to war.

The full idea of martyrdom as a "witnessing of the belief that the life and death of Christ was that of the Son of God" is first found in the account of Saint Polycarp's martyrdom, and it would subsequently be employed in the narrativizing of "passions and legends" of martyrs of the Church, that is, the men and women who suffered and died for Christ and whose deaths were taken to be perfect testimonies to the truth of the faith. Thus were martyrs considered to be, as Cyprian wrote, "treasures" of the Church. They were "glorious," for they sat at the "right hand" of God. They were "superhuman" because their courage in the face of torture and persecution could be explained only as a "manifestation of the power of God." This also explains why the only comic books my parents allowed (ineffectively) in our house were those of the lives of saints. But whereas some early theologians "echoed" the "assurance of God's presence in the manner of deaths of the martyrs," others viewed such convictions as scandalous carelessness by pagans. Though Christians accused so-called pagan and barbarous peoples of holding such scandalous beliefs, pagan officials accused early Christians of similar zealotry (Brown 1981).

Whether paganistic or not, the discourse about martyrdom continued to

be understood and formulated in Catholic theology in terms of the workings of God and the Holy Spirit. Tertullian, echoing Hermas the Shepherd,
saw martyrdom as a "second baptism . . . which removed all sin and assured
an eternal crown." Clement of Alexandria saw martyrdom as sure entrance
into heaven because of Christ's presence with the martyr during his or her
suffering. Origen saw martyrdom as a "proof of Christianity, [since] the
Christian defiance of death was a testimony of the victory already achieved
over evil powers, and an assertion of the resurrection" of the body of Jesus
Christ.

The cult surrounding the veneration of early martyrs had a "relatively
late and slow development" in history. Early Christians, it seems, wanted
merely to give their heroes and heroines—those who died for the faith—
fitting burials in pagan or private cemeteries. But what began as attempts to
bestow fitting burials mushroomed into annual celebrations on what Saint
Polycarp called the "birthday of the martyr" or the anniversary of his or
her death. As might be expected, Catholic teachings require sharp distinctions between pagan and Christian conceptions of martyrdom, especially to
preserve what is taken to be the integrity of the faith and its truth. Whereas
Peter Brown asserted that the cult of saints, of which the cult of martyrs was
a component, did not emerge from Greco-Roman practices per se (1981),
the different origins and practices do not preclude a history of Christian
appropriation of pagan ideas and practices in bids to reconsolidate and
rearticulate Christian identity and its canon of beliefs (consider the history of All Saints' Day and All Souls' Day in the Catholic calendar). For
instance, Christians distinguished themselves from pagans by celebrating
their heroes' *dies natalis* not on the latters' earthly birthdays but on the
anniversary of their deaths, to commemorate their entrance into heaven.
At the tombs, Christians celebrated the "happy deaths," much to the disgust
and horror of pagan officials. Brown explained that Christian celebrations
on the anniversaries of the deaths of their heroes and heroines were driven
by a deep belief that such heroes "breached" the lines between life and
death and between humankind and God. It was for this reason that great
Christian places, such as Rome and the Vatican, emerged, literally, from
tombs and cemeteries.

The history of Christian appropriation of paganistic practices, and continued rivalry with pagans, contributed to the fanaticism that Christians
displayed in their pilgrimages to and venerations at the tombs. Rivalry was
also expressed internally and generated no small anxiety in the Church
over excessive veneration of a given saint's bodily remains or his or her
reliquary, especially when such excesses rivaled the worship of Christ
(Woodward 1990, 53). To guard against such slippage, and to reinscribe the
Church's authority and control, Saint Augustine shifted the emphasis from
heroic suffering and tortures to the profession of faith in Christ (the Apostles' Creed) that was *manifest* in the manner of these individuals' deaths.

For Augustine, martyrdom signaled the "perfection of . . . virtues of a life [led] in full conformity with the spiritual teachings of the Church." It was Augustine who developed the full theological concept of martyrdom still in use today: "*Martyrem non facit poena, sed causa* (It is the reason why, not the suffering[,] that constitutes the martyr" (F X Murphy 1967, 313, 312). As for how to recognize the authenticity of the suffering, or the reason for it, Thomas Gilby outlined the three conditions under which true martyrdom is certified by the Catholic Church: (1) actual physical death; (2) cause of death motivated by *odium fidei* (hatred of Christian life and truth); and (3) the voluntary acceptance of death in defense of Christianity (1967, 314).

This brief summary of the evolution of Church doctrine on sainthood and martyrdom not only illustrates the historical development of the Church's theology on the subject but also provides a sense of how that theology was forged in contested relationship with non-Christian traditions on the one hand, and with competing and even threatening traditions and practices within the Catholic Church's teachings and followings on the other. The penchant for excessive veneration by the laity, or its potential to distract from the Church's view of proper focus (on Christ), for example, is a long and enduring dilemma for the Catholic Church hierarchy. In its understanding of its hierarchy—indeed in the very process of constructing that hierarchy, which is key to the political process of centralizing authority in Rome (see Brown 1981)—Roman Catholicism is extremely conservative and fundamentalist: God is the All Mighty. Next is Jesus Christ the Son, who is also the mediator. As the "direct spiritual descendant of Saint Peter," the pope is also known as the "vicar apostolic" of Christ, or his principle surrogate for temporal matters. One way to maintain this privileged position between the temporal and material world on the one hand, and divine matters on the other, is through control over the discourse of saints and martyrs, those whose fully documented lives of virtue and deaths of heroic happiness are modeled after the exemplary story of Christ. The Catholic Church sees in the lives of saints, especially those who "gave" their lives through "loss" of their lives, signs "of the presence of God in history, of Christ's victory over the powers of evil, and of a fountain of miraculous apostolic abundance" (*Pacific Voice* 1985a, 1). Through the certification of true witnesses of the true faith, the Church reconsolidates its privileged position as the true witness for God.

Narrative Authentication of Blessed Diego's Martyrdom

In declaring San Vitores "blessed" in 1985, Pope John Paul II approved a long and complicated Roman juridical process of beatification, the penultimate step toward sainthood. In beatifying San Vitores, the pontiff accepted the findings of the historical and theological commissions of the Sacred

Congregation for the Causes of Saints, in addition to those of the Congregatio Ordinaire (Congregations of Cardinals), that San Vitores had indeed suffered true martyrdom. It was only then, and after much contemplation, that the pope decreed: "The martyrdom and the cause of martyrdom of the Servant of God Diego Luis de San Vitores, priest, professed religious of the Society of Jesus, is so unquestionably evident that a dispensation has been granted from the requirement of miracles and all other signs and we may now proceed to the further steps in this process" (*Pacific Voice* 1985a, 3). The Archdiocese of Agaña submitted the successful Cause with help from the Congregation of Saints and from the Jesuit order in Rome. Father Agostino Amore OFM served as the postulator, while Father Juan Ledesma SJ, professor of theology, served as the vice postulator. In the 1960s Ledesma was informally recruited to work on the Cause by the late Monsignor Oscar Lujan Calvo, a Chamorro priest and a former student of Ledesma's at the San José Preparatory Seminary in the Philippines in prewar days. The Cause, which is said to have commenced in four formal "processes" immediately after San Vitores's death in 1672, had petered out by 1700 but was revived formally in the late 1960s and 1970s in conjunction with the consecration and installation of Guam's first Chamorro bishop and archbishop, Felixberto C Flores. Flores sought and received formal permission to appoint Ledesma to compile the *Positio,* the Cause for the Beatification of San Vitores.

As stated in the pontiff's decree, the truth of San Vitores's martyrdom was so unquestionably evident as to grant a special dispensation from documenting miracles "and other signs" that are normally required in beatification procedures. Under post–Vatican II law, the requirement of authentic contemporary miracles is waived if the candidate is said to have suffered a martyr's death. Though waived for beatification, authenticated miracles are still required for San Vitores to be fully canonized.

The *Positio* was examined and approved by the historical and theological commissions of the Congregation for the Causes of Saints, which sent the package to the Congregation of Cardinals, which sent it to Pope John Paul II for his final approval. Its successful passage meant that San Vitores's death passed the theological test, which was also predicated on the authenticity of the assassination as a historical act, supported by credible documentation. These requirements are articulated in the executive summary of the *Positio*. Amore writes, "For a servant of God to be judged worthy for the honors of the altar, a model of life and an intercessor for the members of the militant church, it is essentially necessary to know his living human and spiritual image and circumstances surrounding his death" (1981, 23; the following discussion and quotes are also from Amore 1981, 23–35, unless otherwise noted). In line with Church teaching and procedure, the *Positio* seeks to demonstrate that San Vitores's death was in fact that of a martyr. But it also seeks to demonstrate the "authenticity and trustworthiness of the historical documentation" used. It is imperative, argues Amore in the *Positio,* that the supporting documentation be certified as "genuine," as "worthy of historical credence." This is necessary to meet the "essential" requirement of knowing fully the human and spiritual "image" of San Vitores's life and death. The supporting documentation that the Cause "arises hard upon" has to be shown to "be endowed with an amplitude, accuracy and sincerity which any historian or honest researcher can and should demand." I examine this claim in chapter 2.

Theological Correctness

With historical credibility determined, the *Positio* sets out to meet the formulaic definition of martyrdom, what Amore calls "elements which properly constitute the essence of Martyrdom." Dying a martyr's death involved circumscribing the various possible manners, motives, and circumstances surrounding the loss of San Vitores's life. For San Vitores's death to be considered a "perfect testimony and witness," it had to have been caused by *odium fidei* ("hatred for the faith") (on the part of the assassin) and "accepted voluntarily and serenely by the candidate." "Even though there could have intervened other concomitant causes," argues Amore, "the *determining* ones [must be] of a religious character, both on the part of the assassin and on the part of the victim, who accepted his death for the love of God" (emphasis added). And so that it would be "more easy to judge with moral certainty" the essence of martyrdom, Amore urges the reader to ponder two things: first, the necessity of a historical critique, that is, to "take into account and ponder well the historico-environmental circumstances . . . such as the hostility of the natives against the missionaries" that prefaced San Vitores's death. The second necessity concerned the psychological states of the key characters, about which Amore instructs us to "ponder the personality of Matå'pang, as well as the long-standing, and prolonged desire and preparation for martyrdom of the Servant of God."

Of Beasts and Men

To consider these requirements, I reproduce a summary of the political events surrounding San Vitores's death, and his "long-standing and prolonged desire" to die for Christ. This synopsis is taken from the executive summary of the *Positio* (Amore 1981, 1–9). We join the overview, describing the events following San Vitores's arrival in 1668: "The success was beyond expectation. For adding together the baptized on the island of Guam with those of the other islands, it was realized that from June 16, 1668, to April

21, 1669, the resulting total of those who had been baptized was 13,289. Remarks Fr Astrain, 'Rarely has there been a mission to the infidels begun with such prosperity and received with such goodwill.'" After detailing the "fruit of the abundant harvest, which amounted to 30,000 souls" by the beginning of the third year, Amore arrives at the mission's moment of resistance.

> Such fruit could only be harvested at a cost of much labor and sacrifice, of per-
> ilous crossings of stormy seas, in the midst of fratricidal quarrels between rival
> towns. In fine, such labor had to deal with natives who were uncivilized, sav-
> age, barbaric and superstitious. But above all, there was the opposition of two
> principal adversaries, a Chinaman by the name of Choco and the Macanas. The
> former spread the calumny that the Fathers killed the children with the baptis-
> mal waters, and the sick with the holy oils. The Macanas played the part of the
> prophets, promising through skulls that were kept in the homes such goods as
> water, cures, and fish. Together they were the principle causes for the uprisings
> of the natives against the Fathers, including the deaths [of several priests and
> catechists two days before San Vitores's murder].
>
> In view of the massacres of these two last days, the Servant of God, who at the
> time was building a church some distance away, ordered that all should proceed
> [to the central part of the island, where he himself would be on his way]. Pass-
> ing through the village of Tumon [, San Vitores] learned of the recent birth of
> the daughter of a certain Mata'pang. He asked him to let him baptize her. The
> child's father, who had already apostatized from the faith given him in baptism,
> refused and, even uttering blasphemies, threatened the Father with death. This
> he actually inflicted on him with the thrust of a lance into his chest, while a
> pagan fellow native, who had been incited by him, parted his head with a cutlass.
> Meanwhile the Father was begging God to forgive his assassins. Mata'pang cli-
> maxed his crime by snatching from the Father his holy crucifix, and stepped on
> it amid calumnies and blasphemies.

In the reconstruction of the political and personal events and circumstances surrounding the martyrdom of San Vitores, the *Positio* positions
our protagonist face-to-face with an antagonistic Matå'pang. Baptized, but
fallen from grace, Matå'pang is angered at San Vitores's persistent effort
to baptize his infant daughter. Despite Matå'pang's warnings and threats,
San Vitores so proceeds. In the narrative, the Native's anger at God and
priest results in the splitting of the missionary's head with a cutlass and the
piercing of his side by a lance, as in the passion of Christ (figure 2). Thus
emplotted in the *Positio,* the narrative satisfies a determined *odium fidei:*
authentic martyrdom, it might be said, coagulates in the proof that the candidate's death was "religious in character both on the part of the candidate
and especially] on the part of the assassin." Neither an accidental death nor

FIGURE 2. Padre Diego Luis de San Vitores, 1627–1672. Spanish Jesuit San Vitores is credited with (or debited for) founding the Roman Catholic mission among the Chamorros in the Mariana Islands in 1668. In 1672, San Vitores was killed by the Chamorro chief, Matå'pang, of the village of Tomhom, in Guåhan. In his wake, San Vitores's companions launched a movement to canonize him, a movement that dissipated by 1700, only to be revived after World War II by the first generation of Chamorro men ordained as priests, monsignors, bishops, and archbishops. Source: plate 32 in volume 7 of *Galerie illustrée de la Compagnie de Jésus: album de 400 portraits choisis parmi les plus beaux, les plus rares ou les plus importants, et reproduits, en héliogravure par les soins et sous la direction du Alfred Hamy*. Paris: L'auteur, 1893.

plain old murder (and definitely not a suicide) would suffice. In life and death, the candidate's and the assassin's story must be read, respectively, in terms of service to and anger toward God.

The task of glorification involves the peculiar project of rereading the circumstances surrounding San Vitores's death, as we have seen in canonical teaching, as "a perfect testimony" or "witness" to Christ's perfect testimony to the glory of God. To achieve this outcome, among other things, Amore instructs us to "ponder well" an assassin who hates the faith and a political climate that exists as an obstacle to God's immutable plan on earth as "spoken" by San Vitores's death. My objective here is to so ponder how figuring the candidate as a martyr, and the assassin as a hater of faith, converts a historical instance of personal and political opposition to San Vitores into a general symbol of indigenous resistance, only to subsume in the end that particular motive and the wider cultural and political values it exemplifies beneath a determined and determining providential logic. For to have a saint, a model of heroic virtue, and a powerful object of devotion and emulation, you need to have its opposite. To make a hero, you need an antihero, a model of evil, and a powerful subject of everything you must avoid, and against which you would invoke saints and angels—the very heroes and heroines of the Church—to do battle. Indeed, the narrativization of San Vitores into a *beatus* requires the figuration of Matå'pang as beast, and it is in the making of *beati* and their beasts that the effort to canonize San Vitores can be said to work the Native to produce the saint.

To begin, as if to fulfill canonical teachings of martyrdom, and of Christianity, the *Positio* asserts Matå'pang to be an apostate. Like Lucifer, the supreme apostate, Matå'pang had once converted but has now fallen from grace. In this specific narrative, Matå'pang becomes enraged and hurls blasphemies on discovering that San Vitores has gone ahead and baptized his infant daughter. Earlier in the morning, Matå'pang had expressed anger toward God and had instructed the inquiring priest to "go baptize a skull." In the narrative, Matå'pang threatens to kill San Vitores if he persists in baptizing the infant, whom Matå'pang loves dearly. Like a growing number of Chamorros at the time, Matå'pang believed that the holy water and oils used in the baptisms and other rituals were lethal (*Positio* 1981b, 430–439). Three centuries later, Father Fran Hezel, an American Jesuit and historian of Micronesia, explained that baptisms and anointments were linked by illness or death, but not by causation, and certainly not because the water and oils were poisonous; rather, the padres specifically sought out those close to death—newborns, the aged, and the sickly and dying—in the hopes of saving their souls (Hezel 1982). The *Positio* points out that Matå'pang's daughter herself was "in danger of death" and that her mother, "who was a Christian, offered her to the Father to be baptized."

In the narrative, Matå'pang leaves San Vitores to solicit assistance from a companion named Hirao, who balks initially: the *Positio* tells us that even this non-Christian had "recognized the affability and the love with which the Father treated all." But Hirao capitulates after Matå'pang calls him a coward. In the meantime, realizing that Matå'pang is upset, and "so that [he] could cool off," San Vitores goes to gather some children of the village to instruct them in the faith. He also invites Matå'pang, who responds that he is "angry at God, fed up with Him, and irritated by the Father's teachings." Matå'pang leaves momentarily, only to return and discover that the priest has baptized his daughter. It is then that Matå'pang and Hirao attack, first Pedro Calongsor, a Filipino companion of San Vitores, and then the priest himself. In the narrative, Matå'pang's hatred of the faith is further revealed through more blasphemies after the assassination. He is said to have "insulted" San Vitores's crucifix by yelling obscenities at it before eventually smashing it to pieces.

The *Positio*'s stated task with regard to Matå'pang is to "sound out" his character "in order to know better the nature of the violent death" of San Vitores. This sounding entails what Ledesma calls a "recasting" of the events that occurred in the last five months of San Vitores's life. According to Ledesma, Matå'pang was "deeply infected by the same spirit and motivation" that "caused" a period of persecution of the padres and that saw two major outbreaks of war since the establishment of the mission in 1668 and the subsequent deaths of fellow priests and other catechists and assistants before San Vitores's death on 2 April 1672. If the mission enjoyed early success, it would be thwarted by local "sorcerers" known in the vernacular as *makåhnas*, and by a Chinese provocateur named Choco. Jesuit writings refer to Choco and the *makåhnas* as *bonzes* or "masters of death," the same term that Jesuits elsewhere in Asia used to refer to men in similar positions (King 1990). These agents of death, of sorcery, and of the diabolical were viewed as agitators who incited otherwise peaceful Natives, consistently figured as innocent but ignorant children. It was Choco, for instance, who spread the lies about the holy water and oils, but the *makåhnas* were also castigated. As a "class of priests" themselves, according Påle' José Palomo, the first ordained Chamorro priest, the *makåhnas* were competition for the Spanish padres (Palomo quoted in *Guam Newsletter* 1911b, 1).

In short, the "recasting" entailed rereading and subsuming the political motives of the day beneath diabolical agency inasmuch as Choco and the *bonzes*, acting on behalf of the devil, managed to sway Matå'pang and other Natives to likewise resist men who were only doing God's work. Instead of being seen as valiant efforts to defend a way of life against foreign invaders, indigenous acts of aggressive defiance were consistently narrativized by the padres and subsequent historians as "rebellious" and, more insidiously, as the work of "hostile" Natives. Moreover, these hagiographic and historiographic acts of narrativization rendered the encounters more than merely oppositional in logic; they made them dependent for their value and meaning on the heroic presence of the padres. Basically, the *Positio* reasserts this interpretation but focuses or directs the opposition or rebelliousness squarely against God—well, not exactly directly against him but indirectly, through a particular interpretation of Matå'pang's anger. To be sure, there are moments in the narrative when Matå'pang's anger is interpreted as a sign of the "political climate," whereas at other times the political climate is read through the primacy of Matå'pang's anger. And even then, there are times when both Matå'pang and his "hostile" contemporaries are figured as little more than pawns of the devil. At this level of the narrative, however, such contradictions are only temporary, since the immediate question the *Positio* poses is whether or not San Vitores's death can serve as a legitimate witness to providence. Despite the outcome, moreover, Matå'pang plays a role important enough to be singled out for the dubious honor of exemplifying hostilities at the time, because of the singularity of his crime. In fact, Matå'pang is a crucial, mediating sign in a discourse of authenticating martyrdom through *odium fidei*.

The "character and psychological state" of Matå'pang, then, is found in a recasting of the political events surrounding the conflicts in the early years of the mission's presence in the Marianas. "Infected," if not possessed, Matå'pang comes to be the very embodiment of the "spirit and motivation" of general hatred toward the faith. Baptized but fallen from grace, Matå'pang the apostate mocks God before, as, and after he kills San Vitores. Thus, Matå'pang reflects everything that San Vitores is not. If San Vitores is modeled after Christ, hero of mankind, virtue exemplified and perfected, Matå'pang is modeled after Lucifer, who fell from grace, anti-hero extraordinaire and evil incarnate. But evil dwelling in a Chamorro body itself comes to embody the very complexity of indigenous political and spiritual resistance to an intrusive system that sought to consolidate its position in indigenous society by displacing all that did not conform explicitly to its desires and imperatives. Thus, Matå'pang would go down in history as the embodiment of ingratitude, cruelty, and even betrayal to his own people. In its journey into modern historical Chamorro consciousness, the term *matå'pang* remains something negative: arrogant, silly, inane. (In Part Three, I will return to a fuller analysis of the term.) Even a Chamorro Protestant minister, the Reverend Joaquin Sablan, took due note of Matå'pang's troubled legacy among the Chamorro people when he wrote of Matå'pang's notoriety among the Chamorro (1990, 262).

"Death Wish": San Vitores's *Ad Mejorum Servi Dei*

The second criterion used to gauge the authenticity of San Vitores's martyrdom involves what has been called his "prolonged" desire to die in the service of the Lord (Amore 1981, 25). After the death of several assistants and after the brutal beatings of two of his companions, according to Hezel (1982), San Vitores decided to toughen up. At this time, San Vitores appears to have also made another life-and-death decision: having long expressed what one hagiographer called his "longed-for palm of martyrdom" and another called his "pathological death wish," San Vitores might also have very well sensed that it was the right time to die.[6]

In his discussion of the contested effort to canonize the late Archbishop Oscar Romero of El Salvador, Kenneth Woodward examined the importance of timing in the local politics of canonization (1990, 36–49). If it is so important in the local politics of canonizations, and if, as Woodward also asserted, martyrdom is the surest route to canonization, then timing must have import in the local politics of martyrdoms. In a letter to his father general in 1663, San Vitores wrote, "Swords and martyrdoms are not soon found here, nor should we expose ourselves to them *until* the Lord should place us under them, and we should pray that these happen *after* we have brought him many souls in heaven, so that his glory may all the more increase which is the only crown worthy of all desire" (*Positio* 1981b, 224; emphasis added). A similar passage elsewhere in the *Positio* reads: "swords and martyrdom are not soon found . . . *until the Lord does that for us . . . so as to increase more his glory, which is the only halo worthy of all desire*" (1981b, 398; emphasis added).

The *Positio*'s central task on this count is to assess San Vitores's "total personality," which, I argue, also involves navigating the fine line between death as a desire to serve God, and death as suicide (1981b, 678–679). Ultimately, the assessment of his total personality and the reading of the fine line in favorable terms would rest—or double back—on an assessment of his "reputation of sanctity" (*Positio* 1981b, 678). We have already witnessed this self-referential circularity, where one identity finds its truth in the other's existence, which in turn finds its truth in the first. Here, the religiosity of San Vitores's willingness to die is found in his reputation of sanctity, which is presupposed in martyrdom—the religiosity of his willingness to die. At the least this logic requires some explicit justification: though it admits that standard Church practice requires the authentication of a *fama martyrii* in the case of martyred candidates, where non-martyrs require an authentication of their reputations of sanctity in life, the *Positio* concludes that the latter could also serve as a "secondary proof" of San Vitores's authentic martyrdom insofar as "sanctity and heroism are divine gifts that presuppose martyrdom" (1981b, 679). Thus does the *Positio* rely, albeit secondarily, on San Vitores's reputation of holiness in life in order to satisfy the requirement of a death by authentic martyrdom. But the authentication of San Vitores's martyrdom as based on his reputation of holiness in life deploys the circularity linking his desire to die and his desire to serve the Lord: his desire to die is read as testimony of his desire to serve the Lord because his reputation of serving the Lord presupposes the desire to die for the Lord. Moreover, this mirroring—San Vitores's desire to die as reflecting his desire to serve God—itself mirrors God's love for mankind but also reflects, in reverse, Matå'pang's psychological state of mind: the alleged desire to kill as indicative of the desire to no longer serve the Lord. This mirroring, once again, recalls the enmeshment of saints and sinners, heroes and antiheroes, and fundamentalist and absolute ideas of what is good and what is bad. You need one in order to have the other.

Though the *Positio* does not address this point explicitly, I want to also ponder the difference between San Vitores's desire to die as a "sign of his love for God" (and God's love for man) versus his desire to die as a "death wish," which, in the form of suicide, is a cardinal sin. How exactly do you find the fine line between a grave sin and the surest route to sainthood? The conundrum is hefty, and in the narratology, it translates to a nuanced question of timing: It is legitimate to want a "happy death," but it must come when God wills it. Death should not be actively sought. For example, Padre Luis Medina, one of San Vitores's companions, had also desired "a happy death" but heeded San Vitores's instruction to "flee it" (García 2004, 377–378). Francisco García shared the conundrum that Medina, who also happened to be lame, experienced:

> On one occasion he ran, fleeing from one who was following him with a lance to kill him. But he was fleeing with the desire that he be overtaken. He tripped and fell and he thought that he now had what he was seeking. But God prevented his death by means of a woman who detained the aggressor. But who ever saw such a thing? To desire the death from which he was fleeing, and to flee the death that he desired? To die in the act of obedience is a great thing, but it seems as fine a gesture and an even more difficult thing to not die for the sake of obedience, while longing for it, as though Fr. Luis, while fleeing from death, turned his head to see if it was arriving and chided its laziness saying, "Why did you stop running? Why are you defeated by a man without legs? For others you have wings, for me alone you run with fetters on your legs, if you run at all? I cannot wait for you. Make haste and overtake me. See, I trip and fall. Here you have me prisoner, unable to escape. But what ill-fortune is mine! Your running ceases, or someone holds you back from seizing me, and me from seizing what I so desire." (2004, 378)

This rather dramatic re-presentation captures well the predicament and the theological requirement attached to desires for "happy deaths" and their proper outcomes. God, not man's desire, determines properly when and under what circumstance one is martyred. In the same way that Christianity overrides the finality of death by narrativizing it as but a precondition for everlasting life with God through Christ, this narrative overcomes death by rendering it lamer than the lame priest. But in an inverse of the cosmic tale by which a woman compromised man's union with God in eternal paradise by succumbing to temptation, García's narrative produces a woman who forestalls San Vitores's death and thereby man's desire so as to ensure God's proper role in the unfolding dramaturgy. In holding death back from seizing the lame priest from his own desires, the woman functions to make possible a true "happy death," one founded properly on God's desire.

This is the logic that the *Positio* employs (or deploys) in order to navigate the fine line: it converts San Vitores's "desire" into "the most worthy" of all desires: the glorification of God. And if Matå'pang stood no chance in the contest over the meanings of his "psychological" state, San Vitores received in the *Positio's* positioning the full benefit of the doubt in the presupposition that his desire to die was also synonymous with "the most worthy" of all desires. Following García's narrative above, we might also begin to see Matå'pang himself as a kind of feminized rhetorical figure, recruited initially as an ostensibly masculinized aggressor but ultimately nullified, or at least objectified or repositioned, as an object of a subject's active agency and desire, in the way that women (and Natives) often tend to be figured in patriarchal historiographies.

In sum, Catholic theology, God's greater glory, and service toward the goal of increasing that great glory, distinguish between acts of death as carried out by man (murder or suicide) and acts of death motivated by service to, and anger against, God (martyrdom). In the case of martyrdoms, such "happy deaths" are also reinterpreted and celebrated customarily as rebirths, as conditions of possibility for entering into everlasting life in heaven. Furthermore, the conversion of this "desire" into "the most worthy" of all desires is related to a long-standing tradition of viewing life as a gift from God, and particularly a gift whose heroic return to God is understood to be the greatest love of all. Ledesma explains this in the *Positio*: "The heroic love of God, which is supposed by and leads to martyrdom, is a divine gift which God in his ordinary providence does not grant except through innumerable supernatural aids and graces, through the cooperation to these by the Servant of God, which graces . . . his extraordinary virtues. And God, in his infinite generosity, as a reward for them can grant and, when it pleases him, actually grants the palm of martyrdom" (*Positio* 1981b, 678). The gifting, or return, of one's life back to its true owner, the Creator, involves a special relationship between man and God: God gives the gift of life to man, and through a combination of man's "cooperation" (his virtuous acting on "supernatural" aids such as "grace," which is also a gift from God) and God's willingness (if and when it "pleases" God), man can then give his life back. These gifts, in the *Positio's* formulation, become "rewards" to the hero or, more specifically, the "palm of martyrdom." The reward is heavenly. Its initial recognition on earth is declared in a beatification; its final certification on earth, provided it passes certain requirements, is inclusion in the Church's official registry of saints. And so when one's life is "given" back to the Lord, under certain circumstances, the Lord's great message—his love and his gift of life—is acknowledged, made evident. Its truth is laid bare, provided that it is God's and not man's pleasure that motivates a candidate's willingness and desire to die. But authentic martyrdom—the loving return of the gift of life back to its original Giver, for which one is rewarded eternal residence in heaven—is also figured as a gift of love to all people.[7] This gift of love is exemplified in this case by San Vitores's willingness to sacrifice his life so that the baby, as metonym of the Chamorro people, might "live" through her baptism into Christianity. In this way, San Vitores's martyrdom makes him not only like other Church heroes and heroines but also like Christ, the supreme example of self-sacrifice as gift to humankind. But this is also why authentic martyrdoms are glossed as "happy deaths," or "crowning glories": as we have seen, they signify the martyr's death as a glorious witnessing of God's glory and thus the martyr's entrance into heaven. And this is also why saints and martyrs are befriended by the living on earth. Recognized by living mortals as friends in heaven, saints provide guidance for reaching eternal life and can intercede in heaven to provide help, assistance, or protection on earth. This equation, of course, is what permits proponents of Christian missions to self-understand their labor as unselfish gifts of love. In the same way that God gave his only Son to redeem the world, and in the same way that his Son accepted this gift and in turn gave his own life so that others might live eternally in heaven, authenticated imitators of Christ also gave the "greatest gift of love" when they sacrificed their lives for their fellow men and women. This passion is, indeed, a story of love.

The gift of love to fellow men (which has so many redeeming qualities in heaven and on earth for both giver and receiver) constitutes, and is constituted by, the evangelical project. San Vitores's own writings, says Ledesma, reveal such a (pre)occupation, especially those from his adolescent years, as he was preparing for his apostolic vocation. According to Ledesma, San Vitores's writings "manifest his great zeal for the salvation of souls and his readiness and desire for martyrdom" (*Positio* 1981b, 385). So intense was his "esteem for souls," wrote his companions, that San Vitores once told them:

> If crossing from one island to another the boat should break up in the middle of the sea, and [if] there were not enough planks for the safety of all, and [if] someone said that he was in the state of mortal sin and that he had no contrition nor was ready for confession, [then] he [San Vitores] would give his plank to save his life and have enough time to prepare himself for his salvation, and he would let himself drown, happy to die for the salvation of that soul. (*Positio* 1981b, 704–705)

Although he also told them, ominously, that "a thousand deaths should be suffered so that one soul could be granted the grace of God," one could presumably feel secure aboard any vessel with the good padre aboard. San Vitores's companions also said "that there was no death so glorious that he did not esteem it less than the conquest of one soul for God." But San Vitores instructed his companions that "what they should try to do was bring many souls to heaven without caring for martyrdom," for, he would say, "God grants that to him who merits it" (*Positio* 1981b, 704–705).

In the *Positio,* San Vitores is figured as God's agent, while Matå'pang is, like all Chamorros who resisted the missionaries' positions, simply diabolical—except that Matå'pang is made to stand as exemplary, a sort of anti-saint, insofar as it is he who actually kills the future saint. Just as San Vitores's fame for holiness in life and martyrdom at death are conspicuously likened to the life and death, or passion, of the supreme exemplar and most famous Church hero, Jesus Christ, in order to make the case for San Vitores's martyrdom, so too must Matå'pang be compared to the Church's most famous antihero and villain, Satan. In this setup, with San Vitores acting as agent of Christ the hero, Matå'pang stands (or falls) as agent of the antihero, the Antichrist. At best, Matå'pang is, as we shall see, something no good, except, of course, as what might be called "canon fodder"—material for working and realizing San Vitores's heroism and all that is staked therein. These were narrativized in the *Positio* and certified as authentic by the Congregation's theological commission. Before certification, however, the factuality of San Vitores's assassination and the credibility of the source documentation had to be credentialized by the theological commission's historical counterpart. In the next chapter, as I have done in this chapter, I examine this process of credentialization, its stakes, and its costs.

Chapter 2

The Oral Cavity

Providential Historiography and the Silencing
of Native Witnesses

In the previous chapter, I argued that the *Positio*'s narrativizing remakes
Matå'pang as an agent of the devil in ways that allow him to be used as a
kind of negative witness to the authenticity of San Vitores's martyrdom. In
turn, the martyrdom is said to bear witness to God's hand in the life and
death of the saint. In this chapter, I continue to argue that the production
of the historical documentation used to authenticate the veracity of San
Vitores's killing by Matå'pang also involves the simultaneous invocation and
elision of Native voices in ways analogous to Matå'pang's symbolic and discursive treatment, including the familiar circular and self-referential logic
that we encountered in the theological argumentation used in the *Positio*. I argue further that the labor expended to demonstrate the credibility
of the documentation and the veracity of the event mirrors the political
history of colonial subjugation by way of negative historical and cultural
representations of Natives.

The hagiographic tradition, the process of writing edifying life stories
of exemplary and heroic Catholic individuals, did not always concern itself
with questions of "fact" proper, and credibility of sources, although it is true
that efforts to canonize individuals, by San Vitores's time, involved the rigorous collection of testimonies, preferably by eye and auricular witnesses.
Still, and to date, there has also been a long and deep understanding in
Church teachings and practice that tolerated the wondrous, fantastic, if
more excessive, dimensions of hagiographic writing, especially those that
originated from folk communities and their oral traditions and that are
stereotypically dismissed as ignorant or superstitious. But especially among
the learned, there was also a way in which the interest in edifying those
considered worthy, and the pragmatic value of using such edifying stories
to build faith among the flock, operated within a providential logic that
came with its own adamant view about veracity and truth. It did not matter
so much that the stories about a certain hero or heroine were a bit over
the top, much less whether the person in question even actually existed,

if the legends and stories helped build faith in God. The modern concern with factuality, and with credible source documents, was secondary to the belief that if God was working through the individual in question, *that* truth (and its practical value for nurturing faith) was what really mattered. It is not that the Church lacked interest in distinguishing between legitimate and illegitimate cases. But its effort to clean house, removing saints and martyrs who lacked credible documentation, to rely on "facts" and credible evidence for processes of canonization, is a relatively new phenomenon in Church history. This housecleaning tradition is sometimes referred to as the "Bollandist" tradition, a Jesuit-led movement whose principal goal was to purge the registry of saints of fictional individuals or incredible stories (Delehaye 1961).[1]

As seen in chapter 1, Father Agostino Amore, the chairman of the Congregation's Historical Commission, explains that San Vitores's martyrdom needed to "stand out from the documentation" (which "arises hard upon the martyrdom"). Amore also calls attention to the Commission's need to consider the "historical credence of the documents."[2] Three questions are placed before the Commission, to which there are three possible answers: affirmative, suspensive, and negative. The first question is "Are the documents . . . genuine, worthy of historical credence, sufficient and ample enough for a certain historical judgment about the life and death of . . . San Vitores?" (Amore 1981, 26). Questions two and three concern the theological authenticity of San Vitores's *fama martyrii*, which we have already examined. But they also ask explicitly if the event was "historically proven" by the documentation. Amore elaborates: Are the supporting documents "authentic and trustworthy"? Are the documents "endowed," he asks, "with an amplitude, accuracy and sincerity which *any historian or honest researcher can and should demand in this regard?*" (Amore 1981, 24; emphasis added). This chapter takes up the challenge of answering these questions.

Before proceeding, I want to foreground my assumption that the only documents that specifically raise and reconcile the problematic of historical credibility, of the factuality of the martyrdom, are the *Positio* itself, which was begun in the early 1970s and completed as the deposition for the beatification, and another celebratory booklet written in 1985 by the American Jesuit historian of Micronesia, Francis Hezel, under the auspices of the San Vitores Beatification Education Committee. It is true that there are primary source documents that attest to San Vitores's death at the hands of Matå'pang, but they surface first in the footnotes of the *Positio,* and more importantly, as we shall see, they emerge as part of the "processes," or information gatherings, held in Guam, Mexico, the Philippines, and Spain shortly after San Vitores's death and as part of the effort, led by his companions, to canonize him. It cannot be emphasized enough that the only extant primary source documents on the events in question were generated and circulated in a concerted effort to canonize San Vitores in the seventeenth century, and again in the last quarter of the twentieth century. Of equal importance, perhaps as a function of that history, these documents exist only in the form of modern copies located primarily in Church and Jesuit archives. This is not to say that there are not numerous other documents that can count as "primary" seventeenth-century sources. However, to the extent that they comment on these events, they rely principally on knowledge and information as produced and circulated either directly, from these few source documents, or from what can be called the aura, the fame and reputation of the events surrounding San Vitores's life and death as shaped principally by a mission historiography that is also fundamentally hagiographic. Finally, I should make it clear that in scrutinizing the *Positio*'s credentializing of the documentation I am not saying that these events did not really occur, much less that present-day Jesuit and Church historians and archivists are trying to "pull a fast one" in order to honor one of their own. Rather, my critical intent is to reveal the contradictions and dilemmas that accompany efforts to rationalize in modernist sensibilities matters that are largely dependent on faith. At the same time, it would be dishonest of me not to also come clean in my desire to destabilize established truths about the mission, especially about how important dimensions of Chamorro political and cultural meanings have been systematically elided in and subordinated to conventional narratives established principally by the padres and especially by their biographers and hagiographers, and by historians from the seventeenth century to the present. Yet, as will become readily apparent by the second and third sections of this monograph, if not by the middle of this chapter, my own effort to render alternative accounts of San Vitores's name and fame will ultimately rely on such hagiographies and biographies as matters of faith, albeit from radically (one hopes) different angles.

In my reading of two key accounts that were written shortly after his death and that continue to be regarded as primary source documents because they each rely on contemporary reports from the islands (even if neither author actually visited the islands in person), Father Francisco García, in *Life and Martyrdom of . . . Diego Luis de San Vitores* (García 1683, 2004), and Father Charles LeGobien, in *History of the Mariana Islands* (LeGobien 1949), make no special effort to prove the veracity of the event or the credibility of the sources. Neither García nor LeGobien questions the veracity or the authenticity of the martyrdom; both accounts are hagiographic in character.[3] My argument is not that hagiographies are invalid sources for historical understanding. As one who was raised reading *Butler's Lives of the Saints,* I do not see hagiographic writing as less real than "historic" writing proper. Nor is my task to play the devil's advocate. Rather, I inquire if the supporting documentation passes muster, given the modern criteria that the Church has adopted for itself. Personally, and intellectually, I like my stories with mystery and miracles, like the transubstantiation of bread and wine into body and blood, and the wondrous workings of the Holy Spirit, angels, and yes, saints. This confession is necessary for it helps situate my argumentation in this chapter.

How do we know that "in fact" San Vitores was killed by Matå'pang, and killed under the circumstances and for the exact motives that were deemed satisfactory for authenticating the death as one of martyrdom? How do we know that San Vitores did not drown while bathing, or that Matå'pang did not accidentally push him off a cliff in response to, say, a bad joke? And are we so sure that he died when these narratives say he did, and what are the consequences if the true story is different? Though these questions will be directly broached in the final section of this book, they hinge on an unhinging of the established orthodoxies that hinge on the idea of the credibility of the source documents in question.

Hippolyte Delehaye, the famous French Bollandist, warned of the need to be wary of "legends" in the lives of saints, of material that could not be vouchsafed as actual or real (1961). San Vitores's Cause necessitated eyewitnesses, although it is still not entirely clear to me if this was an original or a later concern associated with the Cause. It certainly seems that a robust discourse about eye witnessing was produced. In the *Positio,* and in the booklet produced by Hezel and the Beatification Education Committee (Hezel 1985), there emerge three (star!) witnesses: Mapuha, Bayug, and Ambrosio Hagman. Only the second, Bayug, is "declared to have been present . . . as an eyewitness." (The information and quotations in the following section come from *Positio* 1981a, 474–484, unless noted otherwise.) Mapuha testifies on the basis that the incident "was common statement" of all the Natives, while Hagman is said to be an "auricular witness," to have "heard the facts and details of the crime from the same assassin of Father San Vitores." Remarkably, each recounts the incidents leading up to the moment of passion in the exact same order that we have already seen: San Vitores arrives and searches for a child to baptize; Matå'pang refutes him; San Vitores persists; Matå'pang (later) enlists an accomplice, and together they kill San Vitores's companion before confronting San Vitores himself. Remarkable, too, is that the three testimonies of the actual killing are identical, almost to the word. Here is Mapuha's testimony. The words inserted in brackets are from Bayug's [B] and Hagman's [H] testimonies, respectively, and are the *only differences* between their accounts and Mapuha's wording:

And the Ven Father told him: "May God have mercy on you." And then the native Mata'pang threw a spear at him which penetrated [B=pierced] his chest and the native Hirao gave him a blow with the machete [B=a catana] on the head, with which blow he died. He adds more: that their bodies were thrown into the sea and that these floated up towards the surface two times [H= which came up to [B=towards] the surface twice].

The exactness of the testimonies, we might say, reflects perfectly the logic that Vicente Rafael has shown to structure the entire missionary enterprise in general: the "dissemination of God's Word" (1993, 7).

These testimonies are found in a document identified in the *Positio* as "Authentic Information," which is also identified, rather cryptically, as the "Process of Guam," a juridical process said to have taken place in January 1673, ten months after the assassination (*Positio* 1981a, 474–484). The official who oversaw the collection of these testimonies was Father Francisco Ezquerra, SJ, who was on the island at the time of San Vitores's death, and who succeeded him as the mission's superior. Father Juan Ledesma, the *Positio*'s compiler, tells us that Ezquerra testified at the "Process of Manila" held from 5 October 1676 to 9 June 1677 (see *Positio* 1981b, 522–523n114–116). In the Guam Process, the three Natives are said to have submitted their sworn depositions to Sergeant Major Don Juan de Bozo, who served as the notary apostolic. Three other officers also witnessed these submissions. Ledesma explains that there were only three official witnesses because of the "inhospitable conditions" in the Marianas at the time. Of collecting testimonies in such a climate, Ledesma cites the oldest known source on San Vitores's death, a letter written 26 April 1672 (three weeks after the event) by Father Francisco Solano, SJ, a companion of San Vitores. In this letter, Solano relies on the testimonies provided by the three Natives but apologizes for not making a fuller inquiry because "all the companions were full of fear" (1981, 448). Ledesma surmises that the fathers also did not deem it necessary to conduct more investigation, "principally because of the rush in making and sending this information." We will return to Solano's letter shortly.

Notwithstanding the "rush" to collect information, and the cursory investigation, the testimonies were supposedly gathered, as mentioned, into a single document referred to as the "Authentic Information," which Ledesma christens the "Process of Guam." This twentieth-century act of naming immediately raises the critical question of how much of this history is being narrated into existence along the way. It will also flag how colonialism operates and continues as much through historic and contemporary acts of narrativization as through more familiar processes like warfare or political governance. But let us return to the "Authentic Information" and "Guam Process," which I will now condense and refer to as the "Authentic Guam Information" (AGI). According to Ledesma, the Authentic Guam Information was sent directly to the Philippine Provincial, Father Andres Ledesma (not to be confused with Father Juan Ledesma, the twentieth-century compiler of the *Positio*), and it was subsequently included in a third juridical process referred to as the "Process of Mexico" (held 10 February–30 May 1679; see *Positio* 1981b, 510–521n200). However, Juan Ledesma tells us that there is no record that the AGI ever reached Rome, and that no original form of it exists today, though we have the word of Jesuit historians involved in the Cause, who say that the extant copy they possess contains "authentic information" of that AGI (Amore 1981, 9).

Document 6 in the *Positio*'s chapter 9, titled "The Martyrdom" comprises excerpts from the AGI, the Guam document that contains the all-important Native testimonies. For the purposes of the Historical Commission, this chapter is key because it contains all the pertinent documents that contain seventeenth-century information about San Vitores's death, as guided by Ledesma's commentaries on their historical authenticity. Although there are too many documents to cover here, we need follow only a handful of key documents, like the AGI, which, again, is said to contain firsthand and notarized testimonies from our Native witnesses (*Positio* 1981a; ensuing quotes are from *Positio* 1981a, 474–475, unless noted otherwise). These function to corroborate the existence of the original information contained in key documents such as the AGI.

The full title of the AGI is *"Authentic Information that was made in the Mariana Islands on the glorious death for Christ of the Apostle of Those Islands the Venerable Father Diego Luis de San Vitores. A Copy."* Ledesma explains that the actual document that he worked with, which is currently housed at the Postulation General of the Society of Jesus in Rome, is modern (nineteenth-century) in orthography but is "*a copy of another* made in 1673"; he then asserts, "we could call this information the Process of Guam" (emphasis added). As "proof" that the modern document is a faithful "copy of another" copy of a seventeenth-century document, Ledesma cites a passage, written in Spanish, on the left superior margin, which he translates thus: "The *original* of this information must be sent in the safest vessel." In the final chapter of this book, I will return to the vessel of my choice to render an alternative and even "safe" account of San Vitores and Matå'pang: Matå'pang's canoe.

To return to the matter at hand, Ledesma asserts that this marginal note was also in the margins of "that copy of 1673, and [that] it was copied in this modern copy that we have today." In a footnote, Ledesma explains that this is the opinion of two present-day Jesuit historians of the Historical Institute of the Society of Jesus in Rome.[4] Ledesma's explanation, complete with the backing of fellow Jesuit historians in Rome, is necessary because the beatification (now) mandates veracity and credible sources, and because, he admits, "the original and that first copy do not exist anymore." As it turns out, either the AGI did not make it aboard the "safest vessel" to Rome in the seventeenth century, or if it did, something else happened to it, along with its second contemporary (seventeenth-century) copy and the other possible copies that purportedly were included in subsequent processes in Manila and Mexico (held three and six years later, respectively). Such fate not only denies "historians and other honest researchers" present-day access to seventeenth-century source materials but also means we must take on faith the word of Ledesma's fellow Jesuit historians.

Whatever the documents' fate, Ledesma asserts that proof of the AGI's authenticity—the authenticity of the "Authentic Information," so to speak—is further evidenced in two ways: "the original" was included in the Process of Mexico, and reference to it appears in other contemporary writings. To these, we now turn.

A look at the documentation that comprises the so-called Process of Mexico (Ledesma does not say if this is also his renaming) reveals testimonies by San Vitores's contemporaries during his ministry in Mexico. Of thirty-some witnesses, however, only three provided testimony on his death, and this information, not surprisingly, recapitulates what we have already learned. This is not surprising because, according to Ledesma, they are based on the AGI, which came out of the Marianas. He also tells us that the small number of testimonies on the death itself should not surprise us because news was not widespread on account of the time it took for the ships to arrive from the Marianas. Surprisingly, and contrary to what is asserted in the AGI, Ledesma says only, "We ignore if the original of the minutes of this Process still exist," though he assures us that the extant copy "of the manuscript that we have is a copy of the original" based on an autograph signature of the archbishop "under whose auspices the Process was held" (*Positio* 1981b, 511).[5] Yet, without the benefit of a critical discussion about the original copy of the document (Process of Mexico) that helps authenticate the AGI/Process of Guam, we know only that their original copies do not exist. Still, if we follow the argument, we soon discover that the proofs lie not in the existence of the Guam materials but in other seventeenth-century documents that allude to the information compiled in the AGI.

According to Ledesma, the originator of the Mexico Process was Father José Vidal, SJ, the Procurator of the Mariana Islands, who also doubled as the Procurator of the Mexico Process.[6] It is also from Vidal that additional information about the death of San Vitores gets recorded in the Process of Mexico, but not as part of the AGI documentation per se. In the information that Vidal submits to the Process of Mexico, we encounter a second set of proofs of the authenticity of the AGI (which, again, contains the notarized Native testimonies): other contemporary source documents that repeat information taken by Ledesma to corroborate that contained in the AGI.[7] For example, in Mexico, Vidal presents a letter by Father Lorenzo Bustillo, SJ, one of San Vitores's original companions who helped found the mission in 1668, although it is admitted that Bustillo was not an eyewitness per se and had not even been on the island at the time, having left Guam before the assassination in 1672 and having not returned until 1677. Despite the fact that Bustillo was absent from the archipelago, Ledesma regards him as a credible source witness because he was San Vitores's contemporary and, more importantly, because Bustillo's testimony relied on accounts such as the AGI, or the aforementioned letter by Francisco Solano, San Vitores's predecessor, which letter of 1672 is understood to be the oldest known document on San Vitores's death, written three weeks

after the fact. Yet, neither Bustillo's or Solano's letters make any reference
to something like "Authentic Information" or the "Guam Process"—and
they could not, because they were written before the Guam Process is said
to have occurred.

As additional, secondary proof of the AGI's authenticity, Juan Ledesma
offers two more contemporary documents written by Father Andres
Ledesma (1981a [1674]; 1981b [1672]). Juan Ledesma argues that these,
and a handful of other documents, were written soon after the events in
question and thus were "fresh in mind" (*Positio* 1981b, 452). Their authority is especially shored up by the fact that they drew from various papers
"which have come from the Marianas."[8]

The Solano, Bustillo, and Andres Ledesma letters are primary source
documents whose function is to establish the credibility of other source
documents whose originals do not exist or about whose existence there is no
comment. Indeed, these letters, and others like them, are referenced in the
so-called Process of Mexico, as part of a group of documents that were "contemporary" with the so-called AGI, which contained the testimonies of our
Native eye and auricular witnesses and of which there exists only a modern
copy whose authenticity as a faithful reproduction of a seventeenth-century
copy (of a copy, at that) relies on the words of modern-day Jesuit historians
in Rome. It was precisely to assuage any doubt about the copy's authenticity in the minds of the Commission or reader that we were nodded in the
direction of the Process of Mexico, where it had been sent (but where questions of the original copy are ignored), and where we are directed to these
contemporary letters (by Solano, Bustillo, and A Ledesma). These letters
are said to have informed those other documents/juridical processes. Following information on these sources can be dizzying, not the least for the
circularity that comes with their presentation in the *Positio*. Proof of a document leads to a copy of another copy whose authenticity is said to be proven
in another document that is a copy of another whose authenticity leads
back to other sources that inform the first document. The reader, I would
suggest, is also being circulated in an already familiar way. Let me continue
with another "contemporary" document that takes us from the Process
of Mexico (1679) back to the Process of Manila (1676–1677) in order to
illustrate the circular journey on which the Process of Guam (1673) takes
us. According to Ledesma, Alonzo Lopez, the Procurator of the Process of
Manila, refers to the Process of Guam in a compendium that he wrote on
the life of San Vitores in 1673 (Lopez 1981; *Positio* 1981b, 242–247). In this
compendium, Lopez "speaks of this Process [of Guam]" in references to
the manner of San Vitores's death, and most especially when he described
his sources as "witnesses who were present at such a great cruelty" (*Positio*
1981b, 586). According to Ledesma, Lopez also refers explicitly to the credibility of the information insofar as such knowledge was "constant" in the
islands, and most especially because "Mata'pang himself [had] reported [it]

to many persons from who[m he had] heard" it (*Positio* 1981b, 242). This is the first time that Matå'pang himself is touted as a witness (a confessor, proper). Nonetheless, Ledesma also points out Lopez's own credibility as a primary source: he was on Guam at the time of San Vitores's martyrdom and so "must have been informed already about everything, even before this Process [the Process of Guam] began" (*Positio* 1981a, 475). Along with the compendium on San Vitores's life and death, Lopez co-wrote a histori-cal narrative *(Historica Narratio),* "an original document," Ledesma adds, "since it bears the autograph signatures of six Fathers who were residing in the Mariana Mission . . . though the body of the manuscript is written by another hand whose identity we ignore" (Ezquerra and others 1981). And though the authors do not mention "the source of their information," Ledesma surmises that at least for Fathers Ezquerra, Bouwens, Coomans, and Lopez, their sources are from the AGI/Process of Guam. I do not doubt the authenticity of these or the earlier contemporary documents. I am questioning whether or not they really corroborate the authenticity of the AGI, which is supposed to contain the credible testimonies. I am beginning to wonder, however, if the contemporary documents themselves furnished materiality for a twentieth-century narrativizing of a scenario that could be credentialized after the fact, following modern theological and historiographical imperatives.

The questions of authenticity raised by the AGI are also raised in the status of the so-called Process of Toledo, said to have taken place between 1688 and 1689 (*Positio* 1981b, 565n94). Here, too, we find the circular self-referencing at the level of documents that are held up as credible evidence on which the Cause is based. In this case, Amore, the chairman of the Sacred Congregation's Historical Commission, tells us that "the original of this Process [of Toledo] reached the Congregation of Rites in 1695 . . . but it is not there anymore and we know not of its existence" (Amore 1981, 13). The copy used in the *Positio* is located in the Jesuit Archives in Rome and is labeled an *"authentic"* copy of another document that had been kept in the archiepiscopal archives of Toledo but is no longer there, for it "must have perished in the fire of 1939" (Amore 1981, 13; emphasis added). Accord-ing to Amore, proof of the extant Jesuit copy's authenticity is found in a certification, included in the copy, that was signed by the Secretary of the Chancellor of the Archbishop of Toledo in 1927.[9] I will discuss this certifica-tion shortly, but for now I want to follow the proof of the process's authen-ticity as provided by Ledesma. He reiterates Amore's explanation but elabo-rates by citing two additional documents that "prove" that the "Process [of Toledo] did take place" and that its "original" minutes were sent to the Con-gregation for the Causes of Saints in the seventeenth century (*Positio* 1981b, 94). For convenience sake, I refer to these two documents as Toledo 1695 and Roman Congregation 1692, respectively, after the sites and the dates of their deposits.[10] However, there is a discrepancy between one of these sites and dates, and those indicated by Amore, above: Amore tells us that the Toledo Process reached Rome in 1695 (where it "no longer exists"), but the citation in the Roman archives as provided by Ledesma indicates an earlier date, 1692. This discrepancy might be explained as a mistake on Amore's part, but that answer does not resolve other circularities. In the *Positio,* for example, a footnote for these two documents directs the reader to another footnote: note 220 in document 20 of the *Positio*'s chapter 9. That note, however, has nothing to do with these documents and appears to be a typographical error. Some perusal reveals the correct reference to be document 22 in the same chapter, a document that provides general information on the Process of Toledo. This document contains a footnote (565n139) that again references Toledo 1695 but not Roman Congregation 1692. I have searched the thousand-page "labyrinth" repeatedly and have not found further reference to the second document (Roman Congregation 1692), which we know from Amore to no longer exist in Rome. Here, an important document (that no longer exists in the location where it was supposed to have been deposited) whose burden is to prove the existence of another contemporary document (that also no longer exists) is, in the first instance, referenced to the document whose existence it is supposed to confirm independently. Lacking additional or new information, we are still left awaiting sufficient historiographic information that offers compelling proof, for example, of the location or existence of the documentation that supports the claims of authenticity of the primary source accounts. Where are these documents, or at least how do we know of their existence? In another section of the *Positio,* Ledesma tells us that the documents were sent to Rome (the Congregation), but here he is consistent with Amore: "they do not exist anymore nor is there another original copy" (*Positio* 1981, 94). [11]

Having not found independent, or at least satisfactory, contemporary proof of the existence of the Process of Toledo, we are left only with an extant copy of this process (Toledo 1695). Recall that the "copy" used in the *Positio* is located in the Jesuit Archives in Rome, one that is an "authentic" copy of another document that had been kept in the archiepiscopal archives of Toledo but had perished in a fire in 1939. The discussion of the authenticity of the document that perished in 1939 (that it was in fact Toledo 1695), too, is circuitous: Ledesma tells us that the copy that had been destroyed had been authenticated beforehand, in 1927, by the vice chancellor and the cardinal of the Archdiocese of Toledo. But Ledesma's claim is based on a letter dated 24 September 1974, signed by the diocesan archivist of the time (*Positio* 1981b, 565). Basically, this archivist in 1974, around the time that Ledesma first began to compile the *Positio,* certified the authenticity of the signatures of the prior diocesan officials (the vice chancellor, the cardinal, and the archivist's immediate predecessor). It was this archivist who also speculated that the original of the process "*must have* disappeared in the fire of the archiepiscopal Palace in 1939, for it [had] not been found" (*Positio* 1981b, 565). From the foregoing we may conclude the following: the extant copy of the Process of Toledo in the Jesuit archives in Rome was written by an archivist in Toledo sometime before 1927 and signed by diocese officials sometime before the fire in 1939, which "must have" destroyed that copy. Basically, what we have is a twentieth-century certification of the authenticity of an earlier-twentieth-century copy of a seventeenth-century document that, unlike its twentieth-century authenticated copy, did not survive a fire in 1939. Apparently, neither this seventeenth-century document, nor its contemporary copy, which had been sent to the Congregation in Rome, exists.

Of course, original documents and contemporary copies may perish, unfortunately, but there can be compelling proof of their existence, such as their mention in other documents. This appears to have been the case for at least three of the four processes (those of Guam, Mexico, and Toledo)—and, thus, the dilemma that faced the proponents of the Cause for the beatification of San Vitores. Burdened with proving their existence, however, the proponents held out other contemporary documents that alluded to the information contained in the processes (never direct reference to the processes themselves), or referenced others that referenced others that referenced the originals.

In fact, ultimately, the problem for me is not so much that important supporting documents no longer exist or are missing, or even that we have to have faith in the word of Church historians and archivists following in a long tradition of discovering and certifying truths in which they believe so strongly and genuinely. I do not have a problem with having to have that kind of faith. The problem is that we are being asked to do something else: to abide by modern standards that require criteria other than faith in God (or faith in the words of God's workers), such as in independent, objective sources, and they just are not there to support the claims. It strains credibility when the *Positio* asserts something like, "That the Acta of the Process we are using are authentic is proven by the copy we have, which has been certified by the official archivist of the archdiocese of Toledo" in 1974—a time when preliminary information gathering for reviving the Cause for the Beatification was already underway. I wonder if the Cause would have been better served by making the case explicitly on faith. Whatever the case, I also want to say that what appears to be the Church's enduring dilemma of reconciling articles of faith and articles of reason, or at least of adhering to modern conventions of historiography, is only part of the problem. The biggest part of the problem concerns the "costs" of getting to be a Native witness for such purposes in the first place.

Providential Logic

Thus far I have provided the *Positio*'s discussion of the sources used to discuss the veracity of the details surrounding the death of San Vitores. But in each of these, we must rely on the word of Jesuit scholars today, or else we encounter in supporting documentation disturbing returns to the original document under question. But there is also something not quite right, at least for modern researchers, about the Cause's reliance on providentialist modes of information gathering. In his preliminary notes to the documentation used to verify the martyrdom, Ledesma indexes and hierarchizes the kinds of "sources" employed in the *Positio* thus:

1. Eyewitnesses (Bayug);
2. Immediate auricular witness, who heard it from the criminal himself, Matå'pang (Hagman);
3. Immediate auricular witness, who heard from the eyewitness, Bayug, and from the immediate auricular witness, Hagman (Father Alonso Lopez, Don Juan de Santa Cruz, in the Process of Guam);
4. They quote the eyewitness;
5. They quote auricular witnesses;
6. He was in Guam at the time of the martyrdom;
7. He knows it from Father Alonso Lopez who investigated the matter;
8. He informed himself in Guam from eyewitnesses;
9. He knows it from the mouth of the natives;
10. It is common knowledge; well known; it is of public knowledge and reputation;
11. They learned it from trustworthy persons;
12. From letters of the Missionaries.

As can be seen in this index, the premium sources, occupying the top rungs, are our three Natives, one eyewitness and two auricular witnesses. Though they seem to occupy a privileged location in this hierarchy, it is instructive to see or read specifically how they got to say what they had to say in order to get to where they are in the hierarchy, and then to consider the costs of such testimonies to themselves and to other Chamorros. These costs will show us an alternative history to that narrativized in the *Positio*, for by following the symbolic fates of these Native witnesses we can see how their even serving as witnesses for missionary positions can effectively mute their own, and others', Native positions. We turn first to information from the so-called Process of Manila that furnishes details about the process by which Natives get to testify. Then we turn to instances in which these Natives are valorized for providing such testimonies. Finally, we close by considering the actual costs of such privileged voicing.

In the *Positio,* the questionnaires that were used in gathering the testimonies are excerpted in the documents that comprise the Process of Manila. The question on the martyrdom itself is listed as number 29 of a "long questionnaire." Though item 29 is also rather long for a question, and would not pass muster as a valid research instrument for any modern historian or any honest researcher, it merits full inclusion nonetheless:

> If they know or have heard it said that after the war he continued his ministries and what was the case of his death.
> If the assassin was the native called Mata'pang, whom the said Father had baptized, and the particular circumstances of the cause of his death.
> Especially if the death was caused by his administration of the holy sacrament of baptism to the recently born daughter of the said Mata'pang, whom he asked to baptize her.
> If the assassin said some words which insulted and despised our holy faith.
> And if the Father was preaching to the assassin with a holy crucifix in his hand.
> And if it is certain that after the death of the Servant of God the aggressors struck with a stone a holy crucifix that the Servant of God was carrying over his chest.
> If he pardoned his assassin. What words did he say.
> And how his body was treated. If they threw it into the sea. (*Positio* 1981b, 523–524)

If it is too long and infinitely "barreled" to count as a good social science research question, question 29 is also guilty of "leading" or "structuring" the answer along a prescribed, or better yet, predetermined, pathway. That path, paved in part by the answers sought by the question, circles back to the fundamental truth of providence that is staked in the entire narrative and effort to credentialize its documentation. Not surprisingly, the answers given by the Native witnesses were remarkably uniform, somewhat contrived, and almost perfect, like the perfect imitations for which happy deaths are supposed to bear witness in acts of mirroring the truths of providence.

Mediated if not captured by seventeenth-century efforts to canonize San Vitores, the same Native testimonies are similarly "contained" in and by twentieth-century efforts to credentialize the source documentation used to support the beatification of San Vitores. These Native testimonies are so contained in the double sense of being carried in the documentation but also in being restricted by the historic and contemporary purposes that they are being made to serve: the authentication of San Vitores's death as itself a container proper of God's truth. In this sense, Native voices really do not get to say more than what they are told to say for the purposes of legitimizing someone else's testimony. The actual hierarchy at work in this continuous history can be illustrated by inverting the earlier one presented by the *Positio* thus:

1.   From letters of the Missionaries;
2.   They learned it from trustworthy persons;
3.   It is common knowledge; well known; it is of public knowledge and reputation;
4.   He knows it from the mouth of the natives;
5.   He informed himself in Guam from eyewitnesses;
6.   He knows it from Father Alonso Lopez who investigated the matter;
7.   He was in Guam at the time of the martyrdom;
8.   They quote auricular witnesses;
9.   They quote the eyewitness;
10. Immediate auricular witness, who heard from the eyewitness, Bayug, and from the immediate auricular witness, Hagman (Father Alonso Lopez, Don Juan de Santa Cruz, in the Process of Guam);
11. Immediate auricular witness, who heard it from the criminal himself, Matå'pang (Hagman);
12. Eyewitnesses (Bayug).

Turning the narrative on its head, we can easily see the primacy of Church interests through its interests in canonizing San Vitores in the seventeenth and twentieth centuries. We also see where Native voices are actually positioned in the narrative: at the bottom. But location at *this* bottom does not necessarily enjoy the same status as the "original" bottom of the rankings as presented in the *Positio*. That original bottom has the status of credible "primary source documents"—that holy scripture of modern historiography— again by virtue of "containing," in the sense of carrying, Native witnesses in particular. And again, the only real "containing" that is actually occurring is the ideological confinement of Native perspectives that are paraded as credible witnessing on the condition that what is witnessed is what San Vitores purportedly stood or fell for—God's truth. When stood on its head, the hierarchy of witnesses still does not allow for the Native witnesses to enjoy the status of primary source documentation of the truths offered up by seventeenth- and twentieth-century mission narratives about the seventeenth century, for the only things to which the Native gets to bear witness are seventeenth- and twentieth-century Church narratives. It is as if there is a black hole somewhere out there in the cosmos, or at least here on the written page, that sucks up the power you would think someone at the bottom of a given hierarchy would get by trading places with someone at the top. For some reason, in the logic of providence, the Native cannot seem to get on top and not end up still voicing the truth of the master. Clearly, the difference has to do with the power of writing, through its conceit of stability and superiority by gathering and "containing" oral testimonies. At the same time, the social and discursive processes of gathering and containing oral testimonies also entail the political process of capturing and arresting the possibilities of multiple meanings that inhere in oral traditions. The power of inversion can work only if, to use the concrete illustrations here, the "orality" of the Native eye and ear (or other organ, for orality can be linked to other organs) is considered on par with the written word. Indeed, by inverting the logic and taking Native testimonies at their word—if in fact this is possible and self-evident—we can begin to see, as we will in Part Two, a proliferation of meanings as spied in the histories of Native investments in Christianity, and even in Native investments in San Vitores himself. Not incidentally, Part Three will also show the meanings produced when the favored terms are displaced altogether. But these are in the near future. We need to return to the "past" as it is narrativized in the present *Positio,* or the *Positio*'s present purposes of authenticating its past.

As asserted above, in terms of the specific hierarchy of witnesses laid out in the *Positio,* Natives who are trotted out as privileged witnesses can best be understood as "canon" fodder with and through which heroic Church narratives continue to be articulated. Such articulations occur at the expense of actual Native voicing, insofar as there is a silencing or an emptying of their actual orality even when their primary purpose is to provide testimony in support of missionary perspectives. It is as if Natives get to speak only for, or against, the truths of the Church, except that they do not get to express their own experience because at the end of the day their testimonies are delivered strictly for the purposes of authenticating the testimony that is San Vitores's death. Such constraints are the colonial conditions under which Natives get to "speak" (Spivak 1988).

Natives who speak in support of the Church are valorized, whereas those who defy the Church are demonized. But even if they are not marked as demonic, other Chamorro voices are silenced through the valorization of Native heroes. For instance, Hagman, the auricular witness, is singled out as "deserving of more credit than his elders," presumably for what was taken to be his courage, and presumably because he stood up to his elders, which is a cardinal sin in Chamorro culture. The cost of selectively valorizing a Native like Hagman, however, is the active silencing of all the other Natives who must have feared the Spanish military reprisal sure to follow (and that did in fact follow) in the wake of San Vitores's killing. Or the silencing of other "courageous" Natives, who stood up and defied the foreigners, but whose defiance—think of Matå'pang—gets narrativized only as Native "hostility" toward God, operating under the sway of the devil, at that. *These* Natives do not even get to have full agency in their blasphemous "hostility" toward God!

But as we have seen, being a Native witness *for* the Church can lead to the same result—and these are the Natives who step forth as witnesses! We have seen this cost and negative effect in the ways that their voices have been mediated, indeed in the ways by which their testimonies are captured and contained in print, and for what purpose. We can see it also in the precondition for even qualifying to become a positive witness (unlike Matå'pang and the other "hostiles" he supposedly represented). Such a precondition of capitulation or acceptance was articulated by a group of padres who huddled together in trepidation following San Vitores's assassination in 1672 and decided jointly that they could or would not investigate his death further because of the mounting tension in the wake of the event. Their faith in providence, however, gave them a measure of hope, and in expressing that hope they also articulated the very specific preconditions and terms under which Natives could get to become celebrated "eyewitnesses": "We hope that when, with the favor of our Lord, these natives have settled down and subjected themselves to us, we will find very soon many other eyewitnesses who we have not been able to question for being still our enemies" (*Positio* 1981b, 495).

Bloody Signs

San Vitores had decided to toughen up after several assistants were killed and others were beaten. After these events, according to his remaining companions, San Vitores's demeanor shifted. They said, "The *Father* realized now that the matter had turned serious and that the time had come for promoting the glory of God with blood rather than with words" (Ezquerra and others 1981, 500; emphasis added to call attention to the ambiguity that permits simultaneously referencing God the Father and Father Diego). Interested in promoting the glory of God (and his fellow man), San Vitores welcomed the spilling of his own blood. He needed a Matå'pang. His companions confirmed his bloody testimony: "The voice of his blood shed for the defense of the truth clearly made known with what firmness [San Vitores] believed the divine mysteries. With what glory he proclaimed it is testified by the voice with which, when he died, he professed the faith for which he died" (*Positio* 1981b, 695).

San Vitores's blood also "voiced" another incontrovertible fact of local history: its spilling commenced what may still be the bloodiest episode in Chamorro political history. It was San Vitores who calculated the Native population for the entire archipelago to be about a 100,000 (Higgins 1937a, 20–21). In the 1710 census, the first ever taken by Spanish officials, there were only 3,539 Chamorros left (J Underwood 1973, 1976).[12] At this juncture, the narrative's antagonists—Matå'pang and his accomplice, Hirao—must have had a premonition, perhaps feeling as Pontius Pilate must have felt when he washed his hands of Christ's blood after having purportedly had little choice but to condemn him. At the site of the killing field, they "burnt the ground which had been saturated with [the] glorious blood, lest, in their belief, the air might be infected by its foul odor" (Ezquerra and others 1981, 501). According to Chamorro oral traditions, however, the men failed to destroy all residual signs of their calumny; to this day, on land and sea, the blood, or *håga' Påle' San Vitores,* continues to resurface to remind people of the signal activities of this mid- to late-seventeenth-century event. The resurfacing of his blood and memory in popular discourse continues to bear witness to San Vitores's resurrection via a revived effort by Chamorro clergy and laity to canonize him. With them are eager and enthusiastic members of Guam's civic and business community, seeking to benefit from this "history-making" moment. Taken together, these local Chamorro "discourses"—stories and practices of representing the past, present, and future with real-life political and cultural consequences—also represent meanings that not only invert those of the official Church's efforts but also multiply the meanings, and do so in the competing and contradictory ways that, it seems, only colonized Natives can.

Before we turn to these narratives, however, I want to close this chapter with a scene taken from one of those seventeenth-century documents whose purpose was to corroborate the authenticity, the truth, of the so-called *Authentic Information* from Guam in the seventeenth century. In his letter of 1672, which evoked that same group of padres huddled in fear for their lives in the immediate wake of their superior's assassination, Father Andres Ledesma also found sudden courage and inspiration in news of the arrival of a ship with armed support: "While we were orphans with the absence of our dear Father and surrounded on all sides by the risks that at every moment threatened us, our Lord was served to send us help as if from his own very hands. Because on May 2 of this present year 1672 a ship cast anchor in Guam which came from New Spain for the Philippines" (A Ledesma 1981a, 452). As argued in this chapter, the *Positio*'s task before the Congregation's Historic Commission was to strengthen the credibility of certain seventeenth-century documents by demonstrating their reliance on earlier source materials coming out of Guam during the time in question. For me, however, the narrative imagery of priests as self-described orphans rejoicing over the sudden appearance of a Crown ship amid "Native hostilities" (such as the killing of San Vitores) is also a reminder of the violent colonial context in which this entire episode occurred, and the line that continues to connect it with the present-day effort to authenticate San Vitores's martyrdom. For this image of colonial rescue is not unlike the present-day effort to redeem San Vitores and his companions using a highly selective representation of Native voices and agency to authenticate texts written by and transmitted to non-Natives. It ought to remind us how historiography and historical narrativity can continue to enact the colonial histories they celebrate, at the expense of indigenous testaments of political and cultural difference.

Part Two

From Below
Working the Saint

Chapter 3
The Sweet Spot

Tomhom, Guåhan, 2 April 1672

MATÅ'PANG AND HIRAO return to the village only to discover that Padre San Vitores has already baptized Matå'pang's newborn, against his explicit order.[1] Affronted earlier by the priest, and in the presence of his children and villagers no less, an enraged Matå'pang and his accomplice first attack San Vitores's Filipino assistant, and then turn on the priest, yelling blasphemies. In the vernacular, San Vitores replies serenely, *si Yu'os ma'åse'* (God bless you), a phrase that to this day continues to circulate as a colloquial form of expressing gratitude but whose other form, *si Yu'os in fanbinendisi,* continues to constitute a more formal and customary *blessing* given by *manåmko'* (elders) or *mansainen* (revered elders) to one who greets them with the customary *mangnginge'* (ritual sniffing of the hands), the Chamorro protocol for properly greeting such elders.

For Matå'pang, however, the words coming out of the priest's mouth are not so much respectful as just another instance of San Vitores's mocking him in public. In rage, he and Hirao strike at the priest's head with a cutlass and run a lance through his side, recalling how Jesus himself had been assaulted just before his crucifixion. Eyewitness accounts, according to the padres, say that Matå'pang disrobed their beloved companion and smashed the small crucifix that San Vitores always wore around his neck, but kept the marble one, which Matå'pang would later sell for twenty bags of rice, in order "to play well the role of Judas." The parricides then drag the bodies to the beach, tie heavy stones to them, and finally take them out to sea and dump them. But something strange happened here, in this time and place: having already sunk, San Vitores's body "came twice to the surface" to seize the canoe. Matå'pang is alarmed but manages to loosen the priest's grip and return the body to the depths. The body resurfaces for a third time and again grabs the canoe. A panicky Matå'pang strikes a final blow and "burie[s] in the sea the sacred cadaver," according to the narrative. Back on land, Matå'pang and Hirao return to the scene of the slaughter, where they burn the spot in a frantic effort to destroy all signs of their diabolical crime.

Ann Arbor, Michigan, January 2007

If the effort to canonize San Vitores works the Chamorro to produce the saint, it might also be said that Chamorros rework the saint to negotiate new cultural and social canons for themselves, in ways that produce new meanings for their island. At the very least, Chamorro investments in San Vitores, including local memories of, and efforts to commemorate, his life and death, represent a proliferation of meanings and possibilities of and for Chamorro and Catholic cultural and political life. To better understand the origins and destinations of such local, specifically Native perspectives, one would do well to relocate one's self on Native grounds.[2]

In fact, there is no better spot *on earth* on which to relocate than the one found in the seaside village of Tomhom, where San Vitores's blood was spilled on that fateful day more than three hundred years ago. For despite the perpetrators' best efforts, the priest's blood, like his name and fame, would continue to resurface in time and space in and around that particular spot so as to render the spot an important portal through which we are permitted to see other cultural, political, and historical narratives typically overlooked by official Church rituals and practices (such as the official narratives that reconsolidate themselves through Native witnesses and counter witnesses, as seen in the previous section of this book). And by virtue of the kinds of things we might witness here in particular, this exact plot of land on this specific island can itself be regarded as something of a "sweet spot" in the San Vitores story as it is rearticulated through the political and cultural history of Chamorro Catholicism in Guam. For the purposes of this chapter, and for the remainder of this book's central thesis, I argue that the political and cultural history of this spot in Tomhom gives us a potent vantage point from which to witness the larger truths of San Vitores's legacy among the Chamorro people. As the place in a faraway land in which a seventeenth-century Catholic missionary has in the twentieth century been vouchsafed to have died a happy death, Tomhom offers a vista into the cultural and political possibilities in its inhabitants' historical and cultural negotiations with Spanish and Roman Catholicism, and vice versa, in Spanish and Roman Catholic interests in peoples like Chamorros from places like Guam and the Marianas. Thus, the historical portal is also about cultural portability: this plot of land bears witness as much to the portability of Native culture and land through historical negotiation with *taotao sanhiyong* (people from the outside, like San Vitores) as to the ways people from the outside and their faraway places find temporary "burial" in the cultures and lands of Natives such as *i manChamorro* or *manamorro*

(the Chamorro people).[3] In pursuit of these mutual but unequal appropriations between Native and foreigner, I begin this chapter with an enduring, even endearing, Chamorro folk belief referred to in the vernacular as
håga' Påle' San Vitores (blood of Padre San Vitores) as it surges around past
and present-day foreign skeptics intent on demonstrating the truth behind
the phenomenon and the errors to be found in the historical coupling of
Native and Catholic "superstitions." Next, I turn to a more humanist history of Chamorro and *sanhiyong* efforts to "mark" or lay claim to the spot,
whether for spiritual, political, economic, or even sexual purposes. Such a
historical showering of activities, not surprisingly, reveals competing claims
over the meanings of San Vitores's name and fame inasmuch as any or all
of the attention directed at this spot derives from its notoriety as the hal-
lowed ground where the priest took his spill. With these "local" materials,
this chapter shows how close attention to this spot in particular, given its
holy notoriety, can also display the multiple and multiply layered Chamorro
political and cultural stakes in re-membering San Vitores for indigenous
purposes. But sniffing at this spot for the residual truths that it contains
will also reveal that something strange happened in the intervening three
hundred years. Just as San Vitores's blood keeps bubbling up over time, the
multiple meanings that gush forth from one particular locale continue to
flow through geographic space to implicate other peoples in faraway places
and thus suggest the translocality of this "sweet" spot. Finally, precisely for
the ambulatory character of San Vitores's legacy, my mode of writing and
address will also necessarily require mobility through time and space.

Mache'che', Dedidu, Guam, December 1991

Engracia "Acha" Borja Dueñas Camacho sits in her small kitchen getting
reacquainted with a niece who has lived away from Guam for many years. I
am blessed to also be present, and even happier that "Auntie Acha" allows
me to take notes. She recalls growing up before World War II, and I take
the opportunity to ask her in open-ended ways what she was taught about
Påle' San Vitores in her childhood. She explains: "Some people will say this
is baloney, [that] you must read the books. But the older people said that
there is a spot where San Vitores was stabbed and where, before, *nai,* the
blood keeps bubbling up. They called that *apuyan Påle'* [Padre's belly but-
ton]. That area was red, but now no more. It's all cleared up for the tourists.
This is what I heard from my grandfather around the time of the Nubenan
Santa Cruz" (E Camacho 1991).[4] Our kitchen conversation (fieldwork!) is
interrupted by a telephone call. A *techa* (lay prayer leader) rings to say she is
on her way to pick up Acha for a *lisåyon måtai* (rosary for the dead), for the
well-being of a mutual friend who has just passed on.[5] The session is over
but not before she has shared other matters regarding prewar Tomhom in

general, and most especially, regarding a local Chamorro tradition called
håga' Påle' San Vitores (blood of Padre San Vitores). Maria "Tita" Pangelinan Leon Guerrero Mesa, a *techa* herself, later corroborated Auntie Acha's
understanding: "I am not an eyewitness, but part of the water at San Vitores
Beach turns red during the month of April. This is what my father, Tun Ben
Leon Guerrero, used to tell me when he would fish with his *talåya* [throw
net]" (Mesa 1992). I will return to Tita Mesa in due course.

My field notes from 1991 also include a more formal interview with Mrs
Camacho's brother, John Borja Dueñas, at his home in Leisure World, a
retirement community in Seal Beach, California. Señot Dueñas became
animated at my question about *håga'* San Vitores: "I swear to you I saw it
with my own eyes, I scooped it up with my own hands! *Yes sir,* that water was
bloooood red" (Dueñas 1991). Among the hundreds of young Chamorro
men who enlisted in the United States Navy before the war "to see the
world," Dueñas also recalled infuriating exchanges between US Naval
personnel stationed on Guam and locals like himself around the issue of
håga' Påle' San Vitores (see, eg, A Sanchez 1990). In his *Guahan/Guam: The
History of Our Island,* the late Chamorro historian Pedro "Doc" Sanchez confirmed this particular belief and also the social relations between believing
Chamorros and their doubting Thomases.

> From the time of the killing unto modern time, generations of Chamorros
> have seen red patches around April each year at a spot in Tumon Bay close to
> shore near the site of San Vitores's slaying, and also in East Hagåtña Bay where
> the Jesuit martyr first set foot on Guam. On many occasions, American authorities
> tried to convince islanders that the phenomenon was natural rather than super-
> natural. The latest attempt was at the 1985 College of Arts and Science Research
> Conference at the University of Guam. But the Chamorros, who revered the
> martyred San Vitores and kept his memory alive for some 300 years, had another
> explanation: "haga' Pale' San Vitores," blood of Padre San Vitores, they said of
> the annual occurrence. (P Sanchez 1989, 42)

Estagel, Pyrenees Mountains, France, 1851

Jacques Arago is a French Catholic naturalist who served aboard the famous
Freycinet Scientific Expedition that crisscrossed the Pacific beginning in
1819 (Freycinet 1829). In his 1851 memoir concerning the Marianas, the
illustrator recalls poring over the colony's "sacred book" in Hagåtña, and
finding in its account of the mission this "fanatical embellishment": "The
spot where San Vitores's body fell after this sacrilegious assassination is
always dry and barren; grass will not grow there, and the waters of the cove
into which the body was thrown turn blood red at certain times of the day"
(Arago [1982?], 143). Arago's curiosity is piqued. He questions the sitting

governor, Don Medinilla, who bids him to witness the miracle "for himself."
With assistance from a Chamorro woman named Mariquita and some other
Native companions, Arago proceeds from Hagåtña to Tomhom. Earlier, in
1823, Arago filed a report with the French Academy of Sciences wherein he
lamented the corrupt form of Catholicism he had encountered in the Mariana Islands (Arago 1971). He surmised that only fanaticism and superstition
could result from the violent manner by which the Spaniards planted the
cross, but also scoffed at Native dispositions for such "pretended miracles"
and other Spanish "legends" attributed to San Vitores. He cited examples
such as Juan de la Concepción's *Historia general de Philipinas* (1788–1792),
which Arago considered "a production of ignorance," full of a "multitude
of ridiculous tales of sorcerers and of saints who took part in the conquest
of the Archipelago," and to which any attachment of credibility would be
"absurd" (Arago 1971, 2:42). For example, de la Concepción, a Franciscan,
wrote about how San Vitores's soul, "bounding over space, borne on the
wings of the wind, arrived in his own country, and there announced this
misfortune [ie, his assassination]." De la Concepción also reported the case
of a Chamorro man who was visited by six "aerial females" who were eating
fire and "menaced him with great misfortunes should he refuse to submit
to the new law which has just been imposed on him" (quoted in Arago
1971, 2:42).

Back in Guam, Arago arrives in Tomhom with his entourage.[6] Mariquita
directs him to the plot in question. He sees that, in fact, it is "dry and
barren, and that the naked ground form[s] a silhouette of a human body."

Mariquita prods him, "You see. Isn't it true?"

"What?" asks the scientist.

"That this place is accursed."

"That it is devoid of grass is what it is."

"And why should that be when everything is green around it?"

"I don't know why yet, but I'm going to find out, and then I'll explain it
to you."

Mariquita answers, "You will have to explain it to *heaven*." (emphasis
added)

Arago looks around and discovers a small cabin. He leaves Mariquita
and the others and approaches the cabin, where he meets a fifty-year-old
man who apparently lives there. As Arago approaches, the man gets to his
feet and makes the sign of the cross. A sort of miniature inquisition, but in
reverse, ensues:

"Is this your house?"

"Yes Sir."

"Do you live here alone?"

"Completely alone."

"Because of your *devotion?*" (emphasis added)

"On orders from the governor who sends daily provisions."

"How do you spend your time?"

"I cannot tell you."

"The governor already has."

"He can tell you but I cannot."

"Have you finished your assigned task this morning?"

"I never fail to complete it."

"Nevertheless, I noticed a little grass remaining in the area of the
    head."

"That is impossible."

"My good man, your eyesight is failing. It will be necessary to give you
    an assistant or to replace you."

"For God's sake, don't tell the governor."

"I promise I won't."

Satisfied, Arago returns to the others. He tells them, sarcastically, that
the miracle of the silhouette is "undoubtedly convincing." He then asks his
companions and Mariquita if they have themselves seen the "red water."
They haven't. Arago explains that they will have to wait until later "because
that miracle is not permanent like the one of the grass." They engage in
idle talk while the tide recedes. They all doze off only to awaken to a sea
that is "red, truly red as blood." "*Diablo!* Satan!" they cry out in unison.
"Surely the hermit's power did not reach that far," exclaims Arago, "let's
investigate the phenomenon!" The group launches a canoe to the vicinity
of the red water. They slide an oar into the water so as to lift a bit of sand
to the surface. Arago discovers the sand to be "scarlet, quite scarlet," which
now permits him to "account for the color of the water without resorting
to the supernatural." Turning to his companions, he asks them what they
will report back to Governor Medinilla. "The truth," they retort. "And what
is the truth?" asks Arago. "That we have seen the double miracle," came
the response. And "should we show him the scarlet sand?" presses Arago.
"The blood of fray San Vitores turned it red," is the answer. Arago protests,
momentarily at least: "The miracle should float. See how the tide comes
in and the color disappears, destroying the phenomenon? Never mind.
Tomorrow when it goes out, it will reappear in the cove, and the miracle
of the grass will continue with the daily inspection by the poor man of the
cabin. Señor Medinilla will have triumphed over disbelief."

Ann Arbor, Michigan, 2007

University of Guam marine biologist Ernest A Matson identified the "blood
of San Vitores" as a natural phenomenon more commonly known in his
circles as "unfilial blooms . . . of the algae *Scrippsiella, Peridinium, or Gymno-
dinium*," more commonly known as "red tide" (1991, 95). Matson offered
an overview of the history behind the local legend as his preferred way of

introducing his biological and hydrological analyses of the phenomenon. Relying principally on Mavis Warner Van Peenen, an American folklorist who came to Guam before World War II to salvage "the quaint lore" of a disappearing folk, Matson reiterated a deeply entrenched narrative about the arrival of San Vitores among Chamorros, who were "already decimated by soldiers and ship-borne diseases."[7] He described San Vitores as having "finagled his way . . . to Guam . . . by persuading a bunch of soldiers to sail to Guam instead of to Mexico from Peru." Matson also cited the "first" of what he calls "great Chamorro errors" in the misguided decision by Chief Kepuha, the seventeenth-century *maga'låhi* of Hagåtña who welcomed San Vitores to Guam and who "*allowed* himself" and "another Chamorro named Choco" to be baptized, although Matson admitted that Kepuha may have had no recourse but to "befriend the ruthless Spaniards" (1991, 95). Although the marine biologist's account is erroneous in the historical facts—there is no record of decimation prior to San Vitores's arrival, certainly not by soldiers, who arrived only with San Vitores; San Vitores did not "finagle" his way to Guam the way Matson says; Kepuha did not simply "allow himself" (passively) to be converted; and Choco was not Chamorro—the rhetorical force of the scientist's presumably objective analyses is to at least "correct" the deeper historical error of local belief in the "legend" (as it was first dubbed in Van Peenen 1974) of the "Blood of San Vitores." This was an error presumably rooted in earlier errors of Native conversion, which, implicit in Matson's account, also presumably finished off the process of extirpation begun even before San Vitores's arrival. Nonetheless, as in Arago's previous account, the epistemological confidence exhibited in Matson's recourse to "nature" is itself predicated on viewing Native or religious interpretations in derogatory, or at least patronizing, ways as unquestionably ignorant or simply superstitious. Can anybody be so (positivistically) certain that the algae itself, or any chemical that gave it its scarlet color, was not colored by the blood of San Vitores, as Arago's Native companions pointed out three centuries earlier in response to his skepticism? Can we be so sure that providence, or some spirit, is not here manifesting a moment of divine, or otherworldly, mystery? Can science really prove otherwise? And, what articles of faith mediate science's creed in unmediated objective evidence anyway?

Interestingly, in Tomhom, or more precisely, at the moment he first lays eyes on Tomhom, Arago the naturalist has something of a meltdown or, as he puts it tellingly, "one of those fleeting emotional moments . . . a man experiences . . . when his reason conflicts with the awe-inspiring" ([1982?], 143). The precise moment is in fact when the "peaceful cove" comes into view. Indeed, for many a visitor (and local) before and after, Tomhom inspires awe for its natural beauty and the vista it presents. But it must have been particularly striking for Arago, who, like many others of his time, traveled to places like the Pacific specifically to encounter what nature "in its greatest extent" is said to have provided naturalists of the day: diversity, specifically of flora and fauna.[8] Yet for Arago, nature's extent has slid too far when the "awe-inspiring" appeared to be God's handiwork, and that is precisely why this "man of reason" is thrown, momentarily, for a loop. For a moment, at least, God seems to regain control, and as a result, calls into question that particular form of manliness built on reason.

But before I elaborate on how the man reconfigures his way out of this "fleeting emotional moment," one that sends him back to memories of his "dear mother back in the Pyrenees" and from which he subsequently rationalizes his way back to the engendered present of his preferred identity (there, in view of Tomhom), I want to show how the triggering experience of first "laying eyes" on Tomhom resonates with larger workings of Western colonial discourse through visual encounters with beautiful landscapes and people of the tropics. This particular mode of colonial subjugation, moreover, resonates with the "ecstasy" San Vitores felt when he first laid eyes on the Chamorros in 1662, and the "beatific" vision that was authenticated by the Vatican in 1985. For example, in her analyses of the "erotics of the exotic" found in visual representations of the Pacific Islands and island women in eighteenth- and nineteenth-century pen-and-ink illustrations (by naturalists like Arago) and even in twentieth-century Hollywood and early ethnographic "documentaries," Margaret Jolly described a long and deep colonial tradition that engenders and sexualizes the Pacific Islands as inviting women and emplots their Native women as natural property to possess (1996; see also Jolly 1997). For Jolly, the principal organ for this masculinist operation is the power of a male/colonial gaze, through which islands and their women are reduced to beautiful spectacles to behold (and, I should add, to be held).

In her Native feminist historicization of the bikini bathing suit, Teresia Teaiwa made a similar argument about the colonial sexualization of tropical islands and women through the power of the gaze (2000). The brainchild of US military personnel on leave while stationed in the Marshall Islands during US nuclear testing in the archipelago, the bikini was named after Bikini Atoll, one of hundreds of islands in the archipelago, whose purposeful irradiation—in a shameful and covert effort to gather and build a database with which to scientifically measure radiological effects on humans—also resulted in Bikini's destruction and the tragic removal and resettlement of its Native inhabitants. Thus, wrote Teaiwa, the "bikini" enacts violence as much through its "exposure" of women's bodies for the pleasure of the male gaze, as through its insidious historical and social tendency (through the presumed pleasures and aesthetics of exposed women's bodies) to "cover up" the remarkable violence of US nuclear testing on, and purposeful radiological exposure of, the Marshall Islands and Marshall Islanders.

On Guam, more recently, Christine DeLisle examined the "colonial optic" by which Guam's prewar landscape and Native Chamorro populace had been photographed (in this case, by the wife of a US Naval officer) to convey beauty and innocence on the wane—which doubles, DeLisle argued, for a form of colonial surveillance through nostalgia, and a particular form of colonialism through the agency of the white women who accompanied their military husbands on tour in the tropics (2005). Each of these cases calls attention to the workings of colonial power through the engendering and sexualizing of islands and women through the use of visual practices. Their resonance with the Spanish Catholic legacies of San Vitores will be pursued later.

For the moment, however, I want to return to Arago's way of resolving this momentary internal conflict, a conflict that, as it turned out, would also involve other beautiful lands and significant women whose presumed innocence and tender purity would furnish the material for getting "reasoned" masculinity or manhood back on track. If a spectacularly beautiful Tomhom triggers conflict in the man of reason by evoking God's authorship over nature, it also involves a welling up of memories of his "angelic" mother back home in the Pyrenees. He is compelled to explain, "I was born in a country where one believes in miracles of all sorts and I could quote a few now, more or less true, more or less verified, but which have caused astonishment in . . . my home" (Arago [1982?], 143). This return to his homeland is also a return to feelings of loyalty and fidelity to his mother, which approximates, in my reading at least, the feelings of loyalty and fidelity that Mariquita and company seem to have toward the padres (if not the governor) as they remain "constant" to the miraculous tradition that Arago tries to debunk with recourse to nature. He confesses: "I would be very careful not to place them [miracles] in doubt in the presence of my wonderful old mother, who is nearly as devoted to all the saints as she is to God himself, and who has within her angelic heart a faith so strong that she believes more in the unseen than she does in what passes daily before her very eyes" (Arago [1982?], 143). Though this passage reminds me of how thoughts of my parents kept surfacing while I wrote the previous chapters, I am also struck by the power of Arago's mother's faith "in the unseen," and perhaps more so, by just how powerful it can be to engender faith in maternal terms. Maternalized, Arago's faith can, at least momentarily, disarm manhood staked on reasoned intelligence— a rationality, incidentally, that supposedly distinguishes Europeans from Pacific Islanders. But in the narrative, the disarticulation of this identity as triggered by the breathtaking sight/site of Tomhom is only momentary, and rearticulation is accomplished by rationalizing away the internal conflict thus: "Who could be unaffected after having been tenderly lulled by hundreds of ballads daily, chosen from the Rosellon, none of which are to be found in the martyrology?" (Arago [1982?], 143). In this way, Arago resorts to the power of fond childhood memories, memories of growing up on "hundreds of ballads" of holy men and women, of stories of miracles by persons who may not even have been on the Church's official roll of recognized saints. Such a childhood upbringing, under the influence of a woman whose faith in the unseen far surpassed her faith in the visible, might very well account for the sudden meltdown that made him for a moment at once a lapsed scientist, virtual woman, and virtual Native. But the overall point of this narrative, for my purposes, is to call attention to Tomhom as triggering Arago's desire to investigate the miracle of San Vitores's death while on a scientific jaunt in the tropical Pacific. At this particular site, the French Catholic naturalist suddenly finds himself back in the Pyrenees, before an angelic mother, stripped of the vestiges of his manhood—at least for a moment, before the narrativization of his childhood upbringing in the Rosellon resuscitates his preferred identity.

The martyrology to which Arago refers is the official Roman Catholic registry of saints and *beati*. For all it's worth, the exact number of saints venerated by the universal Catholic Church is unknown, even to the institutional Church. For throughout Catholic time and space there have existed other men and women (or stories about Church-recognized heroes and heroines), venerated in their respective localities, whose lives and deaths are filled with stories that approach the fantastic, the unbelievable, and whose lives are characterized with such color and zeal as to bewilder a Church hierarchy already open to the pragmatic value of such beings for cultivating faith among the populace. In his classic study of terror and healing in South America (1987), Michael Taussig considered the tension—and the analytic possibilities—that lie between official Church (and colonial) discourse and local piety as it is entangled therein. In his account of popular piety in Colombian villages far from national or religious capitals like Bogotá or Rome, Taussig wrote of statues with worldly, even lascivious, appetites that roam about at night. He suggested:

> Perhaps there is a secret life and a hidden Society of Saints and Virgins of which the Church is ignorant. . . . In this society the saints seem more like us, perhaps even like our children, a far cry from the impassive faces they stolidly present to the public when ensconced behind the altar or when posing for portraits sold in the marketplace and streets. And if people like to fill the lives of saints and the virgins with all too human passions, displacing thereby the monologue inscribed by the Church, those same saints and virgins fill the landscape with meanings inscribed by the routes of their interrelations. (Taussig 1987, 202)

Taussig elaborated on the "sacred contouring of the land" that he saw in the Colombian countryside (and that I see in places like Tomhom). In such places, the sacred contours are not simply self-evident, visible to the naked eye, easily coded by the science fiction of objective inquiry, but were also for Taussig "implicit" or "manifested indirectly in the cracks, dreams, and jokes of everyday life" (1987, 203).

What follows may sound like a joke, or maybe a crack in what is supposed to be the high seriousness of an academic monograph, but in turning to the historical and sacred "contouring" of that particular spot in Tomhom, what better guide can I recruit than a blind Chamorro priest? Affectionately known in life as Påle' 'Scot, for the Chamorro pronunciation of the Spanish term *padre* (pronounced by Chamorros *påle'*) and his given name (Oscar, pronounced by Chamorros *Oscot*, and then foreshortened, in Chamorro style, to 'Scot), the late Monsignor Oscar Lujan Calvo is vital to this story not simply because he participated in all the key events and practices that sacralized that particular spot in the twentieth century, or even because it was his idea for the Guam Catholic Church to revive the effort to canonize Påle' San Vitores, but especially because, as we shall see, Påle' 'Scot can articulate all their meanings in formal canonical terms as well as in Chamorro cultural terms (figure 3). Thus, he explained the stakes in pushing for San Vitores's canonization as "our initial tribute of gratitude to our Apostle of the Marianas, in memory of that day when he crowned his work among us with the shedding of his blood, thereby showing us that love greater than

FIGURE 3. Locally known as Påle' 'Scot, Oscar Lujan Calvo was the third Chamorro ordained to the priesthood. The prime mover behind the twentieth-century resuscitation of the seventeenth-century effort to canonize San Vitores, Calvo was also a historian and avid collector of cultural and historical artifacts and print material. Photo courtesy of Ms Magdalena L Calvo and family.

which no other can be. *This is our offering to our people. And through it may the present and future generations come to know whose sons we are, to whom, under God, we owe the faith, the culture, the way of life we enjoy today*" (Calvo 1970, xvi; emphasis added).

Finding the True Cross with a Blind Priest

The name *Tumon* is the Anglicization of *Tomhom,* which is derived from the term *ti åpmam homom* (Kumision I Fino' Chamorro 1992, 59–60), which means "getting dark." As a place once favored by fishermen and hunters from the south, if not from all over the island, this particular fishing ground was, according to one account, so named because it would be "getting dark" by the time the fishermen arrived. Auntie Acha, with whom I began this chapter, related a family *kuenta* (account, story) about her grandfather, also from a southern village, who could defy the odds to get past Tomhom, arrive in Mache'che' (where his great-great-grandchildren live to this day), and return by about sundown. He could do this, said his granddaughter, while carrying heavy loads of produce and game *both ways* (much as how our parents used to walk to school for miles, uphill, both ways). With a twinkle in her eyes and a smile that can stop a scientist, she explained, of course, that he did this with the help of his *ga'chong,* or supernatural friend, a class of helpful beings that many Chamorros still believe in. I did not take her smile as a kind of winking indication that she did not believe in them.

Tomhom is also a "traditional" site of the Nubenan Santa Cruz (novena to the Holy Cross), also known as the Feast of the Finding of the True Cross, which in Catholic tradition is sometimes referred to as the Feast of the *Invention* of the True Cross (Calvo 1991; Mesa 1992). I hasten to add that the use of the term "invention" (Maruchi 1908) here carries absolutely no connotation of inauthenticity and most certainly bears no relationship to a relatively recent scholarly tradition and analytic framework, largely in the disciplines of anthropology, history, and folklore, which consciously sought to "historicize" the culture concept as a highly politicized construct.[9] In general, a novena is a nine-day devotion for purposes ranging from honoring the memory of specific people and events recognized officially in the Catholic Church calendar (like saints or martyrs or any of the numerous manifestations of the Blessed Mother around the world, or the birth of Christ), to honoring the memory of recently deceased loved ones, to praying for any special purpose or reason (Meagher 1967). In her ethnography of the Chamorros before World War II, Laura Thompson observed, "The chant of a novena, primitive as a Chamorro folksong, echo[es] through the ages" (1941, 12). In its own right, the universal Feast of Santa Cruz has been recognized in the Church's calendar since the seventh century and commemorates the discovery of remnants of Jesus's actual cross on 14 September 326 by Saint Helen, the mother of Emperor Constantine.

While there are numerous Nubenan Santa Cruz scattered across the island and the archipelago, and most are maintained as family traditions, the one celebrated in Tomhom was different in two respects: first, it has taken place in the vicinity known or believed to be the actual spot where San Vitores was killed, and second, and in a significantly contested way, the *nubena*'s date has shifted back and forth, in the twentieth century at least, from 2 May, as a Chamorro folk celebration, to 2 April, the anniversary of San Vitores's death, in order to amplify the *nubena*'s formal connection to San Vitores as desired by the remaining Spanish missionary priests on the eve of World War II (Calvo 1991). The difference between Tomhom's Nubenan Santa Cruz and the Santa Cruz novenas elsewhere on the island, and elsewhere in the Catholic world, centers on its geographic and discursive proximity to San Vitores. Regardless of the change in the dates, the *nubena* occurred where it is believed San Vitores was killed in 1672, and typically included a hymn to San Vitores at the end of what was otherwise known as a devotion to the Finding of the True Cross. As a trained priest, and as a participant in the devotion since he was a child, Påle' 'Scot would insist that the Nubenan Santa Cruz had always been first and foremost a Chamorro veneration of the True Cross; but absent substantive knowledge about the man and his ministry, Chamorros knew at least that a man named San Vitores was killed in the vicinity "because of the legend of the blood" and "because of the song in his honor." In fact, Påle' 'Scot insisted on distinguishing the Chamorro folk tradition from the one that more formally recognized San Vitores, because the recent (just before World War II) coupling of the two celebrations left him uneasy: the former (the Nubenan Santa Cruz) followed Church protocol in properly venerating something the Church had authorized, while the latter (Nubenan Santa Cruz as focused on San Vitores) venerated the man prematurely, that is, before he had been properly beatified or canonized. Furthermore, Påle' 'Scot felt compelled to rationalize the apparent connection in the former to San Vitores (as seen through the proximity and the inclusion of the song in his honor) as a possible case of Chamorro confusion, given the long but interrupted history of marking the site with wooden crosses since San Vitores's death in 1672, although he took comfort that "in the end, the cross of the Holy Cross tradition, and the crosses of the San Vitores 'little tradition' are one and the same" (Calvo 1991). Despite Påle' 'Scot's discursive ironing out of little details that ostensibly could get Chamorro Catholics into trouble with the official Church, there are residual contradictions between these two "traditions" that merit further discussion and analysis for what they reveal about important differences between local Chamorro Catholic and *taotao sanhiyong* (outsider) Catholic investments in San Vitores, in addition to the important differences that obtain locally between Chamorro clergy and Chamorro laity. I will return to these revelations momentarily.

This oral history is corroborated in part by accounts written by Spanish padres, and a modern history of the Catholic Church written by an American Capuchin, Julius Sullivan (1957). In reviewing available histories of the eighteenth and nineteenth centuries, I have not found any specific mention of the Nubenan Santa Cruz in Tomhom, whether or not it was conjoined with San Vitores's fame, although there has been a continuous (albeit punctuated) effort since 1672 to mark the spot for both religious and colonial administrative purposes (as we saw of Governor Medinilla during Arago's visit in the nineteenth century), and by *sanhiyong* Catholics. If the Chamorro Nubenan Santa Cruz is in fact several centuries old, it would represent Chamorro markings of the spot.

In the most detailed written account of this novena, Spanish Capuchin Pastor Arrayoz describes in May 1940 the excitement in downtown Hagåtña *as island residents* prepared to travel to Tomhom (which Arrayoz spells Tumhon):

> As early as five o'clock in that morning our Christians, anxious to take part in such a magnificent event, had crowded around the Cathedral of Hagåtña, waiting for the buses that would transport them to the bay of Tumhon. The distance between the Capital and the site of the martyrdom of Father San Vitores is rather minimal, for it does not go beyond five or six kilometers, but a fervent gentleman of the city placed at the disposal of the public some buses for the exceptionally small price of less than twenty five (American) cents round trip. Each bus, full to capacity, had to make up to six trips to bring all the devotees to Tumhon. (Arrayoz 1981, 660–661)

At Tomhom, Bishop Ángel Olano began Mass at 7 a.m. and was assisted by Father Gil de Legaria, the pastor of Hagåtña, with other mission fathers present around the small altar. Father Arrayoz tells us that the Chamorro priest, Father Jesus Dueñas, was "conspicuous among them." Påle' Dueñas was in his late twenties, and was only the second Chamorro ordained into the priesthood, and the first to be ordained in Guam. At this time, Påle' 'Scot was still in the Philippines finishing seminary.[10] Tortured and beheaded by the Japanese during the war, Dueñas is often described by Chamorros as a hero and a martyr for refusing to collaborate with Japanese officials. There is a movement afoot to canonize Dueñas, one that began in the late 1990s and is still in the strategizing stages.[11]

Father Arrayoz also tells us that the children's choir of the Hagåtña Cathedral, accompanied by the whole congregation, sang the Mass. The cathedral's patroness is also the island's patroness and co-namesake (with Queen Mariana de Austria): the Blessed Virgin Mary, who manifests locally as Santa Marian Kamalen, and whose feast day is 8 December, the Feast of the Immaculate Conception, also known among the Chamorros as Misan Santa Maria. In the final chapter of this book, I return to the special significance of Santa Marian Kamalen for Chamorro culture, including the gendered and sexual terms of her relationship with Chamorros. The Hagåtña Cathedral is also known as Dulce Nombre de Maria (Sweet Name of Mary), and it is the linear descendant and co-occupant of the same plot of land on which stood the San Ignacio chapel that San Vitores built in 1668 (on land given to him by Maga'låhi Kepuha). In his homily during the 1940 *nubena* (preached in Chamorro), Bishop Olano narrated "in detail, the history of the evangelization of the Marianas and the martyrdom of Venerable Father San Vitores" which, according to Arrayoz, Olano identified as the very site on which they stood. After Mass, "there took place a long procession throughout the beach of the sea. Several groups sang religious hymns in unison with the public. . . . After the final hymn . . . to the vibrant 'hail' of His Excellency 'long live Pale' San Vitores' the whole people responded with an uproar, which resounded all over Tumhon, thus ending the religious festival of that day" (Arrayoz 1981, 660).

At this point in his text, Arrayoz is overwhelmed. "Praised be the Lord!" he exclaims, "We the old missionaries of Guam wish to see him [San Vitores] soon raised to the honors of the altar" (Arrayoz 1981, 660). San Vitores's value for this particular "old missionary" is explicit in Arrayoz's likening himself to his spiritual predecessor. Like San Vitores two centuries earlier, Arrayoz taught catechism to the children of Tomhom. He also describes his "immense joy" when four years earlier he and a companion found "some remains of a construction, which hardly protruded a few inches from the ground" and which was covered by dense foliage. He believed these to be the remains of a chapel whose construction had begun some twenty years earlier but was neglected after a violent earthquake. In Tomhom, within the tropical foliage, accompanied by a chorus by the Chamorro children's choir, Arrayoz recognized kin. He also found a Guam surrogate of Saint Helen's Finding of Christ's True Cross. I take it from his narrative that it was he who since at least 1936 rescheduled the Nubenan Santa Cruz from early May back to early April to coincide with the anniversary of San Vitores's death.

Precisely because it was conjoined with San Vitores's memory, the Nubenan Santa Cruz "validated" a Spanish missionary on the eve of World War II. In hindsight, this prewar validation marked the virtual termination of the Spanish-era padre, but it also prefigured San Vitores's value in the eyes of the first generation of Chamorro priests and administrators responsible for the spiritual and cultural welfare of a Chamorro Catholic community perceived to be under assault from liberal (modernizing and Americanizing) forces. The Chamorro brain, or heart-thrust, behind the idea to resuscitate San Vitores's canonization was Påle' 'Scot. It was he who first broached the idea to Father Felixberto C Flores, DD, another Chamorro who was ordained shortly after the war, and who would rise up the ranks very quickly to become Guam's first Chamorro bishop in the Roman Catholic Church in 1970 (Calvo 1991). Even before his consecration as a monsignor or papal chamberlain, Flores had already begun the formal legwork to revive the canonization effort, although in fact Påle' 'Scot had already conducted more than a decade of research on the matter, including making personally funded research trips to the Philippines, Mexico, and Spain—all the locations where San Vitores had preached. Påle' 'Scot had also recruited a former companion and mentor from Manila, Father Juan Ledesma, SJ, for initial assistance. Though Ledesma was later brought on board in an official capacity to research and compile the *Positio* that was to be submitted before the Congregation of Saints in Rome, his collaboration with Påle' 'Scot in the early 1960s had resulted in the translation and publication of a popular hagiography by 1970. Though Påle' 'Scot was still in the Philippines during the 1940 *nubena,* one of the first things he did when he returned in 1941 was to visit the Tomhom site to pay homage. Within a month he had his cousin, Tun Jack Lujan, the now-celebrated "master blacksmith," forge and install a bronze plaque at the site (Calvo 1991). In our interviews, Påle' 'Scot told me that although he frequently attended the Nubenan Santa Cruz in Tomhom with his aunt, Mrs Aflague Torres, he never knew of its significance in relation to San Vitores. Only in 1936, in the seminary in the Philippines, did Påle' first learn the truths about San Vitores's ministry among the Chamorros and his death at the hands of Matå'pang. In the seminary, Påle' stumbled on a serialization of Father Alberto Risco's *El Apóstol de las Marianas,* a popular hagiography of San Vitores (Risco 1935). When the war erupted a month after his celebrated return for his ordination as the island's third Chamorro priest—he was in fact (then) Father Flores's senior by four years—the first thing that Påle' did, after helping collect the bodies of Chamorros who had been killed during the invasion, and giving them a proper Christian burial, was to make a beeline to Tomhom to recover and hide the plaque from the Japanese (Calvo 1991).

A vital dimension of the historical sacralization of this cryptic landscape (cryptic in the twin senses of marking a burial and being mysterious or enigmatic in character) is the rather curious dearth of factual knowledge about San Vitores in the prewar and immediate postwar popular devotion "to him." As we saw in the introductory chapter, San Vitores's road to sainthood was billed as the making of history in Guam. Retired US Marine Corps General Ben Blaz, a former Guam delegate to the US House of Representatives (1982–1992), identified San Vitores's beatification and Guam's unresolved political status as a US colony as the two most historically significant events in the island's modern history. For a man so historically significant, and for the sudden fanfare surrounding his beatification in the 1980s, there was for a long time practically nothing known among the Chamorros about San Vitores's own story beyond the fact that he was a priest who was killed by one Matå'pang for baptizing the chief's daughter. Remarkably little information existed, beyond what was produced about him once the formal effort to beatify him was under way. Instead, what was known before the veritable explosion of information in the 1970s and 1980s took the forms of the aforementioned "legend" and the singing of a devotional hymn in his honor at the annual Nubenan Santa Cruz. To be sure, there were scattered historical treatments before the 1960s, especially before the war, but these were written, with one exception, by *sanhiyong*, relying exclusively on *sanhiyong* source documents, and consumed, especially before the war, by *sanhiyong* and by the Chamorro literate elite.[12] Engracia "Auntie Acha" Camacho, her brother Juan Borja Dueñas, and "Tita" Mesa, in their late seventies at the time of our interviews, had attended Guam's public school system under the US Navy before World War II, and none of them recall "history of Guam" classes or curriculum materials.[13] In the modern Catholic school system that was created after the war by German-American Bishop Apolinaris Baumgartner, the effort to incorporate Guam history and Chamorro-language materials, principally through devotional hymns and prayers, coincided with the revived effort to canonize San Vitores. This effort was ratcheted up in 1970 when Father Flores was assigned by Pope John Paul II to succeed Baumgartner and become the island's first Chamorro bishop. Under Flores, the effort to canonize San Vitores, and the production of educational materials about him, charged full speed ahead. The year 1970 also marked the publication, under the imprimatur of the Diocese of Agaña, of Father Alberto Risco's *Apostle of the Marianas,* a pet project of Påle' 'Scot, who served as its editor (Calvo 1970). This was the same serialized hagiography that opened the eyes, and especially the heart, of the *påle'* to the details and motives of San Vitores's ministry among the Chamorros.

The story of the Nubenan Santa Cruz figures into the riddle of the dearth of knowledge about San Vitores outside of devotional materials after 1970. Late in his life, Juan Borja Dueñas was actually dismayed when I pointed out that San Vitores was not in fact the first Native Chamorro priest (Dueñas 1991). I even wondered whether or not this new piece of information might "water down" Dueñas's spirited recollection of his own firsthand witnessing of *håga' Påle' San Vitores.* What accounts for the dearth of information? Mr Dueñas, like so many people before the present generation, explained, "We were never taught history of our island when we were growing up" (Dueñas 1991). Påle' 'Scot corroborated this. "Nil," was how he described the pre- and even postwar level of popular knowledge about San Vitores: "We knew nil" (Calvo 1991).

According to Påle' 'Scot, the only things associated with San Vitores's memory were the Nubenan Santa Cruz—which was held at the site of San Vitores's place of death—and the hymn sung in his honor. This novena was performed mainly by residents of the Tomhom–Dedidu area in which was also located the "San Vitores School," although, as described by Arrayoz above, the 1940 iteration of the Nubenan Santa Cruz entailed island-wide participation, led by the Hagåtña Cathedral's choir, and required all the available taxicabs. Clearly, by 1940 Arrayoz and the other Spanish padres had been playing up that particular local "local" tradition for the entire island. As for the school, Påle' 'Scot explained that though it bore his name, the San Vitores School was actually founded by an American naval governor to "induce" agricultural production on the outskirts of Hagåtña—in places like Tomhom and Dedidu—and not for any substantive desire to venerate San Vitores. The rationale was that the establishment of schools on the fringes would make it unnecessary for the *lancheros* (ranchers) to travel all the way to Hagåtña to attend school. Such treks normally cut into precious time spent tending the fields.[14] Although on the surface it seems that the Americans wanted to teach the Chamorros to be good farmers, their actions were less altruistic than indicative of pity and an arrogant self-possession that was expressed, of course, in a genuine belief in their own cultural superiority and their manifest destiny to uplift simple Native folks. Theirs was, in fact, a secular mission to civilize (and to validate America's colonial presence on faraway soil), and to teach the Native to till the soil as a way to rationalize the colonizers' presence on that soil. But this is a digression, as Påle' 'Scot often depicted his own explanations, a digression about the American mission to modernize, that is, wean twentieth-century Chamorros from the dark ages inherited from old-world Spanish Catholic superstitions. Among the modernizing projects was the building of schools on the outskirts, such as the one the Americans called, ironically, the San Vitores School. Of course, there is no irony in the case of one set of proselytizers embracing the figure that preceded them among the Natives; the irony is that the move to beatify San Vitores by the present-day Church is motivated in large part by a concern to reconsolidate its social and cultural influences on an island and people under assault by modern, liberal (read: Americanizing) forces. In fact, the US Navy's motivation in building the "San Vitores" school in the Dedidu–Tomhom area recalled little of the San Vitores that was laced into the Nubenan Santa Cruz beyond the fact that both sought to impress on the Chamorros altogether different lessons through the invocation of San Vitores's name. But that is actually saying a lot about what San Vitores can stand for in Guam.

Just as the Americans were building the San Vitores School for the aforementioned purposes, Påle' 'Scot was not only discovering details about the life and times of San Vitores in the serialization of Risco's book but had also already begun to consider resuscitating the move to canonize him. A significant part of that effort was realized in 1970 when he published Risco's book—with a translation provided by none other than Father Juan Ledesma, compiler of the official *Positio*, "so that school children would come to know San Vitores's story." In the Philippines, Påle' 'Scot was "moved to tears" by San Vitores's story, especially over the love he had for the Chamorros, as illustrated in his willingness to die so that "we might have the chance to live" in heaven. It was, for Påle' 'Scot, the mode by which the Chamorro priest "for the first time" came to experience and thereby comprehend the truth of Christ's willingness to suffer and die so that man might live (Calvo 1991). As one who heard the calling, and like Arrayoz back in Guam around the same time, Påle' 'Scot realized that San Vitores was his spiritual predecessor, that *he was like him.* But unlike Father Arrayoz, one of the last Spanish missionaries, Påle' 'Scot was Chamorro. He explained to me that San Vitores was especially inspiring to him because San Vitores gave the greatest gift, that of his life, so that his "own people" could live. His personal gratitude to San Vitores was genuine, and Påle' 'Scot's Chamorro cultural teachings around indebtedness prescribed reciprocity and loyalty. Thus would Påle' 'Scot devote the remainder of his life to the service of God through Christ and to a ministry among his own people inspired by his spiritual ancestor of three hundred years earlier. A particular highlight of this ministry was the reciprocal exchange expressed in laboring to revive the effort to canonize San Vitores as a hero for the Marianas and for the Catholic Church. This labor included, as we saw, the commissioning and placing of a bronze plaque in 1941, which involved building a "modest" chapel and erecting a cross at what was taken to be the actual site of San Vitores's assassination. This religious and cultural ministry also involved initiating the historical research and amassing valuable historical mission records and artifacts in preparation for the more formal movement to canonize San Vitores. In addition, public education, such as the aforementioned translation and publication of Risco's book, had to be undertaken.

Alas, to hear Påle' 'Scot's recollection of his almost seventy-five-year ministry is to discover numerous tensions and conflicts: as soon as the chapel was erected, it was vandalized (vandals: barbarians who pillaged Rome in the fifth century; best known for their affinity for destroying holy relics and churches); as well, the prewar shrine was bulldozed by GIs (the same who "liberated" the Chamorros), whose return to the island on 21 July 1944 was widely regarded as a "salvation" in quasi-religious terms and to whom the Chamorros had become culturally indebted in loving and devoted ways. To add salt to the wound, the liberators' halfhearted effort to reinstall the plaque that Påle' 'Scot had hidden during the Japanese occupation saw the plaque not placed "in the actual spot." Furthermore, to hear Påle' 'Scot's story is to learn of the publication of a book that was not enthusiastically received by priests, nuns, and lay educators in the diocese's educational system. "The books just collected dust," he sighed (Calvo 1991). It is also to realize how the fruits of much of his labor ended up in other people's or institutions' collections without his receiving adequate compensation or acknowledgment, and finally, to see the glaring absence of Påle' 'Scot's direct participation in the beatification celebration in Rome and on Guam in the mid-1980s. "I was already sick," he laughed, from his hospital bed in the Philippines, where I interviewed him in 1991. I took his laughter as an ironic acknowledgment that he was both physically ill and fed up with local Church politics. Still, his marginalization is especially remarkable because his own story, his own role in the history of the proceedings, is unanimously taken to be a determining factor in the formal beatification hearings in Rome.[15] But do not belabor the tragic, he warned me, for "I do not do these things for myself. I do this 'for the greater glory of God.'" So devoted was he to this Jesuit, and to his Jesuit teachers and companions in the Philippines, that this diocesan priest adopted the Jesuit motto as his own. The goal of serving the greater glory of God had helped make the Jesuit Order one of the most powerful entities in all of Catholic history. So compelling is the idea, and the purpose, that it translated San Vitores's "desire" to die into a legitimate manifestation of God's will (as discussed in chapter 1.) Calvo's championing of this slogan gives us a sense of how piety in Catholic terms brought by a Spanish Jesuit in the seventeenth century could also be rearticulated with Chamorro cultural and spiritual identity in the twentieth century.

Indeed, belaboring the tragic is not my intent as I call attention to Påle' 'Scot's centrality in the story of the resurfacing of San Vitores's name and fame, or to his own ministry as forged in relation to that of San Vitores. My purpose is to begin to provide a Chamorro-oriented accounting of San Vitores's resurfacing, including the more recent history of the sacralization of that spot in Tomhom, which, I have argued, serves as a useful portal through which we can comprehend both Native and non-Native stakes in the legacy of Catholicism among the Chamorros as identified predominantly by San Vitores's name and fame. Påle' 'Scot's direct involvement in memorializing that spot before the war, and his specific attention to its welfare and concerns afterward, render him a particularly important guide to those seeking to understand the Chamorro investment in San Vitores. Understood in the postwar context of Chamorro cultural anxiety over the social and cultural tensions presented by the island's rapid development and modernization, San Vitores's resurfacing in the twentieth century can also be understood as a sign of Påle' 'Scot's and fellow Chamorro priests' investment in the island's Catholic legacy as an antidote to the ills of modernity.

The multiple meanings and stakes can best be appreciated through the more "local" history of marking the spot of San Vitores's death as the portal to everlasting life. For this reason, following in the wake of the Catholic mission and its traditions of venerating those heroes and heroines deemed to be legitimate witnesses to God, this spot has been marked, literally, by a succession of crosses, shrines, chapels, novenas, and, after World War II, parishes, among which the first was named Saint William's, in honor of an American benefactor from Chicago who enjoyed a special devotion to Saint William. In accordance with San Vitores's beatification in 1985, Saint

FIGURE 4. Formerly known as St William's of Vercelli Parish, the Tomhom edifice was renamed Blessed Diego on the occasion of Rome's beatification of Blessed Diego Luis de San Vitores in 1985. Photo courtesy of Dr Lawrence Cunningham.

William's Parish would be rededicated as the Blessed Diego Parish (figure 4). Before we turn to the particular sets of meanings manifested in the stories of the building of these postwar physical structures, we must resolve what appears to have been a "con-fusion" of traditions of the Finding of the True Cross, as they are bound up with a *nubena* of apparently modern origins.

Cross Findings Crossed

"Traditionally"—that is, according to oral history—the Nubenan Santa Cruz in Tomhom had been celebrated "since time immemorial" on 2 May, to coincide with the wider Catholic tradition of the Finding of the True Cross (Mesa 1992; quote is from Calvo 1991). This oral history indicates a folk tradition that preceded a modern effort to specifically link the tradition to an earlier cross that marked San Vitores's legacy, as we learned in Father Arrayoz's enthusiastic celebration in 1940, and Arrayoz's own discovery, in 1936, of some "remnants" of a cross in the dense foliage. For Påle' 'Scot, the residual fact that the Nubenan Santa Cruz was held on a different date but located in roughly the same vicinity as the site of San Vitores's death did not matter because "the crosses are one and the same." Furthermore, when facing the discrepancy in the dates between the local tradition celebrating the Finding of the True Cross (2 May) and the celebration elsewhere in the Catholic Church (14 September), Påle' 'Scot explained that the latter date was a product of "Vatican II," an important "liberalizing" moment in the history of the Catholic Church in the early 1960s (Calvo 1991). Yet, by 1940, and possibly even a few years earlier, the Nubenan Santa Cruz had been shifted to 2 April, as indicated in Arrayoz's description. This is not surprising, because we have seen how much San Vitores meant to Arrayoz's self-understanding. Thus, there appears to have been a melding of two traditions of "finding crosses" in the twentieth century: that of Saint Helen, of more universal fame; and that of Arrayoz's excited discovery of the "remains" of an earlier cross at the site of San Vitores's death—although, to be sure, the older Nubenan Santa Cruz had already been linked to San Vitores via a hymn, and more importantly, via its sharing the site of San Vitores's death. Sometime after World War II, but definitely by the time of San Vitores's beatification in 1985, the celebration of the Nubenan Santa Cruz reverted to 2 May, and a contemporary, post-beatification novena specifically devoted to Blessed Diego had been invented or "instituted." At least through the early 1990s, according to my notes, the Nubenan Santa Cruz was still being practiced, but among Tomhom's *manåmko'*, and not, according to Calvo, among the younger generation (1991).

As mentioned earlier, as a child, Påle' 'Scot often accompanied his aunt, Mrs Torres, to Tomhom for the *nubena*. The site where the novena was held was owned by the Palomo family, the maternal great-grandparents of local businessman and civic leader Pedro "Sonny" Ada III. The novena was followed by a Mass and a *lukao* (procession) along the beach. Afterward was sung a hymn to San Vitores. As was typical of novenas to village patron saints, the path to the chapel in Tomhom was lit with candles, as for a vigil. Whereas the rituals were typical of those used in the traditional Chamorro novenas to village and personal patron saints, Påle' 'Scot was quick to point out that this particular celebration was *not directed* to San Vitores per se but to the Feast of the Finding of the True Cross, because "Rome does not permit the veneration of an individual who has not been beatified or canonized" (Calvo 1991). This Nubenan Santa Cruz, as he explained, was held "*in conjunction* with the memory of San Vitores" but not "in veneration" of him because he had not yet been beatified. This distinction is significant because, though it is forged through Calvo's training in canon law in the Philippines, it represents a specifically folk Chamorro latent "critique" of Chamorro piety that is ostensibly at odds, but only to a certain extent, with a Spanish priest's enthusiastic conflation of that "little" Chamorro tradition and the finding of remnants of San Vitores's cross, something that clearly had great meaning for mid-twentieth-century Spanish padres on the eve of their being replaced by American and Chamorro priests. This provisional distinction—for Påle' 'Scot, ultimately not too big a deal because "the crosses are one and the same anyway"—nevertheless points to discernable differences and stakes between Chamorro Catholics and foreign Catholic priests in what might otherwise be understood as a unitary history of Catholicism. In chapter 6, when we return to Påle' 'Scot, we will also have an opportunity to consider a case of outright tension between the Chamorro priest, Påle' Dueñas, and two other *sanhiyong* padres, this time Japanese, during the occupation, in yet another layer or dimension of cultural and political alterity and specificity found in Chamorro Catholicism.

Despite his preferred reading of the unity (between the two crosses and traditions), however, Påle' 'Scot still insisted on the antiquity of the Nubenan Santa Cruz for Chamorros, for its indirect role in helping keep San Vitores's memory alive through its location, its short hymn, and most especially, its principal focus on an established and recognized devotion (the Finding of the Holy Cross) that did not transgress canon law. Try as I might, and armed as I was with the critical mantra to "always historicize!" culture, I could not get Påle' 'Scot to agree that the Nubenan Santa Cruz was in fact a modern devotion, one forged in the "aura" of San Vitores's canonization effort (Jameson 1981, 9). In fact, whether it is fifty years or three hundred years of Chamorro veneration of Catholic iconography, there is something quintessentially Chamorro about such "articulated" piety that just throws theories of "inventedness" out the window. In the end, it was I who acquiesced.

Although many individuals among the present cohort of the island's

manåmko' could and would attest openly to the veracity of the story of *håga'*
Påle' San Vitores (blood of Padre San Vitores), few remain who were active
participants in the Nubenan Santa Cruz of the prewar years. Tita Mesa,
the *techa* who inherited the duty of leading the novena from her paternal
grandmother in 1957, is among the aforementioned few. At the time of
my research, she still resided in Tomhom, which was elevated after the war
to the status of "village" for Government of Guam purposes, and to that
of a parish for the government's spiritual counterpart, the Archdiocese of
Agaña. Tomhom, as we shall see below, and in the next chapter, has also
become, since the late 1960s, Guam's version of Waikīkī with its prodigious
number of world-class hotels, shopping malls, eateries, and nightclubs,
including the ubiquitous strip joints that cater principally to Japanese visitors. Equally, Tomhom is a favorite destination for Guam residents for its
after-hours social attractions and its many beaches for family outings. With
deep maternal and paternal "roots" in Tomhom (*familian* Malle' and *familian* Tun Vicentan Leon Guerrero), Tita recalled her mother telling her
that the Santa Cruz novena "was a big, big fiesta" (Mesa 1992). Although
it was not until 1957 that she inherited the formal duties, Tita had been
an active participant in the upkeep of the old chapel during and after the
war. "Masses then were held on Mondays," she recollected, "and we did not
have a full church before the war." But Tita Mesa also recounted a narrative
slightly, but significantly, different from that told by the formally educated
Påle' 'Scot. She said that *i taotao Tomhom* (the people of Tomhom), proud of
the presence of San Vitores's shrine, believed him in fact to be a saint. "Was
he not called 'San' Vitores, like San Vicente, San Antonio, San Ignacio,
some of the other village patron saints on Guam?" she asked. Unlike Påle'
'Scot, who received formal training in theology and canon law, Tomhom's
faithful neither knew nor cared about the finer distinctions between individuals beatified or canonized, on the one hand, and those not properly
certified, on the other.

In fact, there was a collision of sorts during the immediate postwar years
when Church officials sought to correct Tomhom residents' long loyalty to
Nubenan Santa Cruz and its associated would-be saint, San Vitores. This
local melding was reinforced (according to Tita Mesa, and confirmed by
Påle' 'Scot) by the Tomhom belief that what was being celebrated was in
fact the finding of the remains of a small cross *carried by San Vitores* at the
time of his martyrdom, or the recovery of a small wooden cross (or crosses)
that traditionally marked the exact spot of the assassination. This slight distinction and the moment of tension that erupted after the war between
local Catholic officials (including Påle' 'Scot) and the laity are significant
because they register important differences within Chamorro Catholicism
itself. But this is also interesting because, although both Påle' 'Scot and Tita
Mesa have emphasized the independence of the Nubenan Santa Cruz for
Chamorros from the novena(s) that was (were) consciously rescheduled to

coincide with San Vitores's anniversary date (under Arrayoz's tenure before World War II), they differ on the centrality of San Vitores's memory in that the Nubenan Santa Cruz, for reasons, educated priests would say, having to do with villagers' ignorance of canon law. Yet, it warrants pointing out that the mini "schism" between the Chamorro clergy and the Chamorro laity on this count shifts the latter on the side of Arrayoz's desire (as a Spaniard) to identify the Nubenan Santa Cruz with the seventeenth-century Spaniard in ways that Calvo insists run counter to canon law. On this count, the Chamorro laity (and their leaders, the *techa*) are "articulated" with the Spanish priests of the twentieth and seventeenth century, and not with the local Chamorro clergy administrators, including Påle' 'Scot, who nonetheless also self-identifies, on other counts, with San Vitores himself. Indeed, Calvo draws the line between his dutiful service "for the Greater Glory of God" (as a trained priest who is also duty-bound to obey Church doctrine) on the one hand, and Chamorro lay piety, on the other (Calvo 1991).

Of course this local (con)fusion of traditions of found crosses and miracles of would-be saints does not signify the fusion of Catholic and Native ignorance, as folks like Arago observed in the early part of the nineteenth century (or folks like Matson have implied in the twentieth). Rather, such a fusion describes what can be called the interested plots of faith on which, as we shall see, (proud) Spanish, Chamorro, and American Catholic names and identities are staked. In a clear effort to avoid tensions surrounding the Nubenan Santa Cruz, and possibly in a conscious effort to be sensitive to local Chamorro politics (or maybe to not get caught in the crossfire), the new American bishop, Apolinaris Baumgartner, decided to elevate Tomhom to parish status and to build its parishioners a new church. Indebted to a Chicago benefactor and longtime friend and supporter of the bishop's ministry, Bishop Baumgartner named the new Tomhom church Saint William's, after the patron saint of Baumgartner's Chicago benefactor. On an island where "Catholicism is more than just a religion," and where all the island villages and parishes are named after saints, using their Spanish or Latin names (San Juan, Santa Barbara, San Vicente, San Dimas, etc), *i taotao Tomhom* (the people from Tomhom) were stuck with a saint with whom they had no relationship and of whom they had no knowledge, and whose name stuck out like a sore thumb. In what was probably the deepest cut of all, according to Mesa (1992), the new church was not even built "near the place where San Vitores died."[16]

The Saint William's Travesty

Thus the faith that Tomhom villagers expressed toward "their patron saint San Vitores" (before he had in fact been elevated by the Catholic Church, fumed Påle' 'Scot), was fused with the universal celebration of the Finding of the True Cross and was given a severe test in the circumstances immediately following the American liberation of the island in 1945. Even before the war had begun, US Naval officials had been disturbed at what they considered to be the negative influence of the remaining Spanish padres among the Chamorro people and had begun the process of replacing them with American priests, creating local resentment and tension. Påle' 'Scot was the only local Catholic priest left, throughout the greater part of the Japanese occupation. He looked forward to the return of his spiritual superior, the late Bishop Ángel Olano, who, exiled to Japan, was imprisoned there at the time (Olano 1949; Radao 2005). Although Olano did return after the war, an American bishop, the late Apolinaris Baumgartner, who was selected by American church and naval officials, replaced him almost immediately. True to his vows, Påle' 'Scot served his new superior, even though, in his words, the new successor proceeded to do "a great disservice to the people of Tumon" (Calvo 1991). Tita Mesa and other island residents recalled more intense feelings: the people of Tomhom were furious (Mesa 1992).

The "great disservice" that infuriated the Tomhom residents was the razing of the San Vitores marker, and especially the construction of a new parish church, down the street, which was christened "St William of Vercelli Church." In 1945, after the war, and shortly after Bishop Baumgartner had arrived, Påle' 'Scot led a procession in Tomhom to celebrate Nubenan Santa Cruz (Calvo 1991). Using leftover wood from the US Navy, Påle' 'Scot constructed a makeshift "sort of a chapel" that had windows and a door but wasn't really "protected." This structure was vandalized by "these, you know, pranksters and people who go to the beach at night." These vandals broke into the chapel and "used it for their purposes." When I asked him what he meant, he snapped back, "You know what I mean!" When Bishop Baumgartner heard about this, he went out and obtained a piece of property just south of where the makeshift chapel stood. Baumgartner, the first American to head the traditionally Spanish-run mission station, by now a vicariate (*Navy News* 1946, 17; Quitugua 1995), solicited and received financial backing from a stateside benefactor (from Chicago) to build an edifice at this new site. In return, Bishop Baumgartner called this new parish Saint William's, to honor the patron saint of this new parish's new patron. Or was it "to satisfy," as Påle' 'Scot speculates in his typical, blunt way, "the ego or the pride of that American man from Chicago?"

Until the church was renamed "Beatu Diego Church" in 1985 to celebrate the beatification of San Vitores, Tomhom had the dubious distinction of being the only Catholic parish on the island to have an Anglo name. Moreover, the chapel was not even built at the actual spot long revered by local residents. But what aggravated the residents most—and Påle' 'Scot played the role of mediating between the new shepherd and his restless flock—was that they felt that San Vitores had been, in Påle' 'Scot's words, "forgotten

completely" (Calvo 1991). In the postwar years, where Chamorro investments in American institutions have displaced Spanish Catholic institutions
that have displaced other indigenous names and places, the Nubenan Santa
Cruz is celebrated separately from yet another novena specifically dedicated
to Beatu Diego (McGrath 1985).[17] In the 1990s, for instance, the Nubenan
Santa Cruz was led by Mrs Magdalena Perez as authorized by Archbishop
Anthony J Apuron. Then, the Nubenan Santa Cruz had been experienc-
ing problems, celebrated as it is, at the new San Vitores shrine. Enclosed
by a marine recreation concession, a beachside bar, and a Chinese seaside
restaurant, flanked by tennis courts on its eastern end, and dwarfed by the
towering Guam Reef Hotel to its north and northeast, the newly reconstructed shrine is surrounded by congestion and distraction. The annual
novena is now held down the street at the newly renamed and also refur-
bished Beatu Diego Parish. Just as it has shifted spots, some might say it has
shifted languages. In the following section, however, I examine how the
apparent history of shifting tongues does not necessarily point to cultural
demise resulting from (continued) Chamorro investment in Catholicism in
the twentieth century.

Fino' Lågu and Chamorro: Prayers for All at Beatu Diego Church

"You need to know the language to know the novena."
—Tita L G Mesa (1992)

As with the novena, so with language: Which one are we talking about?
Which language will Chamorro articulate itself in now? The Nubenan Santa
Cruz, now led by Magdalena Perez, is not only held at the Blessed Diego
Parish instead of at the site of San Vitores's martyrdom but is held *in English*. The *nubena* itself, described as a local tradition since time immemorial
in the *Positio* and by Church scholars, had in fact been discontinued several
times. Although it was revived briefly in the 1970s in conjunction with the
effort to revive the beatification process (and without Påle' 'Scot's full blessings, for the same reasons he disaggregated the popular Nubenan Santa
Cruz from both popular and Church-sponsored efforts to conjoin the two),
it was only in the late 1980s that the annual observance reappeared. It was
Mrs Perez who asked and received permission from Archbishop Anthony
Apuron to revive the practice. It is still held at the end of April and ends on
2 May. That the Nubenan Santa Cruz itself is conducted in English marks
a key aspect of Chamorro Catholic relations never before studied systematically: the place of language in the conversion of the Chamorro people.
I will outline here the linguistic determinations articulated in one *techa*'s
observations of her craft. Tita's "career" as a *techa* began in childhood, when
she started praying the family's Nubenan Niñu or novena to the Holy Child

during the Christmas holidays. That was "easy," said Tita. Even as a toddler, she delighted in "playing" novena with her younger cousins. Besides inheriting the Nubenan Santa Cruz from Tan Vicentan Unpingco, Tita has also inherited her mother's own Santisima Trinidad (novena to the Holy Trinity). Only a few years ago, at the urging of her older sister, Tita began conducting the novena *in Chamorro* rather than in the *traditional* Spanish language. She did this because "the children were not following it anymore." It might shock a younger generation of Chamorros to know that Chamorro *nubenas* and their *lisåyu* (rosaries) had, before World War II, been conducted in *fino' lågu* (language from overseas; in this case, Spanish).

Recognizing the missionaries' intense interest in Native vernaculars and local cultural practices for their importance in helping them effectively implant Christian doctrine, Vicente Rafael stresses the missionaries' awareness of the risks involved in using Native vernaculars. These include the possibilities of Native mistranslations and misunderstandings, especially when Natives delight in using vernaculars that seemed to delight in meaning making and wordplay. Let us call this version of the epidemic of signification "discursive flourish." To guard against such risks, the missionaries sought as much as possible to define the use of their terms, for example, *långhet* (sky) would be glossed as "heaven." But to be extra certain, the missionaries refused to translate certain names and terms, like God, Jesus, and Mary, into the vernacular because they believed there just could not be any Native equivalents. Although San Vitores was enthusiastic to learn and use the vernacular (see chapter 5), apparently rituals like rosaries and novenas were conducted in Spanish or Latin until the early twentieth century. The shift from *fino' lågu* to *fino' Chamorro* was occasioned, according to Father Julius Sullivan (1957, 118), by a deadly flu epidemic, traced to a Navy transport ship, that hit the island in November 1918. This epidemic killed more than a thousand *manåmko'*, or more than *80 percent* of the *manåmko'* population.[18] According to Sullivan, among the effects was that it "brought to an abrupt halt the use of the Spanish language in Guam." Because English still had not gained "ascendancy," Chamorro became the "medium of carrying on the work of the Church" (Sullivan 1957, 118). This trend was reinforced by the arrival and labor of a new generation of Spanish padres who took a special interest in what was then called *fino' håya* (language from within), now commonly referred to as *fino' Chamorro*, spoken Chamorro, which was still the language of choice for the vast majority of Chamorros, much to the consternation of the American officials who tried to replace it with English. Among the most enthusiastic of the padres, and certainly the one who is recalled with great affection for it, was Påle' Roman de Vera, who showed a special devotion to *fino' håya* by translating many songs and prayers into the vernacular. Not since San Vitores himself has a Spanish *påle'* expressed such a deep concern for the language, and, according to Paul Carano (1975, 12), Påle' Roman hastened the use of *fino' håya*, or Chamorro, for devotional purposes in 1915. It is also highly probable that Påle' Roman composed the hymn to San Vitores that was sung at the end of the Nubenan Santa Cruz, because it is in Chamorro. If this is true, then we need to return to the matter about the provenance of the Nubenan Santa Cruz (suddenly I feel like a Vatican postulator), for it is also highly probable, if extremely provocative, to suggest that the entire Nubenan Santa Cruz, in addition to the particular devotion to San Vitores expressed therein (the song and the procession), might really only have begun early in the twentieth century. Of course this is not to suggest that there were not other forms of upholding the "memory of San Vitores" that are of greater antiquity (but why should "antiquity" be the mark of real history and culture?); indeed, written and spoken record attests to the sanctity of that particular spot in Tomhom and supernatural occurrences there. But if this speculation is true, it would mean that much of what is taken to be the long tradition of venerating San Vitores—especially as upheld in the novena, its hymn, and the procession—is in fact intelligible only within a more recent context of his canonization, and especially as imagined by the last of the Spanish padres in the flux of the prewar years. Or we need to have faith—but now that faith needs to be in what the people are saying of their own traditions.

Still, it is useful to know the histories of *nubenas* and *lisåyu*, to know how they might not have shifted from the *fino' lågu* to the Chamorro vernacular (and increasingly, to English) until the twentieth century. This does not mean, as *taotao sanhiyong* visitors or even longtime residents may think, that there is no such thing as Chamorro culture, that is, that true Chamorro culture vanished long ago. It does indicate, however, the need to attend to the trajectories and forms by which Chamorro culture expresses or articulates itself. In the meantime, in present-day Guam, in a particular spot in Tomhom, down the street from that other place long believed to be the actual spot of San Vitores's martyrdom, there is what might be called a proliferation, a flourish, of *fino'*. For in spite of the need to shift from Spanish to Chamorro to English in late-twentieth-century prayer, Tita described the fullness of praying "in one's own language." She elaborated: "When you pray in your own dialect, your own language, you know, the prayer is deeper" (Mesa 1992). It is for this reason, and not simply because she identifies herself as a Chamorro, that Tita is inclined to lead as many Chamorro songs as possible on a given Sunday Mass at Blessed Diego Parish in Tomhom. But on any (other?) given Sunday, one may also hear songs sung in the *fino' lågu* (at English Masses), and these are also led by Tita L G Mesa. The English Masses serve both parishioners who feel nostalgia for the prewar and immediate postwar days, and the increasing number of Filipinos in her parish (presumably hotel and restaurant workers) who, for their own displaced histories, can join in the chorus of age-old Castilian-Latin hymns. But nostalgia and practicality, too, find good form in *fino' Chamorro* once again. Tita observed that there are more and more of "these Americans and

Filipinos, too, who come to our Mass because we sing *in Chamorro*" (Mesa 1992). Thus, one can find, or hear, *fino' lågu* and *fino' Chamorro* in Anglo Masses at Beatu Diego Parish in Tomhom.

The Beatification Shrine

The proliferation of languages and meanings associated with San Vitores's legacy in Tomhom is also evident in the history of the "Beatification Shrine," which was unveiled on 10 November 1985 to commemorate the beatification of San Vitores. Actually, the shrine consisted of improvements on an earlier concrete chapel (built by the Christian Mothers Organization) and added bronze renderings of the martyrdom. The unveiling followed a Mass and a second novena, a "post-beatification" novena and fiesta in which was celebrated the renaming of Saint William of Vercelli Parish for Blessed Diego de San Vitores. To mark the change of name and its occasion, a towering statue of San Vitores had been unveiled the previous month (on 6 October) on the grounds of the newly renamed church (figure 5). After more than three hundred years, San Vitores finally had "a sacred place named in his honor" (Cates 1985a, 40). The name switch was not a "simple matter in the Catholic Church." According to Sister Francis Jerome, SM, "The matter had to go through the Vatican, and its approval came right after the beatification" (quoted in Cates 1985a, 40).

According to Archbishop Anthony Apuron, the existing shrine in Tomhom was intended to "rally people to continue to pray [for the canonization]" (*PDN* 1985g, 20), to "bequeath to the people of the Archdiocese and their visitors an impressive monument of the martyrdom . . . [and to provide] a fitting place for pilgrimage to the sacred ground" (*Pacific Voice* 1985d, 1). The shrine, and about another $50,000 worth of "improvements" on the existing infrastructure, was also viewed as a "focus of pilgrimage in [the] Archdiocese of Hagåtña."[19] The shrine's total cost (including improvements to the existing chapel) came to about $350,000. The fundraising for the project was spearheaded by the Knights of Columbus, Påle' San Vitores Council 5666, after it was assigned the task by the late Archbishop Flores (*Pacific Voice* 1985d, 1).[20] A "world-class sculptor" from the Philippines designed the beatification shrine, which was built by a local Filipino contractor.[21] The shrine consisted of five larger-than-life statues of San Vitores, Matå'pang, Hirao, and Matå'pang's wife holding a child (figures 6–9). These were erected on "the sacred ground . . . of martyrdom," and were, according to a promotional flyer signed by Archbishop Anthony Apuron, a "testimony to the forces at work in the martyrdom of Blessed Diego."[22] The shrine was seen to "speak plainly of an historical event filled with faith, hope and love shining through human weakness which shaped the culture of the Chamorro people."

FIGURE 5. The larger-than-life statue of San Vitores for a larger-than-life legacy among the Chamorros of the Marianas. This statue is located on the lawn of the Blessed Diego Church in Tomhom. Photo by the author.

Before his death, which occurred a week after the beatification, Archbishop Flores emphasized the significance of the beatification: "It was the first ever in the history of the entire Pacific area wherein a holy martyr [was] elevated to the status of Blessed in heaven, the next step to Sainthood." His successor, Archbishop Anthony Apuron, echoed, "The beatification of

FIGURES 6–9. Built at the site of San Vitores's death in Tomhom to augment a bronze plaque and a chapel, the dramatic portrayal of San Vitores's assassination at the hands of Maga'låhi Matå'pang and his accomplice, Hirao, completes a setting intended, in part, to offer a place of prayer and reflection amid the cacophony of

high-rise hotels, beachside bars, and other modern recreational activities for Asian tourists, US military personnel, and island residents. Photos courtesy of Marita Sturken.

San Vitores is a milestone for the peoples of the Pacific since it [was] the first time in all their history that they will have their own patron saint. Ireland has its own Saint Patrick; the United States has its own Mother Francis Cabrini; Japan has its own Saint Francis Xavier and now, we in the Pacific and Micronesian territories will have our own Blessed Diego." Citing this significance, a member of the Knights of Columbus (San Vitores chapter) quickly added, "For this reason, everyone in this part of the world (as well as Guamanians all over the world) should put in their share to make the San Vitores statue and monument a reality" (*Pacific Voice* 1985c, 1).

Wishing to share in the possession, Guamanians within the region and outside it opened their pocketbooks—and in some rather enterprising ways as well. First, fellow knights each pledged at least a hundred dollars apiece; Guam's business community followed suit. The Guam Visitors Bureau, the organization most responsible for the promotion of the island's prosperous tourist industry, donated $10,000. As with donations to other charities, donations to the religious cause were eligible for tax breaks. Besides personal donations of varying amounts, island residents donated another $12,000 through their participation in a special ten-day extension of the always-popular annual "Fiestan Guam" celebration (*PDN* 1985i, 18). Fiestan Guam—normally a two-week celebration—features a carnival, a beauty contest, a parade, and concessions. More importantly, it commemorates the American liberation of the island from Japanese occupation in 1944. In the next chapter we will see the particular meanings spun out of San Vitores's entanglement with liberation day discourse. In 1985, as was the case with previous "Fiestan Guam" celebrations under the Ricardo Bordallo administration, proceeds were directed toward the much celebrated (and ridiculed) "Latte of Freedom" monument envisioned by Bordallo to memorialize the island's deep commitment to and sacrifice for liberty and democracy.[23] But residents were assured that proceeds from the ten-day extension in support of the proposed improvement to the Tomhom shrine would not go to the "Freedom" monument (*PDN* 1985i, 18).

Perhaps one of the more enterprising sources of donation to the San Vitores shrine involved a Hawai'i franchise department store's contribution of a percentage of a whole month's sales receipts. In an advertisement in the *Pacific Voice* entitled "A Great Way to Help San Vitores Fund," Gibson's Department Store offered "a great opportunity . . . to everyone who is a friend or member of the Archdiocese of Hagåtña to help in the fund-raising." Mixing press release ("Archbishop Flores received word . . . etc") with sales pitch, the advertisement urged:

> Just imagine, every time you deposit your sales receipts when you shop at Gibson's, $.03 out of every dollar you spend for your goods will be turned over to the San Vitores funds under your name. Whether it be on a regular or discount

prices, you as a shopper at Gibson's will DOUBLY benefit. You can take advantage of all the good buys and at the same time, you can be a donor. . . . Remember, the more sales receipts registered, the larger the donation for our beatification project. Please pass on this information to your friends and neighbors so they also may take this opportunity to help themselves and help the cause. . . . *Si Yu'us Ma'ase* for your help! (*Pacific Voice* 1985b, 1)

As its final line indicates, the ad remains indebted both to Chamorro conversion to San Vitores's spiritual legacy and to Chamorro participation in free enterprise and consumerism as introduced by the American legacy. Indeed, investment in San Vitores can pay off. Inspired, perhaps, by the swarm of tourists and their dollars, yet another narrative of the employment of San Vitores in the making of Guam underlies a focal point of attraction and pilgrimage. This possibility of using the site for other tourist attractions was implied in a conversation with a local businessman, Peter "Sonny" Ada III, the great-great-grandson of the original owners of the land in question, whose grandmother had chosen to donate the property—now valuable Tomhom "beachfront" property—to the Catholic Church. At a popular Tomhom bar one night, Sonny approached me, perhaps out of a blend of curiosity and financial interest, and tapped my professional, scholarly opinion: Did San Vitores really die in that place? Are we sure that was the place? Though I may be found guilty of reading too much between the lines, I surmise my friend's question had more than a little to do with imagining the possibilities of some economic *conversions* of his own.

The single most important reason given for why the revived Nubenan Santa Cruz was moved to Blessed Diego Church from its old spot at the shrine is the illicit and inappropriate use of the site surrounding the shrine today. In the 1980s, the parish's pastor reported that visitors to the San Vitores shrine (about half a mile north of the church) might get distracted or irritated by "scantily-clad tourists." The shrine—a "very sacred and very historic spot," according to the pastor—is located between the beach and the tennis courts of the Reef Hotel and is flanked by a popular beach bar that features live rock music, occasional "wet T-shirt" competitions, and beach rental concessions. He also pointed to the difficulties encountered by people who come to the shrine to pray: "Many of the old-fashioned people take offence to seeing girls *in bikinis* near such a sacred area" (quoted in Kemp 1985c, 36; emphasis added). One such old-fashioned person—Auntie Acha—attested as much: "I don't like it there anymore," she scowled, "*too much of these girls with bikinis. Too much Japanese tourists*" (E Camacho 1991; emphasis added). Despite these distractions, the priest predicted that the shrine could "become a very popular *attraction* for tourists" (Kemp 1985c, 36; emphasis added).

Songsong Taotao Tåno' (Chamorro Village), Tomhom, 2005

The newest "edifice" is built about as close to the spot as one can get without actually encroaching on the now-gated grounds of the Beatification Shrine. This addition is actually a set of thatched huts where contemporary Chamorros dressed in loincloths, but also in attire from the Spanish era, mill around, weaving palm hats and fans and birds for tourists and US military folks. In the evening there are two performances by Guam's Pa'a Taotao Tåno' (People of the Land Dance troupe). The re-created village was the brainchild of Frank Rabon, who also founded the Taotao Tåno' dancers and cultural group. Rabon's objective is to render in song and dance indigenous Chamorro culture and traditions from the "precontact" era through the Spanish and contemporary American eras. Part of his definition of authenticity is that if a Chamorro does it, it is Chamorro.

As a "stage," the village itself can be viewed as the latest site of Chamorro cultural performance, one that seeks to capitalize on the visitor industry, but by providing something that the other hotels do not do in presenting their standard Polynesian revues for tourists seeking an authentic tropical paradise—not a generic Polynesian one, but a specifically Native Chamorro song and dance. The emergence in the twenty-first century of a Chamorro village recalling the precontact era (in a spot about as close as one can get to the shrine that commemorates San Vitores's death) may seem to contrast with the surrounding high-rise hotels, restaurants, bars, and nightclubs. They even suggest something of a return of the repressed, oppressed, or suppressed Native, one who after three hundred years of colonization refuses to go away. But because San Vitores's legacy was also ostensibly the legacy of colonialism that has not formally ended, one might say that the spirit of the Taotao Tåno' dancers might also stand (or dance) in sharp contrast to what San Vitores represents. And then again, the stories and rituals of local Chamorro investments that have sacralized this spot into a portal of the translocal and the transcultural also appear to challenge the boundaries between what is Native and what is not in their shared performance of Chamorro indigeneity. In the next chapter, I examine the continuation of such cultural performances, but as they are staged in historic and contemporary narrativizations of San Vitores's legacy among Chamorros. Like the translocal sets of meaning that continue to bubble forth, in time and space, from this particular spot, the historical narrativization of San Vitores's legacy among the Chamorros also yields a proliferation of competing meanings and stories of the sort that challenge any effort—Roman Catholic or Chamorro Catholic—to render a definitive and fundamental reading of this history. To these competing renditions in historical texts and contexts I now turn.

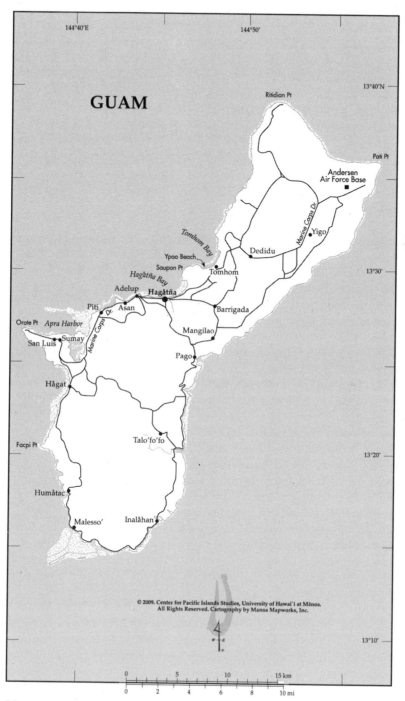

GUAM

13°40′N

Ritidian Pt

Pati Pt

Andersen
Air Force Base

Marine Corps Dr.

Yigo

Tomhom Bay

Dedidu

Ypao Beach
Saupon Pt
Tomhom

13°30′

Hagåtña Bay

Adelup
Hagåtña

Piti
Asan

Barrigada

Marine Corps Dr.

Orote Pt
Apra Harbor
Mangilao

San Luis
Sumay
Pago

Hågat

13°20′

Facpi Pt

Talo'fo'fo

Humåtac

Malesso'
Inalåhan

13°10′

© 2009. Center for Pacific Islands Studies, University of Hawai'i at Mānoa.
All Rights Reserved. Cartography by Manoa Mapworks, Inc.

N
W   E
S

| 0 | | 5 | | 10 | | 15 km |

| 0 | 2 | 4 | 6 | 8 | 10 mi |

144°40′E

144°50′

MAP 2

Chapter 4
Traffic on the Mount

Tomhom Bay, Guam, 1989

Påle' San Vitores Road embraces the gentle curve of a calm and picturesque Tomhom Bay (map 2). On a knoll at the road's southern end, above the Hilton Guam Hotel, there is an upscale neighborhood whose homeowners are miffed. Government of Guam (GovGuam) public works crews are again expanding the road, bringing too much noise, congestion, and even danger to those backing out of their driveway. GovGuam officials ask for patience; this road is the main artery that carries the island's economic and social lifeblood. Sometimes called "Guam's Waikīkī," Tomhom Bay through San Vitores Road is also "hotel row," a lei of edifices built almost exclusively by and for the post–World War II Japanese economy's workers in need of vacation time. There is irony in the prosperity and the taste of autonomy that accompanies economic development based on the Japanese visitor industry: the luring of Japanese tourists into Japanese hotels on a picturesque Pacific island today is seen as an economic antidote to a historic dependence on an American military presence that was responsible for saving the Chamorros from an unwanted, unwelcome Japanese occupation during the last world war. There is also an ironic limit to the irony; it is precisely because of Guam's status as an American territory, a portal into American duty-free markets, estate, and even stereotypically, its western frontier culture, that Japan has invested so much money in the island.

At the northern and opposite end of the bay, in the shadows of another knoll, the four-lane paved San Vitores Road ends in an uninviting path of ditch and gravel. At the end of this road lies Gun Beach, so named for an antiaircraft gun installed by Japanese occupation forces during World War II. But San Vitores Road is also under improvement here because Gun Beach is also the construction site of Hotel Nikko Guam, "the newest Pearl of the Pacific." The road at this end also leads to controversy. Late in 1989, amid groundbreaking, surveyors stumble on remains of a precontact Chamorro village and burial grounds. In compliance with local law, the contractors hire local archaeologists to determine their historical significance and

112

value. Initial digs unearth about a hundred ancestral remains, but also much pottery and other artifacts, rendering the site the largest, most significant and most exciting to date. Discussion among the contract archaeologists, GovGuam officials, and the developer results in the decision to clear the site, temporarily store the ancestral remains, and re-inter them on the lot after completion of the hotel (Superior Court of Guam 1989c). But fearing the worst, Chamorro activists secure a court-ordered halt on "the archaeological survey . . . and continued desecration of the ancestral burial ground" (Superior Court of Guam 1989b). They argue that while "the defendants . . . recognize the burial site's archaeological and historical value, they fail to comprehend [its] cultural relevance . . . as a *way of living* that was built up by [one set of] Chamorros . . . *and passed from one generation to another*" (Superior Court of Guam 1989a). As a compromise, the litigants agree to construct a "memorial" on the hotel grounds.

Ann Arbor, Michigan, 2007

In hindsight, the Nikko incident would only launch a new episode of tension and conflict among militant Chamorros, private developers, and GovGuam officials, with the principal bone of contention being the fate of ancestors continually resurfacing through the land's disturbance by feverish foreign developers and their local boosters in the name of island prosperity and quality of life. Such events have tended to occur in Tomhom in particular because of its noted "beauty," the calmness of its beaches, and the historical fact that there were many villages and settlements in this area. Not merely a coincidence, one beach site, about equidistant between the two aforementioned hot spots along San Vitores Road, had only recently been renamed "Matå'pang Beach Park" due to GovGuam's acquiescence to activists in light of the recent beatification of San Vitores. In the process of developing the site as a "public" recreational ground, of course, ancestral remains would, almost expectedly, resurface to stir things up again.

That these events would occur along such a socially, economically, and politically "congested" road that bears his name signals a cultural and political history of how San Vitores and spots in Tomhom have become virtual conduits for Chamorro historical and cultural self-understanding. As the arterial lifeline that carries the latest currency of Guam's economy and hope for political autonomy, the road is also a kind of portable portal, like the sweet spot where San Vitores was killed, through which bodies and spirits of the ancestors from the pre-mission Chamorro past come bursting through in ways that require attention, and legal action, to (address) the specificity of indigenous culture and tradition, however bound they have become with those that have washed ashore from elsewhere in the past four hundred years.

This chapter examines the heightening and intensification of multiple and competing *manChamorro* (Chamorro) or *taotao tåno'* (people of the land) and *taotao sanhiyong* (people from outside, ie, non-Chamorro) perspectives as they battle over the meanings of San Vitores's legacy among the Chamorro, or of Chamorro Catholicism as it is bound up with San Vitores's mission story. For, as we shall see, *sanhiyong* dwell on the equation in terms of the former, while *manChamorro* dwell on the latter. The same thing looks quite different depending on where and how one is situated. Though situated in a particular site on the island of Guam, the event (San Vitores's death) that took place on land and sea in Tomhom implicates indigenous Chamorro and other residents on Guam but also others outside Guam: the Vatican, Jesuits, European and American historians and colonial officials, and even lay Catholics around the world who are invested in the "universal" Catholic Church but who pay close and informed attention to its matters "overseas." Though transnational and transcultural in character, however, the economic, political and cultural stakes that are themselves "staked" in Tomhom Bay also describe competing indigenous Chamorro histories of "localizing" ideas and practices that originate from beyond their shores. In other words, being on the Native side—whether Catholic or Chamorro—does not guarantee uniform or stable meanings.

In this chapter, I analyze a representative sampling of such transhistorical and transcultural voices in order to continue to demonstrate the competing plurality of meanings associated with San Vitores's name and fame, or Chamorro cultural and political investments in the Catholicism brought by San Vitores. Here, I continue to follow the wider sets of meanings that tend to be arrested or sublimated to a range of *sanhiyong* perspectives—often through competing nationalisms but also through providentialist interpretations—on San Vitores's mission story in particular, and their implications for comprehending Guam's cultural and political pasts and presents in general. Precisely for its concern with the problematic of cultural and historical narrativization and practice, this chapter prevails even more closely on Hayden White's lifelong call to pay critical attention to the "content of the form" and other "tropics of discourse" through whose formal effects historians have narrativized into existence ideas about the historical past that have shaped our historical and present cultural and political consciousness (H White 1973, 1978, 1981, 1987). Riffing on White, I identify and discuss recurring tropes or metaphors, like remoteness and insularity, and "modes of emplotment" like romance, tragedy, and comedy, that structure rivaling narratives or stories about San Vitores. Thus using materiality in and out of Guam, we are afforded just one version of what we might call—again riffing off White—the colonial and anticolonial "discourses of the tropics."[1] In the next section, I survey the romantic and tragic emplotments in *sanhiyong* historiography in order to show that, like the monologic narrative we saw in Part One, canonical historiography of the Catholic mission among the Chamorros leaves much to be desired. In stark contrast, the following sections of this chapter proceed to examine a plethora of indigenous political and cultural "stakes" in Roman Catholicism, whether for Chamorro clergy and laity, or for the Chamorro opposition, which has a discernable legacy. Together, they recall and intensify the competing and contested layers of Chamorro Catholicism as it is forged in relation to San Vitores's mission in these islands.

Romance and Tragedy in *Sanhiyong* Historiography

In the swirl of Guam's present and past, non-Chamorros—Catholics and otherwise—enjoy in print culture, and certainly in academic discourse, a privileged position vis-à-vis Native perspectives. Non-Catholic non-Chamorros in particular have not had much to lose in "dissing" the Spanish Catholic legacy in the Marianas. The slang is appropriate, in this day and age, for these expressions of opposition, given the bond and force of Catholic hegemony in Guam, have also amounted to a rather systematic assault on Chamorro cultural and political agency.

For example, in a letter to the editor of the *Pacific Daily News* during the beatification celebration, one Bob Howe pulled no punches: "It makes me almost sick to my stomach to witness all the pageantry and to hear all the wonderful things said about the so-called martyr San Vitores" (1984, 26). For Howe, missionaries like San Vitores "came to Guam and forced their religion and their will upon the people. The Spanish really [didn't] give a damn about the Chamorros, or the *indios*, as they called them. Wherever the Spanish went in their conquests, they treated the people shabbily, to say the least." Howe called San Vitores "just another punk out of the pages of history," a "selfish" and "religious zealot [who] is directly responsible for imposing his values, religion, and culture upon a people who didn't want it." He concluded (mistakenly or at least prematurely) that "we should not have canonized San Vitores." But Howe's ire was also directed at the "local . . . hypocrites" who "go out to the local Catholic church, genuflect and observe . . . a missionary zealot . . . responsible for . . . the destruction of their heritage." Instead, he touted Matå'pang, who was "brave enough to see that by submitting to him he would lose his freedom and culture." Ultimately, however, Howe's central message in opposing San Vitores was based on a deeply entrenched idea of authentic indigenous cultural and racial demise resulting from a history of foreign (here, Spanish Catholic) colonial encroachment (Monnig 2007). His is a mix of grief and a modern quantum over biological purity and cultural authenticity. Howe railed (or wailed), "Where oh where in the Marianas is a Chamorro? There isn't one! No not

one. Their language is 90% destroyed, their culture is 99% mixed, mutated
or destroyed, and almost 100% of their traditional religious beliefs are lost.
They are now mostly Catholic, ruled by a hoalie [*sic*] pope in Rome." [2]

Howe (and his late-twentieth-century perspective on the demise of
Chamorro purity—as if only on such notions of purity could true Chamorro
culture and language rest) has company in a parade of other non-Spanish
colonial visitors to the Marianas. Together they afford us a sense of the
depth of the terms by which the story of Catholicism (and Native culture)
has been systematically misunderstood, regardless of whether they admire
or vilify "the punk" and his mission. First we examine the discourse of vili-
fication, always tragic, which tragically always ends up obliterating any kind
of meaningful Chamorro agency in this history. We can begin by returning
to Jacques Arago, the French naturalist we met in the previous chapter, to
follow what also turns out to be an international outcry against Spanish
tyranny in an ongoing episode of imperial rivalries.

In 1819, as part of the Freycinet scientific expedition, Arago expressed
pain at "so wretched a condition" as existed in the region. Actually (as we
saw in the last chapter), Arago was ambivalent about this history. Referring
to the Spanish as a people who had "given more noble examples of great-
ness and magnanimity" than any other on the earth (Arago 1971, 1:265), he
also chastised them for having "conquered this Archipelago neglect[ing]
nothing . . . to establish their own manners and customs in their new possessions" (Arago 1971, 2:4). Arago lamented a history in which "armed violence triumphed over timid weakness" (1971, 2:4), in which "[n]ine-tenths
of the inhabitants . . . [had] been exterminated" (1971, 1:268). Sadly, he
concluded, where it "ought to have established in them peace and happiness[, the religion had] covered them with a funeral pall" (Arago 1971,
1:268). His is the kind of source document that indignant modernists like
Howe seem to rely on for their cultural calculus (or geometry, given the
underlying and attendant spatial practices).

Arago was hardly alone in international (European) criticism and conclusion. His contemporary (and fellow naturalist), Russian Otto von Kotzebue, echoed the tragic fate over the "extirpation" of the Chamorro people,
observing that "the sportive, cheerful disposition of the South Sea Islanders
is no longer found among them" and that "all their actions are indicative
of subjection" (1821, 249). Enacting historiographically a longer embat-
tled history with Spain over imperial supremacy, Captain James Burney of
the British Royal Navy took his own potshots when he described the Spanish Catholic mission in the Marianas as "a melancholy exception" to "the
behavior of advanced societies" (1967, 271). Burney explained that, normally, "the disposition to tyrannize . . . becomes tempered by moral and
prudential consideration, and is rendered less sweeping and destructive .
. . than in its more ignorant state of natural society" (1967, 271). In other
words, according to Burney, Spain was more savage than the "natural ones"

it had killed. In fairness, Burney's was only the latest salvo in an enduring international rivalry between England and Spain in a European charter to possess the globe. For Britain, Burney added another tally mark: "Of all the intercourse of Europeans with the natives of the South Sea Islands the settlement of the Ladrones by the Spaniards was the most unfortunate." In fact, Burney did not discriminate ethnically in his aiming at the Jesuits in particular. For example, he called French Jesuit historian LeGobien a "hypocrite" whose writings "color[ed]" and "conceal[ed]" the truth about the Marianas "for the honor of the [Jesuit] society," whose writings were but "the garb and semblance of holiness and compassion to a course of systematic oppression." In contrast, Burney likened his own narrative to a "sound ship . . . [that] sail[ed] under . . . the cause of truth [and was] armed with the proper methods of collecting and offering information to the public" (Burney 1967, 271). Burney himself was also "armed . . . with [the] full conviction that a charge so serious[,] if made upon vague or insufficient grounds[,] would merit severe reprehension." Armed thus, Burney summarized the consequence of Spain's actions in the archipelago: once "[to] the highest degree fruitful and . . . filled with people[, these islands] have been rendered desolate, wild, and wholly bereft of inhabitants" (1967, 274).

In contrast, and perhaps because he was a Spaniard, Señor Felipe de la Corte in 1875 seemed far more ambivalent in groping for a rhetorical maneuver by which to redeem his nation's missionary project among the Chamorros: "One does not know which to admire most, whether the tenacity of the Spaniards in conflict with the elements and against a cunning and treacherous people . . . or that of the natives in pursuing such a cruel and prolonged war that could only end in their annihilation and ruin" (quoted in Olive y García 1984, 3). In assigning blame to the latter, de la Corte's rhetorical admiration can easily be seen as directed to the former.

A decade later, following up on a campaign to "revitalize" this faraway forgotten Spanish colony, Governor Francisco Olive y García concurred with de la Corte's ultimate assessment: "That is exactly what happened—annihilation and ruin" (Olive y García 1984, 3). Olive y García and de la Corte in fact represent a long lineage of colonialist historiography representing San Vitores's mission in romantic terms. Perhaps the earliest synthesis of primary source documents coming out of the Marianas is Padre Francisco García's *Vida y Martirio de el Venerable Padre Diego Luis Sanvitores* (1683). He wrote, "In darkness the Islanders had lived through many centuries when Divine Providence, whose secrets are beyond understanding . . . [called] all nations to the Church as helpers in the vineyard" (Higgins 1937a, 3). In the 1930s, parts of García's work were translated by Margaret Higgins and serialized in the *Guam Recorder* as the "First History of Guam" (Higgins 1936a, 1936b, 1937a, 1937b, 1938, 1939; see also García 2004). The *Guam Recorder* was the US Navy's organ of expression in Guam. According to Higgins and the editors of the *Recorder*, examining this six-hundred-page work was "like *penetrating* a dense forest, where one must make one's own path, selecting as one goes the items of greatest importance as of interest to the general reader, while rejecting for the time being those matters which do not seem important *to our purpose"* (Higgins 1936a, 3; emphasis added). "Our purpose" of course is the US Navy's own missionary impulse to modernize what it considered to be a backward people. García's hagiography of San Vitores and company provided a historical backdrop to America's colonial project and furnished information that would allow a kind of comparison and contrast in styles of administration. Perhaps it even served to validate the navy's presence, or at least its self-perception as a more "enlightened" form of benevolent if secular missionization. The romantic heroism that structured García's hagiography was not lost on his pre–World War II and, later, postwar political descendants. According to the *Guam Recorder* staff, García's narrative was a "heroic epic" whose drama was "the conversion of the Chamorros . . . together with the enumeration of legendary heroic acts of that handful of valiant missionaries and soldiers, who, numbering at times less than thirty souls, were never overcome *by the natives* in the battles" (Higgins 1936a, 3). However comforting it may be for the *sanhiyong* (outsiders) sympathetic to the Spaniards, it is equally revealing to see how even those Chamorros who provided assistance and support to the missionaries and whose loyalty probably accounted for the supposed "Spanish victory" get writ out completely in the foundational narrativization of the heroic few versus "the native" throng. What happened to "the native" on the "Spanish" side? It is as if they were on the wrong side even when they were on the "right" side.

French Jesuit Charles LeGobien also recounted the heroic dissemination of God's Word to otherwise doomed Natives (1949). For LeGobien, the place where God called San Vitores was paradisiacal, "where the sky is always beautiful and serene[, where] one can breathe pure air, and the heat is never excessive" (1949, 8). But there was also trouble in paradise, for though the mountains were covered with trees that were "always green," and were "crossed with streams which flow into the valleys and plains, making this land very pleasant," the islands' inhabitants, in stark contrast, were mired in "a dense darkness" of pride, arrogance, superstition, and "complete freedom" (LeGobien 1949, 8, 21). Two hundred and eighty years later, American Jesuit historian Francis Hezel noted a similar density, but in the Chamorro social terrain, which he described as a dense "political thicket" of rivalry that San Vitores and companions walked into without full realization (1982, 135). Hezel acknowledged the complexity of indigenous political and cultural agency by foregrounding this thicket, the rivalry that existed between Chamorros and the priests, and within each "side."[3] We will return to Hezel shortly. For LeGobien, the import of his narrative was in its perspective on contemporary debates around the pros and cons of man's natural state, and his view that Chamorros would have remained "enslaved" in freedom, had San Vitores not arrived heroically and like Christ, whom God himself sent to save humanity from its original sins.

Twentieth-century narrativizations are not bereft of polemical views on the Spanish legacy in the Marianas. For instance, the *Positio* (examined in Part One of this book) rehearses the providential narrative in which "the Islands were to remain . . . in their uncivilized state and paganism, until . . . 1668 [when] there landed . . . San Vitores" (Amore 1981, 2). This celebration was expressed earlier, in the mid-twentieth century, by the American Capuchin Julius Sullivan (1957), whose postwar Cold War anxiety is remarkable only because canonical twentieth-century historiography by Americans tends to posit fundamental discontinuity between American and Spanish hegemony. In this sense, Sullivan's account is different:

> Spain did not invade these islands to exploit them. No one has ever found gold in these hills. Spain sent her missionaries to Christianize the people and in so doing taught them the ways of western life. Because of the work done by *Padre San Vitores,* this outpost of the United States today can be considered a holding point against the menace of atheistic Communism. This would not be so if the Cross had not been planted firm and upright in the soil of Guam 300 years ago. To plant civilization and to plant the Cross is an achievement that must be applauded by any true lover of the human race. (Sullivan 1957, 22; emphasis in the original)

Such was Sullivan's "tribute to the high spirit of Romance that led Spain to these shores" (1957, 97), a celebration of his Church's history that only echoed America's strategic reasons for possessing Guam before and after World War II.

Not surprisingly, postwar social and historical scholarship from countries other than the United States and Spain also does not spare us the pat dichotomies and their tragic consequences for Natives in particular. In the late 1970s, as indicated in the introduction to this book, anthropologist Douglas Oliver opened his book *The Pacific Islands* with the assertion, "The rape of Oceania began with Guam" (1979, 334). His description marks how the stories of romance and tragedy in Guam's past are also engendered and sexualized by narratives of purity and penetration, whether they come from the pens of churchmen, military men, colonial officials, or modern academics.[4] Thus Oliver's account rehearses the already familiar litany: "Two hundred and thirty years of Spanish-Catholic rule transformed the Mariana Islanders so thoroughly that their Micronesian heritage was barely discernible" (1979, 334). While the anthropologist acknowledged that at least the Chamorro language "had survived" (albeit heavily sprinkled with first Spanish, then American words), Australian social historians Peter Hempenstall and Noel Rutherford found a more thorough Spanish legacy, calling it "one of the worst campaigns of colonial genocide anywhere in the world" (1984, 100). Their article recounts a familiar narrative, that "the Chamorros have been mourned as the victims of a Holy War of conversion to Catholicism carried out by the Spanish garrison at the behest of the Jesuit Order." Though they found no evidence of a "policy" of extermination over what they also called a "mild island people," Hempenstall and Rutherford concluded, "What failed the Chamorros *in the end* was the absence of any centralized organization to coordinate responses to the Spanish, and the always widening gap between their weapons technology" (1984, 100–102; emphasis added). Whether or not there was a conscious policy of extermination, the demise of Chamorro society in the face of foreign encroachment remains, in these oppositional viewpoints, a foregone conclusion, one that cannot fathom organized Chamorro support for the Spaniards as a particularly powerful and effective, if problematic, weapon or technology.

I want to close this brief survey with a modern historiographical account that, perhaps by self-definition as the first "general treatment" (read: neutral treatment) of Guam's history, also conveys modernity's conceit on cultural and historical truth via impassioned scholarship and objective temporal distance. Here, the "American" provenance remains unmarked and disavowed, even as the generic historian is gendered masculine, or at least male. Thus American historian Charles Beardsley wrote: "Whatever the Spanish Historian may have believed to be the truth about the fortunes of the Chamorros, *he* was not enough removed from the event, being Spanish, to judge it impartially" (1964, 135; emphasis added). Beardsley may have labored to be "objective" and "impartial," but Hezel tagged him nonetheless as among those whose accounts remain "unkind . . . to the Spanish" (1982, 115). Hezel's correct assessment is based on Beardsley's penchant for "impartial" observations such as this:

> Now, in the light of modern thinking, the decimation of Guam and the adjacent Marianas Islands . . . shows the colonizing Spanish character at its very worst and leaves even the zealous though meddlesome Jesuits in the rather dubious position of having brought the religion of peace through conquest permanently to a people who were too weak and too polyglot *in the end*, much later, to resist its final triumphant entreaty. (Beardsley 1964, 135; emphasis added)

But Hezel was only partly correct in his assessment that Beardsley was unkind to Spain; also clearly detectable from our vantage point are a form of Christian hostility toward Spanish Catholicism as aided and abetted by Jesuit designs, and a deeply entrenched modernist notion of cultural purity without which Native people like the Chamorro cannot be imagined, much less imagined to have survived. Moreover, the characterization of Chamorro multilingualism refers more to inherent Native cultural weakness than to the possibilities of Chamorro cultural survival through linguistic and discursive flourish.

In contrast to such *sanhiyong* perspectives, the late Chamorro historian "Doc" Pedro Sanchez argued that viewing San Vitores as the "cause of the demise . . . is not completely accurate" (1989, 416). He contended that San Vitores's death, on the contrary, "deprived both the Spaniards and the Chamorros of their best peacemaker" and that "he was the only man who was able to stop the excesses of the military" (P Sanchez 1989, 43). Påle' 'Scot concurred: "We should be grateful to San Vitores" (Calvo 1991).[5] Indeed, Hezel challenged "axiomatic" (including modern) views that the Spanish mission policy was genocidal. He reconstructed the early events of San Vitores's arrival, the souring of relations with the Chamorros, and the tragic outcome of violence that ensued (Hezel 1982, 115, 116). He depicted the priest as "the mildest of men," the "very essence of meekness," and, quoting one of San Vitores's companions, someone "of naturally sweet character" who, to a point of impracticality, carried out his mission "fully trusting in the power of love and meekness to convey the message of spiritual peace" (Hezel 1982, 122, 126).[6] Hezel wrote: "[San Vitores was] so convinced that conversion should be made with the gentleness of the Holy Gospel and without the noise of arms and military operations that he had allowed no forts or military camps to be built and, even after the first Spanish casualties, had forbidden the soldiers to shoot except in self-defense."[7] According to Hezel (1982, 122), source documents show that San Vitores turned to "sterner measures" only after the murder and brutal assaults of several assistants and soldiers. Then San Vitores wrote to Queen Mariana de Austria, his benefactress, for an additional two hundred Filipino troops to bolster the small garrison (Hezel 1982, 122; see letter in Barrett 1975, 38–45).[8] He also sought permission to arrest and deport a Chinese man named Choco who was accused of spreading lies and inciting a "simple and docile people" to rise up against the mission (Hezel 1982, 122).

Thus, Hezel argued, San Vitores began his ministry with love, and only after mounting violence began to use sterner measures, and only for "practical" purposes. His murder by Matå'pang, especially, was a "terrible shock" to the Spaniards, who then mounted punitive expeditions. Blood had only begun to flow. In the first eight years of the mission's existence, Hezel noted, "the mission had suffered terrible losses [and] . . . six Jesuits and another fifteen catechists, most of them Filipinos, had died" (1982, 126). According to Filipino Jesuit historian Horacio de la Costa, the Marianas "remained for many years one of the most dangerous mission fields in the annals of the Society of Jesus" (1961, 45). Hezel and de la Costa differed, however, on the impact of the wars on recruiting more lay workers from across the *imperio*. Hezel said that "there was no dearth" of new volunteers for the Marianas mission, as they were "inspired by the heroic example of San Vitores [and his companions]" (1982, 126), but de la Costa found a "noticeable lack of enthusiasm among younger missionaries, and a certain amount of maneuvering . . . to avoid being sent [to the Marianas]" (1961, 455).

For Hezel, the story was one of unfortunate deterioration, the gradual transformation of a peaceful mission into a bloody but, for the most part, "reluctant" campaign of conquest. He asserted: "There is no question that the Spanish conquest, *in the end,* was *far different from that purely spiritual one* originally intended. . . . Yet if the Spaniards were conquerors and colonizers, they were reluctant ones who were drawn into protracted guerilla warfare to protect the mission" (Hezel 1982, 132; emphasis added). He elaborated:

> The early Chamorro resistance to the mission and attacks on the missionaries themselves led the Jesuits to abandon the *radical pacifist* stance that they had initially taken. Soon they sanctioned the use of Spanish troops for punitive raids in the belief that this would act as a deterrent for future violence. When hostilities continued and the authority over the Spanish garrison was transferred to the civil head of state, soldiers were dispatched to break down centers of resistance and destroy property to forestall further violence. As the contest escalated and the role of Spanish arms became increasingly greater, therefore, the aim of Spanish military forces in the Marianas evolved from the protection of the missionaries in their apostolic work to the outright subjugation of the Chamorro people. (Hezel 1982, 132; emphasis added)

Thus salvaging San Vitores and the Jesuit order from a history of secular conquest and colonization, Hezel offered what can be called the canonical Catholic historical narrative: "The progression in Spanish policy throughout this period was from conversion to conquest—but conquest only in the belief that it was necessary to achieve the Christianization of the people, for the Spanish government's sole raison d'être throughout was to support the missionary enterprise" (1982, 132). But I contend that the history of conversion and conquest cannot so easily be uncoupled, even if we desire it to be. More fundamentally, this history is not finished.

Hezel staked his grounds on primary source documents such as missionary and official reports, accounts, and letters, including key primary and secondary sources like García and LeGobien. And, of course, for engaging these sources, he relied on "modern" studies.[9] His reading of the materials is a faithful conveyance of their perspectives. Indeed, all of these paint a picture of San Vitores as a holy man, initially well received—particularly by specific *maga'låhi* (chiefs) of the stratified Chamorro society.[10] What also paved the way for San Vitores's smooth reception, according to some Chamorros who told him so, was the apparition in 1638 of the Blessed Virgin Mary to a *maga'låhi* named Tåga on the northern island of Tinian (Barrett 1975, 32; Bustillo 1981, 348). The Blessed Virgin Mother instructed this chief to receive baptism and to assist survivors from the *Concepción* (which was shipwrecked off the coast) with a boat "so that," as San Vitores's companion Brother Lorenzo Bustillo related, "they could go [back] to their country and bring them Fathers" (1981, 348). For this reason Tinian had been renamed "Buenavista Mariana." While the padres were generally well received, there is record of at least one *principale* (chief) from "one of the mountain villages" who came down to protest Kepuha's welcoming of the "strangers to the land," but who had a change of heart when he discovered that these were no mere "strangers," but rather "padres" (Plaza 1980, 18). Consequently, this *maga'låhi* invited the priests to his mountain village, and soon thereafter, other chiefs followed suit.

Native conversion to Christianity, at least at the outset, was smooth going for a variety of other reasons: the more influential members of indigenous society were enthusiastic; there was no formal Native religion; and indigenous *supersticiónes* (superstitions) were relatively amenable to Christian doctrine insofar as there were indigenous notions of "souls," of afterlife, and of heaven and hell (Higgins 1937b, 18–21). San Vitores noted that conversion of the Chamorros was facilitated by the absence of the "accursed sect of Mohammed" and of "idolatry" (1981, 268). Elsewhere (Barrett 1975, 19), he added to this facility the absence of snakes or other venomous creatures—although we must be careful not to equate this with the absence of the devil in the Marianas. That the devil's hand was everywhere in the Marianas is everywhere in missionary writings (Barrett 1975, 26). Still, in the Philippines, and anticipating his return to the Ladrones, San Vitores wrote that the Marianas "offers no resistance whatsoever, neither temporal, nor spiritual, nor moral" (San Vitores 1981, 269). And so he could proudly report that after the first two years he "recovered" more than thirty thousand souls to compensate those lost during the Protestant Reformation. Moreover, this number did not include "a large number of catechumens who [were] preparing to receive baptism." Included in that sum were, in San Vitores's own words, "as many as 300 baptized children [who had] died, taken by God to heaven, that they [might] pray for the conversion of their parents and relatives" (Barrett 1975, 19).

Canonical historiography, as seen in Hezel's analysis, also tells us that relations soon deteriorated, and for a variety of reasons: chiefs from other locales became jealous not only at San Vitores's decision to remain in Hagåtña, on Kepuha's turf, but also because the missionaries were baptizing members of the lower classes (Carano and Sanchez 1964, 66). Troublesome, too, were local shamans, called *makåhnas* in the vernacular, and *bonzes* by the Jesuits (Barrett 1975, 26). Alternately glossed as wizards, tricksters, and men of death, the *makåhnas* were despised by the Jesuits—but the feeling was apparently mutual, given the padres' own increasing influence between the elite and commoners, and between Chamorros and their spirits. The *makåhnas* were also said to be swayed by Choco's lies, especially that the baptismal waters and oils were poisonous. A series of skirmishes and retaliations ensued. These quickly escalated into full battles between those who wanted to oust the missionaries and those who saw spiritual and temporal value in their protection. After some of his assistants were beaten and killed, San Vitores decided to toughen up—a sentiment that would lead directly to his death. San Vitores's character and fate were, in this narrative, akin to what we might call an act of "tough love," inasmuch as his death has consistently been figured by proponents of the mission as an act of love modeled, of course, after the greatest love of all.

Spreading the Love

Saint John (15:13) teaches, "Greater love has no man than this, that a man lay down his life for his friends." Påle' 'Scot transposed the good news as a "simple story of love . . . a love *for* the Chamorro people," on whose behalf the "pioneers in 1668 planted the Christian faith, culture, and civilization in *these out of the way, remote islands*" (Calvo 1970, xii; emphasis added). Here, the loving gift of sacrificing one's life, exemplified by Jesus Christ, is itself regarded lovingly by a Chamorro priest whose own "local" name itself is a hybridization of Spanish/American/Chamorro enunciation.[11] We might even say that Påle' 'Scot's name (along with his sense of self, bound up with San Vitores's "simple story of love," as we saw in the previous chapter) itself *names* the cultural and political complexity of Chamorro Catholicism. There is a historical precedent for Calvo's eagerness (in San Vitores) in what has been said of the seventeenth-century Maga'låhi Kepuha, the chief of Hagåtña, who welcomed the missionaries at the outset, and who provided staunch support during the conflicts. According to LeGobien (1949, 22), Kepuha was "pleased at the 'good news' that [San Vitores] brought . . . that . . . [the Chamorros had] been waiting for a long time."[12] But in the twentieth-century counterpart, and perhaps because of the kind of support that Chamorros like Kepuha tendered to the missionaries, Påle' 'Scot seems to have internalized the colonial self-conceit, especially in his recapitulation of the (Eurocentric) marginalization of these islands as "remote" and even "out of the way." Wayward, in other words, not here, out of line, not where they are supposed to be, the Island(er)s almost by definition seem ontologically to await the arrival of a vessel, a device by which they might be pulled back into their proper place in God's order. Indeed, the figuration of Natives as remote, wayward, even lost—and also as greatly enthusiastic— played a central role in the justification and the methodology employed by Spanish missionaries in the heyday of Spain's *imperio*. In his analyses of the role of language and translation in early Tagalog conversion to Christianity (1993), Vicente Rafael has shown how missionaries sought ardently *to relocate* what they presumed to be lost souls, putting them back in their proper place under God's sovereignty while simultaneously trying to maintain as much control as possible over the meanings of the Christian terms and concepts that the missionaries had translated into Tagalog.[13] In re-presenting local and non-local viewpoints, I also attend to the tropes of love and hate, space and place, life and death—and their local reworking—that structure the narratives about Chamorro sentiments about Catholicism.

Indeed, Påle' 'Scot's *loving embrace* of his island's marginal position vis-à-vis European centrality seems to be a classic case of internalizing colonial self-understandings and indigenous cultural (de)valuations.[14] But if the anti-colonial criticism of this psychosocial and historical condition is accurate, such rhetorical maneuvers in the hands of colonized Natives also describe a counter-colonial tactic of localizing—translating, converting, indeed "relocating"; let's just call it repositioning—threatening ideas and practices, as Rafael has demonstrated of Tagalog responses to Spanish missionization. In the Chamorro case, Påle' 'Scot's "internalized" colonial mentality is also marked by hyperbole, overstatement, and excess: The islands are not only out there, but *way out* there; San Vitores's love is *the greatest*. In fact, Påle' 'Scot's loving embrace of San Vitores's great love for uncivilized people (for their geographic and discursive distance from civilized places?) intensifies the suspense and climax embedded in the narrative of Chamorro salvation found in Chamorro gratitude to, and willingness to emulate, San Vitores. Calvo's motto after his ordination in the Philippines before World War II was, "To you from failing hands, we throw our torch. Be yours to hold it high" (Calvo 1991), which can be read as a potent form of colonial mimicry that reverses, replaces, and at times even displaces European agency in favor of indigenous and other positionalities.[15] I will return to this critical idea soon enough; let us first return to the narrative of love.

If Catholic faith, culture, and civilization were "planted" in these remote islands as cosmic acts of love through the selfless sacrificing of one life, the late Sister Felicia Plaza pointed to the spilling of "the blood of martyrs" in the Marianas as commencing a historical cycle, one best symbolized by the phoenix, the legendary Egyptian bird that reemerges triumphantly from the ashes of its funeral pyre (Plaza 1972, 46). San Vitores's posthumous refusal to remain submerged in the depths of Tomhom Bay certainly gives the phoenix a run for its money, but the idea is that they are kin. The modern historiography of Catholicism and key elements of local Chamorro Catholic praxis prevail on the figure of the rising phoenix specifically to represent a cultural and historical "cycle" *of indigenous* survival and durability through and against natural forces like earthquakes and typhoons, and manmade ones like wars and modernization. Thus the color cover of Father Sullivan's history of Catholicism in Guam features a rather striking image of the phoenix rising to signify the principal thematic of that history (Sullivan 1957, 183). The phoenix is also the principal icon of the Father Dueñas Memorial High School, the only all-boys Catholic school named after the second-ordained Chamorro priest who was "martyred" at the hands of Japanese occupation forces during World War II for his refusal to cooperate, and, according to some, for his loyalty to the United States. Påle' 'Scot recalled his companion as a fiercely defiant individual who possessed a "rebellious spirit" (Calvo 1991). The school has also been likened to a breeding ground for Guam's elite civic, business, and political leaders (Stade 1998). Located in Tå'i, a locality in the village of Mangilao, where Father Dueñas was beheaded, the high school might also be viewed as a kind of factory for producing new generations of Chief Kepuhas. At the time of this writing, the present *maga'låhi*, as the territorial governor of Guam is also officially called, is one Felix Camacho, a Father Dueñas graduate.[16]

The late Archbishop Felixberto C Flores, the first Native Chamorro to hold the spiritual equivalent of that office, wrote: "If the blood of martyrs is the seed of Christianity, then we owe the origins of *our* faith to this zealous man" (quoted in Calvo 1970, viii; emphasis added). Flores petitioned us to "ask Fr Diego to foster and cherish from his place in the Kingdom of the Father the faith of his beloved islands of the Marianas, so that as they were once watered by the blood of martyrs, they may continue to flourish as *outposts of the faith, pearls of great price,* in the wide expanse of the Pacific" (Calvo 1970, ix; emphasis added). The fervent desire, through pious petition, is that the once-remote islands become transformed into a surrogate space for the center, a kind of out-posting of the negative connotation that the category "outpost" signifies in colonial discourse. And though it may be stretching it to see the reference to pearls conjuring the pearly gates of heaven, such as to render these islands a virtual portal into heaven, the high price of pearls challenges directly the more secular standards by which the islands have consistently been dismissed or denigrated in colonialist discourse as godforsaken, barren, and economically depressed places. In a move that climaxes the historic transubstantiation from mission station to full-fledged archdiocese via the administrative and geographic category called the vicariate, or in lay terms, Christ's (and Rome's) substitute in the Pacific, the Chamorro-led movement to canonize San Vitores mirrors the process of elevating Chamorro positionality in the Catholic (not global, but *universal, if not cosmic*) world.[17] This indigenously invested reversal is made possible symbolically by a Chamorro veneration—a particular form of articulation—that traffics on the combination of site and action, the place in and manner by which blood was spilled, which accounts for San Vitores's new "place in the kingdom of God."[18] But the name of the place, the region christened "the Marianas" by San Vitores, also expresses the symbolic transaction of reversal from misfortune to favored terrain. Although the archipelago was named Islas de los Ladrones (Islands of Thieves) by Magellan in 1521, its cartographic lay from south to north formed what San Vitores regarded as a "fitting pedestal for Mary," or a set of footsteps to heaven. From the late archbishop's estimation, we might say that, thanks to San Vitores's legacy, Chamorros have gone from being thieves to being nothing less than guardians of the pearly gates. In this sense they may be seen as virtual Saint Peters, or island rocks, so to speak, of the ages.

But what price did the Chamorros pay to serve as such gatekeepers? What is the cost of the solid foundations? According to Påle' 'Scot, "The Chamorro people have always held in their hearts and minds the name of Venerable San Vitores as the leading figure in that long line of martyrs . . . who paid the supreme price with *their* blood" (Calvo 1970, xiii; emphasis added). The emphasis at the end of this sentence marks the ambiguity in its reference; I suggest we keep the subject's referent ambiguous, strategically, in order to better capture a complex and dynamic reality that obscures just whose blood was expended as the supreme price. In the narrative, of course, it is San Vitores's blood that is privileged, with his death standing as that of the martyr. In contrast to his discursive demonization in the *Positio* (see Part One), the villainous Matå'pang is here salvaged, recouped, even reworked. Archbishop Flores explained, "Little did Matapang know that he was doing San Vitores a 'favor' by killing him" (*PDN* 1985e, 19). Flores's positioning of Matå'pang as unwitting accomplice re-scripts Matå'pang from evil incarnate, who serves as one important obstacle to the success of the mission, to necessary agent in the unfolding of providential history, one to whom we should also be grateful. But as we shall see, Matå'pang is also hailed more directly in modern oppositional accounts as a proud hero who fought for Chamorro independence (Benavente 2001). Flores's rewriting of Matå'pang's agency effects one kind of Chamorro redemption, a cashing in on the price of San Vitores's death that other Chamorros might have paid. I will return to this point of redemption soon, in another local account of how San Vitores has become, as another Chamorro priest says, local property if not outright kin. Yet, more than anything outsiders might write or say, these particular Chamorro narratives play a major role in marginalizing other indigenous, competing, oppositional perspectives that would valorize if not lionize Matå'pang and what he might symbolize politically.[19]

In celebrating specifically Chamorro Catholic meanings over errant ones, Flores's view also stands in sharp contrast to *sanhiyong* perspectives on San Vitores's legacy in the Marianas. Those perspectives, as we have seen, oscillate between romanticized celebration (the pro-mission view) and tragic bereavement (the anti-mission view), and their opposition to each other is trumped by their shared inabilities to see the complexity of Chamorro cultural and political agency and their shared assumptions about European and American cultural superiority. In chapter 3, we witnessed nineteenth-century visitor Jacques Arago rail against Father Juan de la Concepción's eighteenth-century description of San Vitores's flight to Spain "on the wings of the wind" at the precise moment that he was being hacked by Matå'pang in Tumon (Arago 1971, 2:42).[20] Arago's repulsion was occasioned as much by the Spaniard's poetic license that "adorned" the history as by the tragic destruction that resulted from it; both of which left in their wake nothing but "tales" of superstitions, such as the "legend" of San Vitores's blood and silhouette in Tomhom. But we can also recognize the value of such poetic flourishes in de la Concepción's hagiography: they serve to memorialize and venerate, and inculcate in their readers—in visceral ways, as good hagiographies are supposed to do—the hand of providence as it also operates through the categorically miraculous and unexplainable in select individuals. We know what Arago thought of it, but how might *we* make sense of pious narratives like de la Concepción's, especially when we appear to be stuck with them as the principal vessels for representing historical truths? Is this a credible narrative, or will the Bollandist excise it for its irrationality? How might the fluidic form and content of this figuration loosen the grip of positivist narrativity and permit us a glimpse into the fluidity of Chamorro agency working through the semiotics of San Vitores's death?

Across the Sea: Rome, 6 October 1985

Across three centuries, two continents, and two oceans, a group of more than one hundred Natives of the missionary's "crystal tombstone" *reverse* San Vitores's historic, geographic, and discursive trajectory by traveling to Rome as "special guests" of Pope John Paul II for the missionary's beatification. With this entourage in particular, Santo Papa shares his "fervent prayer that the life and intercession to San Vitores [would] lead to a strengthened *church in Micronesia*," and his view of San Vitores as "an inspiring *confirmation of the Church in Oceania*" (*PDN* 1985h, 3; emphasis added). The selective lower- and upper-casing of the term "church" and its corresponding area of coverage ("Micronesia," of the lowercased "church"; "Oceania," of the uppercased "Church") recalls Rome's "stakes" in San Vitores's beatification and its attendant and consequent spatial practices. For Rome the value of San Vitores's beatification resides immediately in the fact that the seventeenth-century Cause was in fact revived and motivated by twentieth-century Chamorro Catholics in Guam—which more generally can be seen as a "confirmation" of the universality of God's truth under his temporal surrogate, the Roman Catholic Church. This is what the capital "C" refers to, particularly in contrast to its lowercase counterpart in Micronesia. This, of course, is the dogma that the Catholic Church stands for the universal truth. But the attachment of the uppercase "Church" to the more encompassing term "Oceania" (as opposed to Oceania's smaller parts, like Micronesia, Melanesia, and Polynesia) also signifies the varying degrees of importance through expansiveness that is found in the colonialist scaling from miniscule to small to medium to large as measures of importance and significance. In this particular utterance, Oceania is the more meaningful administrative or bureaucratic category in this part of the globe. It may have been elevated from mission station to vicariate to diocese to metropolitan archdiocese in record time in the twentieth century, but the Metropolitan Archdiocese of Agaña is only one among many in "Oceania," and Oceania in Asia, and Asia in the world. The significance and the attendant spatial meanings and consequences can be better understood by contemplating the theological and pragmatic considerations of San Vitores's beatification: It is the ritual means by which he has been *elevated* to "blessed" status, meaning he has been, by virtue of an authentic martyrdom, vouchsafed to be in the presence of God *in heaven,* and precisely because of this, Chamorros may now properly venerate him and seek his intercession or assistance. But this elevation and honor, and the temporal and spiritual benefits to be had from it, also come with a jurisdictional catch or restriction: the "blessed" may be venerated "locally" by parishioners of the jurisdiction from which they came, but San Vitores is still not eligible for universal veneration. Such a status is reserved for individuals who have been formally canonized. The logic expressed by the (truly) beloved (and missed!) Santo Papa, whose primary job as pope is to speak God's truth, shows a discursive and highly symbolic halting of the Natives in their historic and geographic tracks and a redirecting them back to their proper localities in the cosmos. In terms of the critique of colonial discourse, what we have here is akin to the state's counter-appropriation of a subordinate's appropriation of state discourse.

But for one Chamorro clergyman, "the inspiring confirmation of the Church in Oceania," San Vitores, was also a virtual Chamorro, or at least a possession thereof. Proud that "we finally have a saint that we can call our own," the late Monsignor Vicente Martinez proclaimed that "even though he is a Spaniard, [San Vitores] . . . came to Guam . . . out of love for God, out of love for the people. He stayed . . . he left his heart with us." For all these reasons, Martinez explained, San Vitores "is ours. He *belongs* to us" (Champion 1985; emphasis added). In a view that *arrests* his astral travels, that stops him from upping and leaving the island, San Vitores is kept in what appears to be his proper place, alongside his heart, with the kin he so loved. For some Chamorro Catholics, then, the terms of San Vitores's stay—he left his heart—translate into Native ownership. The price that the islands paid in getting San Vitores a spot in heaven is here redeemed, or we might say "converted," into the value of his ownership by those who must still inhabit the earth. A form of repositioning through re-possessioning, this kinship operation disregards national and ethnic bloodline as a determinant of traditional indigenous Pacific Islander cultural identity (see Linnekin and Poyer 1990). San Vitores's value now lies as a Chamorro convert (or property) who gets to have a place in heaven, a sort of "embedded" (to use an idiom from the present-day media coverage of the Iraq War) virtual Chamorro. In "Chamorrocizing" him, and by bringing the Cause back to the table, the Chamorro now earns a virtual spot in heaven through his intercessor. Now, too, the Chamorro becomes part of the "community of saints," as when one of our own loved ones passes on and we take comfort and joy in the thought that not only is that one in heaven but he or she can work to get us there too. In this Chamorro rearticulation, it is not only the boundaries of cultural identity and kinship that are permeated. Put another way, specifically indigenous stakes in Catholicism in general, and in San Vitores in particular, furnish "natives" with an infinitely wider playing field than is generally acknowledged or permitted of and for the category "natives." And yet, to encounter the official Church's logic is to see how colonial discourse halts Native efforts at world enlargement, even if such efforts are typically appropriated by colonial discourse to accomplish colonialism's purposes.

The way San Vitores "left his heart" with the Chamorro people has deep value for others elsewhere. As we saw in chapter 1, it was the authentication of his death that permitted Church officials to beatify San Vitores. This authentication, including the credentializing of its documentation, also rested on certifying the "religious" motivations of both candidate and assassin (Amore 1981, 24–25). As a result, Blessed San Vitores, like Father Junípero Serra, the famous architect of the California Mission system, is well on the road to sainthood, inasmuch as martyrdom is the "surest route" (Woodward 1990, 52).

San Vitores's elevation officially permits Chamorro Catholics, at least, to venerate him, and to look to him for inspiration and intercession in heaven. Accordingly, the late Archbishop Felixberto Flores authorized a special *nubena* in San Vitores's honor, which was also translated into the vernacular (McGrath 1985, 6). As in the case of the Nubenan Santa Cruz, a *nubena* is a nine-day devotion and memorial to God, the Blessed Mother, Jesus, saints, events, or deceased loved ones (in the form of *lisåyu* [rosary]) and contains special petitions to God, the Virgin Mother, and village patron saints (Ross 1982). "The novena," wrote McGrath, the author and compiler of the special novena, "belongs to the fabric of Christianity in the Marianas" (1985, 6). Moreover, in the Marianas, novenas are celebrated—for there is much food, song, and merriment at the end of the nine-day prayers, called the *finakpo' nubena* (end of novena)—especially those of village patron saints honored on their feast days each year. The benediction to the special novena reads, "O God, You inflamed Your servant, Blessed Diego of the Marianas, with zeal to spread Your name and love in the Marianas, even to water them with this blood. Deign to glorify them with him at Your altar and to grant us through his intercession, the special favor we beg of You" (McGrath 1985, 91). As a novena, the petition is to the saint or spiritual figure to and through whom intercession is being sought. But there is an injunction to the faithful that underwrites the novena: Be properly faithful and your needs will be met. Let us return to the faithful pilgrims, now at the Vatican, and examine the subject and status of their veneration in this place in particular.

"Ringside Seats" for the Pilgrims: The Vatican, Rome, 1985

The Chamorro pilgrims are led by Archbishop Flores. Along the way they stop at famous landmarks in Roman Catholic history: Saint Patrick's Cathedral in New York; Pau and Lourdes, France (in the shadow of the Pyrenees!); and Burgos, Spain (Blessed Diego's hometown). At the tomb of Saint Francis in Assisi, Apuron reminds the group, whose members range from a youngster to an eighty-year-old nun, to "model [their] lives after those of Jesus Christ, St. Francis, and Blessed San Vitores." The tour organizer notes "San Vitores's presence everywhere" (Deville 1985, 1).

San Vitores's beatification is also billed in terms of "Chamorros mak[ing] History" (*PDN* 1985c, 33) and proves to be a powerful source of happiness, pride, and cultural distinction for the predominantly Chamorro Catholic pilgrims composed of "newsmakers and regular everyday folk" (Sizemore 1985, 3). A non-Chamorro non-Catholic journalist for the *Pacific Daily News* writes that "in the local recognition of San Vitores, the people of the Marianas celebrate, and they mark their celebration with a joyous spirit in their souls" (Cates 1985b, 1).

If Santo Papa says anything that upset the Chamorro pilgrims, it isn't evident in the media coverage. But the coverage does return emphasis to Chamorro stakes proper, with attendant and resulting Chamorro spatialities. In print and broadcast "specials," we are treated to enthusiastic coverage by the media whose partiality to the event clearly registered its sense of being co-participant among the blessed. For example, a fifty-six-page supplement in the *Pacific Daily News* is titled, "Biba! San Vitores, Biba!" echoing the familiar Chamorro/Spanish salute "Long Live (San Vitores)!"—a phrase that was commonplace across the Spanish *imperio* in honor of the Crown and God, but which continues to resonate in twentieth- and twenty-first-century political campaigning in Guam (Champion 1985; *PDN* 1985a).

Guam and Chamorro politics are often likened to the "local"—predominantly Chamorro and Filipino—pastime of cockfighting, featuring formal, high-stakes betting on bouts of fighting roosters amid a cacophony of cheering, jeering, and more betting on the side.[21] Fighting cocks are highly prized and cared for; sentiments for the losers range from ridicule from victorious opponents, to utter disdain and repulsion from the loser's owners. Guam and Chamorro power politics are often referred to locally as *gåyu* (from *gallo*, Spanish for "rooster") politics, where it is common to refer to one's political candidate as one's rooster, precisely because of the high stakes in the political contest (Stade 1998).

In the arena of political control over GovGuam, the stakes are not only financial but also cultural, inasmuch as modern government employment, service, and resources constitute important materiality for Chamorro political and cultural rearticulation. In the coverage of the Chamorro pilgrimage to Rome, we can also see how Roman Catholicism provides an analog.

In the 1985 "Biba" special supplement, for example, Chamorro journalist Cathy Sablan Gault filed an essay titled "A Gift from Up There," in which she described herself as "a former reporter who did the 'Pope Beat' earlier in the decade" but whose essay is "more than a follow-up story . . . detailing what was happening in Rome." It is, she explained, a "Thank You." The subject of her heartfelt gratitude is especially telling. Gault began by describing the experience as "humbling," because "coming from a tiny place to a big crowded place . . . we were so few compared to the thousands-strong European delegations." But Pope John Paul II knew Archbishop Flores; Gault noted, "He knew we existed, and that made all the difference." Amid the boisterous Spaniards, "it was Archbishop Flores and the Guamanians *who stole the show*." With "quiet dignity that set us apart from the crowd [we] took [our] seats in the reserved section. We had *ringside seats* in Catholicism's most significant church." She continued the allusion to arena culture, writing, "Of the three Jesuits beatified, *our man got top billing*." For Gault, the *"tiny delegation of Guamanians . . . witnessed history in the making"* and *"seemed to command an important presence in the Eternal City,"* and she speculated that it was "perhaps because of the strength of our collective faith and the Jesuit missionary who brought it to us" (Gault 1985, 32, 37–39).

In advance, Church organizers had approved the inclusion of Chamorro hymns to be sung at the Mass (celebrated by Santo Papa) and allowed representatives of the Guam contingent to participate in its various liturgies.[22] The *sound* of Chamorro songs was especially moving for the "tiny" group from a "tiny place," who no longer felt out of place amid the boisterous throng of Spaniards at Saint Peter's Cathedral, the spiritual foundation of the Catholic world. "Chamorro words reverberated in the huge basilica," recalled Gault, and they sent "goose bumps" up her spine and sent her heart to her "throat." In Chamorro, the word for goose bumps is *fugu*, and, as in other parts of the indigenous Pacific, they can register otherworldly presences. For Gault, such reverberations also sent a "strong and clear" message: *"Skeptics keep predicting the demise of Chamorro, but here it was in the Vatican ringing out strong and clear and very much alive"* (1985, 32; emphasis added). But there was also "a certain sadness" amid the cultural pride of being a Chamorro at this particular moment, in this place in particular, with such "ringside seats," no less. Gault's meltdown, like Arago's in his jaunt to see San Vitores's miracle two centuries prior, invoked sudden memories of religious mothers in one's life. With heart in throat, Gault's hand wrote, "I kept thinking about my grandmother, a fiercely religious woman who remained close to the Church until she died; my mother who died a year after the pope's visit to Guam; and my Auntie Lola, who died just the day before I left on this trip. None of them had even been to Rome. None of them even had the chance to be where I was." In a moment of selflessness that approximates "the greatest love that man could give," Gault said, "I would have gladly given up my spot for them" (1985, 39).

Through this particular register we can easily see a strong and powerful circularity that has historically been produced between Chamorros
and Roman Catholicism through the vehicle of San Vitores in the seventeenth and twentieth centuries. Because their "man received top billing,"
Chamorros were also given "ringside seats." But like the Chamorro words
that "reverberated" in the huge Basilica, there is also *a specific* Chamorro
perspective and cultural value that gets "top billing" in this "making of
history." When Gault shared a genuine desire to "give up" her seat to the
genealogical mother figures of her life— Chamorro historian Laura Marie
Torres Souder identified the figure as *si Nåna* (the Chamorro mother), who
is the real "agent" in Chamorro "herstory" (1987, 3)—it was not that she
wanted to go to heaven but that she was willing to die so that they might
return to experience temporally, viscerally, in person, the concrete magnifi-
cence of their spiritual investments as "fiercely religious" Chamorro Catholic women. They might already be in heaven (the addressee is "up there"),
but their good daughter was recalling them to earth in acknowledgment of
something she knew to be valuable and important to them.

In her study of contemporary Chamorro women organizers and activists in the 1970s and 1980s, Souder pointed to the relative homophony
between the term *håga'* (blood) and *håga* (daughter) (1987, 3). Combined,
she asserted, *hagan håga'* (blood daughter) best captures the cultural and
political power that has characterized maternal Chamorro genealogy in
Guam's history (Souder 1987, 5). According to Souder (1987, 37), through
relations of love, obligation, and duty to *si Nåna, hagan håga'* embodies a
dialectic between two other principal dialectics in Guam's history: the "dialectic between colonizer and colonized" on the one hand, and that between
"tradition and modernity" on the other. Precisely because of the weight
of all these dialectics, Souder paid special attention to the "intergenerational" tensions and conflicts between Chamorro women and their daughters in the colonial context, and has virtually predicted some of the most
volatile events to shake island cultural politics in the subsequent decades,
most notably, the highly publicized mother-and-daughter showdown over a
remarkably conservative antiabortion bill passed in the early 1990s (Souder
1987, 215; see also Dames 2003; Diaz 1993; Stade 1998). In Part Three, we
will return to this showdown and consider how the embodied subjectivity
called *hagan håga'* engages the gendered terms of kinship and identity associated with Santa Marian Kamalen, the local manifestation of the Blessed
Virgin Mother, which San Vitores set into play in the seventeenth century.

For the moment I want to tease out a bit more the political and cultural
stakes manifest in Gault's "Thank You" essay and connect them to the practices of narrativizing Guam's history in particular. I do this through the
image of Chamorro women's hands writing down things that are important
to their mothers, grandmothers, and aunties. Such hands are the central
imagery and topic of an essay titled "Tumuge' Påpa' (Writing It Down):

Chamorro Midwives and the Delivery of Chamorro History," by Christine Taitano DeLisle (2007). A Chamorro historian, and an active participant in *hagan håga'* subjectivities as a mother and grandmother of four *hagan håga'* herself, DeLisle has reflected critically on the promises and liabilities to be found in the venerable Chamorro women's tradition of "writing down" whatever it happened to be that one's mother, grandmother, or auntie needed recorded at the moment. Her essay draws from both white and women-of-color feminist theory that focuses specifically on the power of recouping "maternal narratives" from patriarchal and colonial histories and practices. Following the feminist scholarship of Marian Hirsch, for instance, DeLisle wrote, "to the extent that they involve a 'tradition' of 'maternal narratives,' contemporary writings that define themselves as daughterly traditions in relation to a complicated maternal past, . . . *tumuge' påpa'* . . . become for me authentic and legitimate modes of . . . articulating Chamorro histories. They are authentic and legitimate because, as a daughter and granddaughter, I am only the latest in an ongoing process of 'writing down' what a Chamorro matrilineage deems important" (2007, 5).

The point of DeLisle's essay, however, is to register both hope and caution: hope for a specifically indigenous and female-oriented practice of documenting and expressing "that which continues to be marginalized," but caution because, as Toni Morrison has observed of such writing in particular, women of color like herself tend also to be guilty of perpetuating oppression via romanticization and nostalgia (DeLisle 2007, 6–7). DeLisle specifically tied this predicament to her simultaneous identity as an academic historian and a Chamorro *hagan håga'*, both of which account for and intensify her interests and stakes in *tumuge' påpa'* as an "authentic" and viable Chamorro form of historical and cultural narrativization. Citing theorists like Michel-Rolph Trouillot, DeLisle explained that while generally the process of remembering and writing down certain historical truths also always entails the forgetting and erasure of other truths, and thus the scholarly imperative to exercise critical judgment by discerning the valid from the invalid, *tumuge' påpa'*, as deployed in and as a Chamorro cultural or familial imperative, also will entail the privileging of certain family narratives over others. But the scholarly imperative to make selective, critical judgments also means that *tumuge' påpa'* will lead to a questioning of one's, or another's, mother, auntie, or grandmother (DeLisle 2007, 6–7).

Yet while this may be culturally inappropriate, DeLisle concluded that the risks of not writing what Chamorro women desire outweigh those of being culturally inappropriate (2007, 10). And so, though the Chamorro investment in San Vitores, as I will continue to illustrate, comes principally from the good Chamorro "fathers" of the Guam church, good Chamorro *hagan håga'* have also weighed in through *tumuge' påpa'*, through the obedient and dutiful "writing down" of matters they know to be of importance to the Chamorro mother figures of their lives.

Another such weighing can be spied in an article titled "Notes from a Participant Observer" in the same "Biba" supplement: "A friend once asked me which I was first—a Chamorro or a Catholic. I said, and still say, the two can't be separated. They're complementary, as I see it. I was born Chamorro and baptized Catholic at about the same time. I've been both all my life and see no reason whatsoever to change" (*PDN* 1985f, 2). In simultaneously "marking" the narrator's indigenous cultural and Catholic religious identities as virtually one and the same, as "complementary," the account reinforces not only the theme of indigenous survival through a common history with Catholicism ("I was born Chamorro and baptized Catholic at about the same time") but also intones defiance against possible skeptics, whose likes we have already seen. But this remarkable passage also helps us appreciate how history writ large can also be history writ small, that is, embodied in the life stories of particular people and events, and archived through their narrativizing practices—like *hagan håga'* who *tumuge' påpa'.* (In the next chapter, I return to this theoretical and methodological theme in relation to my interviews with Påle' 'Scot.)

Shortly after San Vitores's beatification, Archbishop Felixberto Flores— Chamorro Catholicism's first modern *maga'låhi*—made explicit the stakes for Chamorros in particular: "The beatification makes me very happy, really, for *the people's sake.* . . . It's the culmination of what *our ancestors* believed in. . . . We finally have someone who lived and died *here* who will be *our* intercessor" (*PDN* 1985e, 19; emphasis added). The "here," of course, refers to the Marianas, though it appears that Flores was interviewed either in Rome or San Francisco at the time. The "we" might ostensibly be "the people," but, following DeLisle, we need to heed the dilemmas of representing specificity and the erasures that can come with it, particularly when culture through genealogies are at stake. What, exactly, are the truths of these desires? Exactly who are "the people," the "we"? And who is left out, and why?

Ann Arbor, Michigan, 2007

Archbishop Flores's happiness was derived from viewing San Vitores's beatification as a gift of acknowledgment that was long in coming, an acknowledgment of a long history of Chamorro faith ("the culmination of what our ancestors believed in") but whose principal purpose was in service ("for the people's sake") to specifically local Chamorro concerns and particularly Chamorro provenance in the subject matter ("we finally have someone who lived and died here, who will be our intercessor"). Like Påle' 'Scot and other clergy, Archbishop Flores called specific attention to the prominence of the Islanders and their islands, and in so doing repositioned Chamorros and the Marianas in the center. They are no longer far away. If anything, their history is redeemed, thereby rendering San Vitores's elevation a kind of surrogate cultural space for Chamorro signification. This new status also constitutes a kind of arrival point for Chamorro Catholicism, a point of pride, distinction, and happiness, in addition to everything else that comes with having a saint of one's own.

Sadly, Flores died in a San Francisco hospital only days after the beatification and accompanying jubilation. The coincidence of the archbishop's death and San Vitores's beatification was the source of other interpretations that would continue to fuse Spanish, Roman, and Chamorro Catholicism and their historical and cultural significance for newsmakers and everyday folk in Guam and the Marianas—and locales here, there, and over there, in the beyond. For instance, in an "inspirational homily" at a celebration Mass in Tomhom, Walter Burghardt, SJ, likened the lives of Jesus Christ, San Vitores, and the late archbishop to "a grain of wheat" that "when alive, is alone," but when dead, "is buried in the earth [and] grows and flourishes." Burghardt concluded his analogy by recalling Chamorros and their island field of labor: "Both the Archbishop [Flores] and Diego have been grains of wheat for you and fell into the ground for you. If Agaña is to live and the Marianas are to flourish, then it is now *you* who must fall into earth and *you who must live God's life*" (quoted in G Perez 1985, 1; emphasis added). Burghardt's metaphor of planting—an old tradition in Christianity—traffics on the powerful idea of Guam and Chamorro Catholicism being important witnesses to God's truth. In 1970, the director of the Jesuit Martyrs Museum of Nagasaki, Japan, likewise identified Guam as "the witness of the heroic virtues of Fr San Vitores" (*Umatuna Si Yuus* 1970, 4). This status is the consequence of San Vitores's own martyrdom here; indeed, the director himself had come to Guam as part of the celebration of Archbishop Flores's ordination, which also marked the formal commencement of the beatification movement. For the occasion, he presented what Jesuit and local Church officials believe to be the actual soutane (robe), complete with bloodstains, worn by San Vitores at the time of his assassination in 1672.

Another person who viewed Chamorro as a testament to the Church's validity was Palauan Jesuit Felix Yaoch (1985, 35), whose homily, printed in the "Biba" supplement, also gives us a sense of the event's significance for other Islanders in the Church in Oceania. For Yaoch, San Vitores's ministry had particular appeal to him and others "from Micronesia [who] have seen how political factions, economic inequalities, and social status have divided people and kept them apart from one another." He implored the faithful, "Let the spirit and the works of San Vitores continue in us and make us effective instruments of peace and reconciliation in our communities and societies. Let our positions, our talents, our wealth, not become barriers but opportunities for building bridges and bringing about harmony and peace among our peoples, following the examples of Father San Vitores." Drawing out the specific connections between San Vitores and the cultural, political, and social stakes of fellow Micronesians, Yaoch singled out the "Chamorros from the Marianas Archipelago" as "living tributes to San Vitores and his companions," and beamed that "today, the people of the Marianas Archipelago can boast of the Marianas as *the* Catholic islands in Micronesia, with an archbishop, two bishops, and many priests and religious, all natives of the islands" (1985, 39). But Yaoch's sermon had been delivered just before Flores's untimely death (and although the supplement came out after Flores's death, had not been edited accordingly); without their beloved archbishop to "boast" along with, Chamorro Catholics were not entirely in the mood to celebrate. Nonetheless, in the wake of San Vitores's beatification, and in light of the impending "wake" occasioned by Flores's death, the Chamorro "participant-observer" (above) noted the auspicious coincidence and took comfort therein: "Yes, we, the people of the Marianas, and the Catholic Church have lost a dedicated servant and strong leader in Archbishop Flores. No words can tell of our sorrow. Yet we take comfort in knowing that we have gained another intercessor" (*PDN* 1985f, 2).

The Other "We"

Shortly before his death, the archbishop pulled together all the Chamorro "stakes" in San Vitores's beatification thus: "It brings to reality a dream the people of the Mariana Islands have prayed for: These islands . . . have retained many features of Spanish Catholicism. Fiestas in honor of our patron saints for each village, public processions, rosaries and novenas are all woven into our cultural traditions. All of these are a part of the legacy that Blessed Diego and his successors brought to us—the people of the islands they converted. . . . Today the faith that Blessed Diego brought to the islands is embraced by virtually all the local population of the Marianas" (F Flores 1985, 1).

For Flores, Chamorro cultural history is a woven tapestry, a Chamorro "fabric" composed of major Catholic rituals and practices—fiestas in honor of patron saints (and rosaries and novenas). The legacy of Blessed Diego and "his successors," the ones who "converted," is that "today the faith . . . is now embraced by virtually all the local population." But is it really? Implying otherwise, a brochure for a 1990s traveling public exhibit on Guam's political history asserted: "The death of San Vitores initiated the systematic killing of all Chamorros who refused to give up their customs and practices" (Guam Museum 1991). The exhibit also sought to show the "tenacity and resiliency of the Chamorro desire to regain their freedom and liberty as expressed in the documents." Juxtaposing excerpts from Spanish, American, and Japanese proclamations of colonial authority with seventeenth- and late-twentieth-century indigenous voices of opposition and resistance, the exhibit portrayed San Vitores as a symbol of the tragic demise of Chamorro culture and freedom. It questioned the (heroic) Catholic narrative of death as a precondition of eternal life, associating San Vitores directly with the violent legacy of political conquest and genocide. Chamorro lives (and liberty) were, indeed, heavy prices to pay.

As in the contemporaneous effort to canonize Junípero Serra, the eighteenth-century Franciscan who founded the California Catholic mission system, there *has been* indigenous opposition to the effort to canonize San Vitores, although it tends largely to be constrained, even muted.[23] In an effort to gauge the range of sentiments around the beatification, a local reporter interviewed Chamorros "on the street" (Kemp 1985b, 3). Many expressed "mixed feelings" but specifically asked to remain anonymous, "fearing what their families and the church might think about their comments." Chamorro historian and statesman Robert Underwood explained that Chamorros "are very proud of their Catholic traditions, and they don't want to seem disrespectful of the religion, but it's not a 100% sentiment of euphoria." Historically, he continued, Chamorros who resisted the mission have been portrayed as "villains," whereas those who assisted the missionaries have been portrayed as "heroes." Thus, he pointed out, the "goodness of the ancient Chamorro is determined by his cooperation with the Spanish" (R Underwood quoted in Kemp 1985b, 3). One person who questioned the movement to canonize San Vitores was local artist, activist, and archaeologist Alejandro Lizama, who in the late 1990s served time in a federal facility for "terrorist" acts when he protested a federal oversight hearing on land issues. In his fieldwork and career, Al is known as a passionate supporter of research and preservation, but in the service of Chamorro heritage rather than for science, a particularly entrenched binary opposition whose terms are habitually racialized and engendered as the pitting of "emotional" Native activists against "dispassionate" (read: white) scientists (usually contract archaeologists and private developers). In the street survey mentioned above, Lizama invoked the decimation of the Chamorro population in the wake of San Vitores's arrival. Though he admitted that it was not necessarily San Vitores's fault, per se, Lizama clearly cast a shadow of doubt on the effort to canonize him: "How do you celebrate the arrival of the Spaniards when depopulation occurred?" (quoted in J Kemp 1985b, 3).

For Chamorro Catholics in particular, public opposition to San Vitores's beatification lacks sufficient political and cultural capital to express itself freely and openly. However, there is opposition, and it is mounting. Moreover, this vocal opposition is articulated in terms of a rebellious and defiant cultural nationalism and anticolonialism that increasingly dates itself back to the side that "lost" the Spanish–Chamorro wars of the seventeenth century. Whereas much of its (legitimate) ire is directed at "America," an undisclosed (and difficult to ascertain) amount of the anger is directed at the Spanish Catholic legacy. The openly defiant tone is still relatively rare, given the Chamorro Catholic hegemony in Guam, but public expressions are increasingly audible (and visible): "I don't care anymore. And you can identify me if you like," asserted a member of the grassroots activist organization Nasion Chamoru, "But, no way; I do not support San Vitores!" (Benavente 2001). But where the United States is begrudged the insidious effects of its military presence in the form of environmental degradation, and most especially the unhealed wounds inflicted by its postwar land tak-ing—a topic that could convert the most "mild-mannered" Chamorro into an "activist" (R Underwood 2001, 211)—Catholicism tends to be decried as the cause of near genocide and cultural destruction.

And yet, to speak against the Church is to also speak against Chamorro Catholic hegemony, a mixed system through which indigenous Chamorro culture has historically come to "speak" through largely Catholic rituals and practices. Following Underwood's comments in the 1985 interview (Kemp 1985b, 3), to defy the Church is to run the risk of transgressing normative ideas of proper cultural behavior as institutionalized through a long history of colonialism. This colonial valuation, according to Underwood (1977), is evident around the island, in public memorials and monuments such as the larger-than-life-sized statue of Maga'låhi Kepuha, the Hagåtña chief who welcomed the missionaries (figure 10), and whose Christian burial—the first among the Chamorros—was viewed an "edification" of the Catho-lic Church in the Marianas (LeGobien 1949, 27–28). For Underwood, this public inscription, on land and consciousness, is likewise etched in the depiction of Kepuha's contemporary Chamorro other, Maga'låhi Matå'pang from Tomhom, whose murder of San Vitores had also been memorialized dramatically in bronze, in a highly dramatic "encounter" of statues of the priest (holding Matå'pang's infant daughter), of Matå'pang and his accom-plice Hirao, and of Matå'pang's "wife."[24] If Kepuha is lionized (let us just say that he has muscles where there are no muscles), Matå'pang is demon-ized. Standing behind a kneeling and angelic-looking San Vitores, who is holding the baby up toward heaven (as Matå'pang's wife looks on almost helplessly), an angry Matå'pang prepares to run him through with a spear, while Hirao similarly clutches a *catana*, or cutlass, high overhead.

Through these (muffled) public sentiments of opposition (who wants to be connected to Matå'pang?), one gets a rather clear sense of social and cultural protocol that can be traced to a kind of post-traumatic syndrome, the profound aftereffects of the aforementioned Chamorro–Spanish wars that raged in the final quarter of the seventeenth century. As explained in the introduction to this book, the conflicts began shortly after San Vitores's founding of the mission in 1668 but escalated quickly after his death in 1672. The misnamed wars might be better viewed as a kind of civil war between traditional rivals and/or classes, but with the novel and fateful presence of Spanish priests and a Crown-sponsored garrison sent to protect them.[25] The wars and their aftermath ushered in a period of intense social and political transformation, which, due to warfare, disease and, by all accounts, a deep-rooted collective melancholia, resulted in the Chamorro equivalent of what Hawaiian scholars have called in a post-missionary Hawai'i a "population collapse."[26] At the height of the conflict,

FIGURE 10. Overlooking Marine Corps Drive at the traffic loop in the heart of Hagåtña, Guam's capital, the bronze statue of Maga'låhi Kepuha lionizes the seventeenth-century chief of Hagåtña. In death as well as life, Kepuha provided important strategic support to the Catholic mission. Kepuha gave land and military support to the missionaries, and his death and, especially, his Christian burial, were described by a seventeenth-century padre as the foundations of Christianity among the Chamorros, inasmuch as the Christian burial displaced burial practices considered paganistic. Photo by the author.

particularly under the command of conquistadors who took it as a holy mission to extinguish any and all forms of opposition and resistance, any outward expression of opposition could be a real risk, to say the least.

Thus, as a result of such a fraught political and social history of Chamorro conversion to (and conversion of) Catholicism, any opposition against the Church is also an opposition to the family, to Chamorro culture. In the political calculus of this cultural history, to oppose Chamorro culture is to oppose God. In his interview (Kemp 1985b, 3), Underwood drew attention to the cultural prescriptions of "pride" and "respect." Both *banidosu* (cultural pride, as opposed to vanity, in Spanish) and especially *gai respetu* (having respect) are key values in *kostumbren Chamorro*, that syncretism of ancient Chamorro and Catholic cultural values and practices that emerged in the eighteenth and nineteenth centuries and that persists to this day. These are closely linked to other cultural prescriptions and practices, known in Chamorro as *tåhdong* (deep, in antiquity and level of meaning) (PSECC 1994, 9–11). Examples are values like *mamåhlao* (shame), *nginge'* (deferential sniffing of an elder's or a priest's hand), and *chenchule'* (reciprocity). Deep in indigenous time/discursive space, these values have come to underlie if not inform manifest social rituals and practices connected to the Catholic calendar, such as fiestas, novenas, *fandånggos* (wedding feasts), *lisåyu* (rosary), and the *kompaire* (godparenthood) system. While known customarily, the particularity of this Chamorro mixture has also recently been codified around another *tåhdong* principle called *inafa'maolek* (interdependence), which also connotes balance and proper behavior or correct living, a cultural value that bears a strong similarity to other value systems across the Native Pacific (such as *pono* in Hawai'i) (Department of Chamorro Affairs 2003; PSECC 1994, 9–11; PSECC 1996a). Indeed, in recent years *inafa'maolek* has been codified into something of a "system" itself, certainly an authentic tradition, that has been rearticulated by a movement to write "Chamorro history by Chamorros" for rather conspicuous political purposes pertaining explicitly to ongoing efforts to "decolonize" the island by changing its political status with the United States.[27] These views "relocate" in compelling ways Chamorro *tåhdong* values and practices as the underlying basis of a *kostumbren Chamorro* cultural system whose outward social manifestations are Spanish, Mestizo, or later, American, in appearance and form, but whose driving force or agent remains identifiable aboriginal values and principles that, for the most part, retain their aboriginal names and terms. Finally, these "revisionist histories" are diametrically opposed to the written *sanhiyong* "canon," which consistently re-inscribes a history of Native cultural and social death and decay as the pat result of superior forces of "Hispanicization" or, later, "Americanization."

But given this history, we might well ask what Chamorro will dare speak out openly against the status quo, particularly one that has made big claims to all that is Native and Right, and in terms of a Catholic order. What Chamorro will risk the consequences of being associated publicly with all that is Catholicism's "other," that is, of being godless, less Chamorro, errant, diabolical? Matå'pang? A Chamorro atheist might, but there is just no redeemable political or cultural capital in that. One may as well live in the mainland United States, but that would not get you very far either, given the conservative religious backlash today.[28] A more "acceptable" location or positionality—or at least a more culturally negotiable one—would be a Chamorro steeped in a Christianity other than that of Spanish Catholicism, a social and cultural positionality that in Catholic Guam has its own history of persecution, no doubt, but is still recognized within the cultural order. A position that has been associated, according to Underwood, one of its most prominent members, with a peculiarly nonconformist Chamorro sensibility (R Underwood 1997).

The Chamorro Protestant most "public" on the San Vitores celebration is also Guam's first Chamorro ordained minister and one of only three ordained Chamorro religious leaders who administered the needs of the faithful during the Japanese occupation.[29] In his memoirs, the Reverend

Joaquin Flores Sablan, who also taught the history of Guam course at the University of Guam for many years, *praised* San Vitores as a man whose words of peace and gentleness "won the hearts" of the Chamorro and thus "diminished the horror they entertained of the Spanish name" (1990, 260). For Matå'pang, however, Sablan reserved even greater praise. The man held in disdain by local Catholic Church officials—"He is a coward," said Påle' 'Scot, "he couldn't even kill San Vitores by himself" (Calvo 1991)—was instead lionized by Sablan: Matå'pang was "the most nationalistic leader [in Chamorro history, who] did all he could to expel the foreign intruders from the island" (J F Sablan 1990, 261).[30] According to Sablan, Matå'pang has been derided only by his own people, a mistreatment that actually prevents them from seeing him as "a proven and well-tested hero [for] the *Brown* Power Movement." Sablan pointed out that the derision is evident in changes in the meaning of the word *matå'pang* itself: in the vernacular it means "insipid, idiotic, and deranged," and Chamorros use it generally in a "derogatory manner, usually accompanied with giggles and laughter" (1990, 261). Sablan was quick to explain that this usage was a post-mission shift; its "original meaning," the exact opposite, can be found in use in its Filipino cognate: "brave, heroic, and courageous" (Sablan's sources were his Filipino students at the University of Guam, but the Chamorro–English dictionary confirms this older meaning [Topping, Ogo, and Dungca 1975, 139]). It is partly from these Chamorro Protestant historians (Sablan, Underwood) and partly from Chamorro Catholic priests (Calvo, Flores) that we can sense in the San Vitores–Matå'pang relationship the makings of a Chamorro Catholic hegemony: What had once been valued brave and heroic has in the hands of Catholic missionaries and their Native supporters become reversed—which is itself a powerful way to canonize the Catholic mission and their Chamorro supporters (like Kepuha). Refusing to defer total Chamorro-ness to Catholicism, and assisted by radical ideas furnished by liberal American Protestantism (and its racialized ideas of national progress, or perhaps more properly speaking, a US civil rights struggle), Sablan's analysis reverses and subverts the prevailing discourse by which a heroic Catholic history is reworked in the interest of Chamorro political and cultural survival. Interestingly, Sablan likened Matå'pang to "the great Indian chief Crazy Horse" (Red Movement hero?), who defeated General Custer (White Movement hero?) in the battle of Little Big Horn, with "the only difference being that the Dakota Indians have memorialized their hero and their culture, "while the Chamorros wanted to *retain their* culture and at the same time deride and denigrate their only real Chamorro hero."[31] Wishing to redress this "paradox," Sablan called for the erection of a statue in Matå'pang's honor, and for it to be placed in "the most conspicuous place on the island to represent the Brown Power Movement *as well as its culture*" (J F Sablan 1990, 262; emphasis added).[32] For Sablan, such a place was none other than Adelup Point, the present location of the *ufisinan maga'låhi* (governor's office), as the term is now glossed in the territory's politics.

Locating the governor's office at Adelup was the brainchild of the late Governor Ricardo Bordallo, a particularly flamboyant Chamorro nationalist who built many "public landmarks to house the spirit of the Chamorro people" (Ige 1990, 3). He once defended the Adelup complex as "a monument which allows us to cross over that cultural gap which has been widening to a point where our heritage was being threatened with extinction. It allows the people to cross over the past so that we may cross back over into a better future. Adelup links us with one another" (Ige 1990, 3). But in 1990, rather than giving himself up to federal incarceration after being found guilty of corruption charges, Governor Bordallo committed suicide at another key public monument that he built, also in Hagåtña: the park of the (ennobled and hypermuscularized) Chief Kepuha (see Diaz 1993). Only five years earlier, Bordallo had been among the "pilgrims" who attended the beatification of San Vitores at the Vatican, and he even offered, appropriately enough, a bronze statue of Kepuha to the late Pope John Paul II in the special audience that the pilgrims had with the Holy Father (Champion 1985). Kepuha, you will recall, was the seventeenth-century *maga'låhi* from Hagåtña who offered staunch support to San Vitores. Despite or perhaps precisely because of the fact that he chose to express his nationalist sentiments so dramatically at the Kepuha statue, Bordallo has himself been memorialized in a life-sized bronze statue fronting the *ufisinan maga'låhi* complex at Adelup.[33] Bordallo's memorialization at Adelup, by way of his dramatic "crossing" at the Kepuha Park, is unfortunate for the Reverend Sablan insofar as it would appear to preempt any movement that might be mustered in favor of building a monument in honor of Matå'pang in such a "conspicuous" public space in Hagåtña. Such blockage is less about clutter than about a cultural politics that still heavily favors the island's Catholic heritage. Though these particular conspicuous spots have been usurped, a dissatisfied Reverend Sablan, in his memoirs, pursued his point: "May Mata'pang soon be vindicated by his people who call themselves Chamorros, for to continue in the present attitude toward him would be considered by historians as a 'Monumental Littleness' for a people who are unable to give honor to whom honor is due" (1990, 262). A real Chamorro, following the late Reverend Sablan's logic, should honor Matå'pang, not Kepuha, and much less San Vitores. Any other course deserves any belittlement that historians can muster (and certainly have mustered) toward a people "unable to give honor [where] honor is due."

For the Chamorros who imagine themselves to be the political and cultural heirs to Matå'pang and other rebels of the seventeenth century, the battle continues. In the late 1990s, as Guam's "non-voting delegate to the US House of Representatives," Robert Underwood had entered into the *Congressional Record* the text of a rousing seventeenth-century nationalist war cry attributed to Maga'låhi Hurao (not to be confused with Hirao, Matå'pang's accomplice). "The Hurao speech," as it is better known among Chamorro cultural nationalists (and those who scorn them), sounds a rousing battle cry for Chamorros to rid the island of all foreigners. The speech first appeared in French in 1700; its author, the French Jesuit Charles LeGobien, had never visited the islands and relied solely on reports and letters the Jesuits there filed. After World War II, LeGobien's book was translated into English by American priest-historian Paul Daly (LeGobien 1949). In the 1980s, Hurao's speech was subsequently translated from English into Chamorro by cultural nationalists. In fact, the speech was imagined by LeGobien to represent the kind of liberal sentiment that plagued places like the Marianas and people like Chamorros at the time, and it thereby justified for him the noble and corrective work of his Jesuit companions. But if there was some kind of inauthenticity about it in its original form, Hurao's speech, I would assert, gained cultural, and certainly political, legitimacy (if not authenticity) in its jaunt from the seventeenth to the late-twentieth century, that is, from an antiliberal Catholic Counter-Reformation ideal in French to a resurgent Native Chamorro oppositional consciousness in the Chamorro language, even as it passed through an English translation provided by an American priest-historian (Daly), whose only interest was to make LeGobien's hagiography accessible to modern-day Guamanians. Apparently, for increasing numbers of Chamorros, the accessibility of such hagiographies seems to backfire for the Church.

A Journey of Faith in Reverse: Hagåtña, Guam, August 1974

Reflecting on the formal decision to proceed with the beatification process, Jesuit postulator Paolo Molinari explained that the Church "has a duty to look into [candidates'] lives and try to capture the message that God tries to convey to us through the exemplary manner of their lives." That message, he said, involves the Church's "lively concern for *the people out here*" as he likened Chamorro Catholic history to a plant whose "seed" was first sown by San Vitores centuries ago but which "now grows and grows *vigorously*" (*Pacific Voice* 1974b, 1; emphasis added). But this vigor—the intensity I have described in this chapter—also has a "return effect," as he called it, one beyond Roman public relations: In making Chamorros "look at their faith again," the Cause to canonize San Vitores will also strengthen the intimate bond between the universal Church and its individual members throughout the world. In describing its value for both the universal Church and local Catholics, Molinari revealed how the Cause to canonize San Vitores can also be seen as something of a loaded vessel or, in terms opened in this chapter, a particularly congested road through a commercial district. The commerce—the investments and the returns—on *this* San Vitores Road, however, are not to be measured in dollars or yen, but in souls. Souls, and Chamorro cultural and political identities and possibilities.

Part Three

From Behind
Transgressive Histories

Chapter 5
Disrobing the Man
A Second Peek

Madrid, 1660

Looking down, Padre San Vitores squirms in his seat. The person with whom he meets is first amused, then annoyed, and now impatient: "Padre please! Sit up and keep still!"[1] In his biography of San Vitores only two decades later, Francisco García wrote that the priest was "so confused . . . so embarrassed . . . that they had to give the painter the authority of a superior to command him to raise his face and open his eyes so that they could get a good likeness" (2004, 74).[2] García wrote that later, when San Vitores returned to Mexico from the Philippines in 1667, his friends in the Sodality of San Francisco also tried to have his portrait painted, albeit in secret, "since they knew he wouldn't grant permission." Outside the room for a scheduled meeting with his superior, Father José Vidal, and in which a painter remained hidden, San Vitores "seemed to know" something was amiss, and refused to enter. Though San Vitores was "dragged in" and "covered his face with paper," García said the painter managed to get the priest's "likeness, and it turned out to be a very good one" (2004, 154–155).

Ann Arbor, Michigan, 2007

This chapter renders an alternative portraiture of San Vitores's life and death as a witness to alternative understandings of the man, his mission, and his legacy from those presented by canonical and monological narratives. Here I reread stylistic elements of San Vitores's ministry in search of multiple and competing meanings spied in non–Church-sanctioned narratives and in those within the competing forms and layers of Chamorro Catholicism in the ensuing centuries. This counter-witnessing is transgressive, not oppositional, in that it does not diametrically oppose or invert the Church's preferred meanings so much as run angular to and away from them and their opposing perspectives.[3] Thus, this chapter foregrounds and examines the problematic of San Vitores's image and self-awareness as recalled by his immediate companions in the seventeenth century and his spiritual and political descendants in the twentieth century. First I turn to moments in the twentieth century in which the priest's image itself is called into question, only to be resolved in manageable terms. Then I return to the seventeenth century to examine the form of San Vitores's ministry in light of the spectacle it presented, and the sounds and scents it transmitted, through the particular embodied techniques San Vitores employed to teach God's word to Natives in particular (because Natives were infantilized and so were thought to require simple and graphic forms of teaching to effectuate their true conversion). Although I agree with his contemporaries and their twentieth-century successors that there was something profoundly visceral about it, I suggest perpendicularly that the deeply embodied dimensions of his ministry also embody other spiritual, and political, possibilities not necessarily in line with those of Church teachings. As a sight to behold, sometimes a laughter to evoke, even an essence to whiff—though ultimately these are not funny, given the deadliness of his seriousness—San Vitores was in fact an intensely "determined" man who left few if any stones unturned in his zeal to do God's bidding (McGrath 1972, 43). But whereas the Church has determined that his true character, especially his desire to die, was in line with God's greater plan, San Vitores can also be viewed as a particularly passive-aggressive individual who used guilt, threat, and, when needed, military force, against *anybody* who obstructed what he took to be God's will. I suggest that this passive aggression can also provide an alternative way to comprehend the epic tension that needs to be discerned between the desires of San Vitores "the man" and those that originated in and from God, properly speaking. We saw this tension in chapter 1, in the Vatican's authentication of San Vitores's "desire to die" as a faithful witness to God's will. But to say "determination" is another way of saying that if you do not support him, you are not supporting God, and this is precisely what San Vitores communicated consistently to those who opposed him either outright, or indirectly, if they did not assist him. This figuration of opposition to him as equivalent to opposition to God is best illustrated by the fact that Chamorros who opposed San Vitores and the missionaries were repeatedly depicted as "hostile," Matå'pang being the supreme example. Furthermore, seeing San Vitores as a vessel of God whose death exemplifies his willingness to serve as a gift to the Chamorros whom he loved also obfuscates the violence that comes from passive forms of aggression and enacts another form of violence in the continued silencing of fundamentally different cultural and political motivations and principles that underlay or informed, and continue to inform, historic and contemporary "opposition" to San Vitores and the Church's views. To be sure, mine is a portrayal of San Vitores in humanist terms, but there are other indigenous spiritual and political stakes attached to it as well. Therefore, and given the terms of San Vitores's canonical legacy, I am well aware that my work transgresses or digresses from the Church's line. For this sin, but also for theoretical and methodological reflection necessary for matters simultaneously academic and personal, intercultural and intergenerational, scholarly and spiritual, I head for the confessional as a theoretical preface. To serve as my confessor, but also as my key Native witness and the channel through which/whom to sound the concerns of this chapter, I return to Påle' 'Scot, the blind Chamorro priest who, as we saw in chapter 3, ought to be properly credited as the one whose idea it was to resurrect San Vitores's canonization in the twentieth century. In Påle' 'Scot's story we find a likeness to the portrait of San Vitores as I see it, and even, in all honesty, to the likeness I sometimes see when I look in the mirror.

Confessions of Digressions: Makati, Philippines, January 1991

Late in the life of the earthly vessel that is his physical body, Påle' 'Scot has returned to the Philippines, which is something of a second home, and has been convalescing at the Makati Medical Center. Besides his native Chamorro, Påle' is also fluent in Spanish and can converse in Tagalog. The Philippines provides him a certain *familia*(r) social and cultural environment. He speaks with much nostalgia about the place and is as incensed at local and national politics here as at those on Guam—and incensed, too, by their peoples. Medical staff, including custodians, have quickly learned not to mistreat him, for although he is soft-spoken and very deliberate in speech, he is also "irascible, you know." "I get like this," he grimaces, clenching both fists, and shaking as in a fit of rage. In fact, this is exactly how he responded to some of my questions, causing me such great fright, not for my safety but for his physical and emotional well-being so late in his years.

Our typical sessions consist of spending much of the mornings in conversation. I manage to tape about half these "conversations" and end up choosing not to do any videotaping. I place quotation marks around "conversations," because he does most of the talking. He grants me permission to record him, but only on the condition that the information be used for educational and research purposes and not for profit. In my notes I write down "if any royalties to the book, redirect to Påle''s finances." In this regard, he refuses to grant me permission to do a story on him for a local magazine edited by my brother, Tony. Påle' prefers to deal with the magazine directly, although I think that when I tell him of my connection to Tony, he will capitulate. (He did not. But he did grant an interview. See E Santos 1991.) Påle' 'Scot also initially refuses to allow me to use any of the material for a public television video project on the Church for which I was writing a script. This refusal comes on the first day; by the end of the week, he changes his mind. I think I have earned his confidence, though I am nervous about the responsibilities that come with his opening up to me.[4]

In our "conversations," I quickly learn that Påle' "digresses" often and is self-conscious and light-hearted about it. His meanderings are always interesting and often redirect my initial questions to unexpected but significant and sometimes profound places and issues. Case in point: I asked a straightforward question about Catholicism's relationship to Chamorro culture. I want to hear how he would describe *kostumbren Chamorro* and the family, how he would define novenas, rosaries, and the godparenthood system, all of which are central social and cultural elements that revolve around the Church's calendar but that also express indigenous Chamorro cultural and political alterity. Instead, he snaps at me: Why do I ask such "intrusive" questions that are not germane to my "study"? In my initial correspondence with him, I explained my interest in why the effort to canonize San Vitores was revived in modern Guam and what it meant for Chamorros. Just tell the truth about San Vitores, he replied over the phone then, for there are too many "detractors" out there. At the moment, he is angry with me, though he proceeds, nonetheless, to vent about events and individuals in Guam's history, including those inside and outside the local Catholic Church hierarchy who, as I understand him, "let the Church and Chamorro culture down" by failing to do this or that. Clearly, the "straightforward" question about the "relationship" between Catholicism and Chamorro culture struck a nerve. As it turns out, this discovery leads me to a productive way to think about the topic: To what extent is the history of the Catholic Church and the question of Chamorro culture about residual, festering wounds?

For many such digressions, it was not simply that we run out of tape, or that I shut the recorder off to save tape; I have my pen and pads but often put these down too. Sometimes I am simply mesmerized in and by his wanderings—he gets off the point of an initial question and talks of his travels around the world in search of material to help the San Vitores Cause. He talks of things long ago and then all of a sudden is referring to something going on today, maybe in the Philippines, on Guam, or over there, in the Middle East, which is uppermost in his mind. Forsaking pen and pad, I find myself slouched in the chair, sometimes with my face buried in my hands in deep and silent concentration. Once, when I have not said anything for a while, he suddenly asks if I am sleeping. For the record, I never fell asleep during any of his digressive soliloquies. Although I can condense, summarize, or paraphrase "information" or "data," I find it impossible to convey the truths of what he has to say without also evoking his demeanor and style, which are vessels of sorts. They alternate between deep peace and tranquility on one hand and restless energy and anxiety on the other. His stories begin here and go there, and then there, and come back here, in time and space. I am tempted to say that he embodies the beatification effort, or at least the more interesting elements of culture and history that often get ignored because they are considered either too unwieldy to deal with or not credible enough to garner attention, or because they are just unknown to authorities. Perhaps this is also why a mirror, or an inverse relationship, characterizes the dynamic between him and San Vitores: San Vitores enjoys official attention although his place in popular consciousness is actually slight; Påle' 'Scot's relative erasure from more recent coverage of the beatification of San Vitores is striking, given the Chamorro priest's role as originator of the movement earlier this century.

Somewhat like San Vitores three hundred years earlier, I squirm in my seat, looking down, seated before the man. Sometimes I want to cover my face. Sometimes I feel penitent before this Chamorro priest who stores so much historical and cultural knowledge. Why penitent, I do not know. But I also come away refreshed from these long and winding sessions of listening to him speak on and on. Refreshed (as in the way that confessions result in renewals), I have also become deeply fond of the monsignor—the self-described "irascible" person he is. His demeanor is captured in a story he tells of a recent exchange with a "poor fellow," a young and reportedly brilliant Filipino psychiatrist with whom Påle' 'Scot requested a session. "I wanted to know why," explains Påle', "every time I think of something that makes me angry, I get like this." He is grimacing and shaking his fists again; in this, he is just like my own father. In their first session, the good doctor proceeded to "ask, you know, these silly questions." "Like what?" I ask. "For instance," Påle' explains, "he asks what I liked the most when I was a kid." "What did you tell him?" "Well, the best times of my life were when I was in the seminary. You know, they ring the bell and it's time to get up. They ring the bell and it's time to eat. They ring the bell and it's time to work. Wouldn't you call that heaven?" If heaven is the bliss of submitting oneself to what one believes is good and true, then yes, I can see his point. But as he himself confesses, Påle' 'Scot also has his antsy moments. He proceeded to answer the doctor's remaining questions but concluded that it was a waste of time. The doctor wanted to set up a second session, but Påle' thanked him politely, and told him, "I'll call you." Then he says to me, "My gosh, Vincent, I'm only a priest but I could ask those nonsense questions too. What did they have to do with my condition?"

I also find it very difficult to leave him at the end of our sessions. One day, for example, I arrive at the usual time only to discover that his doctor has told him to take a break from "all the excitement." My first reaction is guilt. In fact, his blood pressure had been rising from the combination of our meetings and the start of "Operation Desert Storm," the US bombing of Baghdad. When my brother Carl and I first arrived at the hospital, we walked into his fifth-floor room to find him clutching a rosary and listening to news of the war on the radio—a surreal image of the priest who almost single-handedly tended to the spiritual needs of the Chamorros during much of the Japanese occupation fifty years earlier. Though that war began with the Japanese allowing only himself and Påle' Dueñas to remain "free" (the other priests, Americans and Spaniards, including Bishop Ángel Olano, were imprisoned in Japan), Dueñas refused to meet with Japanese officials, was charged with harboring American fugitives, and was subsequently tortured and killed. In the shadow of this local hero and would-be martyr, Påle' 'Scot was by implication figured as a "collaborator" because, by default, he was forced to work with Japanese officials, including two Catholic Japanese priests who were assigned to replace the exiled Spaniards.[5] Someday I will write Påle''s biography. In it I will detail how the intensity of his Catholic faith had the effect of making him look like a traitor to his people (and dismissive of their loyalty to America) during the Japanese period. His removal of the crucifix and other religious icons from the cathedral (on Japanese orders) stunned Chamorros, who saw the act as blasphemous both to God and to these symbols of Chamorro faith and culture. But, as Påle' explains, it would have been unconscionable for a priest to allow unconsecrated hands to desecrate such holy objects. If they were to be removed by anybody—Chamorro or Japanese—it had to be done with respect, by someone sanctified. "Instead, these ignorant Chamorros accuse me of assisting the Japanese," he recalls.

Påle' Dueñas was Calvo's superior and was Bishop Olano's "vicar apostolic," or apostolic substitute. But Dueñas did not want to deal with the Japanese, and delegated the office to Påle' 'Scot, who refused it because, as he had learned in Church canon law, "that which has been delegated cannot be sub-delegated." So, according to Påle' 'Scot, Dueñas kept the title but chose instead to seclude himself in the south, as far away as possible from the Japanese. And who can blame him? Even there, as it turned out, he was not safe. Hearing complaints from his parishioners about two Japanese priests who were preaching their country's propaganda, Dueñas incurred the ire of occupation officials by writing a curt letter of disapproval. But these two individuals "were good priests," explains Påle' 'Scot. They helped him tend to the spiritual needs of the whole central and northern parts of the island. And they arrived, as canon law requires, with a bona fide letter of permission from Bishop Olano. But there is another "tradition" still circulating in Chamorro oral histories of the war that exonerates Påle' 'Scot from charges of collaboration: Observant Chamorros who attended the wartime services conducted by the Japanese priests claim that whenever they had to use the pulpit for Japanese propaganda purposes, the priests would conspicuously remove their rings in full view of the congregation in order to signal to them that they were speaking *ex categra* or "outside the office."

During one of our sessions, Påle' 'Scot recites these words, for which he had once won an oratory contest as a seminarian almost seventy years earlier in Manila: "To you from failing hands, we throw our torch. Be yours to hold it high." Sensing its deep significance for him, I interpret the passage to mean that as a historian I need to convey faithfully the truths that he understood and labored to champion in his own right. Certainly I am well aware of my obligation to attune to his investments in me. Indeed, in our very first session, he made it clear—disarmingly clear; in fact, I thought he was giving me the thumbs down—that he did not grant interviews to just anybody. He specifically said that he does not play "native informant" to the "latest, enterprising researcher who will profit at [his] and Guam's expense." I got the clear sense that he has had his share of enthusiastic interviewers who ended up never giving him anything in return. His exact words varied, though all were crystal clear: "quid pro quo," "fair exchange," or most pointedly, "I give you something, you give me something back." I recall *chismes* (gossip) about him: that the monsignor is selfish, even greedy (especially for a priest). From what I know of him already, I react the way he does: "Ignorant people!" though I do not know all the gossip, or its basis. I do know that Påle' 'Scot is hardly a self-serving man; his ideas and history in fact provide a rather complicated context and explanation for alleged instances of "selfishness" and "greed." I shall get to this shortly, but in the meantime, I had to consider what I had of value that I could reciprocate for his insights. First, we agreed that if I wanted to videotape the interviews, I would furnish him with questions beforehand. In fact, I taped these questions for his convenience. Protocol also required that I formally ask the archbishop's permission to interview the monsignor. This was necessary because Påle' 'Scot is a "secular" priest or, more specifically, a "diocesan," whose loyalty and obedience is to a diocese rather than to a religious order, such as the Capuchins. These considerations alone put to rest *chismes* about his alleged greed or selfishness: diocesans take vows only to celibacy and obedience, not to poverty, as do other "religious." Thus, Påle' is not only permitted to own personal property and have a source of income, but, like most of us, he needs these because as a secular priest he lacks the support that their respective orders provide other priests later in life. Traditionally, diocesan priests also look to their diocese for financial support, but this support depends on the availability of resources in the diocese.

So, despite what some people might say and no matter the rumors that circulate, I have become convinced that his "story" is not only worth telling but is a prerequisite for understanding the complexities of San Vitores's (and the Catholic Church's) cultural and historical relationship with the Chamorro people and how the former has been internalized and reworked by the latter. It may perhaps even temper our reliance on the written record, that holy scripture of Western historiography, except that Chamorros themselves have an archive of written testimonies to this history, and Chamorro perspectives are interpellated in and by, and can be interpolated from, the writings of *taotao sanhiyong* (people from the outside). But if the beatification of San Vitores is something of a historical event today, whether one supports the effort or not, then it is especially important to learn a little about the person most responsible for bringing knowledge about San Vitores into modern local (and Vatican) consciousness. Påle' 'Scot is that person. He embodies Chamorro Catholic cultural and historical relations. His words, his gestures, his body, his vision, are archival.

Archival work, especially on real, live bodies and reputations, requires utmost caution, respect, and responsibility. Besides obligations to my own family and friends in a small island community, and besides those straight-forward agreements I mentioned, I am obliged to contextualize properly any information Påle' 'Scot provides me. I also feel a connection between my desire to (re)write local history and his digressions. It is his influence that makes me conceptualize Chamorro priests as points of synthesis and points of rupture in Chamorro Catholic history. Their particular role as mediators between the local parish and the global Church must yield some truths never even considered in modern historiography. Their backgrounds, their knowledge, are keys to the archives. Once in our conversation Påle' had asked me to clarify my project, my thesis. I summarized it as concisely as possible. He erupted. I was not to discuss anything controversial. I was ask-ing too many irrelevant questions of the Church and of Chamorro culture. I should simply focus on the facts of San Vitores's story. What were these facts? I asked. He replied that San Vitores brought the light of truth to the Chamorros and that he loved the people so much that he gave his life so that they might live. For that we should be thankful and proud. Though he could not see me, I think he knew that I was again squirming in my seat. It was not that I doubted Påle' 'Scot. Nor did I doubt San Vitores's faith. I do not think he was a bad man or that the mission was singularly responsible for the supposed death of Native culture. And I certainly did not think Påle' 'Scot was disingenuous, and most certainly did not think he had sim-ply been brainwashed by Catholicism. But at this stage in my research I had already sensed that the task of accounting for love through martyrdom and its various costs was not a simple story. Moreover, the conceptual task was particularly difficult because I was working from scratch, in that the only other models of analysis and remembrance in San Vitores's case were so oppositional and left so much to be desired in terms of understanding the political dynamics of cultural exchange between Native and missionary. Above all else, at that moment I certainly did not dare tell him the title of my dissertation, not the least for the mental image he might get of me.

Belaboring the Tragic: Tomhom, Guam, 1985

David L Sablan is a Chamorro artist whose paintings of precontact Chamorro life grace many residence and office walls in the region. A bronze star Vietnam-war "hero," Sablan found that his stint forced him to question his armed presence in the country (face-to-face with a Vietcong he had just shot, he held the man in his arms and thought, "I don't know you . . . you and I have nothing against each other") and his loyalty to the United States (D Sablan 1983, 13, 19). This questioning got him into trouble (he wound up, as many Chamorro vets had, in "the slammer"), and led to art and to a born-again patriotism as a citizen of "Nasion Chamoru."[6] By the mid-1980s, Sablan was already making an impression in the community as an artist, so it was not surprising that Archbishop Felixberto Flores commissioned him to paint a life-sized portrait of San Vitores in anticipation of the beatification, a painting that would be unveiled on 6 October 1985 along with a twenty-foot-tall statue of the priest (see figure 5; Cates 1985a, 40; *PDN* 1985j, 32). What Flores did not realize was that his own championing of Chamorro culture would collide head-on with Sablan's. The collision occurred on the day of celebration, before a throng of parishioners and others, and more precisely, at the moment when the archbishop unveiled the life-sized painting that showed a realistic portrait of the murder, complete with San Vitores's head being split open and blood gushing down his face (figure 11). Below the image, in big, bold lettering, were the words, "Martyred At Last!" According to an eyewitness who asked not to be identified, the archbishop's face had blanched as he quickly threw the cover

FIGURE 11. Twentieth-century depiction of San Vitores's 1672 "martyrdom" at the hands of Maga'låhi (chief) Matå'pang and his accomplice, Hirao, of Tomhom. The painting was commissioned for the renaming of Tomhom's St William's Parish for Blessed Diego as part of the celebration of San Vitores's beatification in 1985, but Archbishop Felixberto C Flores considered its realism too graphic and in "bad taste." The artist, David L Sablan, retorted that it was in fact faithful to a seventeenth-century account. Print reproduced with permission of David L Sablan.

back over the "tasteless" image and had it hurried away.[7] In a coffee-table commemorative booklet on the beatification, commissioned by Archbishop Flores to Guam Atlas Publications, the illustrator was specifically instructed to "not belabor the tragic" (Hezel 1985). Accordingly, the graphic that illustrates the martyrdom is a pen-and-ink portrayal of San Vitores lying on the ground before his assailants, whose feet are visible in the painting, along with part of the spear at the painting's margin (Hezel 1985, 31).

A decade and a half earlier, on the occasion of the Guam publication of Alberto Risco's popular hagiography of Padre San Vitores (Calvo 1970), Flores foregrounded San Vitores's seventeenth-century "image" against the backdrop of the 1960s and 1970s cultural and political happenings, and in providentialist teleology:

> To a generation attuned to rock music and the hippie and the psychedelic, this Life of Fr Diego might conceivably offer no great attraction. And yet, with a bit of ingenuity, phases of Fr Diego's life as a missionary could easily be reshaped so as to make of him a glorious hippie saint. His manner of dressing, for example, during his missionary travels, in outlandish suits of palm leaves, would probably make the most far-out hippie today turn green with envy; and his penchant for putting Christian doctrine into song would delight our guitar and combo generation. (Calvo 1970, viii)

Though Flores would quickly point out that a peeling away of the visual stylistics would reveal the timeless truth and substance of San Vitores's legacy, it was the residual image of a "far-out" hippie saint decked in an outrageous outfit that made a lasting impression on this post–Vatican II generation kid, who wanted only to play electric guitar at church.[8]

A Spectacle (and More) to Behold

Padre San Vitores was, by choice, a spectacle to behold, but he also produced a sound that could make you wince, or else draw you closer in curiosity or amusement. And he was something to smell, which is significant for Chamorros, because the continued practice of the *mangnginge'*, or the sniffing of an elder's hand to take in the "essence" (in the olfactory sense of the term) and to show deference and respect, is another of the *tåhdong* or culturally and historically "deep" and profound practices that continue to inform the surface layers of Catholic ritual and practice.[9] To appreciate how smell figures into San Vitores's truthful "image," I highlight a larger historical context in which the sense of smell has been marginalized systematically in favor of metaphors and practices of sight and vision as standards for ascertaining truth and knowledge (Classen, Howas, and Synnott 1994). In the late twentieth and early twenty-first centuries, the central paradigm as based on mass media, including cyberspace and virtual reality, is one of visuality as the principal mode of cultural production and consumption, through "ways of seeing" (Berger 1972) and "practices of looking" (Sturken and Cartwright 2001). But in the days of San Vitores, the scent of things was as much a witness to truth, especially divine truth, as were stimuli from any of the other sensors. For example, Father Diego Ramirez on 31 July 1648 wrote about "a small trifle which called no little attention of many and which caused in me no insignificant admiration" for the young San Vitores (quoted in *Positio* 1981b, 80). Ramirez was San Vitores's confessor, and the two had been traveling overland from Madrid to the Jesuit seminary in Villarejo, Spain, where they arrived on the eve of the Feast of Saint Ignatius. We pick up the story before supper on the night of their arrival:

> among other mortifications that were practiced after the manner of those held at lunch, one was to kiss the feet of the community as is usually done. When they came to kiss the feet of our guest [San Vitores,] they noticed the excellent smell they exuded, so that for only that reason they deliberately and repeatedly looked at him and recognized him among the rest. Many marveled at such novelty and later told me about it as if it were something mysterious. I for my part[,] intending to see if he went to bed, entered his room while he was disrobing and quietly took one shoe and tried to smell it. I must confess that it did smell extraordinarily well. No tanned hides that I had ever smelt in my life gave me such comfort. (quoted in *Positio* 1981b, 81)

Ramirez went on to explain that the two had been traveling for days, under the heat of the season, and that it was a physically demanding journey for which San Vitores had "sweated excessively—a thing that is not conducive to good odor, much less of the feet." For these reasons, Ramirez concluded that "whether this was natural in the boy . . . or whether it came from a higher source . . . which is my personal belief[,] considering the quality of the smell . . . only God knows." What Ramirez was sure of, however, was that he "later . . . was sorry that [he] did not take with [him] one or both shoes" (quoted in *Positio* 1981b, 81). Of this incident, San Vitores's biographer, Francisco García, asserted, "God wished to testify to the good odor of virtue and sanctity that those feet were to spread in preaching the gospel of peace, drawn by the unguents of the spouse" (2004, 33). This passage, according to Father James McDonough, editor of García's 2004 publication, refers to a specific verse in the biblical Song of Songs (Song 1:3–4, cited in García 2004, 33). According to the official Web site of the United States Conference of Catholic Bishops, the Song of Songs refers to the mutual love and relationship between man and God and often characterizes this relationship as a "marriage," although there is also "a consistent application of the Song of Songs to the Blessed Virgin Mary."[10] I will return shortly to the terms of kinship in relation to the special kinship between

Father San Vitores and Mary the Mother of God, who is locally venerated as Santa Marian Kamalen, Holy Lady of the Shed. Santa Marian Kamalen, according to Marilyn Anne Jorgensen (1984), is Chamorro Catholicism's "key symbol," whose temporal and physical manifestation (other than her statue) is the archdiocese's cathedral, now known as Hagåtña Basilica.

In another instance, in May 1670, San Vitores returned to Guam from Tinian. In Hagåtña he discovered that a fellow priest had become "very ill," his body covered with open sores "from which there ran continually a filthy and ill-smelling humor, which offended the sight as well as the olfactory sense" (García 2004, 225). Moreover, the man's shirt was considered "so repugnant" that his attendant "would not touch it, even if he was a good and charitable man." So, in order to "overcome in himself all repugnance," San Vitores took the priest's shirt, went into another room, and put the shirt on. Then he returned to the sick priest, who asked San Vitores to cure him, to which San Vitores proclaimed, "My hands, of themselves, are worth nothing, unless, because they are the Superior's hands, they possess some virtue of those of Christ." San Vitores then proceeded to the proverbial (or parable-like) laying on of the hands, but according to García (2004, 225), "to dissimulate his part in the miracle, he applied a signature of Venerable Father Luis de Medina (a companion who had been killed earlier) to the patient . . . and immediately his health was recovered."

In the above incidents, suddenly encountering smells from sources that should normally not emit them, such as a pleasant fragrance from sweaty feet (or, as typical for other saints, the scent of roses from putrid sores) or observing the ability to heal are signs of something other than nature at work (Bell 1984). Indeed, San Vitores's biography is saturated with what García called unusual "auspicious signs" in nature that coincide with San Vitores's doings, which García consistently read as providential in origin and signification. For example, a painting of Saint Francis Xavier in Mexico began to "sweat" as a sign of something that was about to happen in the Marianas; García speculated it was an omen of either the "Great War" (of 1670) or San Vitores's martyrdom in 1672. For García, the other "connection" was that San Vitores was also a "living image" of Saint Francis Xavier, the proto–Jesuit missionary (2004, 234, 235). There is also a class of "auspicious signs" that features what García called "remarkable correspondences" in dates and events (2004, 28), including the following examples:

- Both his deaconate ordination and his martyrdom occurred on 2 April (in 1650 and 1672, respectively). García said, "He was killed preaching the Gospel on the day he was given power to preach it," which also meant that he preached the Gospel "even better with the *voice of his blood*." As additional support, García also pointed out that his death occurred "one week before Palm Sunday" (2004, 42, 252; emphasis added).

- His mother died on 19 July 1657, which was seventeen years to the day from her capitulating to her son's entrance into the Society of Jesus. For García, there was something even more remarkable: in 1640, she took San Vitores to the Saint Ignatius chapel in Madrid specifically because she sought Saint Ignatius's intercession for her salvation in exchange for her son's entrance into the order. Thus, explained García (2004, 59), the coincidence of her death and her "capitulation" is also "a sign of the salvation she had asked for from God, via the intercession of St Ignatius."
- San Vitores was released from the infirmary on the feast day of Saint Francis Xavier, to whom San Vitores prayed for his recovery (García 2004, 60).
- San Vitores took his vows for the mission ministry on 12 November 1657, thirty years to the day that he was baptized (García 2004, 61).
- A "blood red comet" streaked across Mexico's skies and an earthquake rumbled on 13 March 1668, the date of San Vitores's departure from Acapulco to the Marianas (García 2004, 158).
- Earthquakes rocked Manila, Mexico City, and Acapulco on 7 August 1667, the day San Vitores left Manila. García pointed out that this was also the "Octave of the Feast of St Ignatius, Founder of the Jesuit Order" (García 2004, 148–149). ("Octave" refers to the eighth day of a given feast.)

A final example features a whole slew of coincidental dates as "auspicious signs": On 12 October 1659, while undergoing the Spiritual Exercises of Saint Ignatius, San Vitores wrote to the Jesuit father general, Gowen Nickel, asking to be sent overseas. He received Nickel's favorable reply on 18 December 1659, the Feast of the Expectation of the Blessed Mother. Furthermore, he received positive news from the provincial father, and the "blessing" of his own father, Don Jerónimo, on 2 January 1660, which García pointed out was the "Octave of the protomartyr Saint Stephen" (2004, 72). I do not wish to discount belief in auspicious signs, or in God, the Blessed Mother, or the saints, or to write off the rather complex history of the significance of the eighth day in Catholic doctrine, but given the prodigious numbers of saints in (as well as those not recognized formally by) the Church, and not counting the innumerable other days commemorated in Catholicism, there is no single day of the (itself significant) Gregorian calendar that can be seen as insignificant, not "auspicious," and therefore not evidence of providence.

In fact, San Vitores's "humors" comprise only a part of the spectacle (and specter, since spirits, like humors, are miasmic) he presented deliberately, so deliberately in fact that it is composed of what I will refer to as a bundle of "techniques" he employed.[11] His "sounds"—spoken and sung—are no less remarkable as evidence of his, and other, truths implicated in his memory and legacy. First we turn to the facility he was said to have had with the

Chamorro language, which his companions consistently attributed to the Holy Spirit, in classical Christian fashion. Next we turn to songs he used as part of a special kind of ministry that he and his companions called "the mini-mission," which included a particular form of preaching they referred to as the *acto de contrición*. This ministry involved sporadic treks to the villages or paths in the hinterlands, where the mission hoped to catch Natives off guard, and attract others to God's word by singing holy verses, often referred to in Spanish as *ejaculaciónes*, which San Vitores himself likened to "holy darts" he would fling expertly into the innocent hearts of otherwise ignorant and unsuspecting *indios*. According to García, the particular effectiveness of the mini-missions had been proven in the Spanish countryside, in Mexico, and in the Philippines, but they relied for their success on the use of the vernacular and the element of surprise. Finally, we turn to San Vitores's demeanor and its political and cultural implications to round out this portrait.

As he had done in the Philippines with Tagalog and other languages, San Vitores is said to have learned Chamorro "with such facility and in such a short time" that his companions deemed it the work of the Holy Spirit (García 2004, 93). The biblical reference is to the "Tongues of Fire" in Acts 2:3–4, something that San Vitores affirmed when he attributed the success of his ministry to the Holy Spirit (García 2004, 98). Antonio Nieto, the captain of the ship that carried San Vitores from the Philippines to Mexico, testified that his passenger was so fluent that he "corrected other nationals in the use of their own languages," including, ironically, a Filipino he had retained as one of his Chamorro-language teachers and translators because the Filipino had spent time in the Marianas (García 2004, 149). By the time San Vitores finally made it to the Marianas for his eagerly awaited return on 17 June 1668, he is said to have "impressed the natives by speaking fluently in their language" (de Viana 2004, 21). On the ship, he readied himself by composing hymns in Chamorro. García said San Vitores learned Chamorro "so thoroughly that eight days after arriving . . . on the feast of St John the Baptist, [he] gave a sermon in Chamorro . . . with such elegance and propriety that the Natives marveled" (2004, 159). In addition to such compositions, and with help from his Filipino assistants, San Vitores translated into Chamorro the Apostles' Creed, the Ten Commandments, and the Holy Mysteries, and composed a Chamorro grammar and *vocabulario* (dictionary) (Burros 1954; García 2004, 186, 192). And in response to his companions' anxieties about not knowing the vernacular well enough, San Vitores told them not to worry, for God and the Blessed Mother would "give them words" (García 2004, 186). Captain Juan de la Cruz himself attested to the power of San Vitores's use of the Chamorro language. A frequent witness to baptisms (which may explain the origins of the frequency of the names Juan and Cruz in Chamorro history), de la Cruz instructed one mother, who had been hearing the protestations of the *aniti* (ancestral spirits), to rid them with the sign of the cross and a prayer to the Holy Trinity and to Jesus as translated by San Vitores (García 2004, 192). And finally, moments before Matå'pang and Hirao slaughtered him, San Vitores called out to them in Chamorro, "May God have mercy on you, Mata'pang!" (García 2004, 252). Interestingly, nowhere is the Chamorro phrase recorded. However, the phrase he probably used was *si Yu'os ma'åse'*, whose colloquial meaning is simply, "thank you," but in other contexts also means "God bless you." In this latter sense, the phrase resonates with the acknowledgment, *si Yu'os in fanbinendisi håga-hu* (or *låhi-hu*) (God bless you my daughter [or son]), as spoken by *i manåmko'* (the elders) when a younger person shows proper respect through *nginge'* (ritual sniffing of the hands).[12] This digression continues to illustrate the important historical and complex intermingling and entanglement between Chamorro and Spanish Catholic terms of cultural acknowledgment in language and ritual, and the historical and even messy entanglements that militate against efforts to reduce the legacy to a singular, definitive meaning.

Vicente Rafael has shown as much in his study of the role of language and translation in the mutual but unequal appropriations between early Tagalogs and Spanish priests in the Philippines (1993). Through the painstaking work of translating Christian doctrine into the various vernaculars with which they had to contend, the padres were time and again confounded by differential and competing counter-appropriations of Spanish and Catholic terms and practices by various classes of Natives interested in furthering or reconsolidating their own social, cultural, and political positions. An example is the fate of specific dogmatic concepts ("Dios," "Santa Maria") that were deliberately kept in the original Latin (the language of God), either because the padres believed that they could have no possible equivalent in the vernacular, or to guard against the possibility of Native mistranslation. Despite these measures, Natives appropriated these concepts. One example that is germane here is the Filipino counter-translation, or, as Rafael put it, the "contracting" of prayers to the Holy Trinity, or to the Holy Family, into what he calls an indigenous "inoculation" against the threat or the shock of danger (as posed by colonial officials, soldiers, and priests), so that "Jesus, Maria, and José," as a Catholic invocation (as Captain Juan de la Cruz urged of the Chamorro woman who heard the *aniti*) becomes "contracted" in the double sense of being negotiated and foreshortened into *"Susmariasep!"* According to Rafael, *"Susmariasep!"* continues to be a commonplace expression that registers "shock" at the unexpected or surprising. These were exactly the kinds of politicized transcultural processes that trafficked on San Vitores's fame among the Chamorros. We can bear witness to it in the layers and modes of "spectacle" presented in the particular form of his ministry called the mini-mission, which contained a particular device called the *acto de contrición*.

Emissions and Omissions in the Spectacle
of San Vitores's Mini-Mission

The "mini-mission" was a form of ministry that involved sporadic treks to the villages or paths in the hinterlands to attract the heathen to God's word. Employed and said to have been perfected in San Vitores's ministries in the countryside of Spain, Mexico, and the Philippines, the mini-mission used numerous devices, such as the animated singing of *saetillas* or *saetas* ("darts" or "arrows"), often glossed as "flying darts" (Calvo 1970, 50) or "flying sermons" (*Positio* 1981b, 211), and which consisted of *ejaculaciónes* or "holy maxims," sung in Latin or in the vernacular. Also in the tool kit was the conscious use of "spectacle" and surprise to attract and hold a throng, and specifically to engage it with the *acto de contrición*, a special form of confession and devotion. A typical scene would involve the sudden appearance of San Vitores, hurling or throwing these *ejaculaciónes* into the hearts and minds of the unsuspecting witness, who would then be expertly and skillfully led into the recitation of the *actos*.

According to Father Horacio de la Costa (1961, 471), San Vitores was a follower of Father Jerónimo Lopez, founder of the *acto de contrición* movement in Spain. According to de la Costa:

> Lopez had found in the course of giving innumerable missions to the simple folk of the Spanish countryside that one of the most effective means of drawing them to a better life was to march through the streets of a town or village carrying a crucifix and crying out the act of contrition in a loud voice, varying this with short extempore ejaculations expressive of sorrow for sin, and wherever a crowd collected, at street corners or in the squares, expanding the formula into passionate exhortations to repentance. Usually people who merely stopped to stare stayed to pray, and soon the missioner was being followed by a vast procession singing hymns and shouting the act of contrition with him, often with sobs and tears. He led them in this manner to the church, where, after a brief instruction on how to make a good confession, he sent them to the priests waiting in the confessionals. (1961, 471)

De la Costa added, "It must all have been very much like a Protestant revivalist meeting, but it was extremely effective. Moreover, we must not forget that the Catholic Church does not disdain such manifestations of religious enthusiasm, as long as they bring people closer to God. Indeed, the Church had been making use of them in the Middle Ages and even earlier" (1961, 471). De la Costa also told us that for his ministry in the Philippines, San Vitores translated "the most powerful verses" from Lopez. We can assume he brought these to the Marianas.

In the Marianas, according to García (2004, 98), the *acto* was San Vitores's basic instrument for "daily talk with the indios" and that he even "went to it

. . . if at any time he was at a loss." Though these were used in the country-side, San Vitores quickly discovered that elements could also be helpful in the (new) villages whose residents were already Christianized because the problem of their "constancy" to the faith was always a devil's battleground for the missionaries. In these villages (as in the Philippines, Mexico, and Spain), San Vitores would suddenly appear in a location, hoist a banner, and then walk the streets singing the doctrine in Chamorro, sometimes even using just an "invented tune." On these walks, San Vitores always sought out children, who were, as García put it, "wax in his hands." No doubt because he always had little presents and sweets for them, the children also fol-lowed San Vitores from village to village, and in time San Vitores seized on the idea to organize contests among them involving the recitation of the doctrines; the best participants would be given titles like "captain" and be permitted "the honor of holding the banners" (2004, 202). In fact, San Vitores was reportedly "never seen without children," whom he referred to as "tender plants" (García 2004, 184). It would not be long before this kind of throng would evolve into what San Vitores called a "squadron of Mariano Infantry" that was "weak in the eyes of men, but as formidable to demons as it was agreeable to angels." He also said that this squadron "laid siege to the villagers" (García 2004, 203), thus introducing into our critical history an important Chamorro demographic that supported the padres.

There is some indication that, in the villages, San Vitores preferred to use Spanish phrases, whereas he used Chamorro in the countryside "for those Chamorros [read: recalcitrants] who remained hidden" (García 2004, 54–55). Whether in Chamorro, Spanish, or Latin, inside or outside the confines of these villages, San Vitores relied on the aforementioned *ejaculaciónes,* or holy arrows, darts, or sermons, such as: "Awake, sinner and hear! Awake, death is near! Confess your hidden sins! You end when day begins!" (García 2004, 254). US Naval Captain William Safford, a natural-ist and philologist fluent in Spanish who basically served as Guam's first lieutenant governor in 1900 (technically, he was an aide-de-camp), took a strong interest in the history of the Chamorros, especially the work of San Vitores and his companions. Of *these* mini-missions, Safford wrote that "in imitation of the songs of the natives [San Vitores] would repeat these words to the rhythm of clapping hands, and the people round about him, catch-ing the inspiration, would fall to dancing with him." He also explained San Vitores's use of the language and dance thus: "Naturally, it was impossible for the good padre to explain the doctrines of the Church to these simple-minded people whose language he understood but imperfectly" (Safford 1911, 6). Though Safford misses the point about why San Vitores used these techniques—regardless of his fluency, after all, San Vitores did believe that God and the Blessed Mother would furnish the right words when needed—Safford's patronizing view of the "simple-minded" people registered only the navy captain's affinity with the padres, despite the space of three hundred years that separated them, and the secularism of his own mission. For San Vitores did consciously seek out "tactics" that he thought were appropriate to Natives in particular, tactics whose desired effects, wrote Augusto V de Viana (2004, 23), were most likely not understood by the Chamorros of the time.

San Vitores was indeed mindful of what the Chamorros were capable, and incapable, of comprehending. According to García, the "means" he used within the framework of the mini-mission "followed the natural order suggested by God . . . the invisible known via the visible." As he did in the Philippines, San Vitores relied on things that the Natives "saw with their own eyes."[13] Thus he prevailed on festivities and celebrations in chapels and churches to help them "appreciate the beauty and meaning of the sacrament," and performed deeds of charity "in order to banish their fear [that] the Spaniards would deceive . . . and enslave them . . . and to demonstrate and prove the sincerity and unselfishness of the missionaries" (García 2004, 118). In outlining the specifics of the form by which the doctrine had to be taught to *indios* in particular, San Vitores also confirms the legitimacy of specifically *indio* fear toward the Spaniards: fear of slavery, deception, and tributes and taxes, and fees for marriages, baptisms, and funerals (García 2004, 119).

San Vitores also sought "simple and coherent narrations of [the] Faith," such as "the story of God," the creation, sins of angels, fall of man, devil's envy, birth/passion, and "the death of Our Lord to expiate the sins of men." He told them that man had "offended God by rejecting the light given to do good," and asked how it is that man "who is so low . . . might offer expiation to the Lord of Heaven who is so high." The answer: only by being "as high as God, being both God and Man!" And he said that the *indios* were as "deeply moved" by these as they were by "temporal objects [like blankets] to illustrate the power of God and the usefulness of novel things" (García 2004, 119). San Vitores also taught the Natives the progression of doctrines, using images and signs, especially earthly signs: there is "drift" between man and beast; man is of heaven, beast of the earth. (The ensuing progression is from García 2004, 183, unless otherwise noted.) The narrative he told: Real treasures are in heaven. God "the Father" sent his Son, Jesus, to the "land," and so the "road" to heaven is through Jesus in the "arms" of the Blessed Mother. (San Vitores would add that he himself was sent by "the Father" to these islands to teach God's "children" to follow Jesus to the "treasures" of heaven). Christ was born of a virgin named Mary. He died for us. Mary was beautiful, powerful, and holy. As the mother of Jesus (the Holy Infant), she was also Mother of God. Jesus was God and a man. So Mary is also Queen of Man. God loves the Chamorro as a father loves a son. (San Vitores loves God and loves the Chamorro as a father loves a son.)

The "simple," the "visible," and the "easily grasped" were conjoined with what San Vitores believed the Chamorros loved best. And as they were "naturally fond of singing, dancing, and buffoonery," San Vitores sought kindred means to "attract them" (García 2004, 183). So, when he saw a group of Natives, he would suddenly begin to dance about and sing in their language, clapping his hands, and exclaiming, "Joy, Joy, Joy! Good Joy, Jesus and Mary! Our Joy, Jesus and Mary! Amen, Amen, Jesus, Mary and Joseph!" (Safford 1911, 6). García said that "San Vitores would *repeat the last words* ['Jesus, Maria, José!' in Spanish], beating out the rhythm with his hands, singing all the while and dancing as they joined in happily, 'Oh, How Good is Jesus, Mary, and Joseph, and how good is the Great Padre, How happy, *how amusing'*" (2004, 184; emphasis added). Putting them "in good humor," San Vitores would "seize the opportunity to explain the mysteries and commandments, [and] exhort . . . them to believe them and observe them." Finally, wrote García, "He would end this ritual with the same dance . . . so that they would be happy to the end" (2004, 184).[14]

"Sus!"

From San Vitores's calculated and repeated ejaculations while jumping up and down and consciously "playing the buffoon," according to García, we can imagine in the Chamorro who first encounters him initial shock, then amusement, and even happiness "to the end."[15] The shock might have come from the sudden surprise, but surely it was also a reaction to the image he presented, for not long after his arrival, and in order to better empathize and thus gain the trust of the Natives, San Vitores discarded his robe and fashioned for himself an "outlandish" outfit made of palm leaves. Around his neck he wore a rosary of Our Lady, but around his waist was a rope by which an assistant led him about. He wore this because he wanted to "fit" in, because similarly, he had quickly ceased wearing his spectacles so as to be on the same level of the heathen, whom he described as "blind" to God's word.[16] Unfortunately for him, however, the immediate consequence was simply that he could not see and thus needed, in order to get around, the rope tied to his waist and an assistant to pull him along (García 2004, 202). This image collides head-on with that portraying San Vitores as capable of "scaling [hillsides] like a deer" to outpace the *indios* (García 2004, 132).

Finally, there is one other important detail about San Vitores that is seldom mentioned, the implications of which receive virtually no commentary by primary or secondary sources that I have seen: San Vitores had no teeth! (See Calvo 1970, 102–103.) Before I get to the implications of this rarely mentioned tidbit, we need first to consider the "humors" of his apparel.

San Vitores's dress version of "doing as the Romans do"—a Guam version of "playing Indian," as Philip J Deloria described the cultural and political history of Anglo-American self-fashioning via appropriating Native American identity and regalia (1998)—had precedents before his arrival in the Marianas. In 1660, as he was preparing to leave Spain for Mexico, San Vitores gave a farewell speech and sermon at a hermitage in San Sebastian. According to García (2004, 73), the festivities included the "traditional" custom of students and masters dressing "in ridiculous clothing" and going about in procession "to inspire veneration and humility." (The Chamorros whom San Vitores first confronted about the clothes thought they were "absurd in appearance and custom," and they simply refused to wear them, although Maga'låhi Kepuha was said to be "very much pleased" with the hat, among other things he was given [García 2004, 189]). It was not only the Natives who found San Vitores's appearance absurd. Arriving on 13 June 1669, Don Manuel de Leon and another priest, Padre Pimental, were "moved to laughter" when they saw San Vitores and a companion approach the ship in a canoe, although the source of this quote quickly recovered and asserted that "while they were laughing . . . they also felt a wave of respect and veneration . . . well up in their hearts" (Risco, in Calvo 1970, 141).

In Chamorro "nakedness," San Vitores saw ignorance but also the tremendous "hardships" that awaited his ministry (Calvo 1970, 113). These hardships were the sexual license he saw, particularly in regard to the *guma' uritao* (young men's houses), which reminded him of houses of prostitution in Europe.[17] The *guma' uritao* were places where *uritao* (young men) congregated and where parents often sent their young daughters in return for goods or services. San Vitores saw this as scandalous, and let it be known. As one might imagine, the *uritao* did not respond well to San Vitores's scolding, and at least one major battle spilled blood over this particular matter. Indeed, San Vitores listed resistance from the *uritao* as one of the major "obstacles" that the devil had strewn in his path, and was scandalized because the activities that occurred in the *guma' uritao* contradicted what the Church deemed to be the "proper" relations between man and woman. The proper relationship, of course, was that of husband and wife as bound together in the presence of God and in imitation and realization of God's commitment or marriage to humankind, as we saw earlier expressed in the Bible, in the Song of Songs. And if the relationship between humankind and God was figured as a "marriage," and heaven was its "banquet," then man and woman needed "proper attire" before they could be invited in. Or rather, invited *back in*, for as we know, by giving in to the forbidden fruit of desire, Eve, along with Adam, fell from paradise, one consequence of which was the tainting of nudity as a sign of sexual temptation (Pagels 1987). The Chamorros' "nakedness" played into this discourse, and the only solution to their predicament, according to San Vitores, was to clothe them properly, which was to say in "proper attire" for the wedding feast. To "wear proper attire" was also to accept God's word and convert, remaining "constant" to that word through piety and devotion, respect for the name of God, attention to doctrine, and fulfillment of the obligations prescribed by the Father through the father (García 2004, 506). Most of all, "proper attire" entailed proper relations through holy matrimony, which, along with schools for boys and girls, was another institution that San Vitores used to replace the *guma' uritao*. But a curious thing happened on the way to the chapel. Where initially the *uritao* had resisted the padres' efforts to terminate *their* institution, the padres began to notice a favorable change in their demeanor when the *uritao* themselves began to notice a behavioral change among Chamorro women in their new status as "wives." Henceforth, the *uritao* themselves began to abandon the *guma' uritao* in favor of the new arrangement, while young women, much to the consternation of the padres, began to defend the older Native tradition. Clearly, those Chamorro women believed that the new arrangements—the new attire—spelled the demise of the status and prestige they had enjoyed before the missionaries' arrival.

There still remains the matter of San Vitores's teeth. Have you ever heard anybody with no teeth speak? If not, curl your upper and lower lips around your upper and lower teeth and try to say "Maria!" It is funny enough to speak your own language this way, but consider that San Vitores was speaking Chamorro mediated by Filipino translators. The point is more substantive than a funny sight (or sound) to behold (or hear). The point is that if we are to render an account of San Vitores's life and death in humanist terms and not continuously refer to God or the Holy Spirit, we begin to see the quotidian realities and implications that raise other images of his mission. It was not, for example, out of some presumed "natural" intellectual shortcoming that Natives could not understand what the missionaries were trying to teach, as much as it was the multiple mediations that various (and variously mediated) languages and discourses threw at efforts to transmit truths across huge cultural divides. More than three hundred years later, it is still uncertain, to my mind, whether or not the Catholicism that was co-constructed by both missionary and Native can be vouchsafed as the one the missionaries were trying to teach. Sometimes it seems as if we are all speaking to each other without teeth, except that some "tongues" seem to be assisted by more teeth to enforce their utterances. San Vitores's *ejaculaciónes* had such teeth.

San Vitores's Demeanor

The foregoing portrayal of San Vitores is no laughing matter when we consider the level of violence, the number of deaths, and the social upheaval that resulted from the historical collision of differences but that apparently saw Chamorro capitulation, at least on the surface, to Spanish Catholic discourses. Continuing the task of painting an alternative portrait of San Vitores, I take a closer look at San Vitores's demeanor to argue that he was what is today commonly called "passive-aggressive," but his case was a particularly intense one. In my working definition, passive aggression is a form of personality or character—not to say these are inherent or immutable— that might otherwise be understood as "laid back" or passive, except for a particularly formidable resolve to achieve a goal in the face of any form of obstruction. Indeed, San Vitores's zeal may be seen as excessive. In fact, he was an intensely "determined" man who left few if any stones unturned in his zealous response to what he genuinely believed to have been God's bidding. This fierce determination, as I've suggested earlier, reflected the view that opposing San Vitores was tantamount to opposing God and explains why Chamorros who opposed him were, and continue to be, depicted as "hostile," and even diabolical. Inasmuch as San Vitores's determination and sentiments continue to be cast in benevolent and even heroic terms, they obfuscate the violence of passive forms of aggression and enact another form of violence in the continued silencing of different cultural and political motivations and principles that may not conform to, or even directly oppose, San Vitores and the Church's views. In the next chapter, I explore the political and cultural meanings that drive that opposition.

San Vitores's passive aggression is driven by his genuine desire to serve "for the greater glory of God," as the Jesuit motto goes. This is not to say that all Jesuits are passive-aggressive, nor is it to say that the Jesuit desire to serve God's greater glory, or the authenticity of the love to serve God generally, necessarily leads to violence. I do have serious qualms, however, with that variety that says that if you are not with me, then you are against God, and I protest especially if that group wields control and uses violent forms of enforcement.

San Vitores's zeal is best seen in his garb, specifically in terms of a theology of clothes, and more specifically of "wedding garments," as we saw above. If the relationship between man and God is understood to be that of a marriage, and if heaven is figured as its banquet, then the prerequisite for attendance is "proper attire," or "wedding garments." This garb, as we saw in San Vitores's theology for Natives, was woven out of a life of devotion and zeal, including obligations to God's laws and customs. Another "auspicious sign" involving his apparel attests to this semiotic reading and the hierarchies involved therein. García shared an incident in a canoe in which, "because of his nearsightedness," San Vitores fell overboard but his clothes remained dry. According to García (2004, 132), this incident "caused greater veneration for the Servant of God, who was now considered a man of Heaven rather than a mere earthly human."

His presence in (or out of) a Chamorro *galaide'* (outrigger paddling canoe) halfway across the globe, of course, testifies to the kind of devotion that set San Vitores and his companions apart from the rest of the pack. Though, like many—most?—Stephen Neill considered the founding of the Jesuit order "the most important event in the missionary history of the Roman Catholic Church . . . [because of] . . . Jesuit devotion to the reconversion of heretics, and the conversion of pagans" (Neill 1986, 126–127); San Vitores heard and answered the vocational call, to spread the word among heathens in the far corners of the world in particular. While there were many others who answered the call, not all had the zeal he displayed.

Indeed, he was more than "a man determined," as Father Tom McGrath once depicted him; he was so determined that he let nothing get in the way of his desire to serve God. No temporal matter, or being, that is. For, as we already know, that which belongs or emanates from man must be subordinated properly under God's agency. San Vitores's relations on earth can thus be seen as a battle over whose will prevailed in a temporal and spiritual contest to represent *God's* will. If, for his labor among the Natives, San Vitores wielded a spectacle of a tool kit, his weapons for dealing with potential detractors from within his own social circles involved that classic Catholic form of passive aggression commonly referred to nowadays as "guilt-tripping," backed by a particularly heavy threat of damnation. We can see this in his relationship with his parents. In his letters, in hagiographies, biographies, and histories of the time, we see that San Vitores sensed from an early age that his calling was to go to the mission fields to shed his blood for Christ.

As we can imagine, his parents were quite concerned about this. From his childhood through his adolescence, San Vitores's mother, Doña María Alonso Maluenda, registered strong disapproval until, he said, she saw an apparition. His father, Don Jerónimo, resisted much longer, but he too capitulated under similar circumstances. These capitulations, in light of San Vitores's repeated pressings, would prefigure his relations and the outcomes of these relations with many other individuals who registered opposition to his, or God's, desires. His mother's turning point occurred, for instance, when Saint Ignatius and a young boy "covered with blood and wearing a crown," appeared to her. According to Doña María, the boy resembled San Vitores. In the apparition, Saint Ignatius looked at the woman and said, "I want him in my house as a saint," and García wrote that from this point onward the mother "becomes an agent for her son's entry into religion" (García 2004, 25). For San Vitores's father, the battle took a little longer because Don Jerónimo suspected rather early on that the local Jesuits were behind his son's ideas and were even writing his son's pleading (and threatening) letters (García 2004, 16–18). But San Vitores was "adamant" that he was their author, or at least their vessel, and his subsequent letters were "written in the presence of his mother" to prove they were his words, "or more accurately, [those] of the Spirit" (García 2004, 10, 19). Don Jerónimo finally capitulated to his son's desire to join the order after an incident in Madrid, where San Vitores contracted another of his mysteriously recurring fevers and doctors again "los[t] all hope." On his deathbed, with his father at his side, San Vitores told him that if he wanted to see him live, he should "consecrate [San Vitores's] life to the service of God and of souls in whatever part of the world God might want [him] through the disposition of [his] superiors" (García 2004, 63). His father agreed "at once," and San Vitores was immediately and miraculously cured. But Don Jerónimo was still pensive about his son's desire to leave for foreign missions, especially in the Far East, which had already become notorious for the number of padres "who [had] laid their bones" in those foreign lands (Neill 1986, 127). Soon after his ordination in 1650, San Vitores had already begun to express his desire to die in God's service overseas. Apparently, there was also debate among the Jesuits in the province about sending San Vitores abroad. In 1659, San Vitores wrote to the father provincial, Father Gowen Nickel, again stating his desire to "spill his blood" abroad. San Vitores also sent a copy to his own father, in which he offered this "deal": "If you allow me to go to the Indies, I will assist you at your death bed. I give you my word and I will keep it. I have a deep interior feeling that this must come to pass. But if you delay my departure, I will not assist you" (García 2004, 72). García explained, "With this threat and promise, the father was both frightened and consoled." That same copy of the Nickel letter that San Vitores sent to his own father included the particular form of pressure called "playing on one's conscience" as it involved the slew of "auspicious signs," according to García, which we saw earlier in this chapter:

> I wrote this letter in the hands of the Blessed Virgin on the Feast of the Visitation [2 July] and I received the very happy answer on the Feast of the Expectation of the same Holy Mother, December 18, the year 1659. This answer and the letter of Father General to Father Provincial were written on October 12, a day when I was making the spiritual exercises of our father, Saint Ignatius, and asking our Lord most earnestly that he give an answer that would be to his greater glory and the greater good of my soul and of the most abandoned souls. Finally through the great goodness of God and the mercy of the Blessed Virgin, I was told of the very happy resolution of the province and of the blessing of my father [Nickel] and lord, both on January 2, Friday, the octave day of the protomartyr Saint Stephen, in the year 1660. May God and his Blessed Mother grant that I may not ruin it all by my sins. To which end I ask my father and lord, don Jerónimo, to whom in obedience to my superiors I entrust these papers, that he intercede for me before our Lord Jesus Christ crucified and his Blessed Mother, that their holy purpose may be accomplished in me to his greater glory and the good of our souls and our neighbors. (García 2004, 72)

Risking the loss of Christ as a personal intercessor when death is imminent, and facing the prospect of having to personally account to God the Father, the Blessed Mother, the Holy Infant, Saint Ignatius, and Saint Stephen, this temporal father (Don Jerónimo) had no real choice but to finally render his love and support. Besides, as the letter above conveys, San Vitores had already been given the green light.

As he had done with his parents, so San Vitores did with Church and secular officials who might have had plans other than what he desired in wanting to serve God. These spiritual bribes and guilt trips, including playing on the Catholic conscience, were nothing to discount in a milieu in which service to God legitimated nothing less than the existence of the Crown and its imperial project. Acting against God could get Spaniards killed, too. San Vitores, for instance, once proclaimed that it was precisely because the Marianas had no gold or silver or resources other than souls that the Crown should direct to him all the *socorro* (assistance) he needed for converting those souls, lest the king be left wanting when it came time to account to the Lord for why he did not help the Lord's son, San Vitores, in his holy labor. These are reflected explicitly in his campaign to obtain permission to return to establish a permanent mission in the Marianas. Writing from Manila in 1665, San Vitores sent a letter to King Philip IV, to which he appended an endorsement from Father Manuel Poblete, the archbishop of Manila, and a letter addressed to his father, Don Jerónimo, both of which are signed "Saint Francis Xavier" (García 2004, 140–143). Ventriloquizing—some would say "plagiarizing"—Saint Francis Xavier, San Vitores cited Scripture, *redde rationem villicationis tuae* (give an account of your stewardship) (Luke 16:2), and *quid prodest homini si universum mundium lucretur, animae vero suae detrimentum patiatur* (what does it profit a man if he gains the whole world and suffers the loss of his own soul?) (Matthew 16:26). The targets of these exhortations from "Saint Francis" are both the secular powers and "the religious who are not doing enough for the Indies" (García 2004, 140–141). In the same year, San Vitores wrote to Father Johann Eberhard Nidhard, Queen Mariana's confessor, to ask him to apply personal pressure to the queen to execute a royal *cedula* (decree), which had been promulgated earlier but had never been put into operation, on behalf of "the thousands of perishing children . . . as she would for one child within the palace" (Lévesque 1995, 163–171). In the letter, San Vitores compared the "power" of these particular souls to the "*niños* of wax" for whose protection parents offer votive candles at church (García 2004, 141). In addition to elbowing Church and Crown officials into action by channeling a holy bigwig, this letter continues to reveal the gendered ways that mission discourse consistently infantilized the Chamorros: when addressing men like King Felipe IV or his own father, San Vitores invoked metaphors of business and commerce; writing to the queen, he shifted from economics to an appeal to filial and maternal sensibilities for innocent children.

Capable of shifting from passive to active modes of aggression, San Vitores was not beyond expressing anger and, if we are to believe the "auspicious signs," making good on threats that ranged from the cautionary to the deadly. When news arrived in 1667 that Queen Mariana had activated the *cedula* and promised financial support for the Mariana mission, officials in the Philippines and Mexico organized a plan, stipulated in the *cedula*, that called for San Vitores to travel back to Mexico to collect the *socorro* and then return to the Marianas. A date was set for him to travel aboard the *San Diego*, built specifically for his Mariana mission, and named after then Philippine Governor Diego Salcedo. But before the scheduled departure, the ship's captain announced that the *San Diego* was to redirect for Peru on a commercial venture. San Vitores became "angry" and, according to García, "threaten[ed] Manila with calamities and misfortunes of every kind." The ship itself began to capsize but ended up listing and "resisting every human attempt to right it." San Vitores explained calmly that the only corrective measure was to reinstate the original purpose; Salcedo promptly complied, and the ship immediately "righted . . . all by itself" (García 2004, 146).

Instances such as these reveal activities and sentiments that beg an alternative reading of San Vitores's zeal and a rethinking of his description as meek and mild-mannered but "determined" (Coomans 1997, 2; de Viana 2004, 27–28; Hezel 1982, 122, 126). Coupled with the (gendered) passive aggression through which he held family members, companions, and secular officials spiritually hostage, the more active forms of aggression begin to directly conflict with extant beliefs and sentiments about proper forms of zeal and devotion as represented in the virtues of humility, obedience, and modesty. San Vitores himself appeared to confess as much, at least provisionally, when he later wrote the father provincial to give an account of the *San Diego* incident and his role in it, including the fact that he "felt no shame" in it, even though it was "in poor conformity to the ideals of the Society." What allowed him "no shame" in risking transgression was his belief, once again, that the entire event was "an opportunity from the hand of God" (García 2004, 64). Alas, this was also the preferred narrative he took (and his successors take), when, in the face of mounting tension from "hostile" *indios* (read: recalcitrant or opposing Natives), San Vitores began to call for military expansion: Though the faith was first "planted without arms . . . the devil intervenes, arms the barbarians . . . [and] it became necessary, in order to preserve the work once begun and continue its progress, to resort to arms . . . in order that the infidels and apostates might not silence the sound of the truth" (García 2004, 504). Citing Isaiah 2:4, García explained:

> It has been necessary in this spiritual conquest, as experience has shown it is always necessary among barbarians, that our Spanish zeal carry in its right hand [the ecclesiastical hand] a plow and the seed of the gospel, and in the left [the secular hand] the sword and the lance, with which to prevent anyone from interfering with the work, until that time shall come when in the new lands the prophecy of Isaiah be accomplished for the law of grace, that they shall make plowshares of their lances and sickles of their swords. (2004, 504)

In Spanish the phrase is *"a Dios rogando y con el mazo dando"* (Praying to God and striking with the hammer") (quoted in Calvo 1970, 92).

Isla Buenavista (Tinian), late 1671

San Vitores hovers in midair, in the throes of another fever. Suddenly the Blessed Mother appears to him and informs him that his time is at hand. San Vitores is taken aback and *protests:* "This is not *our* plan! *This* is not what you promised me!"(García 2004, 225; emphasis added)

Ann Arbor, Michigan, 2007

Just before this incident, San Vitores faced near death in a conflict for which he had felt he needed to travel to Tinian. Then the fever hit, followed by the visitation and the news. In my read, San Vitores's outburst to the Blessed Mother was not over the danger but over the realization that he was going to die in Tinian, and even worse, of a fever. In the chronology, San Vitores had an "epiphany," and in it, what we might call an unguential moment of the bride, or even a garb of a balm that soothed, if not enraptured, him. The epiphany, he concluded, was "a confirmation . . . of the place of his future martyrdom." Thus he "made all haste in returning to Guam, which he looked upon now with special affection as the scene of his final battle and victory" (García 2004, 225). Actually it would take a few more months before he would find Matå'pang, challenge him directly, and thereby earn what he had desired all these years. But for my purposes here, something else is witnessed in the visual narrativity of this ecstasy. Coming dangerously close to arguing with not just one's mother, but *the* most powerful Mother of God, and in a narratological device that subordinates his human desire to God's, San Vitores's epiphany also explicitly identifies Guam in particular as the privileged site for the unveiling of God's design for him. In the official Church narrative, as we have seen thus far, *both* the form of San Vitores's death and the significance attributed to the site of that happy death by generations of Chamorros themselves would be touted as significant "vessels" that carry God's will in ways that provide mutual benefits to the Roman Catholic Church and to the local Church on Guam. This was the "return effect" that San Vitores's beatification provided both Rome and Guam, according to Father Paulo Molinari, the one whereby San Vitores's modern-day beatification bears witness to the strength of contemporary Chamorro Catholicism, which in turn bears witness to the enduring truths manifest in San Vitores's ministry among the Chamorros more than three hundred years before. I have no qualms with that, but there are, in the climax of San Vitores's death at the hands of Matå'pang on the island of Guam, still other images, other narratives, which I believe can also serve as vessels, can bear witness, to yet other cultural, political, and historical truths, even for Catholic Natives in the new millennium. To these I now turn for a final look at the terms, but from the vantage point of Matå'pang and aboard the vessel called his canoe moments before he disposes of San Vitores's body once and for all. Or so he had hoped.

Chapter 6

Kinship with Matå'pang

Something like this must have been thought sometime, somewhere, by at least some Native person in the Mariana Islands shortly after 1668:

> Okay. So he can't sing and dance. And he smells bad. He talks funny, and, for the ancestors' sake, man, lose the outfit. But about this Yu'os business. As the all powerful and all mighty, who is also good and loving. Who lives in such a special place that I am supposed to want to go there. And can, but only if I change my so-called evil ways. And what of this Queen Maria, sitting next to him. Beautiful, loving like a good mother should be, and so powerful that she can grant whatever her subjects ask if they honor her properly? And their son, Jesus, another powerful person and spirit who Påle' says loves us so much that he gave his life so that we too can live in the riches of heaven? Is it really that good, and is it worth it to change our ways? And are we really little more than children who know no better than to be swayed by the bad spirits (and what happened to the good spirits of our ancestors?), who cause us to do evil things that hurt this Holy Family, and cause them to retaliate with typhoons, earthquakes, scourges, and other signs to punish or warn us about our errant ways? Are they stronger than our ancestors' powers? And hell, what the . . . ? And if they love us so much, why do the padres have armed men with them?

There has to have been at least one person who pondered along these lines, for not too long after his arrival San Vitores would write to his superiors excitedly that he had baptized more than thirty thousand souls but would remain sober enough to recognize that "in the *infancy* of Faith, God wishes that the tender infant Christians should be raised on the milk of devotion to the Blessed Mother" (García 2004, 182; emphasis added). There has to have been at least one person who thought along these lines, for not too long after his arrival San Vitores also wrote to his superiors *for more arms.*

Ann Arbor, Michigan, 2007

We saw in the previous chapter how San Vitores labored to teach these lessons in terms simple and graphic enough for *indios* to comprehend. Whatever the actual numbers of *indios* who seriously pondered and submitted to (or defied!) such "simple" lessons, what we *can be* certain of is that San Vitores infantilized the Chamorros, figured them in need of the Blessed Mother's milk, and fancied himself in a special role nudging the Chamorros to her breast, if not succoring them with his hand on the metaphorical breast. I introduce this final chapter with an imaginative act drawn from San Vitores's mode of teaching the doctrine in "simple" and "appropriate" ways because I see it as one of those proverbial "teaching moments" that can help us understand the rather difficult historical and cultural material embedded in the story of Catholicism among the Chamorros. The difficult material, one of three interrelated foci of this chapter, concerns the gendered terms of kinship that structured the teaching of Catholic doctrine to the Chamorros in the seventeenth century, especially the relationship between them as children, San Vitores as their "father," and the Blessed Virgin Mary as *Nanan Yu'os,* or God's Mother, who would sooner or later become Chamorro Catholicism's most powerful and loving *Catholic* spiritual figure as Santa Marian Kamalen. Perhaps more importantly, the kinship that was taught and forged among the Chamorros, the padres, and the Blessed Mother furnished an important and lasting cultural lexicon, which the first generation of modern Chamorro priests (as spiritual "fathers") would later use to shepherd the island's Catholic spirituality and Chamorro identity through Guam's social and cultural upheavals following the devastation of World War II and the chaos and challenges wrought by the unbridled economic development and demographic revolution of the ensuing decades (see again the photo of Påle' 'Scot with the statue of the Blessed Mother, figure 12). To understand this claim, we need to better understand the terms of kinship that San Vitores put into play among the Chamorros, and a good way to understand them is to see how they play in relation to the import of his martyrdom. For it was precisely through the authenticity of his martyrdom that San Vitores is said to have "[risen] to Glory" as a "Vessel of Expectation," an ascension that has been likened to San Vitores's ritual elevation to the status of the "Mother's or Virgin's page" (Calvo 1970, 45; Risco 1935, 39). In dying a martyr's death, in other words, San Vitores was raised or "elected" to the honorific status of a bona fide "page," sometimes a "handmaiden," to the Blessed Mother. This particular relationship recalls his conviction about the need for "nursing native infancy in the Faith with the milk of devotion to the Blessed Mother." But the relationship, and the imagery, illustrate once again San Vitores's privileged position as mediator between Chamorros and the Blessed Mother insofar as "the milk of devotion" is one and the same with the truth of his devotion to God: what brought him to the Chamorros to teach them God's word in the first place, and what got him killed in the second place. The diabolical perpetrator, as we saw, was Maga'låhi Matå'pang, and despite the tendency to cast him in unflattering terms, it merits pointing out that, for his role in "handing" San Vitores over to God, Matå'pang also remains a vital mediating figure or device in the narrative. Though he oscillates between being an antihero on the one hand, and to a far lesser extent (at least publicly), an under-appreciated political if tragic hero for certain Native Chamorros on the other, Matå'pang's range of meanings and values remains circumscribed by the orthodoxy and the requisite opposition that the "doxa" (the accepted social convention or prevailing view) needs in order to continue to articulate itself. Because of this endless circularity, and in search of alternative meanings of and for Matå'pang, the second part of this chapter returns to the "scene of the crime," so to speak, and sifts for narratological clues and evidence that might nod us in the direction of new historical and cultural ways of understanding him. These I find in an important scene of San Vitores and Matå'pang's final moments together in a canoe in Tomhom Bay, including a remarkably detailed scenario featuring parts of the canoe. Ending this book as I began it—in a canoe—I close this chapter and the book's analyses proper with a meditation on Matå'pang as vehicle, more specifically, as narratological canoe or vessel for alternative meanings and stories associated with San Vitores's legacy.

The Awesome Threesome: Spreading the Love of Spiritual Kinship

In his *Life and Martyrdom of . . . San Vitores*—a seventeenth-century publication that Fran Hezel says has "no modern equivalent" in that it is "part history," "part hagiography," "part devotional," and "part travel adventure"— Francisco García explained that the elegy section is "organized" along three "halos" or "crowns": that of a martyr (of the Marianas), of a doctor (of the people), and of a virgin (of purity).[1] García explained that San Vitores's "rise to Glory" on these three counts "obliges the Queen of Heaven to look upon them [the Marianas] as her own, and to make them look upon Mary as their Queen" (2004, 253). I will return to the historical and cultural consequences of this mutual and reciprocal gaze momentarily. For now, the important thing to understand is how San Vitores's martyrdom, predicated as it is on the "truth of his devotion," and on Matå'pang's "anger to God," also positioned him as an important mediator between the Native and the Blessed Mother, and how this relationship was gendered and sexualized in some very particular if not already familiar ways.

The gendered terms that structured Catholic doctrine also structured how San Vitores taught that doctrine to the Chamorros in the seventeenth century. These terms are easy to comprehend because they have been cir-culating for millennia through teaching, ritual, and practice, and because we also saw them in the last chapter in the form of San Vitores's simple and graphic teachings: God is the Almighty Father, the Virgin Mary is the Almighty Mother and Queen, and Jesus, the Man–God, is their loving and obedient Son. Moreover, God's relationship to man is understood similarly as a holy marriage, with God's house as its feast or banquet. In pointing to San Vitores's election to "Vessel of Expectation," García's elegy helps us understand how his martyrdom, earlier understood in terms of service to God in imitation of the Son (and through the workings of the Holy Spirit), is also expressive of his service to the Blessed Virgin Mary. Whether as "handmaiden"—midwife, even—to an expecting (or lactating) Mother, or glossed as page to Queen Regent of the cosmos, San Vitores "rises to Glory" in the annals of Church history by hand delivering the Chamorros to their true spiritual Mother, who in turn becomes obligated to their care (García 2004, 253). Later we will have occasion to examine the reciprocal relationship between the Chamorros and the Blessed Mother in the form of her "local" veneration as Santa Marian Kamalen, Guam's "key symbol" of its Chamorro Catholic faith and culture (Jorgensen 1984).

In imitation of Christ the Son, San Vitores reflected the "apostolic" tradi-tion, that long and powerful genealogy that runs from Jesus's followers and disciples as key witnesses to his life and death as the "New Testimony" of God (as prefigured in the Old Testament of Judaism). This apostolic tradi-tion gave the disciples a privileged position as the founders and foundations of Christendom in the form that, for our purposes, deposited itself into the Roman Catholic Church. In dutiful and faithful service to God, the Church is not only referred to as a universal Catholic Church but is maternalized as our Mother on earth, through the work of its fathers in the hierarchy, and those "religious" fathers and brothers in fraternal organizations and sisters in female orders and sororities. Here men and women who dedicate their lives to Christ as priests and nuns ritualize these commitments through vows of marriage to God exclusively, which is one reason that the Church con-tinues to balk at the prospect of marriage for priests and for nuns, let alone come clean on the topic of homosexual unions (Curb and Manahan 1985; Kennedy 2001; Maguire 2004; Stevenson 2006). The central inheritor and primary figure of this apostolic tradition is the pope, referred to lovingly as Santo Papa, Holy Father, and spiritual heir to Saint Peter. Beginning with the pope and the Vatican in Rome, the Church's gendered hierarchy is replicated in title and logic in a complex chain of command downward and outward, through an intricate global network consisting of dioceses (and larger or more important archdioceses) with jurisdiction over local parishes, churches, and chapels. This network is administered by an equally complex and intricate male network of "fathers" with reverential titles like cardinal, archbishop, bishop, monsignor, and pastor, which network is typically composed of "fathers" ("secular" or "diocesan" priests, who belong to no one religious order; or "religious" priests, who belong to any number of religious orders). They are assisted by "brothers" or their assistants, or originate from the laity as formally ordained "deacons" and lay ministers. This chain (of fathers and brothers) is augmented by other Catholic men in devotional societies such as the Knights of Columbus or the Knights of Saint Sylvester, in addition to a virtual university and legal firm of Church scholars, theologians, and lawyers, although by calling attention to the wider network I do not by any means suggest that there are no heated contestations within the "family." Moreover, this male chain is assisted by an equally formidable network of Catholic women, as nuns or sisters, led by their respective mother superiors, who belong to an impressive number of religious orders, and who are joined by a female laity who might serve formally as members of devotional sororities and orders. To this "family," of course, we must add the parishioners, all God's brothers and sisters "in Christ."

Forged in imitation and dutiful service to God Almighty, the temporal Church replicates the terms of kinship and the hierarchy that they represent. However, in the seventeenth century the Church enjoyed, and suffered from, a special relationship with various European monarchies whose service to God, as we have seen, furnished their legitimacy, just as these monarchies furnished the Church and religious orders with financial help, military protection, and administrative support. In practice, the actual relations between them were not always—perhaps were seldom, if ever—smooth (Hezel 1982; Hezel and Driver 1988). Nonetheless, the missionary fathers who followed, and blazed, the path for the Spanish empire, could in theory count on the assistance of the Catholic monarchs.[2] But the relationship between the sword and the cross also entailed a spiritual *conquista* (conquest) that was inextricably temporal and political as well, notwithstanding Fran Hezel's uncoupling of their relation and character (Hezel 1982; Hezel and Driver 1988).

Although Miguel Legazpi formally claimed the archipelago for the Crown (with a Mass) in 1565, it was not until San Vitores arrived more than a century later to establish the Catholic mission that Spain established a real colonial foothold in these islands. Indeed, as the mission's superior, "Father" San Vitores was also the head of the garrison and, for all intents and purposes, was the archipelago's first colonial governor, whether Church historians and sympathizers will own up to it or not. The formal colonization of the Chamorros, which included requiring them to swear an oath of political allegiance to the king as an outward sign of capitulating to the padre in 1681, operated through the gendered terms of spiritual kinship that San Vitores introduced and implemented (PSECC 1994, 29). When San Vitores "connected" the infantilized Chamorros to their spiritual Mother-cum-Queen, he also connected them to their temporal regent in Queen Mariana de Austria, the reigning queen monarch of Spain. His petition to the queen (via her intercessor) may have used metaphors of motherhood over those of commerce used in his correspondence with King Felipe and his own father, but such maternal terms were no less colonizing than the patriarchal or paternal ones. Nonetheless, through San Vitores's fatherly love, the Chamorros became formally figured, if not institutionalized, as obedient children to loving parents represented by fathers who take care of the Mother Church.

The form of kinship that was taught in the seventeenth century became the cultural lexicon that was part of what the first generation of modern Chamorro priests used to help form Guam's Chamorro Catholic spiritual identity during the island's social and cultural upheavals after World War II, especially during the conflicts and tensions accompanying the unbridled economic development and demographic explosion of the postwar period. Thrown into positions with island-wide power as monsignors, bishops, and later, archbishops, and assigned to administer and manage a modern Church bureaucracy, a generation of Chamorro priests, exemplified by the late Monsignor Oscar Lujan Calvo, the late Archbishop Felixberto C Flores, and his successor, the present Archbishop Anthony S Apuron, faced the daunting task of ensuring the island's Catholic spiritual and Chamorro cultural well-being as the community wrestled with the challenges of modernity. It was Påle' 'Scot, as we have already seen, who conceived of and laid the groundwork for the resurrection of San Vitores's Cause by caring for the chapel in Tomhom, by editing and publishing Risco's hagiography of San Vitores, and by beginning to collect documentation and contacting his former mentor in the Philippines, Father Juan Ledesma. And even before he was ordained as Guam's first Chamorro bishop in 1970, the late Archbishop Flores also mobilized Church resources and activities in honor of San Vitores, as we saw in chapter 4 (figure 12). The annual novena and fiesta to San Vitores at the Blessed Diego Church in Tomhom continues as a major celebration under Archbishop Apuron. We also saw these and other Chamorro clergy and civic leaders seize San Vitores as a powerful device to rally Catholic faith among the Chamorros. These men forged ahead even in the face of a populace that in fact had little knowledge and active memory of San Vitores (except for observing the Nubenan Santa Cruz and knowing the "legend" of San Vitores's blood). Among rank-and-file Chamorros, San Vitores simply never enjoyed the popular devotion and veneration that Santa Marian Kamalen has enjoyed over the centuries.

According to Marilyn Anne Jorgensen (1984, 5), Santa Marian Kamalen is and has been the key cultural symbol of Chamorro Catholicism on two levels: the personal, in that she grants favors or provides intercessory help "in times of personal crises," and for the island as a whole, particularly as protectress "against threats posed by natural disasters such as epidemics,

Figure 12. Statue of Archbishop Flores standing in the Chalan San Antonio traffic loop, at the top of San Vitores Road in Tomhom. The statue's left palm holds the likeness of Santa Marian Kamalen, the islands' patroness and manifestation of the Blessed Mother in the Marianas. In the right hand is a figure of San Vitores, the founder of the Catholic mission in the Marianas. Photo courtesy of Dr Lawrence Cunningham.

earthquakes, or typhoons." For example, the earliest Chamorro novena on record is the *nubenan linao*, a *promesa*, or special promise or vow of devotion, to Santa Marian Kamalen in return for her protection against earthquakes, after a particularly powerful one struck in 1767 (Farrell 1991, 281). More than a century later, the late Chamorro historian Pedro Sanchez recalled the "unease" that observant Chamorros felt when peering up at the skies and observing the environment just before the Japanese bombing of the island on 8 December 1941: *Baba sinatna i långhet* (bad signs in the skies), said some *manåmko'*; the animals are restless, said others. *Si Yu'os ha tumungo!* (Only God knows!). The Feast of the Immaculate Conception, the island's most important feast day, celebrated in honor of Santa Marian Kamalen, falls on 8 December (P Sanchez 1989, 169). The fact that Japan formally surrendered on 15 August 1945, on the Feast of the Assumption of Our Blessed Mother, was not at all lost on the Chamorros. They read the first as a sign of the Blessed Mother's unhappiness with the complacency of Chamorro faith in modern times, and the second as the Blessed Mother's protective intervention to preempt more destruction (Sullivan 1957, 176). In the mid-1980s, Jorgensen also found that, across the island, and across all demographics and walks of life, Chamorro Catholics were "quite open about their respect for and faith in their island patroness." She noted the significance of the "widespread belief [in] and reliance on . . . their Blessed Mother" and the influence this belief had on local politics. For example, on Guam, 8 December is a *legal* holiday, thus making the island "the only locale under the American flag where a religious holy day of obligation is also a legal holiday" (Jorgensen 1984, 5–6).

The 1980s also saw a local event make national headlines, not the least for the "fine line" that a stateside journalist noticed between local Catholicism and politics (Goodman 1990). The event was the passage of the nation's most restrictive antiabortion legislation, which, among other things, criminalized pro-choice counseling to pregnant women by local organizations such as Planned Parenthood (Dames 2003; Diaz 1993; Stade 1998).[3] The late Senator Elizabeth "Belle" Arriola, a Chamorro mother of eight, introduced the bill. Arriola got her start in local politics by organizing the island's largest women's religious organizations (the Christian Mothers and the Catholic Daughters) to defeat pro–casino gambling initiatives. Local attorney Anita Arriola, Senator Arriola's daughter, called the legislation and the climate it created "stifling" and joined forces with the American Civil Liberties Union (ACLU) to challenge the law in the Guam courts for its infringement on the right to free speech. Interestingly, before the younger Arriola went public, mother, daughter, and siblings held a family meeting and decided that the two could battle it out in public if they remained "respectful" to one another and to the family, thereby subordinating each one's own political and ideological (and generational) cause to two enduring Chamorro cultural values and institutions: *gai respetu* (respectful behavior) and *i familia* (the family). Earlier, during the legislative hearings, Archbishop Anthony Apuron allegedly threatened to excommunicate any local senator who opposed the bill. Most recently, in 2005, the archbishop led a protest against the (first-time) local production of Eve Ensler's *Vagina Monologues* (2001) at the University of Guam, an action (the demonstration, not the theater production) in which members of my own immediate family played lead and supporting roles, much to the consternation of my other siblings, who could very well have participated in the stage production.[4] These events in recent history give a taste of some of the epic clashes between the island's Chamorro Catholic values and sensibilities and social and cultural and political transformations—widely glossed as "modernization"—under US colonialism. They certainly indicate how families can find themselves on opposite sides in battles around issues of faith and sexuality.

Another tension between the island's indigenous Catholic legacy and American-style modernity began in 1970 and led to the demise of what had been for several decades the island's most popular television show, *The Family Rosary Hour*. Recorded at the small KUAM studio in the village of Ordot, the half-hour broadcast, which started in the late 1950s and was going strong until the early 1970s, aired every Sunday afternoon. In it, a priest or nun led alternating groups of students from the island's Catholic school system in a recitation of the rosary. The broadcast saw virtually the entire island's Catholic community dutifully stop what it was doing at the prescribed time to head indoors and pray along with a television program that featured dazzling pans and tilts, close-ups and zoom-outs of schoolchildren's solemn faces and praying hands dissolving into close-ups and medium shots of the statue of Santa Marian Kamalen on a makeshift altar. But suddenly, in 1970, Guam was invaded by what I believe now to be the most insidious force ever to have hit the island: the simultaneous introduction of color television and cable programming, or more accurately, one-week-delayed videotaped broadcasting from Southern California. Like the Japanese forces that occupied Guam from 1941 to 1944, this more recent invader would need only a few years to accomplish what the US Naval colonial government could not do in the fifty years before World War II: glue Chamorros to America like there was no (Chamorro) tomorrow, and inspire the island's slogan of "Guam, Where America's Day Begins." Though we received cable television a week late, we took comfort in always being a day ahead of the "mainland" by virtue of being on the "other side" of the International Date Line. In one fell swoop, America displaced Spanish Catholicism through the agency of shows like *The Brady Bunch*, *The Wonderful World of Disney*, *Sonny and Cher*, and *The Dating Game*. In "living color." However, American television programming was in fact introduced to Guam by returning Chamorros who, in the 1950s, constituted the first generation of California-born and -raised Chamorros, and who now thought it interesting and profitable to bring their technical skills and commercial acumen "back home" (*Guam Daily News* 1970, 1). By 1975, the *Family Rosary Hour*'s producer and founder could no longer secure sponsorship and even had trouble getting some religious to agree to come to the station to lead the rosary. I know this for a fact because my father was the producer, and I felt the consequences of its decline rather directly. By 1975, I was already in high school and something of a jock when my father would drag my brothers and me to the station to fill in, and we would beg him to instruct the cameraman to focus only on the statue of Santa Marian Kamalen atop the makeshift altar. The *Family Rosary Hour* was part of my father's own *promesa* to the Blessed Mother, a vow he took as a prisoner of war (he survived the Bataan Death March) during the Japanese occupation of the Philippines.[5] The other part of the promise was to name his six daughters Mary something. By 1975, the *Rosary Hour* could no longer compete with what tape-delayed cable programming from Southern California had to offer—although I thought it was cool that by then I already knew which freeways and which off-ramps I would have to take to get to the different Cal Worthington Ford dealerships or to the Los Angeles Forum or Coliseum before I even knew what a freeway was, let alone how to drive. And though my own ethnic and cultural roots are in the Philippines and Pohnpei, the fact that both places were once under Spanish Catholic influence meant that my family's Catholic roots permitted me to feel kinship with the Chamorros with whom I came of age. For all of us, without denying important ethnic and cultural differences, Catholicism, especially as shown through our deep devotion to the Blessed Mother, was as much a reflection of our indigenous investment in Catholicism as it was a Catholic investment in indigenous souls. Importantly, this mutual but unequal investment is forged historically through natural and man-made catastrophes like earthquakes, typhoons, wars, and television.

Jorgensen explained how Santa Marian Kamalen is a(nother) portal into Guam's Chamorro and "Guamanian" (non-Chamorro) Catholic culture:

> The Feast of the Immaculate Conception is important to Guamanian culture because it contributes to social cohesiveness and continuity in a society with a long history of mixing of ethnic and cultural identities, of political subordination to off-island powers, and of struggles for survival brought about by the threat of large-scale extermination of the population either by conquering armies or by natural forces such as earthquakes, typhoons or epidemics. The statue that is the object of veneration on the day of the Feast of the Immaculate Conception . . . has a long "life history" itself that is found in the island's oral tradition. . . . One can gain a sense of historical continuity that this statue of the island's patroness symbolizes—for the statue has survived essentially the same challenges that generations of post-contact Chamorros have faced. The challenges have been great, but the Chamorro people, their culture, and their symbolic statue have survived all of them. (1984, 21–22)

In her study of the various traditions that focus on Santa Marian Kamalen (stories, rituals, plastic arts), Jorgensen examined an annual "Little Miss December 8th contest," which is basically a modern beauty contest but for little girls (in some ways recalling the pre-mission *guma' uritao,* the young men's houses to which parents sent their girls in return for payment or services, a practice that scandalized the padres; but for the Little Miss December 8th pageant, the offering is to the Blessed Mother and enjoys the enthusiastic support of the priests). Inasmuch as beauty contests and culture were introduced by US Naval personnel in the prewar era and were just as quickly appropriated by Chamorros (DeLisle 2008), the Little Miss December 8th pageant is also an amalgamation of Spanish Catholic and modern American legacies among Chamorros. The critical point is that the socializing that was staked on the religious and political process of introducing the Chamorros to their new "queen," as we saw earlier, continues in the late twentieth century. A "particularly important feature of the celebration," according to Jorgensen (1984, 21), was "one in which honoring [by Chamorro women] is a predominant theme":

> The [queen] contest involves Chamorro women in the organization of an event that honors both the female patroness of the island and the young girls of the society who participate in the fundraising. A close examination of the honoring activities . . . reveals that this is one more example of Chamorro women continuing to perform a vital and key role in the preservation and reproduction of Chamorro culture, as they are known to have done throughout the many adverse circumstances of post-contact Chamorro history. For this reason . . . the study of Guam's Virgin patroness as she is honored on Her Feast Day that celebrates Her purity (including a simultaneous honoring of present-day Chamorro virgins in the queen contest) is of special interest to those concerned with the active and important roles that women can play in cultural enactments and in the reproduction of a society's traditions and values. (Jorgensen 1984, 22)

In light of the "honoring" rituals in this particular beauty queen contest, and in consideration of local narratives, stories, legends, and other traditions, Jorgensen concluded by calling specific attention to the stakes for Chamorro women in particular:

> The honoring of Santa Marian Kamalen . . . cannot but help to give an added sense of dignity to female Chamorros, especially when they already identify strongly with Her in Her role as the Blessed Mother of Christ and also as a nurturing mother figure who is the Protectress of her Guamanian children. There is much personal identification with the Virgin Mary among the Catholic Chamorro population of Guam—not only among females, but also among males. Mary is deemed a "model" for every Catholic virgin, mother, and wife by the Church,

and it is in this modeling of behavior role that the working of the key symbol . . .
is made apparent. (1984, 245–246)

Through their strong "identification" with Santa Marian Kamalen as "a
nurturing mother" and "Protectress of Guamanian children," Chamorro
women rearticulate their own maternal and protective identities and ensure
through rituals and practices such as the pageant that their daughters are
likewise socialized sufficiently for when their time comes to be protective
mothers. This socialization occurs through the girls' "honoring," which,
according to Jorgensen, "emphasizes the importance of the social interaction that takes place [in the Feast] and its significance to the reproduction
of the society's most important values and ideals." But the "larger point,"
she added, "*is that in honoring Mary one honors self,* and that there is a reproduction of society's most important values and ideals" (Jorgensen 1984,
251; emphasis added).

By now we should be able to recognize not only the kinship between this
"larger point" and San Vitores's meaning for the Chamorro people but also
the seldom appreciated fact that these mutual expressions were enabled
by San Vitores, with nothing less than the "reproduction of society's most
important values and ideals" at stake. Yet, while we might appreciate the
gendered terms of San Vitores's "true devotion" and his serving as a vessel
for historical and contemporary Chamorro Catholic rearticulations, and
perhaps take comfort in or congratulate ourselves on the Church's recognition of this Chamorro "journey of faith in reverse," there remains something profoundly lacking, or too partial—and even violently repressed and
repressive—in all this gendered spreading of love and purity. This critical
point brings me to my kinship with Matå'pang. Sensing in Matå'pang something of a political and spiritual kindred soul, I have grown increasingly dissatisfied with the role that he is relegated to play as nothing but a negative
witness to San Vitores's martyrdom, his valorization as defiant anticolonial
hero in some circles notwithstanding. Moreover, although there is clearly
contextual evidence to "elevate" his actions to a political level and thus free
it from its subordinated position under the "mission *Positio*," I am still bothered by the inescapable and profound fact that the only mention we have
of Matå'pang as a real-life Native person is in documentation produced by
taotao sanhiyong in the context of canonizing San Vitores, and the only information we have of him is in the scripted role in which he kills the priest
in a show of direct anger toward God. This is his only *fama*, despite the
intriguing fact that his name also occurs as a term for "strong" and "brave"
in Tagalog and a few Filipino dialects, as I will discuss in fuller detail later.
At the end of this chapter, too, I will return to other cultural, political, and
analytical meanings and possibilities of the term *matå'pang*.

Despite his less than flattering positionality in the canonical narrative, even considering the confines of that narrative, Matå'pang, by helping San Vitores achieve his lifelong goal of spilling his blood for God in imitation of Christ, is also something of a handmaiden or page to the father, and to all the other Chamorro and non-Chamorro fathers, mothers, brothers, and sisters staked in this narrative, given the circular self-referencing and returns already demonstrated in this book. Thus Matå'pang is something of an intermediary, not unlike San Vitores, who mediated between man and God at one level, and between Native and the Blessed Mother on another, particularly by bringing the metaphorical child to the metaphorical mother.[6] The critical and political difference, however, is that, with respect to Matå'pang, there just has not been an interest, beyond demonizing or valorizing him, in considering other ways of thinking about his important positionality and its meanings. To remedy this, let us return to the scene of the famous crime and sift for narratological clues that might nudge us in the direction of other meanings staked on the vessel of Matå'pang's agency.

At the Scene of the Crime

What follows is taken from Francisco García's reconstruction based on "original" information drawn from the first reports and letters out of the Marianas following San Vitores's death on 2 April 1672. (In the ensuing sections I draw from García's coverage of this climactic moment [2004, 246–254]). Where canonical narratives typically begin with the "murder scene" proper and the moment of San Vitores's entry into Tomhom in search of a newborn, I rewind the narrative's chronology a few months and set the lens a bit wider geographically to view San Vitores's return to Guam immediately after his ecstatic episode with the Blessed Mother in Tinian, where we find him hovering, literally, in mid-air. In what follows, I also continue to benefit from hindsight to enter and exit the chronology in question in order to make specific analytical connections and critical points.

18 December 1671

It is the Feast of the Expectation of Our Lady. San Vitores has returned to Hagåtña from Tinian, which he has just renamed "Isla Buenavista," ostensibly in memory of the Blessed Mother's appearance to Maga'låhi Taga more than thirty years earlier, but perhaps also because Blessed Mary had visited San Vitores himself only days ago. In Hagåtña, San Vitores discovers that things are "in good hands" under Father Solano's capable supervision, so he decides to perform his spiritual exercises. In light of the earlier visitation, and marked by the "auspicious" coincidence of San Vitores's return on this day in particular, García concluded that "the severity of his fasts, disciplines, and chains clearly showed that he was preparing for the martyrdom that he saw close at hand." García also told us that Nature, according to Native testimonies, would attest to his martyrdom: following San Vitores's death at the hands of Matå'pang, Chamorros said that the "skies became enraged" and "lightning struck where he was killed." According to García (2004, 254), the Natives attested to these as "signs of God's anger," saying that "[h]eaven made war against earth and fired the artillery of its anger against the island when the execrable cruelty had been committed." But this was still in the future, to which we ourselves now draw nearer.

Friday, 1 April 1672 (Another Auspicious Sign?)

San Vitores receives word of the attack and murder of a companion and his assistants while he is out in the field in a stepped-up search for newborns and especially for a "lost sheep" in the form of an *indio* from the Visayas, in the Philippines. Accompanying San Vitores is another *indio*, also from the Visayas, named Pedro Calongsor, whom—in contrast to his wayward *kababayan* ("countryman," that is, from the Visayas)—García described as "well-merited to share in San Vitores's martyrdom" (García 2004, 251). García explained that the wayward (read: bad, or at least inconstant) *indio* was among those who had been shipwrecked on the wreck of the *Concepción* off Tinian in 1638, the same year (a suspicious sign?) that the Blessed Mother appeared to the Tinian Chief Taga. Precisely because he had lived among the Chamorros long enough to learn their language and the lay of the islands, the wayward *indio* had initially been "contracted" by San Vitores as a language instructor, translator, and guide. But of late, either because of his own *indio* penchant for "inconstancy," or in light of the mounting assaults on the padres and their assistants, the translator had decided to "return and live the unrestricted life of the natives" (García 2004, 251). Because of this, San Vitores decides to include the search for this "lost sheep" in his search for children to baptize. These baptisms he did "in caves and [on] hillsides," which had by this time already become "traditional" hiding places for recalcitrant Natives. With the good *indio* (Calongsor) at his side, San Vitores finds the bad *indio*, who promptly repents. San Vitores then sends his other assistants back to Hagåtña but chooses to have Calongsor remain with him to search especially for newborns. True to "merit," the good *indio*, Calongsor, would also be beatified by Pope John Paul II in 2000, precisely by virtue of the Filipino's status as an ordinary "lay" individual who willingly suffered a martyr's death alongside San Vitores, and on the credentials of the priest's authentic martyrdom and its supporting documentation (Arévalo 1998).

Saturday, 2 April 1672, One Week before Palm Sunday

Around seven in the morning, San Vitores and Calongsor arrive at Tomhom, where he quickly learns that the village's *maga'låhi*, Matå'pang, a known apostate, has a newborn daughter. San Vitores and Pedro go to Matå'pang's residence and ask the chief for permission to baptize his daughter. Matå'pang responds sarcastically, "Go baptize a skull in there," referring to the widely circulating "calumnies" that the holy waters and oils used by the padres were lethal, and exhibiting spiritual and political resistance insofar as skulls were commonly venerated as vessels housing ancestral spirits.[7] San Vitores decides not to press the issue at the moment, and leaves in order to gather children and give the chief time to calm down. According to García, however, San Vitores, in the presence of the children of the village, calls out to Matå'pang to join them. Already predisposed to suspicion and wavering in faith, Matå'pang becomes enraged at what appears to be a public scolding or mocking.

Chamorro physical anthropologist Dr Vince Diego argued that such encounters between missionaries and key Chamorro men in the seventeenth century, and across the subsequent three hundred years, were ripe occasions for triggering a deep (and enduring) Chamorro cultural value known as *matakña* (Diego nd). Before I elaborate on this cultural value, it merits pointing out (in the uncanniness of Guam's cultural history) that *this Diego*, like his Catholic *tukåyu* (namesake) (Blessed Diego, not me!) also experienced the lightning rod of a religious epiphany and call to vocation, although unlike his seventeenth-century namesake, his was a clarion call to Protestantism rather than to the Catholic priesthood. For *this* Diego (nd, 2), *matakña* is "a Chamorro cultural 'form of courage,' [which describes] a person who stands up for himself or herself with a certain fierce or staunch determination . . . [and which is] encapsulated by the modern slang 'attitude.' Thus, a woman who stands up for herself 'with attitude' would be described as matatnga. Alternatively, it may be the courage to stand your ground under not-so-favorable conditions." I imagine that many a *manåmko'* during the antiabortion scandal saw the younger Arriola as *matakña*. Ditto for the women, especially the Chamorro women, who participated in the local staging of *Vagina Monologues*. According to Diego (nd, 4–5), *matakña* interacts "synergistic[ally]" with two other core Chamorro values: *emmok*, which is "like but not fully coextensive with [Anglo meanings of the term] 'revenge,' and *manhihita* [which is] an understood form . . . for active solidarity" approximated in the phrase "*we are in this together to the end.*" Following Diego, and for the transhistorical and transcultural qualities of the San Vitores story, and the consequent intermingling of personal, scholarly, and political elements raised in my project, I offer this customized definition of *matakña*: the value of an in-your-face defiance forged and sustained by the political principle of and need for watching each other's backs in the presence of unwarranted threats to oneself.

In hindsight, informed further by the politics and analytics of historical situations in which Natives must watch each other's backs if they want to protect themselves from cultural affronts and outright attacks, we return to the narrative's denouement. Affronted in the presence of his village's children (the "wax" in San Vitores hands, which also constituted "a formidable army that laid siege" to the villages), Matå'pang is probably feeling, as his village's "first" or "top" male, that his authority and person have been mocked publicly. Following Diego's framework, we might say that Matå'pang culturally synergizes *solidarity (manhihita)* and *revenge (emmok)* by first recruiting his "backer," Hirao, and then launching the now familiar (anti-ejaculatory?) outburst: "I don't want to learn, I'm fed up and angry at God." In *response*—this is where modern oppositional accounts offer the "death wish" theory—San Vitores proceeds to baptize the infuriated chief's infant. Exhibiting all the cultural dynamics and imperatives of *matakña* (which Diego saw in contemporaries such as Hurao and other "rebels" of the time), Matå'pang and Hirao turn first and kill Calongsor, who stands his ground in an apparent act of heroic defiance, in response to which García spurts, "Fortunate Boy!"[8]

By now, we should fully understand the cultural and spiritual reasoning behind García's *ejaculación*. Pedro's fortune is also that which soon awaits San Vitores, and in the circularity of things in the providentialist logic, Pedro's fortune is also the Church's, and following the Church's certification of San Vitores's martyrdom, is also the fortune of Filipino Catholicism as staked in his subsequent beatification. But if the spreading of Pedro's love is predicated on his heroic defiance and courage in the face of a diabolical Matå'pang, the Tagalog term for such cultural behavior also happens to be a form of the Chamorro term. However, in the Tagalog tongue, the word is pronounced with an accent on the first syllable, *mátapang*, and lacks the *glotta* or glottal stop (before the *p*) that it has in Chamorro. In fact, in Tagalog, *mátapang* not only means "bold" and "courageous," as any Filipino from the lowlands (and some highlands and provinces) will readily attest, but more than likely also circulates in a constellation of social, cultural, and political meanings linguistically and discursively "related" to Dr Vince Diego's Chamorro theory of *matakña*—but with an important difference. The difference is mission history in the Marianas, or a narrativization of that history, which inverts the earlier sets of positive meanings that Chamorro and Tagalog probably shared as "sister languages" under the parentage of the Austronesian language family. From that fateful morning in Tomhom, in other words, the culturally significant Austronesian term *matapang*, as it occurred until this point among the Chamorros, would become converted by inversion to something glaringly "not" bold or courageous, and certainly not *matakña*.[9]

When I asked Påle' 'Scot what he thought of the call by (the Chamorro Protestant minister) the Reverend Joaquin Sablan to honor Matå'pang as the island's true hero, he replied with anima worthy of his hero's religiously engendered ejaculations: "Matå'pang was a *coward!* He would not even kill San Vitores himself! He had to call a friend [Hirao] into it!" Påle' 'Scot did not, I should point out, say anything derisive about his spiritual counterpart in Sablan, although he did direct his defensive anima toward me rather aggressively—making me now wonder if his is the Chamorro Catholic masculine version of *matakña.* Thus Påle' 'Scot proceeded to scold me for such "provocative" questions that "strayed" from what he presumed to be the straightforward scholarly documentation of the life and times of Blessed Diego but that was now coming dangerously close to attacking the faith itself. This may seem like a digression, but I assert that the exchange constitutes a moment of rearticulated cultural and historical continuity.

"Happy over the fate of his companion," San Vitores, according to García, now prepares for "a similar *end.*" But is this not just *the start of a history* that simultaneously marginalizes but does not entirely destroy the deeper cultural principles and values that inform both "rebellious" and "heroic" Chamorro political and cultural consciousness, even if the latter are staked on "capitulation" to Catholic values and rituals? In preparation for the end (which will become the beginning of Guam's history, for all intents and purposes), San Vitores removes the crucifix that he always wore around his neck, and begins to preach, as Matå'pang and Hirao turn their attention to him. García wrote, "Seeing them approach and knowing that they were about to kill him, [San Vitores] wished to imitate the meekness and charity of his Lord when he died." San Vitores exhorts, in Chamorro: *"May God have mercy on you, Mata'pang!"* In rapid progression, in narrative as in act—or is it in act as in narrative?—Hirao strikes San Vitores with the cutlass, "dropping his head forward on his neck." At the same time, Matå'pang "runs" the priest through with a lance. According to García, it is in this manner and at this moment that San Vitores's "spirit, released from the prison of his body, flew to heaven." It is also at this point in the narrative that García identified and interpreted the auspiciousness of the coincidence of San Vitores's death on the day of his deaconate ordination, which empowered the would-be priest to preach the Gospel. It was not only the coincidence of the dates but the manner of the death that inspired García to observe poetically that henceforth "the voice of his blood" would preach the Gospel better than anything San Vitores could ever say in life.

For García, there would be other "auspicious signs" in the progression that immediately followed San Vitores's death. Let us follow these but sift for clues to permit counter-readings and alternative meanings, for signs regarded auspiciously can also be treated suspiciously both for the meanings they signify and for those they obscure as a consequence or even as a precondition. Indeed, suspicious signs can be read auspiciously. For example, Matå'pang and Hirao begin to strip San Vitores and discover three iron belts "at which they marveled." The devil, so to speak, is actually in the details: First Matå'pang takes the crucifix from San Vitores's neck and proceeds to chop it into pieces; yet, earlier in the narrative, San Vitores had removed the crucifix and held it up to Matå'pang and Hirao as they approached him. García also had Matå'pang "breaking . . . *the other one also,* cursing it as he worked, saying, "This is what the Castillas venerate as noble Lord and Chief." The immediate reference is to a second crucifix that San Vitores had affixed to a staff, which he carried on his treks; the greater signi-fication, however, is that Matå'pang's anger is directed to Christ. This moti-vation, as we saw in chapter 1, is necessary in order to satisfy the theological test of martyrdom. Lest the reader somehow miss it, García confirmed: "No one doubted that Christ was the motive in his having followed and attacked the Servant of God, and *that Christ wished to suffer in his image, when his servant suffered in his body"* (emphasis added). Still, in this passage, there is an inter-esting ambiguity in the subject reference, at the tail end of the sentence. Where the first occurrence of the stand-in "his" clearly refers to Matå'pang, the final three can work in reference to either Christ or San Vitores to rep-licate, or reenact, in language and discourse, what is ritually reenacted in Catholic Masses. As yet another example of the materiality of language and discourse, and the discursive and linguistic meanings of concrete social and political practices in colonial and religious acts of translation and conver-sion, this ambiguity constitutes an eclipsing of Matå'pang's own potential to serve specifically as an indigenous form of cultural mediation and signi-fication (Rafael 1993). In fact, just for such clarity's sake, García reiterated Matå'pang's proper positionality in the very next sentence, where the chief is purported to have "tak[en] the crucifix . . . [and] later [sold] it for thirty bags of rice, lest he fail to play the part of Judas up to the hilt." Despite the effort to clarify, however, there remains a residual slippage in the narrative, as when Matå'pang is figured as traitor (Judas) rather than the antihero (the devil), although the difference is short-lived because the devil is also the supreme example in Christian discourse of "the traitor."

Interestingly, even in such a devotional passage as this, there is hidden in plain view an indigenous penchant for mocking authority—hidden so that the subversive intent and effect can evade the colonial gaze of the padre, the colonial official, or the historian sympathetic to the latter's cause. Maybe this passage is not merely a rhetorical flourish in the service of a devotional point after all. Maybe Matå'pang *really* did sell the crucifix for thirty bags of rice, and did so precisely to register his awareness and oppo-sition to Catholic narratives of betrayal that he already suspected would be his legacy. Perhaps he wanted to play it to the hilt. Perhaps Matå'pang was "playing Apostate," was articulating a subaltern form of resistance, a "weapon of the weak," by simulating nonindigenous subjectivities even as he battled the priest head-on (Scott 1985). Even Matå'pang, the quintessential figure of resistance to Catholicism, gives us a glimpse into a history of Catholicism that reveals indigenous cultural continuity through simulating Catholic precepts and practices.

Still, what are we to make of these ambiguities and inconsistencies? Was García's claim about Matå'pang merely a rhetorical flourish to bolster or reinforce the greater truths that the priest believed to inhere in the event? Is this merely another instance of that religious sensibility of the time, and of hagiographies in general, that says that if something is not true, it may as well have happened, if it is in the service of a higher truth? Or is this an "authentic" account of what happened, either in direct testimony to the truths as claimed by García, or indirectly, as an indicator of the same event, with motives and purposes not in line with those of García? And what about the inconsistencies in the details involving the crucifixes? Should details not matter—not least for their abilities to betray underlying fault lines in the structure of overarching narratives?[10] And what are the implications and consequences of my own positioning vis-à-vis these narratives? Will I be viewed the skeptic or a heretic? Or will I be viewed as a good Bollandist trying to disaggregate empirical fact from legend? Is my critical interrogation helping strengthen the case for veracity and thus preempting future embarrassment for the Church? Am I not saving it from the sharper tools and weapons of its true enemies? Or is mine a mere mocking of story elements that can be fashioned any which way, despite their provenance in, and their witnessing of, the fundamental truths held by the Church? Are there in fact indigenous meanings and political possibilities that are not given a fair and honest shake when diametrically opposing perspectives square off? In examining my conscience, as God is my witness, I understand this work to be in the authentic service of that fair and honest shake. Yet, in this vein, let us continue to shake down the narrative for details that might point to other cultural and political positionalities and possibilities.

For García, San Vitores's death itself did not satisfy "the cruel parricides," who proceed first to burn the pools of blood at the site of the murders, then to bring the two bodies to the beach, where they tie heavy stones to their feet, place them in a "light boat," and take them "out to sea," to be thrown overboard. But, said García, "a strange thing happened" out there: "The body of Father San Vitores, having sunk, came twice to the surface, and the hands seized *the outrigger of the canoe, which the natives use here to counterbalance the sail*" (emphasis added). If the first-time reader is struck by the miraculous resurfacing of San Vitores's lifeless body, I am struck by the fact that García not only bothered to include technical details of Native vessels, including their names and their function, but that he knew them in the first place. His troubling to explain the function of the outrigger ("which the natives use here to counterbalance the sail") almost made me expect more technical explanation, even something such as, *but in counterbalancing the sail, the outrigger also produces a drag that turns the nose of the canoe back into the wind, for which the Chamorro craftsman must then compensate ingeniously with the concept and production of an asymmetrical hull.*[11] Because *that kind* of technical elaboration would stand in striking contrast to this description of Native craft that García provided much earlier in the book:

> The . . . canoes of these islanders, even for a smooth sea, are dangerous enough and look more like things cast up from a shipwreck than any kind of craft in which to sail. They are made of one or two boards tied together with cords, with no shelter from rain or sun, in which the poor sailor goes as if he were clinging to a log . . . and one cannot move from one place to another, but must sit, soaked continuously by sea water and often also by the rain. . . . The greatest happiness that one may dare to hope for, not being a fish like these natives, is to escape with his life, for death is always before him, the imminence of it not permitting him to eat or sleep, and when dire necessity makes him take some sustenance, the fare is nothing more than a few roots, which together with seasickness serve rather to purge the stomach by vomiting than to succor his needs. In this type of boat, in continued danger, or rather experience of death, the Apostle of the Marianas sailed with only two companions. They felt safe, because they were in his company, and because he was carrying the light of the gospel to those who lived in darkness. (García 2004, 212)

My own suspicion is that García knew otherwise but nevertheless furnished this unflattering and erroneous description in the interest of playing up the power of the Gospel, and the role of San Vitores, as the more superior vessels. So it is especially curious when García switched modes in the canoe scene that follows San Vitores's death. If the miraculous is all we need, why switch now to a realist modality? Why bother to point out the technical details by naming parts of the canoe and their function and how they play realistically in an equally realistic and remarkably graphic, and chilling, passage that follows: Matå'pang is alarmed. Twice he loosens the grip with a "stick," but, according to García, "the body rose a third time and grasped *the stern* of the small craft, *where Mata'pang was stationed.* By now he was so frightened and aghast that he did not know what to do. He wanted to throw himself into the sea, believing that the father was going to climb into the boat" (García 2004, 252; emphasis added). Here the details multiply as the narrative crescendos: in rapid order, two times he tries; a third time the body rises to grasp not just the outrigger, but the stern, where, I should add from experience, Matå'pang would, in fact, be "stationed," and where a body fallen overboard might very well grasp the canoe's stern, if the conditions of direction and strength and length of canoe were met. We discover, furthermore, that Matå'pang quickly regains his nerves and strikes "one heavy blow at the head with one of the oars" only to quickly depart and thereby "leave . . . that sacred body buried in the sea, to the perpetual grief of those whom he left behind." Thus, recovering quickly,

Matå'pang, according to García, has the presence of mind to now use an oar, rather than a stick as used earlier, to strike the head (as opposed to the hands) in a much more effective solution. But perhaps more striking (pun intended) in the realism of these details (details that can now be seen as a kind of "embellishment," but only in the service of authenticating the more mystical signs at work) is their plausibility and thus their believability. San Vitores may in fact have been alive. And maybe Matå'pang himself realized it quickly enough after the initial shock—at which precise time he may very well have ejaculated something like "*SusMaria!*" Indeed, I do think San Vitores was still alive, and that the "calm" waters of Tomhom Bay jolted his own shocked body to action; most likely in autopilot mode, San Vitores clutched desperately for the closest thing he could reach, which could have been the outrigger, and then, as the canoe proceeded forward, the stern, where Matå'pang would in fact have been stationed if he had wanted to take charge of the direction of the canoe. (Hirao would have been paddling or working the sail.)

In examining this information we could take an entirely different critical tack and ask of the narrative: How do we even know these things happened in the canoe, beyond the sight of others? It is a good question, but I have been operating on my faith in the documents examined since Part One of this book. More in keeping with this faith then would be the question, what does it do to the posthumous canonical narrative of martyrdom if San Vitores was still alive at this time and actually fighting for his life? García might say that Matå'pang still ended up killing him. But is it not possible that Catholic historiography had already left San Vitores for dead much earlier, and did so by a narrative strategy that required a device like Matå'pang to serve the infinitely more noble project of making a hero out of a man?

Matå'pang's Canoe

Surely, Påle' 'Scot would turn over in his grave at that final rhetorical question, one so far-fetched from the point of view of established orthodoxy.[12] Murdering San Vitores in a narrative act was certainly not Francisco García's intent when writing this biography—or history, or hagiography, or travel adventure, or whatever Fran Hezel would call it in the absence of a modern equivalent category. No matter what anyone calls it, I am not convinced that *any* classification would diminish the soundness and credibility of this or any other "primary" source document that might have been written in the metropoles by men who never visited the islands (LeGobien 1949). They are authentic expressions of the discourses of the time that can also be reread as commentaries of today. Speaking historiographically, Greg Dening would call these profound historical performances that comment as much on the cultural present as on the historical past (1996). Somewhat similarly, Jim Clifford and George Marcus would view such ethnographic narrativizations as real fictions (1986). Such historical, historiographical, and ethnographic discourses wend their way into modern consciousness *despite* or, better yet, *because of* the fact that their meanings may be opposed, inverted, subverted, simulated, dissimulated, and even ignored, in the multiple perspectives and interests with which they come into contact.

García himself alluded to the possibility of multiple and even conflicting meanings at different times in his attempt to foreclose the ultimate meaning of San Vitores's passion proper. Returning us to a set of predicaments in the immediate wake of San Vitores's death, García invoked God as the ultimate arbitrator of all temporal questions and conflicts: "Now they [the companions] had not even the company of his venerable relics, unless the Lord determines, as we may hope, to let the sea restore this treasure, which it guards, to appease the envy that the earth now has for the sea and to give the precious body the veneration it deserves for having been the repository of that blessed soul" (2004, 253). As creatures of a benevolent and Almighty Father in the Judeo-Christian genealogy, and as offspring of the cosmic siblings Puntan and Fuuña of pre-Christian Chamorro cosmology, land and sea enjoy (or suffer), we might say, a form of sibling rivalry (Coomans 1997, 16–17; Genesis 1:6; Risco 1935, 96). Or a love triangle, if you include San Vitores in the picture. Though land and sea squabble over possession of San Vitores's body and reliquary, whose value lies as the "repository," or I prefer, the *vessel(s)* of "that blessed soul," it is ultimately for God, like the good father that he is, to decide if the priest's body and reliquary will ever be restored to the land, and by extension, to the priest's companions so that they may once again be in his "company." We know *this* story, the one forged in the *wake* of San Vitores's death—"wake" being understood as both the aftermath of San Vitores's legacy and also as the ritual devotion that immediately precedes the final interment of a deceased in Catholic tradition. A death, especially that of the man or woman fortunate enough to be recognized as a bona fide servant of God, is but the prerequisite for everlasting life in heaven, according to Catholicism.

But I think there is another set of stories and meanings, which does not necessarily have to terminate in hell, even if it does not end up in heaven (or purgatory) either, especially if these stories and meanings do not happen or want to align with the "straight and narrow" interpretation prescribed by Roman theologians and historians, or their "brothers" in Christ across the "universal" Catholic Church's map. I want to close this chapter by meditating on alternative meanings of and for Matå'pang as they present themselves not in the wake of San Vitores's death, but in the wake produced by Matå'pang's canoe. To begin to understand this, it would be useful to consider first the position of canoes in Chamorro discourse and then consider Chamorro discourses of *matå'pang* as itself an important vessel for such alternative possibilities.

A cursory glance at the Chamorro people and language alone, both said to be thoroughly acculturated by colonial history, reveals strong and enduring traces of a seafaring legacy that is interpellated in interesting ways in *sanhiyong* systems of meanings following three hundred years of continuous colonial rule. Explorers and visitors from the sixteenth to the end of the eighteenth century marveled at the Chamorro crafts, some claiming them to be unrivaled in all of Oceania in speed and manageability, appearing to fly, or at least skim the surface (Dampier 1729; Pigafetta in Barratt 1996, viii).[13] The *sanhiyong* also described the Chamorros themselves as virtual sea creatures in their being as comfortable and skillful on the water as on land.[14] Observations by foreigners were not always flattering, and by the time of the Chamorro–Spanish Wars, the accounts were filled with anxiety and include record of canoes being destroyed to prevent rebels from using them. There are also intriguing accounts of canoes being used as shields and many complaints dating back to Magellan of Native "duplicity" in transactions between canoes and ships, and especially treachery, as when canoes were used to lure priests and soldiers into the water, where Chamorros felt they had a tactical, material, and martial advantage. Clearly the priests and soldiers did not feel comfortable in canoes, as we saw earlier in this chapter. San Vitores, I believe, was actually killed at sea as he tried to climb aboard Matå'pang's canoe, and Matå'pang himself was killed in a canoe as he was being returned to Guam after fleeing to a northern island.

For all the assertions about Chamorros being overpowered by acculturative forces—forces blamed for the disappearance of the canoe, and with it, Chamorro culture—indigenous Chamorro discourse to this day contains significant referencing to seafaring culture. For example, one possible origin of the term "Chamorro" is found in the phrase *tcha mu ulin* (do not use your rudder [*umurin* or *umulin*] anymore), which dates to the earliest days of contact, when *sanhiyong* vessels entered Chamorro waters (Freycinet 1829; Russell 1998, 203 and 249n219).[15] The notorious British privateer Thomas Cavendish in 1587 noted that the "images carved into, and standing at the head of the canoes contained one or two knots of hair" atop their heads, an anthropomorphic reference to the Chamorros themselves who wore such hairstyles (*Guam Newsletter* 1911b, 1), which have become something of a cultural symbol of resistance among activist Chamorros today. In the nineteenth century, Freycinet was still able to record the indigenous terms for the Chamorro calendar, and identified in the population names with seafaring meanings, including the following: Gofsipik (skilled fisherman), Taiagnao (intrepid), Faulosgna (skillful navigator), Mesngon (patient; able to endure), Massongsong (he who settled a village), Gofhigam (skilled with adze), and Agadgna (skilled canoe tillerman or steerer) (cited in Russell 1998, 241n136). Påle' 'Scot translated the name Kepuha as "a dare . . . like dare to overturn this canoe" (Calvo 1991). Kepuha, it would seem, was *matakña* (*taiagnao*, above?). But to whom? Kepuha, you will recall, was the *maga'låhi* of Hagåtña who *welcomed* San Vitores, who was one of the first converts, who continued to provide the mission with vital material and military assistance against other Chamorros, and whose Christian burial was said to have provided "the cornerstone" for the edification of the Catholic Church (LeGobien 1949, 27–28). We can imagine him "daring" rival clans or villages to overturn "this canoe" of Christianity that carried his motives and reasons for supporting the padres. I would bet my tenure on this: Had Kepuha—already lionized in the most prominent spot in downtown Hagåtña, at the center of the traffic loop, where cars traveling in all four directions must encircle him or pass him by—been allowed to become a priest in the seventeenth century, he, and not San Vitores, would be Påle' 'Scot's principal spiritual hero. But do not count on me to launch his canonization.

From the earliest days of the mission to the present, canoes were also consciously seen as highly symbolic, which is to say that they were signs of matters significant and substantive. In 1565, Legazpi's ritual claiming of the archipelago for Spain included planting the flag beachside and celebrating the Mass—the first in the Marianas—inside a large canoe house (Carano 1975, 3; Russell 1998, 27). The very holding of the first Mass in a canoe house indicates the need to consider the history of Christianity among the Chamorros in more culturally mobile ways. Moreover, the possibility that the *kamalen* in Santa Marian Kamalen refers to a canoe house in particular most certainly would make us pause to consider the depth of indigenous investments in the Blessed Virgin Mother. Archivist Rodrigue Lévesque has pointed out the habitual use of such canoe houses for holding Mass, and certainly the early Spaniards defined a *camaren* as a "boat shed."[16] Such a framework might even help account for the discovery, also in 1565, before there is any record of missionaries among the Chamorros, of a large and "unusual" *canoe* house that could hold two hundred people and was shaped like a cross (Lévesque 1993, 164; Russell 1998, 226). San Vitores himself wrote of his first encounters with Chamorros on canoes, saying, "They came out to meet our vessels, tacitly to tell us the grave charges which will be made against us for leaving them in their blindness, we who come to bring light to the Gentiles" (*Positio* 1981b, 279).

Even three hundred years later, long after the outrigger canoe had been displaced by landlubbing practices and inter-island restrictions, both the product of colonial policies, the *galaide'* and *sakman* (the Chamorro name for the outrigger canoe, depending on the size and function) reemerge in interesting ways that index colonial, counter-colonial, and even post-colonial dynamics. For example, Christine T DeLisle noted colonial nostalgia in the form of the image of the sailing canoe emblazoned in the center of the Guam seal, which came directly from the central icon of the

Guam flag (DeLisle 2005; Rogers 1995, 140–141). (The ensuing discussion is from DeLisle 2005.) The seal and the decision to make it double as the principal iconography of the Guam flag were projects of prewar US Naval personnel. It was designed and submitted by one Helen Paul, the wife of a naval officer, for a contest conceived and sponsored by the naval governor, Roy Smith, in 1917. A landscape photographer who also took many photos of "quaint" and "charming" children making handicrafts, Paul evidently took her inspiration for the design from a specific photograph of Hagåtña Bay with a patch of land, a palm tree, and a corrugated tin-roofed hut in the foreground. In her design, Paul reframed the bay shot within an upright, football-shaped outline, which, she said, symbolized the similarly shaped sling stones for which the ancient Chamorros were famous for adeptly using during battles against the Spaniards and each other. But Paul chose to remove the (modern) hut and insert in the bay, at the center of the image, an outrigger canoe under sail. Reading this image against the backdrop of Paul's photography of Guam's "pleasing sights/sites," which DeLisle located within a deeply problematic and not innocent tradition of the landscape painting and photography of "aesthetically pleasing" or "beautiful" content, DeLisle argued that the removal of the hut in favor of a sailing canoe registers a specific form of nostalgia for the precontact Native life, a nostalgia born of colonial guilt or a wish to disavow colonization. Incidentally, because the Guam seal and flag have also become for Chamorro cultural nationalists symbols against US colonialism, DeLisle examined the dissonance and dilemma presented by the fact (or claim) that a white American wife of a naval officer designed the seal and flag. There has been a range of responses, the most common and compelling being that a certain Chamorro man had shared his artwork with the American woman, who submitted it in tweaked form. Whatever the truth of the matter, my point in this story is the symbolic function of the canoe in twentieth-century colonial and counter-colonial and even postcolonial discourse.[17]

Indeed, the use of the canoe as a potent symbol recurs in the history of the Church in the Marianas. In the seventeenth century, García's unflattering depiction of the canoe, mentioned above, served to highlight, in relief (in the double sense of sharpness in contrast, and respite or comfort), the potency of San Vitores's presence, while in his 1957 history of the Church in the Marianas, Father Julius Sullivan, an American, described the Spanish mission at end of the nineteenth century to be in a moment of "stagnation," saying it was "merely holding on to a thread of life" and "the time had come for New blood *and a fresh breeze to lift the drooping sails of Spanish Culture in the Orient*" (1957, 97; emphasis added). On the other hand, Vince Diego's analyses of the *matakña* complex at play in seventeenth-century Chamorro battles against the missionaries were deployed by him as a rebuttal to "repugnant" claims about the "docility" of the Chamorros that he saw perpetuated in the works of present-day historians and anthropologists

(Diego nd, 2; Hezel 1982; Rogers 1995; Stade 1998).[18] In contrast to their interpretations, Diego's offered *matakña* as "the proverbial sails . . . of the 'proas' of Chamorro agency," whose fundamental character, he explained, was never lost "across the turbulent course of over three centuries of antagonistic interaction with Western powers" (Diego nd, 2).

With such an enduring legacy, and in light of the centrality of both the literal craft, and the entire story as vessel in the story of San Vitores's death (including the symbolic limitation or reduction of Matå'pang's significance in it), it should not be peculiar at all to consider the figure of the canoe as a particularly heuristic device. For example, San Vitores might be viewed productively and provocatively as a virtual canoe that *carried* a distinct form of Christianity to the Chamorros from Spain and Rome, by way of Mexico and the Philippines three hundred years ago, only to return three hundred years later *to carry* the inspiring (perspiring, to some) story of Chamorro Catholicism for Chamorro culture and spirituality back to Rome in a form that excites Rome for its value, precisely as a local story, to bear witness to the universal, catholic, and eternal truths of providence. In this complex voyage, we can easily see how the elevation of San Vitores to the Church's highest altars is also a vessel that carries and circulates the heroic and political story of Chamorro cultural survival. To see San Vitores as such a historical canoe also permits us to apprehend abstract, complex, and certainly politically fraught processes of cultural construction through ideas and material furnished by colonialism and imperialism. The virtual canoe that looks like San Vitores gives witness to the messy ways that indigeneity rearticulates itself by "navigating" the local and global (Diaz 2005). It helps us understand the mix of foreign and local Native processes of bridging otherwise disparate spaces and so re-signifies the meanings of these spaces and the subjectivities that are forged in relation to each other. But what might sailing in the wake of Matå'pang's canoe *in particular* do for us? The answer lies in a twofold maneuver involving, firstly, understanding the value of displacing San Vitores as principle sign in favor of Native perspective, in this case, Matå'pang, and secondly, understanding Matå'pang, like his canoe, in discursive terms. The first operation is that of the Chamorro cultural nationalist who opposes head-on the history of foreign encroachment and domination, notwithstanding the fact that many Chamorro nationalists will not openly oppose Catholicism, whether out of cultural respect, ambivalence, or even agreement, insofar as Catholicism has become such a part of the "fabric" of Chamorro culture. One Chamorro who had no such reservations, as the first ordained Chamorro Protestant minister, was Joaquin Sablan, who singled Matå'pang out as the "race's" true hero. But even then, among some members of Nasion Chamoru, the Chamorro grassroots movement begun in the late 1980s and active through protests and actions against the US military and the Government of Guam, there had emerged, at least for a time, a "Mata'pang Society," a more or less underground organization or movement whose principle function was to defend Chamorro culture and values against institutional and colonial assaults.[19] The aggressive defiance in defense of one's cultural face and one's cultural property recalls the enduring Chamorro value and concept of *matakña* —aggressive boldness and courage, that operates in a threesome, or in kinship with *emmok* or "defense" and *manhihita* or "solidarity," which I discussed earlier in this chapter in relation to Vince Diego's analyses. But where Diego saw Matå'pang's contemporary, Maga'låhi Hurao (not to be confused with Matå'pang's accomplice, Hirao), as the supreme example of *matakña* in the seventeenth century, I think Matå'pang is as good a candidate inasmuch as what little we actually know about him satisfies, nonetheless, all of the definitions and connotations of the *matakña* cultural complex. Perhaps more than satisfies them, which prompts a second way of approaching Matå'pang: as a sign of discursive or semantic flourish.

Inasmuch as Tagalog and Chamorro are virtual "sibling" languages of the mother Austronesian language, it is reasonable to assume that the Chamorro term *matå'pang* is, or *was once*, the same as *mátapang* in Tagalog, which means "bold" or "courageous," like *matakña*. At least until 1672, when Matå'pang killed San Vitores. If in fact *matå'pang* was synonymous with its Tagalog homophone *mátapang*, then his reputation reversed and then went downhill as a direct result of his bold and courageous opposition. Today there are more Chamorros who would prefer not to be called *matå'pang* than those who would, though I believe that the numbers in the latter category are on the increase.

As a Filipino and Pohnpeian born and raised on Guam, and in light of the long and often vexed historical and political relationship between Chamorros and Filipinos, I can personally attest to the moments of Chamorro unease on matters Filipino on Guam, and the innumerable historical and cultural reasons that might trigger such sentiments (Diaz 1995a). My suggestions of a more or less direct link between the Tagalog and Chamorro homophones, for instance, could be misconstrued as yet another Filipino claim of Chamorro "origins" in the Philippines (which is not my claim) (Abella 1962).

Although there is no doubt that the Tagalog and Chamorro homophones are siblings, or cousins—in most of Micronesia, if not among Chamorros, the term for "first cousin" is one and the same with the term for "sibling" —there is no consensus among linguists about their exact relations, particularly on the question of whether or not the Chamorro term is borrowed from a Philippine language. In response to a recent inquiry from Vince Diego about the term *matå'pang* for a research paper he was writing, but also because I wanted to update my notes for this book, I e-mailed Dr Lawrence Reid, an Austronesian and Philippine language specialist. I started by saying he probably would not remember me, but that I had taken an introductory linguistics class of his (twenty-seven years ago!) and was now wondering if he could confirm my theory that the Chamorro and Tagalog *matå'pang* and *mátapang* were one and the same, as Austronesian cognates. His prompt response was "Dear Vince, You are Right! I don't remember you!"

Dr Reid graciously shared his assessment, although he explained that he was writing from abroad, which I took to mean that he did not have access to all his notes, or that his was a preliminary set of findings. He did give me permission to share his findings with Vince and my other colleagues at the University of Guam. Reid theorizes that the Chamorro *matå'pang* (with the glottal stop before the *p*) appears to be a loan word from Tagalog or some other Philippine language (that might still retain it) because, as he explained, the *mátapang* in Tagalog has a stress on the first syllable, which "can indicate that the word may have originally had a glottal stop in it, but was lost in Tagalog, with compensatory vowel lengthening" (Reid, pers comm, 23 Nov 2006). But what convinced him that it "is clearly a borrowing" is that the Chamorro *matå'pang* "doesn't have the appropriate reflexes to indicate that it was inherited from Proto-Austronesian (PA) or Proto-Malayo-Polynesian (PMP)" and "(since PMP *p > Chm f)!"[20]

In response, however, Chamorro linguist (and former director of the Government of Guam's Kumision Fino' Chamorro/Chamorro Language Commission) Professor Rosa Palomo of the University of Guam displaced the terms of the debate by pointing out that the Chamorro *matå'pang* is actually composed of two separate morphemes, "the passive marker *'ma,'* and *'ta'pangi','* to cleanse with water" (R Palomo, pers comm, 5 Dec 2006).[21] Reid may be a major figure in Austronesian linguistics, especially in Filipino languages, but I should point out that Palomo is a (UCLA-) trained linguist who is also a native speaker of Chamorro. Palomo's analysis quickly morphed from morphology to semantics, and in ways that also displace, at least partially, but still respectfully, the official semiotics provided by Church officials: "It is very easy to understand how Chief Mata'pang got his name . . . for it literally means 'one who was cleansed with water,' or baptized. *It does not matter who did the cleansing/baptizing,* what is important is that he was cleansed, made pure, with water and holy water at that! We use the word *'ta'pangi''* to mean to baptize, and *'mata'pangi''* to mean one who was baptized" (R Palomo, pers comm, 5 Dec 2006; emphasis added).

In shifting from morphology to historical semantics (and back), Professor Palomo simultaneously engaged and deflected Church ideology by conceding to the mission origins of the chief's name by identifying processes of cleansing and purification through the holy waters of baptism as the significant markers of his name. Here, however, *San Vitores* is actually subordinated to another Chamorro discourse of baptism with holy water in ways reminiscent of or analogous to Chamorro claims to Christianity (recall the Reverend Joaquin Sablan), without recourse to the Catholic Church in general or to San Vitores in particular. In other words, Palomo

rendered a meaning of *matå'pang* that is neither defined in opposition to
San Vitores nor dependent on him at all. What is particularly interesting
to me is that *this Chamorro linguistic* operation, working at a meta-level, as
Hayden White would say, moves from morphology to historical semantics
but returns to morphology—"*we use* the word *'ta'pangi''* to mean to baptize,
and *'mata'pangi''* to mean one who was baptized"—to emphasize Chamorro
meanings, in the passive form no less (*"ma"* is a passive marker), to assert
Chamorro agency! We might even view Palomo's argumentation here to be
a decidedly non-*matakña* Chamorro style of subtle assertion, the very kind
that allows indigenous cultural and even political agency to endure, if not
reconsolidate itself with materiality from without (Christianity; advanced
college degrees in linguistics), without incurring the wrath of the authorities. To top it off, Palomo returned to the initial query and Reid's preliminary (cursory?) findings, and again, from an angle other than direct, or
oppositional: "It is *also* highly possible," she surmised, "that as well as being
homophonic, the word is also polysemous" (R Palomo, pers comm, 5 Dec
2006).

As it turns out, Matå'pang is both polysemous (ie, has multiple meanings) and homo*phonic* (emphasis added in light of the Church's views on
same-sex unions). In Chamorro, *matå'pang* also means "tasteless," or as Påle'
'Scot put it, "you know, neither this nor that" (Calvo 1991). The connotation refers to food, and not to lack of style or couth. But there is another
set of meanings that I recall from childhood banter on the playgrounds
and streets of the 1960s and early 1970s: *matå'pang* as rude, "stuck up," silly,
or uncooperative. The term's inclusion and definition in a popular publication in the late 1980s titled *English, The Chamoru Way*, corroborates my
memory: "Matå'pang: Silly; Inane" (Images 1987, 37). This definition also
incurred the wrath of Påle' 'Scot, who clearly was annoyed, to say the least,
with what he believed to be a new (postwar?) generation of Chamorros who
did not know their language. But I must defend Chamorros of my cohort:
My continued informal survey on this term reveals that even among those
who are not as fluent as they might wish, they still know that there are multiple meanings of *matå'pang* and consistently cite the older definition pertaining to the taste of foods, no doubt because of the vitality of Chamorro
cuisine in everyday life and rituals (mostly local Church-related!) such as
fiestas, novenas, *lisåyus*, *måtais* (funerals), and *fandånggo*.

I want to close on the fact that the homophonic terms' polysemy was not
lost on Professor Reid. This *matå'pang* ("tasteless") is a "different story."
He explained, "It has the appropriate reflexes of Proto-Malayo-Polynesian
*mata'bang 'tasteless' (since PMP **b* > Chm p) with reflexes in the languages
of Batanes as *matavang*, and in Cebuano as *tab-ang* 'tasteless.' So even though
the two Chm forms are homophonous, they have different origins. The one
for brave is a borrowing from some Central Philippine language (possibly

old Tagalog), while the other is a reflex of an inherited word" (Reid, pers comm, 23 Nov 2006).

Cyberspace, 25 November 2006

Dear Vince,

I hate to muddy the waters any further, but I found another form of *matapang*, this time in an unpublished dictionary of Central Cagayan Agta, which has the meaning "dirtied, stained." This may be a completely different lexical item, although it could be derived from a form with glottal stop, since syllable final glottal stops were lost in this language (as in all the Northern Luzon languages). Larry (Reid, pers comm, 25 Nov 2006)[22]

Professor Reid is wrong. He has not muddied any waters with the new, possibly different lexical item from the Northern Luzon. For in the wake of Matå'pang's canoe, this much is clear to me: no waters of meaning pertaining to San Vitores's legacy, be they the seas of Tomhom or the holy waters of baptism, have ever been so historically clear, so spiritually pure, as to not have also been guilty of staining Matå'pang's reputation and arresting the fluidities and possibilities of his cultural and political legacies.

Epilogue

In the Shadow of Mass Destruction

Ann Arbor, Michigan, 2007

In Guam, as in Rome, the official Catholic Church's position on San Vitores is that he is a virtual vessel whose life and death served "the greater Glory of God," as understood by the Jesuits, who take pride in their rigorous ministry that has made them perhaps the most powerful, and sometimes the most controversial, of the Catholic religious orders. For rank-and-file Chamorro Catholics, including non-Chamorros like myself whose families emigrated to Guam and consider it home, San Vitores's story is a relatively recent one, whose climax with his formal beatification in the mid-1980s plunged the saint into island consciousness in ways that eclipsed prior "legends" and traditions that were better known among a quickly passing generation of elders. My bet is that most folks had never heard the term "beatification" and knew very little of San Vitores's life and death before then. An elder with whom I spoke was even dismayed to discover that San Vitores was not Chamorro, notwithstanding the adamant view of this elder's contemporary, a Chamorro monsignor, that the Spaniard "belongs to us" and "is ours" specifically for the way that he spilled his blood on Guam.

This discrepancy within the Chamorro community resonates with others within the local community and even between Rome and the Guam Catholic community. These socially layered and geographically interconnected discrepancies compose a local and a Catholic global history of mutual but unequal investments in and benefits obtained from celebrating San Vitores's legacy. Locally, for example, San Vitores's social and cultural resurfacing in the twentieth century reveals a complex mix of harmony and cacophony. Clearly, San Vitores has been generally and respectfully received by the faithful, not only because they are faithful to the Catholic Church but also because tradition demands that Chamorros show love and respect toward and defer to the authority of Chamorro clergy. In turn, these Chamorro spiritual "fathers" clearly see San Vitores as their spiritual kin, whose faith translated into love and concern for the spiritual well-being of the Chamorros. To be sure, this paternal, sometimes maternal, love and concern in relation to the archipelago's "children" translated into the gendered terms

204

of Chamorro faith as mobilized in social and cultural codes and practices. Clearly, too, the Chamorro church leaders saw the value for Guam and Chamorro culture itself in San Vitores's elevation to the Church's highest honors. In this view, San Vitores is a powerful witness to the importance of the Catholic faith for the island and, in particular, for the survival of Chamorro culture, an enduring indigenous culture that is consistently silenced by an enduring legacy of writings by Church detractors, historically mostly foreigners making racist and patronizing assumptions about "Native" cultural authenticity and purity. Such presuppositions, of course, left/leave no room for comprehending the complex histories of how Natives, in the interest of cultural and social rearticulation and survival, can also convert those who come to convert them.

Perhaps precisely because of this historical opposition over San Vitores's legacy in the Marianas, but ultimately because of the strength of Chamorro Catholicism, the Vatican received the movement to canonize San Vitores with enthusiasm and support. But, as well, the Vatican exhibited measured caution, born from the long-standing dilemma presented by relying on saints and martyrs to encourage popular devotion and piety while having to deal with the popular penchant for excess. Absent excess in the popular reception of San Vitores (except for a local and relatively harmless tradition of asserting that the priest's blood colors a portion of Tomhom Bay near the area of his death), the Church has in fact welcomed the revival for what a cardinal called the "journey of faith in reverse." This, of course, is the story by which San Vitores's children in faith have reversed his geographic and chronological trajectory by returning to the Vatican to push for his "elevation." According to that cardinal, this journey in reverse had important "return effects" for the universal Catholic Church to the extent that this local success story can attest to the universal and eternal truths of God the Father as witnessed by Santo Papa, his temporal and spiritual surrogate, through the apostolic tradition that reaches back to Saint Peter's privileged role as witness and scribe for the Good News that is Jesus.

But through this transhistorical, translocal, and transcultural lovefest, we also witness, in the various investments in the San Vitores vessel, competing and sometimes conflicting interests and perspectives, not all of which get to circulate and enjoy equal airtime. From "above," for example, the official and juridical imperatives to authenticate San Vitores's martyrdom in order to attest to its legitimacy required the simultaneous invocation and subordination of Chamorro agency, first via Matå'pang, the infamous chief who is said to have murdered San Vitores, and second, via Native eye and auricular witnesses, as a prerequisite for certifying the providential truths at stake in San Vitores's life and death. The first operation involved the rhetorical and discursive conversion of an angry Chamorro into an agent of the devil whose motive was shown to be religious in character and, more specifically, hostile to God in particular. This, and the second operation, also entailed the conversion of Chamorro cultural and political codes of defiance and protection—directed at the missionaries and their local sympathizers—into an epic battle against God as orchestrated by the devil. Yet, this figuration and characterization contrasts rather sharply with "local" discourses that are, at best, ambivalent about the figuration and (over)simplification of their cultural traditions in diabolical terms. Furthermore, local investments in San Vitores, whether by the Catholic populace or by the clergy, for the most part do not belabor the Matå'pang story but call attention to the positive history of Catholicism in the survival of Chamorro culture, particularly against the aforementioned discourses of its denial or dismissal. More pointedly, the local investment in San Vitores can be understood as a postwar social and cultural "alliance" (detractors might say an "unholy alliance") between Native culture and Catholicism against what is widely perceived and lamented to be the deleterious effects of postwar modernization under the mantle of American forces of liberal individualism and uncontrolled materialism.

Whatever it may mean, the form and manner of San Vitores's resurfacing in the postwar years features a proliferation of meanings that contrast sharply with the singular narrative wielded by the Vatican, and by local supporters of the Cause. Just as we can sense a substratum of specifically indigenous values and practices—locally known as *kostumbren Chamorro*—beneath the surface forms of distinctly Catholic rituals and practices, so too can we identify local Chamorro Catholic interests as a second subterraneous set that bellows beneath the official Church "position" from on high. And whereas the two local layers testify to Chamorro cultural continuity, they also involve their own sets of actual and symbolic marginalization and suppression of other Chamorro and Native positionalities. *Kostumbren Chamorro*, for example, obfuscates indigenous investments in systems other than Spanish Catholicism, such as Protestantism, or even other cultures of modernity, such as liberal American culture, or even contemporary Chamorro investments in cultural nationalisms as they are understood to have been at work in the seventeenth-century rebellions against the padres. Most certainly, the hegemony of *kostumbren Chamorro* leaves little cultural traction for traditions of defiance directed at a political patriarchal lineage that is modeled explicitly on the terms of kinship brought by "father" San Vitores on behalf of the "Father Almighty," a system that finds expression in a formidable *familia* system modeled on the Holy Family and that, therefore, leaves no room for nonnormative relations. Likewise, the alliance between *kostumbren Chamorro* and the Vatican offers even less room for the increasing number of Chamorros who are consciously linking their social and political plight as a colony of the United States to a longer history of subjugation by the Catholic Church. To speak against San Vitores, in other words, is to speak against God, and to speak against God is to also strike at the island's political, cultural, and social nerve centers. This is why Chamorro resistance and opposition to the Cause is muted, even if it clearly exists in varied degrees of intensity; it is also why those few Chamorros who can speak out do so from relatively safe positions as non-Catholic Christians (like the late Reverend Joaquin Sablan, who championed the public honoring of Matå'pang as a "true" Chamorro hero).

Across these discourses from above and below, and in an effort to articulate a position that explicitly highlights the processes of narrative construction in hindsight but also in sight of issues of power and vantage point, I have labored to find alternative meanings in San Vitores's past and present that are neither simply celebratory nor diametrically oppositional—for we are now at a moment in our histories where we know what will happen if you oppose formidable power head-on: it only reconsolidates itself in relation to its oppositions. We need such alternative stories and meanings, furthermore, because whoever we understand ourselves to be and wherever we end up calling home, we will continue to be at the mercy of those who speak in the name of God and who have at their disposal the smallest, or the largest, weapons of mass destruction to unleash on those who are not with them in their holy crusade.

Notes

Prologue

1. Hanlon 1999 offers a critical treatment of such colonial commemorations in Micronesia.

2. San Vitores's significance in the Jesuit story in the Philippines is treated in de la Costa 1961, 455–457, 470–472, and 510–511.

3. The other two Spanish Jesuits were Francisco Gárate and Jose Rubio (Libreria Editrice Vaticana 1985).

4. Contrast this with the apology in 1998 by the Catholic bishops of the Philippines for the clergy who sided with Spain and opposed the Philippine revolutionaries in the Spanish–Filipino War in 1898: "Truth be told," wrote the bishops, "we are still in the process of liberating ourselves" (Teves 1998, 13).

Introduction

1. Examples of this Native Pacific cultural studies movement are K Camacho 2005; Clifford 2001; Deloughrey 2007; Diaz 2002a; Diaz and Kauanui 2001; Gegeo 2001; Jolly 2001, 2003; Kauanui 2007, 2008; Najita 2006; Osorio 2001; Teaiwa 2001a, 2001b; Tengan 2008; and G White and Tengan 2001. Critical assessments are in Hviding 2003 and Wood 2003.

2. The "field" of cultural studies is identified with a post–World War II leftist intellectual movement in Britain, first in public education and media studies, and then more broadly in other areas of cultural production. Its most famous figure is Stuart Hall, with important genealogies to Raymond Williams, Louis Althusser, and Antonio Gramsci. For this connection, see Hall 1986a and Hall 1992. Hall's theory of articulation is in Hall 1986b, Hall 1996, and Morley and Chen 1996. Good introductions to cultural studies are in During 1993; Gilroy 1987, 1993; Grossberg, Nelson, and Triechler 1992; Nelson and Grossberg 1988; Sardar and Van Loon 1998; and Story 1996.

3. The field of "postcolonial" studies is also immense, with introductions in Ashcroft, Griffiths, and Tiffin 2000; Lazarus 2004; Lewis and Mills 2003; Loomba 1998; and R Young 2001.

4. This peculiar phrasing comes from a response provided by a Chamorro journalist to the question: Are you Catholic or are you Chamorro? See chapter 3.

5. An example of the "hispanicization thesis" can be found in Mayo 1984, 17–25; at one point Mayo said that the Chamorros "became Spaniards" (1984, 32). For criticism of this thesis, see Stade 1998.

6. Kayoko Kushima examined the trope of insularity in Guam's historiography (2001). Robert A Underwood called this the "size matters" aspect of Guam's colonization (2001).

7. As late as 1951, the US Navy continued to use the term "mongrel" to refer to the Chamorros (see United States Navy 1951, 1). A full analysis of this racial formation is in Monnig 2007.

8. Critical scholarship on political reform during the prewar US Naval period can be found in Bordallo Hofschneider 2001; Diaz 2004; Hattori 1995; PSECC 1993a, 1993b, 1994, 1995, 1996a. In response to the agitation, one governor facilitated the "absorption" of dissent by creating a "Guam Congress" of appointed "representatives" who had neither been elected nor been given lawmaking powers.

9. Critical treatments of Chamorro commemoration of the Japanese occupation are, in reverse chronology, K Camacho 2005; Bevacqua 2004; E Flores 2002; Diaz 2001; C T Perez 1996; A Santos 1991b; Souder 1989; and R Underwood 1977. Chamorro oral histories of the war in Guam are in T Palomo 1984 and P Sanchez 1979.

10. The movement for Chamorro self-determination of this period is treated in Alvarez-Cristobal 1990; Bettis 1993b; M Perez 1997, 2005; Perez-Howard 1993; Rivera 1992; A Santos 1991a, 1991c; Souder and Underwood 1987; and R Underwood 1990, 1984. See also the essays in PSECC 1993a.

11. Chamorro anxieties about immigration are in Souder and Underwood 1987 and R Underwood 1985. Leland Bettis identified immigration as a US colonial policy (1993a). See Diaz 1995a and Monnig 2007, chapters 6 and 7, for contextualizations of these sentiments within colonial and US racial formations.

12. The latest example of this oxymoron can be found in Caryl 2007.

13. For a critical commentary on the relationship between indigenous histories and theories of creolization, see Diaz 2006. The most sustained critical treatment of Chamorro culture in the throes of a racialized history of "mestizo" mixings is found in Monnig 2007.

14. For the international makeup of the seventeenth-century mission, see Tueller 2000; for Filipinos in the history of Guam, see de Viana 2004.

15. See Diaz 2005 for a way of thinking about indigeneity through pre- and post-European contact histories of mobility and contact based on indigenous seafaring concepts, practices, and histories.

16. "Religious" belong to an order (the Franciscans, the Capuchins, etc), while "secular" do not.

17. There is no comprehensive history of other Christian denominations among the Chamorro people. Places to begin include Forbes 1997; Pesch 2002; J Sablan 1990; and the Chamorro Bible Project Online (see http://www.rlenelive.com/Chamorro%20Related%20Articles/Chamorro%20Bible%20Articles/chamorroBible2ndDiscovery.htm [accessed 13 December 2008]).

18. The pro–San Vitores, pro–United States stance is exemplified in then US Congressman Ben Blaz's effort to have the US Postal Service issue a commemorative stamp in San Vitores's honor: "This [beatification] is a tremendous honor for the United States because it recognizes the historic importance of San Vitores's work and elevates towards sainthood a man from an American community" (quoted in

Pacific Voice 1985e, 1). Besides serving several terms as Guam's delegate to the US Congress, Blaz is also distinguished as the first Chamorro soldier to reach the status of brigadier general in the US Marine Corps. He is also a graduate of Notre Dame. Somewhat opposite of Blaz, the late Angel (Anget) Santos's political trajectory exemplifies a subaltern and oppositional Chamorro consciousness. Santos was a decorated veteran of the US Air Force who was honorably discharged, and proceeded to agitate against US colonialism and militarism in Guam. Santos served briefly in the Guam Legislature in the late 1990s after founding the grassroots nationalist movement, Nasion Chamoru. He and other members led a major protest in the mid-1990s that forced the local government to activate a Chamorro land-trust program. He once scaled a military fence and aggressively confronted armed military guards before being subdued and arrested. For more information, see Monnig 2007 and Stade 1998. For all apparent differences, Blaz and Santos were also both staunch Catholics, with Santos always clutching a rosary in his pants pocket.

19. Critical assessments of the "invention of tradition" thesis in Pacific studies are in Clifford 2001; Diaz and Kauanui 2001; Hau'ofa 2000; Jolly 1992; Jolly and Thomas 1992; Lindstrom and White 1993; Linnekin 1991a, 1991b, 1992; Tobin 1994; and Trask 1999.

20. This exchange is reproduced, conveniently, in Hanlon and White 2000.

21. In Hawai'i, see Linnekin 1983. In New Zealand, see Hanson 1989 and H B Levine 1991.

22. For analyses of the "breakdown" of the *familia* system, see K Aguon 1977 and Munoz 1977.

23. She was the sister of Mensila, Nahnmwarki en Kitti.

24. I elaborate on this entanglement, as on that between indigeneity and colonial patriarchy, in Diaz 1993 and Diaz 2002b.

25. For a discussion of syncretism, see J Murphy 1988, 116, 120, and note 12, 170.

26. In Melanesia, see Trompf 1987.

27. For instances of fugitivism and its futility, and the rigorous campaign of pursuit, see LeGobien 1949, 10, 85–86, 110, 114, 118–120.

28. The word *reducción* is also glossed as "settlement"; see Driver 1971, 19.

29. For examples of missionary anxieties over what García considered the "natural inconstancy" of the *indios* (Higgins 1939, 124), see García 2004, 361, and LeGobien 1949, 14, 128. A good discussion of churches as physical places of refuge is Carano 1973, 18. World War II furnished an interesting reversal of sorts when Japanese invasion forces used the cathedral as a makeshift prison to hold American servicemen and Spanish priests (Olano 1949). During the occupation, under the pastoral care of two Japanese priests, many Chamorros refused to attend Masses (Olano 1949, 49). Finally, Pope John Paul II's visit to Guam included an address about the Catholic Church's value as protection and answer to a modern world that "is often confused and misled" (*L'osservatore Romano* 1981, 19).

30. Robert Priest provided a critical assessment of the phrase in modernist and postmodernist usages (2001).

31. Likewise, neither here nor in my analyses across these pages do I understand colonial and counter-colonial discourse *ultimately* as patriarchal and phallic. Without dismissing their endurance and force in history and historical representation (phallogocentric), we also need not see colonial and counter-colonial power being

the exclusive domain of patriarchy and masculinity, nor their effects as essentially effeminizing.

32. Classical feminist critiques are Daly 1985 and Ranke-Heinemann 1990. In the historiography of Christianity, see Pagels 1987.

33. The idea of "situated knowledges" is virtually paradigmatic of feminist cultural studies scholarship. Influential for me were Behar and Gordon 1995; Haraway 1991, 1989; and from anthropology, Rosaldo 1989. Early works by radical Chicana theorists who foreground gender and sexuality continue to help me specify and situate critically my own work. I remain indebted to Anzaldúa 1987; Moraga 1983; Moraga and Anzaldúa 1981; and Sandoval 2000. For Pacific Islander critiques of gender and sexuality see Hall and Kauanui 1994; Te Awekotuku 1991; and the essays in Jolly 2008.

34. This insistence underwrites Native historiography in the past two decades in the two areas with which I have working familiarity: Chamorro studies and Hawaiian studies. Across this monograph, where appropriate, I cite critical work by Chamorro scholars and activists. Works of Native Hawaiian historiography, political, and cultural criticism from the past two decades that have influenced my thinking are Kame'eleihiwa 1992; Kauanui 1999, 2005, 2008; McGregor 2007; Osorio 1992, 2002; Silva 2004; Stillman 2001, 2003, 2004; Tengan 2008; Trask 1999; and K Young 1998. For a critical assessment of spatiality between Native Pacific studies "in" the islands and cultural studies "for" the islands, see Teaiwa 2001. See also Teaiwa 1997 for a radical reworking of the "ground" of Banaban history and identity. For Native Hawaiian footing in the US continent, see Kauanui 1998 and 2007.

Chapter 1: The Mission *Positio*

1. Robert Foley has criticized my pointing out this "imagined" contradiction by asserting that I miss "*the rather obvious point* . . . that it is not possible to write about *the martyrdom* . . . until after his death and that the closer to the event such documentation is, the more reliable it can prove to be. This is surely what is meant by the phrase 'hard upon the martyrdom'" (2002, chapter 2; emphasis added). I leave it to the reader of this chapter to judge if my argument has merit. I do want to point out that Foley himself presumes the martyrdom (see italics above). He also finds need to correct my theological understanding of *fama martyrii* by pointing out that this is a reputation in life, which is categorically different from the authenticity of a martyred death. I know the distinction, and find it very clearly articulated in the *Positio*. But it appears that Foley missed the point in the *Positio* where Father Ledesma, its compiler, resorted to San Vitores's *fama martyrii* as a "secondary proof" for helping substantiate the candidate's "true character," which constituted part of the test for authenticating martyrdom.

2. Biblical references: "Holy One par excellence" (Is 6.3); "Proper Name" (Is 1.4; 5.19; 41.14); "His apartness and inaccessibility" (Lv 33.20, 21.18–21); "Covenant . . . Chosen People . . . Communication" (Ex 19); "purification, worship and obedience" (Lv 11.44–45, 19.2, 20.7, 21.8, 26); "spiritualization . . . through separation from profane through renunciation" (Is 1.26, 4.3, 5.16, 6.3, 6.5).

3. Biblical references: "Holy nation" as "the Church" (1 Pt 2.5, 2.9; see also Dn 7.18); Christ as "Holy One" (Mk 1.24; Lk 4.34; Acts 3.14, 4.27, 4.30); saints as "the

faithful" (Acts 9.13); "dominant personal attitude . . . perfection . . . moral effort" (Eph 5.3; Col 1.21–23; Rom 6.19, 6.22, 12.1; 2 Cor 7.1); "union with Christ as sharing in Divine holiness" (1 Pt 1.15; Apoc 1.6, 5.10, 20.6); "consecration of divine service" (Eph 5.26; 1 Pt 2.5, 2.9); service in "love" (Eph 1.5; see also Rom 5.5); "plea for personal moral goodness"(1 Jn 3.3; 1 Pt 1.15; see also Lv 11.44–45); "vision" of God (Math 5.8; 1 Jn 3.2; 1 Cor 13.12); "bodily resurrection with Christ" (Phil 3.21–22; Jn 6.35–39).

4. For an analysis of this accounting system within a larger colonial discourse, see Rafael 1993.

5. My understanding and the ensuing discussion of the historical and theological development of martyrdom come from F X Murphy 1967, 312–313, unless otherwise noted.

6. Alberto Risco, SJ, quoted in Calvo 1970, 154. The idea of San Vitores's "pathological death wish" is from former Jesuit Ronald Haverlandt (nd).

7. The critical idea of God as "Eternal Creditor" is from Rafael 1993.

Chapter 2: The Oral Cavity

1. For an introduction to the formal processes of canonization used in the Sacred Congregation of Rites, see Blaher 1949; Green 1967, 193; and Molinari 1967. Alan Riding referred to the Congregation as "the saint factory" because of the increase in the number of canonizations under Pope John Paul II (1989, 5).

2. The documents used in the *Positio* "have to do more explicitly and directly with the person, the life, the virtues, the apostolic labor, and the glorious death of the Servant of God" (*Positio* 1981b, 712). Its bibliography begins with materials starting in 1672, the year of the martyrdom. Indeed, one can surmise that virtually all the information about San Vitores's life and death was gathered in the context of the movement to canonize him.

3. But see Hezel's assessment of García 2004 (on the back of the book's dust jacket), identifying it as more than a hagiography.

4. Fathers Felix Zubillaga and Josef Wicki (*Positio* 1981b, fn 78 at end of chapter 9, after p 591).

5. This archbishop was Fray Payo de Rivera, OSA. That copy is in Biblioteca del Instituto de Antropología e Historia de México, Sección de Manuscritos, Colección Jesuitas, Dossier 18, and is excerpted and translated in *Positio* 1981b, 511–521. According to the late Archbishop Flores, Father Angel Hidalgo of the Jesuit Curia in Rome discovered the Process of Mexico only in June 1974 while working in collaboration with Ledesma. Hidalgo came across the 300-page document at the Anthropological Archives in Mexico City during a research trip sponsored by the Institute for Hispanic Culture in Madrid (*Pacific Voice* 1974a, 1).

6. Elsewhere, Ledesma identifies Father Alonzo Lopez as the Procurator of the Guam Process, and Father Francisco Ezquerra, San Vitores's successor, as the "immediate Official of the Process" (*Positio* 1981a, 475).

7. Ledesma also cites a later Alonzo Lopez document as additional proof of the existence of the *Authentic Information*/Process of Guam document. Quoted in *Positio* 1981b, chapter 9, footnote 80, after 591.

8. As found in the title phrase of A Ledesma 1981a.

9. This was Dr Francisco Vidal.

10. The exact citations in the *Positio* are, respectively, Pos Decr et Rescr 5 Martii, 1695, Toletana, f 1–2, and Reg Decr Beat et Can 1692–1702, 159–160.

11. In my 1991 interview with Father Juan Ledesma, I was not able to get to this question because his advanced age and physical condition left him exhausted and short of breath.

12. Hezel has challenged modern claims that this "enormous decline" in the Native population was due to the "reckless slaughter of large segments of the population" by the Spanish (1982, 133). Citing J Underwood 1973, Hezel speculated that early population estimates, including San Vitores's own, are unreliable. Chamorro loss of life in battle, by all accounts, he said, was "light" (Hezel 1982, 133).

Chapter 3: The Sweet Spot

1. In this section, I paraphrase Margaret Higgins's (1938, 15) paraphrasing of García 1683. A recent translation is García 2004.

2. This is not just a maneuver to capture some essential "Native perspective." My aim here is to join other Pacific theorists who call for grounding oneself in the specificity of place conceived not as an ontological given but as a site through which localities and identities are produced in relation to each other. In Pacific history, see Hanlon 2004 and the essays in Lal 2004. See also Lal and Hempenstall 2001. For a critical reflection of place in Pacific studies' intellectual production, see Teaiwa 2001a. The most thorough study for Guam is Stade 1998.

3. On Pacific history as process of identity construction, see G White 1991. On the "portability" of place, see Gegeo 2001. For understanding cultural identity as portable, through discourses of movement, see Clifford 1997. In Diaz 1989, I meditated on place and history in relation to Christian missionaries and social sciences in Pohnpei.

4. Engracia Camacho's reference to Tomhom as the site of *apuyan påle'* conflicts with another site of the same name in southern Guam, between the Humåtak and Hågat (Siguenza 1992).

5. During a University of Guam Humanistic Studies colloquium, 4 April 1989, Chamorro linguist Dr Benit Dungca Camacho explained that *techa* means "to begin," and more substantively is the embodiment of "the transference by chant of what we know from the ancestors."

6. The following quotes are from Arago [1982?], 142–143.

7. See Van Peenen 1974. For a critical treatment, see Diaz 2000.

8. On Western science's debt to the Pacific, see MacLeod and Rehbock 1988.

9. A sampling from the "critique of the invention of tradition" in the Pacific: Handler and Linnekin 1983; Keesing and Tonkinson 1982; Linnekin 1990; Linnekin and Poyer 1990; Van Meijl and Van der Grijp 1993. See also notes 19–21 to the introduction of this book.

10. The first ordained Chamorro priest was Påle' José Palomo in 1859 (Sullivan 1957, 148). In a letter to one Father Ricart in 1894, Palomo expressed his "remembering with gratitude" San Vitores for "having liberated the aborigines, our ancestors, from the yoke of Satan" (quoted in *Positio* 1981b, 635).

11. Conversation with William Hernandez, curator of the Hagåtña Basilica National Museum, and member of the organizing team, August 1991.

12. These are Carano and Sanchez 1964; Dugan 1956; Higgins 1936a, 1936b, 1937a, 1937b, 1938, 1939; LeGobien 1949; Safford 1903–1905, 1905, and 1911; Sullivan 1957; Thompson 1941; and Van Peenen 1974. Carano and Sanchez 1964 is the only work in this list that did not rely exclusively on *sanhiyong* sources, and only Higgins's 1936–1939 items in the *Guam Recorder* would have been relatively available to (literate) Chamorros before World War II. After the war, the works of LeGobien, Sullivan, and Carano and Sanchez could also have been obtained relatively easily.

13. But see Searles and Searles 1937, which was published by the US Navy's Department of Education. For a memoir of prewar education, see Carter 1997. In 1951 the Department of Education, now under a civilian government, published a history of Guam (R Perez and Wygant 1951). In the Catholic and public schools that I attended in the 1960s and 1970s, no history of Guam courses were offered, although Guam scholar Dr Lawrence Cunningham informed me that he and a few others, like Janice Beatty, Mike Musto, Jim Kessler, and Tim Tishler, had by the late 1960s begun to put together their own curricular materials for the public school system (see Beatty 1968). For his own work on Chamorro precontact society and kinship, see Cunningham 1984, 1992. My intent here is only to convey the general absence of history of Guam courses for Guam's students before World War II and up until the late 1970s.

14. Such schools were built in the outlying areas because, although the majority of Chamorros lived in Hagåtña and Sumay, they traveled daily with their children to their *lanchos* (ranches) in the countryside to tend to their gardens and livestock. Thus it had become impractical to require the children to return to town for compulsory schooling. The San Vitores School in Dedidu was therefore established to bring compulsory education to the Natives, in ways symbolic of the sending of Spanish missionaries to the islands three hundred years earlier. For information on San Vitores School, see Sullivan 1957, 135, 137.

15. In a 5 September 1985 press release, the Micronesian Area Research Center attributed "the initiative . . . of the cause" to "Archbishop Flores, as a young priest," with no mention of Calvo's seminal role (MARC 1985). But drawing from *Positio* 1981b, the *Pacific Daily News* acknowledged Calvo's role of "reviv[ing]" it (*PDN* 1985b, 55).

16. On this count, Påle' 'Scot was on Mesa's side.

17. According to Tom McGrath (quoted in Kemp 1985a, 31), it is "the only . . . novena to San Vitores known of in the world." The novena was based on information from the *Positio* 1981b.

18. It is not clear if Sullivan was including the entire Marianas. Robert F Rogers cited a Navy report of 858, or 6 percent of the total population for Guam (1994, 143).

19. Quoted from a promotional flyer in the "San Vitores" Files, in the Micronesian Area Research Center's Vertical Files.

20. The Knights of Columbus is the world's largest Catholic fraternal organization. It was extended to Guam in 1965.

21. The sculptor was Eduardo Castrillo; the contractor, Fred Arizala.

22. Quoted from a promotional flyer in the "San Vitores" Files, in the Micronesian Area Research Center's Vertical Files.

23. Latte stones were upright stone foundations of important precontact Chamorro houses or structures. They consisted of pillars ranging from several feet to thirty feet in height and were capped with semispherical "capstones." The Latte of

Freedom was envisioned as a towering latte stone lookout and was ridiculed as frivolous and a waste of public money.

Chapter 4: Traffic on the Mount

1. Elsewhere I have tracked US Naval colonial anxieties in and on the "tropics" in discourses about recreation and public works; see Diaz 1998 and 2002a.

2. The Hawaiian term *haole* (here spelled "hoalie") is usually translated "foreigner."

3. For a sense of the fuller complexities of the mission story, including the tensions and conflicts mentioned here, and the international or transnational makeup of the missionaries, see Tueller 2000. For an analysis of the ambivalences and contradictions that the missionaries themselves faced, including their hesitations and reservations about their own zeal and labor, see Clifford 1982. For a useful reflection on the history of conversion and missionization in Pacific history, see Hanlon 2001. Readers familiar with Guam's history will notice the conspicuous absence of Rogers 1995 in my sampling. My views of this book, particularly on the question of Chamorro agency, have been published already; see Diaz 1996.

4. My observation is not intended to dismiss how colonialism is, in fact, gendered and sexualized. For two good treatments from radical women of color, see Tadiar 1993 and Smith 2005.

5. Påle' José Palomo also expressed gratitude to San Vitores for freeing the Chamorros from "the yoke of Satan and for changing the unjust name of Ladrones into that of the Marianas" (*Positio* 1981b, 635).

6. The companion quoted was Pedro Coomans (1997, 2). Augusto de Viana wrote that San Vitores "adopted a policy of appeasement towards people like Hurao . . . and that he wanted to win their hearts through kindness and mild treatment" (2004, 27).

7. Hezel cited a dispatch from Queen Mariana to the viceroy of New Spain, 12 November 1672.

8. For a history of Filipino participants in the Mariana mission, see de Viana 2004.

9. See also the references in Hezel and Driver 1988, the sequel to Hezel 1982.

10. See Plaza 1980, 17, which presents a translation of book 3, chapters 1–4 of García 1683.

11. His maternal and paternal surnames are Spanish; however, in the Marianas such names do not necessarily signify Spanish ancestry but rather centuries of baptism, or other *Indio* ancestry from elsewhere in the *imperio*, especially the Philippines and Mexico.

12. The Chamorro term *maga'låhi* translates as "first male" and connotes the top-ranking male of a clan, a set of clans, or a village, and thus has been translated as "chief." For caution in interpreting the category "chief" in colonial contexts, see G White and Lindstrom 1998.

13. Lévesque 1995 indicates the same in explaining why *Yu'os* (*Dios*) is a Castilian term.

14. Classic critiques of this are in Fanon 1965 and Memmi 1965. Chamorro critical treatment of Chamorro colonial internalizations are in Aguon 2006; Bevacqua

2004; C T Perez 1997; Perez-Howard 1993; Souder 1991, 1989; and R Underwood 2001, 1990.

15. The classic study of counter-colonial mimicry is Bhabha 1984. See Diaz 1993 for mimicries of this framework in relation to other moments in Guam cultural history.

16. Perhaps as a sign of the modernizing influences, Camacho's conversion to a non-Catholic denomination raised eyebrows in the Catholic community.

17. For a study of the elevation of the Mariana mission into a vicariate, see Quitugua 1995.

18. Michael Goodich discussed the historical basis of piety as cultural self-fashioning (1982, 7–8).

19. I return to a fuller treatment of the term *matå'pang* in chapter 6.

20. San Vitores's *fama martyrii* includes "astral traveling" and bilocation, the supernatural ability to be in two places at the same time.

21. For a classic cultural "reading" of cockfighting, see Geertz 1973. See also Marvin 1984.

22. Beloved songs, like "Maria Nananmagof" and "Matuna I Ginasgås-mu" (which "brought tears to the *manåmko'*"). Two other Chamorro hymns that were sung: "Korason Santos," which the pilgrims were surprised to learn was an old Basque song, and "San José," which borrowed the tune from a Jesuit theme song (*PDN* 1985d, 27).

23. On opposition to canonization efforts among indigenous people from California, see Costo and Costo 1987 and Fogel 1988.

24. I mark the category "wife" to question the particularity of marriage and matrimony as defined in Catholic terms at the time. In addition to being a fundamental part of the Catholic calendar/cosmos in general—with its attendant views on normative sexuality—the institution was also seized on by the padres as a substitute for what they understood to be the customary terms of relations between men and women, especially as these were institutionalized in Chamorro society in the *guma' uritao*, or young men's houses, which were abhorred by the padres as "houses of debauchery" (LeGobien 1949, 109). Initially, Chamorro men resisted the priests' efforts to abolish the *guma' uritao*, but one priest observed a transformation and willingness among the men when they realized how "obedient and circumspect" the Chamorro women became in their new identities as "wives." For discussion of the power that Chamorro women wielded in precontact society, see Jorgensen 1984; Lawcock 1977; Souder 1987; McGrath's foreword in Souder 1987; PSECC 1994, 1995. Chamorro women themselves began to oppose the abolition of the *guma' uritao*, an abolition that presumably sought to protect women. It was as if the women understood the implications of their domestication as "wives." For a Chamorro "herstory" of women's power, particularly on the home front, see Souder 1987. The Chamorro term for a woman of the *uritao* was *maulitao* (Freycinet 1829, 164). According to Freycinet, "in general a maulitao of any age was more respected than an older girl who was chaste" (1829, 164).

25. See Diaz 1995b for a post-structuralist interpretation of this war.

26. Haunani-Kay Trask, quoted in the film *Act of War* (Nā Maka o ka 'Āina 1993). Lilikalā Kame'eleihiwa attributed the collapse to the Hawaiians' internalization of the missionaries' insistence that baptism and conversion are the only paths to *ola hou*, or everlasting life (1992). I am grateful to Dean Saranillio for drawing this possible comparison.

27. The Government of Guam in 1991 created the Guam Political Status Education Coordinating Commission (PSECC), to "develop a curriculum of political status studies for Guam Schools." The commission was composed of representatives of the (then) Guam Department of Education, the University of Guam, the Guam Community College, the (then) Guam Commission on Self-Determination, and the Community-at-Large (PSECC 1994). An unstated objective was the recuperation of Chamorro perspectives from *sanhiyong*-produced and -oriented histories. Under its imprimatur, PSECC produced eight volumes for kindergarten through high school, including anthologies typically used at the postsecondary level. Because PSECC favored collective research and authorship, none of the volumes are credited to any single author, and every volume was pored over, word for word, by members of the commission. In 1996, PSECC was absorbed into the Chamorro Heritage Institute Planning Group (CHIPG). In 1999 CHIPG was absorbed into Dipåttamenton I Kaohao Guinahan (Chamorro/Department of Chamorro Affairs), where it continues to produce curricular materials. I served as PSECC's historian from 1992 to 1996.

28. See Micklethwait and Wooldridge 2004; but see Smith 2008 for radically progressive political possibilities between American Indians and the Christian Right in the United States. For a broader call for American Catholics to return to Catholic theologies of social justice and Progressive Catholicism, see Maguire 2008. A call for a Chamorro Liberation Theology is in J Diaz 2007.

29. The other two were the Catholic priests Oscar L Calvo and Jesus Dueñas.

30. I forgo here an extended discussion of Chamorro nationalism except to say that sometimes it appears to be "modern"—as when it is articulated in relation to liberal ideas of individual and collective civil "rights" (such as calls for "self-determination")—while at other times the idea of nationhood is invoked perhaps as the only term available in western discourse, that is, with recognizable and enforceable capital, to describe a fierce sense of people-hood that existed for millennia before the arrival of the *sanhiyong* and that resisted efforts to subjugate it.

31. The reference to Crazy Horse at this time challenges the primacy in Guam of US civil rights discourse in favor of a distinctly Native American struggle for sovereignty.

32. My added emphases are meant to highlight Chamorro insistence on cultural continuity despite or through political discontinuities and colonial socialization.

33. The contradiction between Bordallo's suicide as a mortal sin—at the feet of Kepuha, the staunch Catholic, no less—and his lionization in bronze at Adelup was short-lived. Bordallo was allowed a state and Catholic funeral because, according to Archbishop Apuron, as reported in a local daily, Bordallo never recanted his faith.

Chapter 5: Disrobing the Man

1. The verbal exchange is the only license I take in representing the scene in García 2004, 74.

2. That portrait is the frontispiece of García 2004.

3. I thank Phil Deloria for suggesting the differences between inversive and angular kinds of (counter-) discourses.

4. Two years later, in Guam, Påle' 'Scot asked me to head a nonprofit corporation that he had created for the purposes of inventorying his library and collections. We never succeeded because of "local politics," but this is another story.

5. Nobody is going to come right out and say it, but for what can be construed as the implicit figuration of Påle' 'Scot as a Japanese collaborator, see Sullivan 1957, 163. Påle' Dueñas's unfavorable views of the Japanese priests are related in Olano 1949, 48–50.

6. Nasion Chamorro is treated in Stade 1998, 196–200, 252–255; see also Monnig 2007.

7. I have not found any written sources on this incident. I also do not know what became of the original painting but suspect it was destroyed. However, a limited number of first-run poster prints were produced by the Guam Museum.

8. And play football, as I did with the Santa Barbara Parish touch football team under the mentorship of Father Bob Phelps, an American Capuchin. Father Bob may attribute the sins in this book to the fall I took in a game that split my own head and spilled some of its contents. For the social and cultural costs of the tackle football that we played under the watchful eyes of Hawaiian men against US military teams at the time, see Diaz 2002a.

9. Christine DeLisle reminded me that the *mangnginge'* is also featured at Christmastime, during the Nubenan Niñu (novena to the Christ Child). Here, but also after Masses during the season, and in rounds in the village led by the priest and altar boys, a statue of the Blessed Child is passed around and sniffed while the faithful sing a hymn with the line, *ta nginge' ta adora* (let us adore) Jesus, to the tune of "O Come, All Ye Faithful."

10. The official Web site of the US Conference of Catholic Bishops is at http://www.nccbuscc.org/nab/bible/songs/intro.htm [accessed 1 February 2007]

11. Along with goodies, such as chocolate, sugar, and preserves, which the padres used as "bait to attract the Marianos to the Christian doctrine" (García 2004, 379).

12. In their *Chamorro-English Dictionary* (1975, 215), Topping, Ogo, and Dungca translated Yu'us as God. (*Yu'os* is an alternate spelling.)

13. Though the reference in this quote is to the Mangayans in the Philippines, García quickly asserted that "this was the method he was to always use in the Mariana Islands" (2004, 118).

14. See Burros 1954 for a discussion of San Vitores's Chamorro catechism.

15. Of his buffoonery, García wrote: "Other people admire him for his great miracles; as for me, I admire him for the great zeal which made him do things so contrary to his nature, modesty, and seriousness. He played the madman, when he was most sane; and he played the buffoon, though he was so serious and religious" (2004, 184).

16. García said that San Vitores "thought he was doing nothing as long as he was not among Indios and the abandoned Gentiles. To him, these were the poorest and the blindest" (2004, 95).

17. A good synthesis of available information on the *uritao* is in Russell 1998, 148–152.

Chapter 6: Kinship with Matå'pang

1. The quote from Hezel graces the book's dust jacket.

2. But see Rafael's analyses of the administrative and bureaucratic headache that the Patronato Real created for itself by trying to maintain its "fiction" of representing God and king across the empire (Rafael 1993).

3. The antiabortion flap erupted only months after another event, former Governor Ricardo J Bordallo's dramatic suicide, the consequences of which also contained elements that exemplify the fine line between religion and politics in Chamorro political and cultural consciousness. For an elaboration, see Diaz 1993.

4. The *Vagina Monologues* is a national and international phenomenon, involving the theatrical staging of monologues from Ensler 2001. Based on hundreds of interviews with women of different ages, walks of life, and ethnicities, the *Vagina Monologues* offers powerful testimony to the violent effects of patriarchy on women's perceptions of their bodies, especially their vaginas, and was forged by inspiring stories of their political reclamation of these and other organs.

5. The *Family Rosary Hour* was conducted in English despite the fact that island-wide *fino' Chamorro* was still the principal medium for the majority of the Masses, novenas, and *lisåyus*. This difference marks the limits of comparing my own family's Catholic heritage to that of the Chamorros.

6. Or, in terms of the last chapter, one might envision San Vitores as the tailor who furnishes the Chamorro heathen the "proper attire" to attend the wedding banquet (by shedding his own robe and removing his glasses).

7. I thank my colleague Lawrence Cunningham for this observation.

8. Like Chamorros, Filipinos were infantilized.

9. For the moment, I am withholding accent marks to the term *matapang* because it is not yet clear how the older term was pronounced. Later in this chapter I return to some options as they implicate yet other meanings.

10. Another interesting discrepancy in details involves the way in which the local church has come to embrace the *catana* (machete), and San Vitores's (blood-stained) cassock, as holy reliquaries despite the fact that, in the written record, he was killed by a spear or a lance and his cassock was reportedly burnt. I thank Lawrence Cunningham for pointing out the discrepancy involving the *catana*.

11. I base this description on personal experience and study of traditional voyaging. A technical description along these lines is in Lewis 1994, 76–77. From 1994 to 1998, I served as the coordinator of the Micronesian Seafaring Society, a regional association of traditional canoe builders and navigators from every political entity in Micronesia. In 1999, I also co-founded with Dr Lawrence Cunningham the University of Guam traditional seafarers society, which included formal coursework, and building and sailing such outrigger canoes in 1997, 2000, and 2001 under the mentorship of the late Polowat navigators Sosthenis Emwalu and Chief Manipy, and in collaboration with *utts* (canoe houses) Wenemai and Wenebuku in Polowat. In 2001 we raised our own *utt*, the Sahyan Tasi Fachemwaan, at the Paseo in Hagåtña, where the group continues to hold courses and build and sail canoes under the mentorship of Manny Sikau, also from Polowat.

12. There are exceptions: Jesuit hagiographer Alberto Risco speculated that San Vitores was still alive in the canoe (1935, 163). Risco's is also the only account that indicates that San Vitores had no teeth.

13. Anson in Tinian provided a detailed description of the crafts while observing their "prodigious degree of swiftness" (Walter 1928, 322). As late as 1771, Crozet supplied another detailed description of Chamorro canoes and remarked that the Chamorros "preserved perfectly the art of making canoes from their forefathers" (Ling Roth 1932, 149). Although he recorded that the only canoes to be found in Guam today are the *galaide'*, the outrigger paddling canoe, Freycinet in 1821 was still able to record from his "informant" the names of the five other categories of Chamorro canoes, their riggings, and their designs. In his account, "canoe houses," "pilots," and "canoe launchings" pop up rather casually, considering that the canoe was supposed to have disappeared (Freycinet 1829, 75, 81, 95).

14. In 1829 Freycinet wrote, "They are still tireless swimmers and skillful divers"; he described "swimming games" and fishing skills (1829, 29–30, 97–98, 121–130). See also Russell 1998, 186, 195.

15. Another theory is that it derives from the phrase *hay chammu miya* ("welcome" or "come here") as it is said in the Itbayat dialect in Batanes, Philippines. This meaning was proposed by Dr Florentino Hornedo, professor of history at the University of Santo Tomas (de Viana 2004, 15–16n24).

16. Lévesque in conversation with author, May 1992. See also Jorgensen 1984, 38.

17. On the topic of technical accuracy, Cunningham observed correctly how the placement of the mast in relation to the sail and outrigger in the icon is erroneous and would cause this canoe, at least, to swamp (1992, 150). This fact alone could attest to the non-Native provenance of the design, unless the Native designer did not have knowledge of rigging an outrigger canoe.

18. I disagree with Diego's lumping together of Hezel, Rogers, and Stade. Each author has, in different ways and with different consequences, acknowledged Chamorro agency in their work. I discuss Hezel's work in chapter 4, and Rogers's in Diaz 1996. Stade's analysis of a distinct Chamorro cultural agency, which admittedly seems to be overpowered by the emphasis he places on the structuring agency of world cultures (namely, Spanish/Roman Catholicism and American liberalism) in Guam's history, is strongest in his discussion of Chamorro vernacular identity and culture.

19. This information derives from conversations with a former member of the Matapang Society whose name I will not divulge.

20. Reid, pers comm, 23 Nov 2006. By the latter argument, he means that the Proto-Malayo-Polynesian [*p*] is older or greater than the Chamorro [*f*].

21. Palomo had the benefit of seeing Dr Reid's initial findings before she made her own response.

22. Dr Reid also located "a matapang 'brave' with stress on the final syllable" in Casiguran Dumagat, a Negrito language, but he assumes it to have been borrowed from Tagalog ("with stress change") because this language "has been very heavily influenced by Tagalog" (Reid, pers comm, 25 Nov 2006).

References

Abella, Domingo
1962   *Vignettes of Philippines-Marianas Colonial History.* Manila: International Association of Historians of Asia.

Ada, Joseph, and Leland Bettis
1996   The Quest for Commonwealth, The Quest for Change. In *Kinalamten Pulitikåt: Siñenten I Chamorro (Issues in Guam's Political Development: The Chamorro Perspective)*, 125–203. Hale'-ta (Our Roots) Series. Agaña: Political Status Education Coordination Commission.

Aguon, Julian
2006   *Just Left of the Setting Sun: Essays for a Decolonizing Island.* Guam: Blue Ocean Press; Tokyo: Aoishima Research Institute.

Aguon, Katherine B
1977   Changing Patterns Due to Urbanization. In *Women of Guam*, edited by Cecilia Bamba, Laura Souder, and Judy Tompkins, 15–19. Agaña: The Guam Women's Conference.

Alvarez-Cristobal, Hope
1990   The Organization of Peoples for Indigenous Rights: A Commitment Towards Self-Determination. *Pacific Ties* [UCLA Asian Pacific American Magazine] 13 (4): 10–24.

Amore, Agostino, OFM [Order of Friars Minor (Capuchin)]
1981   Report of the Chairman of the Historical Commission. In *Positio* 1981b, 1–26.

Ansaldo, Marcelo
1971   Events that Transpired on June 15, 1668, on the Arrival of the Sanvitores Mission at Agaña Bay: An Eyewitness Account by Brother Marcelo Ansaldo, SJ, translated by Felicia Plaza, MMB. Reprinted in *Guam Recorder* 1 (1): 14–17.

Anzaldúa, Gloria
1987   *Borderlands/La Frontera: The New Mestiza.* San Francisco: Spinsters/Aunt Lute.

Apuron, Archbishop Anthony S
1991   Audiotaped interview with author. San Ramon, Guam, 3 April.

Arago, Jacques
1971   *Narrative of a Voyage Around the World.* New York: Da Capo Press.
[1982?] Recuerdos de un Ciego. Selecciones del Capitulo XXXIII, Islas Marianas. Viaje al Rededor del Mundo. Madrid: Gaspar y Roig (1851). Transcribed

and translated by Marjorie G Driver. Manuscript in Spanish Documents Collection, Micronesian Area Research Center.

Arévalo, Catalino G
  1998   *Pedro Calungsod: Young Visayan "Proto-Martyr," † 2 April 1672.* Manila: Archdiocese of Manila.

Arrayoz, Pastor
  1981   Extract from Monumento a un Misionero. In *Positio* 1981b, 658–661.

Ashcroft, Bill, Gareth Griffiths, and Helen Tiffin, editors
  2000   *Postcolonial Studies: Key Concepts.* New York: Routledge.

Attwater, Donald
  1986   *The Penguin Dictionary of Saints.* Harmondsworth, UK: Penguin Books.

Barratt, Glynn
  1996   *The Chamorros of the Mariana Islands: Early European Records 1521–1600.* Saipan: CNMI Division of Historic Preservation.

Barrett, Ward
  1975   *Mission in the Marianas: An Account of Father Diego Luis de Sanvitores and His Companions, 1669–1670.* Minneapolis: University of Minnesota Press.

Beardsley, Charles
  1964   *Guam: Past and Present.* Tokyo: Charles Tuttle.

Beatty, Janice
  1968   *Guam, Today and Yesterday.* Agaña: Guam Department of Education.

Behar, Ruth, and Deborah Gordon, editors
  1995   *Women Writing Culture.* Berkeley: University of California Press.

Bell, Rudolph
  1984   *Holy Anorexia.* Chicago: University of Chicago Press.

Benavente, John
  2001   Audiotaped interview with author. Inarajan, Guam, 6 March.

Berger, John
  1972   *Ways of Seeing.* London: Penguin.

Bettis, Leland
  1993a   Colonial Immigration of Guam. In *A World Perspective in Pacific Islander Migration: Australia, New Zealand and the USA,* edited by Grant McConnell and John Connell, 265–296. Kensington, NSW: Centre for South Pacific Studies.
  1993b   Commonwealth: Our Hope, Our Dream, Our Liberation. *Pacific Daily News,* 21 July, 32–33.

Bevacqua, Michael L
  2004   These May or May Not Be Americans: The Patriotic Myth and the Hijacking of Chamorro History on Guam. MA thesis, University of Guam, Mangilao.

Bhabha, Homi
  1984   Of Mimicry and Man: The Ambivalence of Colonial Discourse. *October* 28: 125–133.

Blaher, Damian J
  1949   *The Ordinary Processes in Causes of Beatification and Canonization: A Historical Synopsis and a Commentary.* Canon Law Studies 268. Washington, DC: The Catholic University of America Press.

Bordallo Hofschneider, Penelope
  2001   *A Campaign for Political Rights on the Island of Guam, 1899–1950.* Saipan: CNMI Division of Historic Preservation.
Brown, Peter
  1981   *The Cult of Saints: Its Rise and Function in Latin Christianity.* Chicago: University of Chicago Press.
Burney, James
  1967   *A Chronological History of the Voyages and Discoveries in the South Sea or Pacific Ocean.* Volume 3. New York: Da Capo Press.
Burros, E J
  1954   Sanvitores' Grammar and Catechism in the Mariana (or Chamorro) Language. *Anthropos* 49:934–960.
Bustillo, Lorenzo
  1981   Summary of the Events of the first year of the Mission in these Mariana Islands. May 15, 1669. In *Positio* 1981b, 337–353.
Calvo, Oscar L
  1991   Audiotaped interviews with author. Makati, Philippines, 13–18 January.
Calvo, Oscar L, editor
  1970   *The Apostle of the Marianas: The Life, Labors and Martyrdom of Ven. Diego Luis de San Vitores, 1627–1672,* by Alberto Risco. Translated from the Spanish by Juan M H Ledesma. Guam: Diocese of Agaña.
Camacho, Engracia D
  1991   Interview with author. Mache'che', Dedidu, Guam, 18 December.
Camacho, Keith Lujan
  1998   Enframing I TaoTao Tano': Colonialism, Militarism, and Tourism in Twentieth-century Guam. MA thesis, University of Hawai'i, Mānoa.
  2005   Cultures of Commemoration: The Politics of War, Memory and History in the Mariana Islands. PhD dissertation, University of Hawai'i, Mānoa.
Carano, Paul
  1973   The Heart of Guam: Dulce Nombre De Maria. *Guam Recorder* 3 (2): 17–18.
  1975   Who's Who in Guam's History. *Guam Recorder* 5 (1): 3–15.
Carano, Paul, and Pedro Sanchez
  1964   *A Complete History of Guam.* Rutland, VT: Charles Tuttle Co.
Carter, Rosa Roberto
  1997   Education in Guam to 1950: Island and Personal History. In *Guam History: Perspectives,* edited by Lee Carter, William Wuerch, and Rosa Roberto Carter, 1:181–218. Mangilao: Richard F Taitano Micronesian Area Research Center.
Caryl, Christian
  2007   US Military Embraces Guam: Why the US Military Is Pouring Forces into a Remote West Pacific Island. *Newsweek International,* 26 February. Also online at http://www.msnbc.msn.com/id/17202830/site/newsweek/ [accessed 27 Feb 2007]
Cates, Karl
  1985a Church Named for Blessed Diego. Biba, Sanvitores, Biba! *Pacific Daily News,* 10 November, 40.
  1985b San Vitores Legacy Intensifies. *Pacific Daily News,* 9 November, 1.

Champion, Greg, producer
   1985   *Apostle of the Marianas: Blessed Diego Luis de Sanvitores.* VHS, color, 30 min-
            utes. Agaña: Guam Cable TV.
Classen, Constance, David Howas, and Anthony Synnott, editors
   1994   *Aroma: Cultural History of Smell.* New York: Routledge.
Clifford, James
   1982   *Person and Myth: Maurice Leenhardt in the Melanesian World.* Berkeley: Uni-
            versity of California Press.
   1988   *The Predicament of Culture.* Cambridge, MA: Harvard University Press.
   1997   *Routes: Travel and Translation in the Late Twentieth Century.* Cambridge, MA:
            Harvard University Press.
   2001   Indigenous Articulations. *The Contemporary Pacific* 13:468–490.
   2003   *On the Edges of Anthropology (Interviews).* Chicago: Prickly Paradigm Press.
Clifford, James, and George Marcus, editors
   1986   *Writing Culture: The Poetics and Politics of Ethnography.* Berkeley: University
            of California Press.
Coomans, Peter
   1997   *History of the Mission in the Mariana Islands: 1667–1673.* Translated and
            edited by Rodrigue Lévesque. Occasional Historical Papers Series No 4.
            Saipan: CNMI Division of Historic Preservation, Department of Commu-
            nity and Cultural Affairs.
Costo, Rupert, and Jeannette Henry Costo, editors
   1987   *The Missions of California: A Legacy of Genocide.* San Francisco: Indian Histo-
            rian Press.
Crumrine, N Ross
   1982   Praying and Feasting: Modern Guamanian Fiestas. *Anthropos* 77:89–112.
Cunningham, Lawrence J
   1984   *Ancient Chamorro Kinship Organization.* Agat, Guam: L Joseph Press.
   1992   *Ancient Chamorro Society.* Honolulu: Bess Press.
   2005   Pre-Christian Chamorro Courtship and Marriage Practices Clash with
            Jesuit Teaching. In *Guam History: Perspectives,* edited by Lee D Carter, Wil-
            liam L Wuerch, and Rosa Roberto Carter, 2:60–80. Mangilao: Richard F
            Taitano Micronesian Area Research Center.
Curb, Rosemary, and Nancy Manahan
   1985   *Lesbian Nuns: Breaking the Silence.* Tallahassee, FL: Naiad Press.
Daly, Mary
   1985   *The Church and the Second Sex.* Boston: Beacon Press.
Dames, Vivian L
   2001   Out of the "Circle of Belonging": Rethinking American Citizenship from
            the Perspective of the Chamorros of Guam. PhD dissertation, University
            of Michigan, Ann Arbor.
   2003   Chamorro Women, Self-Determination, and the Politics of Abortion in
            Guam. In *Asian/Pacific Islander American Women: A Historical Anthology,*
            edited by Shirley Hune and Gail Nomura, 365–382. New York: New York
            University Press.
Dampier, William
   1729   *A Collection of Voyages.* Volume 4. London: Knapton.

de la Concepción, Juan
  1788–1792   *Historia general de Philipinas. Conquistas espirituales y temporales de estos españoles dominios, establecimientos, progresos y decadencias.* 14 volumes. Manila: Imprenta de los Dominicos.
de la Costa, Horacio
  1961   *The Jesuits in the Philippines, 1581–1768.* Cambridge, MA: Harvard University Press.
Delehaye, Hippolyte
  1961   *The Legends of Saints: An Introduction to Hagiography.* New York: University of Notre Dame Press.
DeLisle, Christine Taitano
  2001   Delivering the Body: Narratives of Family, Birth, and Prewar Pattera (Chamorro Nurse Midwives). MA thesis, University of Guam, Mangilao.
  2005   Navy Wives, Native Lives: Race, Gender, Empire and American Colonial Sentiment in Guam. Paper presented at the "Sovereignty Matters" conference, Columbia University, 15–16 April.
  2007   Tumuge' Påpa' (Writing It Down): Chamorro Midwives and the Delivery of Native History. In *Women Writing Oceania,* edited by J Kēhaulani Kauanui and Caroline Sinavaiana. Special issue of *Pacific Studies* 30 (1/2): 20–32.
  2008   Navy Wives/Native Lives: The Cultural and Historical Relations between American Naval Wives and Chamorro Women in Guam, 1898–1945. PhD dissertation, University of Michigan, Ann Arbor.
Deloria, Philip J
  1998   *Playing Indian.* New Haven, CT: Yale University Press.
Deloughrey, Elizabeth M
  2007   *Routes and Roots: Navigating Caribbean and Pacific Island Literatures.* Honolulu: University of Hawai'i Press.
Del Valle, Maria Teresa, MMB
  1972   Guam as Part of the Spanish Overseas Empire. *Guam Recorder* 2 (2–3): 41–43.
Dening, Greg
  1996   *Performances.* Chicago: University of Chicago Press.
Department of Chamorro Affairs
  2003   *Chamorro Heritage: A Sense of Place; Guidelines, Procedures and Recommendations for Authenticating Chamorro Heritage.* Agaña: Dipåttamenton I Kaohao Guinahan Chamorro (Department of Chamorro Affairs, Research, Publication and Training Division).
de Viana, Augusto V
  2004   *In the Far Islands: The Role of Natives from the Philippines in the Conquest, Colonization and Repopulation of the Mariana Islands, 1668–1903.* Manila: University of Santo Tomas.
Deville, Janice
  1985   Rome Pilgrimage Ends; Return Journey Begins. *Pacific Daily News,* 14 October, 1.
Dhareshwar, Vivek
  1989   Toward a Narrative Epistemology of the Postcolonial Predicament. *Inscriptions* [UC Santa Cruz Center for Cultural Studies] 5:135–157.

Diaz, Jonathan Blas
  2007   The Liberation Theology of the Chamorros of the Marianas. No Rest for the Awake: Minagehet Chamorro. Blog posting on 12 August, at http://minagahet.blogspot.com/2007/08/hafa-na-liberasion-4-liberation.html

Diaz, Vicente M
  1989   Restless Na(rra)tives. *Inscriptions* 5:5–75.
  1993   Pious Sites: Chamorro Culture Between Spanish Catholicism and American Liberalism. In *Cultures of United States Imperialism,* edited by Amy Kaplan and Donald E Pease, 312–339. Durham, NC: Duke University Press.
  1995a   Bye Bye Ms American Pie: Chamorros and Filipinos and the American Dream. *Isla: Journal of Micronesian Studies* 3 (1): 147–160.
  1995b   Grounding Flux in Guam's Cultural History. In *Work in Flux,* edited by Emma Greenwood, Andrew Sartori, and Klaus Neumann, 159–171. Melbourne: Melbourne University History Conference Series 1.
  1996   Review essay of *Destiny's Landfall,* by Robert Rogers. *Isla: Journal of Micronesian Studies* 4 (2): 179–199.
  1998   Paved with Good Intentions: Roads, Citizenship and a Century of American Colonialism in Guam. Paper presented at the "Legacies of 1898 Summer Seminar," Obermann Center for Advanced Studies, University of Iowa, July.
  2000   Simply Chamorro: Tales of Survival and Demise in Guam. In *Voyaging Through the Contemporary Pacific,* edited by David Hanlon and Geoffrey White, 141–170. Lanham, MD: Rowman & Littlefield. First published in *The Contemporary Pacific* 6:29–58 (1994).
  2001   Deliberating Liberation Day: Memory, Culture and History in Guam. In *Perilous Memories: The Asia-Pacific War(s),* edited by Geoff White, Takahashi Fujitani, and Lisa Yoneyami, 155–180. Durham, NC: Duke University Press.
  2002a   Fight Boys till the Last: Football and the Remasculinization of Indigeneity in Guam. In *Pacific Diaspora: Island Peoples in the United States and the Pacific,* edited by Paul Spickard, Joanne Rondilla, and Deborah Hippolite Wright, 167–194. Honolulu: University of Hawai'i Press.
  2002b   Pappy's House: History and Memory of an American "Sixty-Cents" in Guam. In *Vestiges of War: The Philippine American War and the Aftermath of an Imperial Dream,* edited by Luis Francia and Angel Shaw, 318–328. New York: New York University Press.
  2004   Political Rights on the Island of Guam. Review Essay on *A Campaign for Political Rights On The Island Of Guam, 1899–1950,* by Penelope Bordallo Hofschneider. *Micronesian Journal of the Humanities and Social Sciences* 3 (1/2): 94–100.
  2005   Moving Islands of Sovereignty. Presented at the "Sovereignty Matters" conference, Columbia University, 15–16 April.
  2006   Creolization and Indigeneity. Commentary on V Munasinghe. *American Ethnologist* 33 (4): 576–578.

Diaz, Vicente M, and J Kēhaulani Kauanui, editors
  2001   Introduction. *Native Pacific Cultural Studies on the Edge.* Special issue of *The Contemporary Pacific* 13:315–342.

Diego, Vincent P
nd   Matatnga: A Cultural History of the Concept and a Homage to Chief
      Hurao. Manuscript. Copy in author's files.
Driver, Marjorie G
1971   Historical Documents from Mexico. *Guam Recorder* 1 (1): 18–19.
1972   Mariana de Austria. *Guam Recorder* 2 (2–3): 39–41.
1988   Cross, Sword, and Silver: The Nascent Spanish Colony in the Mariana
       Islands. *Pacific Studies* 2 (3): 21–51.
Dueñas, John Borja
1991   Interview with author. Seal Beach, California, 24 August.
Dugan, Paul F
1956   The Early History of Guam, 1521–1698. MA thesis, San Diego State
       College.
During, Simon, editor
1993   *The Cultural Studies Reader.* New York: Routledge.
Ensler, Eve
2001   *The Vagina Monologues.* Revised edition. New York: Villard.
Ezquerra, Francisco, Gerardo Bouwens, Pedro Coomans, Antonio Maria de San
       Basilio, Tomas Cardeñoso, and Alonzo Lopez
1981   Historical Narrative of Events in the Mariana Islands from 1667–1673. In
       Positio 1981b, 496–501.
Fanon, Frantz
1965   *The Wretched of the Earth.* New York: Grove Press.
Farrell, Don A
1991   *History of the Commonwealth of the Northern Marianas.* First edition. Saipan:
       CNMI Government.
1994   The Partition of the Marianas: A Diplomatic History. *Isla: Journal of Micro-
       nesian Studies* 2 (2): 273–301.
Flores, Evelyn S M
2002   Rewriting Paradise: Countering Desire, Denial, and the Exotic in Ameri-
       can Literary Representations of the Pacific. PhD dissertation, University
       of Michigan, Ann Arbor.
Flores, Felixberto C, DD
1985   Blessed Diego San Vitores. Pastoral Letter. *Pacific Voice*, 6 October, 1.
Fogel, Daniel
1988   *Junípero Serra, the Vatican, and Enslavement Theology.* San Francisco: ISM
       Press.
Foley, Robert C
2002   Motivation for Martyrdom: The Death of Diego Luis de San Vitores. MA
       thesis, University of Guam, Mangilao.
Forbes, Eric
1997   The Origins of Protestantism in Guam. In *Guam History: Perspectives,*
       edited by Lee Carter, William Wuerch, and Rosa Roberto Carter, 1:123–
       140. Mangilao: Richard F Taitano Micronesian Area Research Center.
Freycinet, Louis Claude de Saulces de
1829   *Voyage Autour du Monde.* Volume 2. Paris: Phillet Aine. Microfilm reel 58,
       unedited translation. New Haven: Yale University Human Relations Area
       Files Ms 1410. Located in Micronesian Area Research Center, Mangilao.

García, Francisco
  1683   *Vida y Martirio de el Venerable Padre Diego Luis de Sanvitores de la Compania de Jesus, Primer Apostol de las Islas Marianas.* Madrid: Juan Garcia Infanzon.
  2004   *The Life and Martyrdom of the Venerable Father Diego Luis de San Vitores of the Society of Jesus, First Apostle of the Mariana Islands, and Events of These Islands From the Year Sixteen Hundred and Sixty-Eight Through the Year Sixteen Hundred and Eighty-One.* Translated by Margaret M Higgins, Felicia Plaza, and Juan M H Ledesma; edited by James A McDonough, SJ. Mangilao: Richard Flores Taitano Micronesian Area Research Center.

Gault, Cathy Sablan
  1985   A Gift From Up There. Biba, San Vitores, Biba! *Pacific Daily News,* 10 November, 32, 37–39.

Geertz, Clifford
  1973   Deep Play: Notes on the Balinese Cockfight. In *The Interpretation of Cultures: Selected Essays,* 412–453. New York: Basic Books.

Gegeo, David
  2001   Cultural Rupture and Indigeneity: The Challenge of (Re)visioning "Place" in the Pacific. *The Contemporary Pacific* 13:491–508.

Gilby, Thomas
  1967   Martyrdom, Theology of. *New Catholic Encyclopedia* 9:314–315.

Gilroy, Paul
  1987   *There Ain't No Black in the Union Jack: The Cultural Politics of Race and Nation.* London: Hutchinson.
  1993   *Black Atlantic: Double Consciousness and Modernity.* Cambridge, MA: Harvard University Press.

Goodich, Michael
  1982   *Vita Perfecta: The Ideal of Sainthood in the Thirteenth Century.* Stuttgart: Anton Hiersemann.

Goodman, Amy
  1990   Guam: Territory in Turmoil. *On the Issues* [upstate New York quarterly on women's health issues, published by Choices 1980s–1990s] Winter: 14–15, 37–38.

Green, A E
  1967   Beatification. *New Catholic Encyclopedia* 2:193.

Grossberg, Lawrence, Cary Nelson, and Paula Treichler, editors
  1992   *Cultural Studies.* London: Routledge.

Guam Daily News
  1970   Color, Cable TV Starts Next Week! *Guam Daily News,* 26 August, 1.

Guam Museum
  1991   I Minagahet: An Exhibition of Selected Prints and Documents Depicting A Glimpse of Guam's Political History. Traveling Exhibit Brochure, 3–4 August. Agaña: Guam Museum.

Guam Newsletter
  1911a   Guam in the Future. *Guam Newsletter* 3 (3/4): 1–2.
  1911b   Guam in the Past. *Guam Newsletter* 3 (2): 1.

Hall, Lisa, and J Kēhaulani Kauanui
  1994   Same-Sex Sexuality in Pacific Literature. In *Asian American Sexualities,* edited by Russell Leong, 113–118. New York: Routledge.

Hall, Stuart
  1986a Gramsci's Relevance for the Study of Race and Ethnicity. *Journal of Communication Inquiry* 10 (2): 5–27.
  1986b On Postmodernism and Articulation: An Interview with Stuart Hall. *Journal of Communication Inquiry* 10 (2): 45–60.
  1992 Cultural Studies and its Theoretical Legacies. In *Cultural Studies,* edited by Lawrence Grossberg, Cary Nelson, and Paula Treichler, 277–294. New York: Routledge.
  1996 Race, Articulation, and Societies Structured in Dominance. In *Black British Cultural Studies: A Reader,* edited by Houston A Baker Jr, Manthia Diawara, and Ruth H Lindeborg, 16–60. Chicago: University of Chicago Press.
Handler, Richard, and Jocelyn Linnekin
  1983 Tradition, Genuine or Spurious. *Journal of American Folklore* 97:273–290.
Hanlon, David
  1988 *Upon a Stone Altar: A History of the Island of Pohnpei to 1890.* Pacific Islands Monograph Series 5. Honolulu: Center for Pacific Islands Studies and University of Hawai'i Press.
  1999 Magellan's Chroniclers? American Anthropology's History in Micronesia. In *American Anthropology in Micronesia: An Assessment,* edited by Robert Kiste and Mac Marshall, 53–78. Honolulu: University of Hawai'i Press.
  2001 Converting Pasts and Presents: Reflections on Histories of Missionary Enterprises in the Pacific. In *Pacific Lives, Pacific Places: Bursting Boundaries in Pacific History,* edited by Brij V Lal and Peter Hempenstall, 143–154. Canberra: The Journal of Pacific History.
  2004 *Wone Sohte Lohdi:* History and Place on Pohnpei. In *Pacific Places, Pacific Histories,* edited by Brij V Lal, 195–215. Honolulu: University of Hawai'i Press.
Hanlon, David, and Geoffrey M White, editors
  2000 *Voyaging Through the Contemporary Pacific.* Lanham, MD: Rowman & Littlefield. Publishers, Inc.
Hanson, Allan F
  1989 The Making of the Maori: Culture Invention and Its Logic. *American Anthropologist* 91:890–902.
Haraway, Donna J
  1989 *Primate Visions: Gender, Race, and Nature in the World of Modern Science.* New York: Routledge.
  1991 *Simians, Cyborgs, and Women: The Reinvention of Nature.* New York: Routledge.
Hattori, Anne
  1995 Righting Civil Wrongs: The Guam Congress Walkout of 1949. *Isla: Journal of Micronesian Studies* 3 (1): 1–27.
  2004 *Colonial Dis-Ease: US Navy Health Policies and the Chamorros of Guam, 1898–1941.* Pacific Islands Monograph Series 19. Honolulu: Center for Pacific Islands Studies and University of Hawai'i Press.
Hau'ofa, Epeli
  2000 Epilogue: Pasts to Remember. In *Remembrance of Pacific Pasts: An Invitation to Remake History,* edited by Robert Borofsky, 453–471. Honolulu: University of Hawai'i Press.

Haverlandt, Ronald
nd   Of Ocean Foxes and Guilty Wolves: The Beforetime People, Their Epic Response To Modern Power. Literary Agent. Manuscript available at the Micronesian Area Research Center and the Guam Bureau of Planning.

Hempenstall, Peter, and Noel Rutherford
1984   Violent Protest. In *Protest and Dissent in the Colonial Pacific*, 87–118. Suva, Fiji: University of the South Pacific.

Hezel, Francis X
1982   From Conversion to Conquest: The Early Spanish Mission in the Marianas. *Journal of Pacific History* 17 (3): 115–137.

1985   *Hinanao I Hinengge: Be'atu Diego di Marianas (Journey of Faith)*. Education Committee for the Beatification of Blessed Diego of the Marianas. Agaña: Guam Atlas Publication.

Hezel, Francis X, and Marjorie G Driver
1988   From Conquest to Colonization: Spain in the Mariana Islands 1690–1740. *Journal of Pacific History* 23 (2): 137–155.

Higgins, Margaret M, translator
1936a   *Recorder* to Run New Series: First History of Guam. *Guam Recorder* 13 (6) [Sept]: 3, 5, 39.

1936b   First History of Guam, Part 2. *Guam Recorder* 13 (8) [Nov]: 10–11, 27.

1937a   First History of Guam, Part 7. *Guam Recorder* 14 (1) [April]: 18–21, 36, 38–39.

1937b   First History of Guam, Part 8. *Guam Recorder* 14 (2) [May]: 18–21.

1938   First History of Guam, Part 19. *Guam Recorder* 15 (2) [May]: 14–16, 38–40.

1939   First History of Guam, Part 31. *Guam Recorder* 16 (3) [June]: 101–103; 122–124.

Hinnebusch, W A
1967   Rosary. *New Catholic Encyclopedia* 12:667–670.

Howe, Bob
1984   Letter to the Editor. *Pacific Daily News*, 21 April, 26.

Hviding, Edvard
2003   Between Knowledges: Pacific Studies and Academic Disciplines. *The Contemporary Pacific* 15:43–73.

Ige, Ron
1990   Bordallo Known as Dreamer, Builder: Lived life of Triumph and Loss. *Pacific Daily News*, 1 February, 3.

Images
1987   *English the Chamorro Way*. Agaña: Images.

Iyechad, Lilli Ann Perez
2001   *An Historical Perspective of Helping Practices Associated with Birth, Marriage, and Death Among Chamorros in Guam*. Lewiston, NY: The Edwin Mellen Press.

Jameson, Fredric
1981   *The Political Unconscious: Narrative as a Socially Symbolic Act*. Ithaca, NY: Cornell University Press.

Jolly, Margaret
1992   Specters of Inauthenticity. *The Contemporary Pacific* 4:49–72.

1996   From Point Venus to Bali Ha'i: Eroticism and Exoticism in Representations of the Pacific. In *Sites of Desire/Economies of Pleasure: Sexualities in Asia and the Pacific,* edited by Lenore Manderson and Margaret Jolly, 99–122. Chicago: University of Chicago Press.

1997   White Shadows in the Darkness: Representations of Polynesian Women in Early Cinema. In *Representation and Photography of the Pacific Islands,* edited by Max Quanchi. Special issue of *Pacific Studies* 20 (4): 125–150.

2001   On the Edge? Deserts, Oceans, Islands. *The Contemporary Pacific* 13:417– 466.

2003   Our Sea of Islands or Archipelagoes of Autarchy? Some Preliminary Reflections on Transdisciplinary Navigation and Learning Oceania. Paper presented at the "Learning Oceania: Towards a PhD Program in Pacific Studies" workshop, Center for Pacific Islands Studies, University of Hawai'i, Mānoa, 13–15 November.

Jolly, Margaret, editor
2008   *Re-membering Oceanic Masculinities.* Special Issue of *The Contemporary Pacific* 20:1.

Jolly, Margaret, and Nicholas Thomas
1992   The Politics of Tradition in the Pacific: Introduction. *Oceania* 62 (4): 241–248.

Jorgensen, Marilyn Anne
1984   Expressive Manifestations of Santa Marian Camalin as Key Symbol in Guamanian Culture. (Also found under the title "Guam's Patroness: Santa Marian Kamalen.") PhD dissertation, University of Texas, Austin.

Kame'eleihiwa, Lilikalā
1992   *Native Land and Foreign Desires: Pehea Lā E Pono Ai?* Honolulu: Bishop Museum Press.

Kauanui, J Kēhaulani
1998   Off-Island Hawaiians "Making" Ourselves at "Home": A (Gendered) Contradiction in Terms? *Women's Studies International Forum* 21 (6): 681–693.

1999   "For Get" Hawaiian Entitlement: Configuration of Land, Blood and Americanization in the Hawaiian Homes Act of 1921. *Social Text* 17 (2): 123–144.

2005   Precarious Positions: Native Hawaiian and US Federal Recognition. *The Contemporary Pacific* 17:1–27.

2007   Diasporic Deracination and "Off-Island" Hawaiians. *The Contemporary Pacific* 19:138–160.

2008   *Hawaiian Blood: Colonialism and the Politics of Sovereignty and Indigeneity (Narrating Native Histories).* Durham, NC: Duke University Press.

Keesing, Roger M
1989   Creating the Past: Custom and Identity in the Contemporary Pacific. *The Contemporary Pacific* 1:19–42.

1991   Reply to Trask. *The Contemporary Pacific* 3:168–172.

Keesing, Roger M, and Robert Tonkinson, editors
1982   *Reinventing Traditional Culture: The Politics of Kastom in Island Melanesia.* Special issue of *Mankind* 13(4).

Kemp, Jamie
1985a   Sanvitores Beatification Tomorrow; Novena to End. Biba, Sanvitores, Biba! *Pacific Daily News,* 10 November, 31.

1985b   Sanvitores Not a Hero to All on Guam. *Pacific Daily News,* 4 October, 3.

1985c   Shrine Not in Ideal Location. *Pacific Daily News,* 21 September, 36.

Kennedy, Eugene C
2001   *The Unhealed Wound: The Catholic Church and Human Sexuality.* New York: St Martin's Press.

King, Noel
1990   Interview with author. Santa Cruz, California, 1 May.

Kumision I Fino' Chamorro
1992   *Nå'an Lugat Siha Gi Ya Guåhan (Guam Place Names).* Hagåtña: Kumision I Fino' Chamorro.

Kushima, Kayoko
2001   Historiographies of Guam and Discourses of Isolation: Canonical and Alternative Historical Narratives. MA thesis, University of Guam, Mangilao.

Lal, Brij V, editor
2004   *Pacific Places, Pacific Histories.* Honolulu: University of Hawai'i Press.

Lal, Brij V, and Peter Hempenstall, editors
2001   *Pacific Lives, Pacific Places: Bursting Boundaries in Pacific History.* Canberra: The Journal of Pacific History.

Lawcock, Larry
1977   Guam Women: A Hasty History. In *Women of Guam,* edited by Cecilia Bamba, Laura Souder, and Judy Tompkins, 7–11. Agaña: The Guam Women's Conference.

Lazarus, Neil
2004   *The Cambridge Companion to Postcolonial Literary Studies.* Cambridge, UK: Cambridge University Press.

Ledesma, Andres
1981a   Account of the Happy Death of the Venerable Father Diego Luis de Sanvitores taken from various papers which have come from the Mariana Islands [1674]. In *Positio* 1981b, 450–463.

1981b   Events in the Mariana Islands from the year 1669 up to the present year of 1672. [1672]. In *Positio* 1981b, 465–469.

Ledesma, Juan
1991   Audiotaped interview with author. Santa Ana, Philippines, 18 January.

LeGobien, Charles
1949   *Histoire des Isles Marianes.* Paris: Pepie (1700). Translated from the French by Paul V Daly. Manuscript in Nieves Flores Library, Agaña.

Lévesque, Rodrigue
1993   *History of Micronesia: A Collection of Source Documents.* Volume 2: *Prelude to Conquest 1561–1595.* Quebec: Lévesque Publications.

1995   *History of Micronesia: A Collection of Source Documents.* Volume 4: *Religious Conquest, 1638–1670.* Quebec, Canada: Lévesque Publications.

Levine, H B
1991   Comment on Hanson's "The Making of the Maori." *American Anthropologist* 93:444–446.

Lewis, David
1994   *We, the Navigators: The Ancient Art of Landfinding in the Pacific.* Second edition. Honolulu: University Press of Hawai'i.

Lewis, Reina, and Sara Mills, editors
   2003   *Feminist Postcolonial Theory: A Reader.* New York: Routledge.
Libreria Editrice Vaticana (Vatican Publishing House)
   1985   Misa De Beatificación De Tres Siervos De Dios: Diego Luis De San Vitores
          Alonso, José María Rubio y Peralta, Y Francisco Gárate Aranguren. Hom-
          ily by Holy Father John Paul II, Sunday, 6 October. Available online at
          http://www.vatican.va/holy_father/john_paul_ii/homilies/1985/docu-
          ments/hf_jp-ii_hom_19851006_beatificazione-tre-gesuiti_sp.html#top
          [accessed 20 Aug 2007]
Lindstrom, Lamont, and Geoffrey White
   1993   Introduction: Custom Today. *Anthropological Forum* 6 (4): 468–473.
Ling Roth, H, translator
   1932   Crozet's Voyage to Tasmania, New Zealand, the Ladrone Island, and the
          Philippine Islands in the Years 1771–1772. *Guam Recorder* 9 (11): 130–132,
          137; 9 (12): 148–151, 156.
Linnekin, Jocelyn
   1983   Defining Tradition: Variations on the Hawaiian Identity. *American Ethnolo-
          gist* 10: 241–252.
   1990   The Politics of Culture in the Pacific. In *Cultural Identity and Ethnicity in
          the Pacific,* edited by Jocelyn Linnekin and Lin Poyer, 1–16. Honolulu:
          University of Hawai'i Press.
   1991a Cultural Invention and the Dilemma of Authenticity. *American Anthropolo-
          gist* 93:446–449.
   1991b Text Bites and the R-Word: The Politics of Representing Scholarship. *The
          Contemporary Pacific* 3:172–177.
   1992   On the Theory and Politics of Cultural Construction in the Pacific. *Ocea-
          nia* 62 (4): 249–263.
Linnekin, Jocelyn, and Lin Poyer, editors
   1990   *Cultural Identity and Ethnicity in the Pacific.* Honolulu: University of Hawai'i
          Press.
Loomba, Ania
   1998   *Colonialism/Postcolonialism.* New York: Routledge.
Lopez, Alonzo
   1981   Compendio de la vida del Apostolico Padre Diego Luis de Sanvitores de
          la Compania de Jesus y apostol de las islas Marianas donde derramo su
          sangre por la santa fe de Cristo [1673]. In *Positio* 1981b, 582–586.
L'Osservatore Romano
   1981   Meeting With the People. *L'Osservatore Romano* [*The Roman Observer;* Vati-
          can newspaper], 2 March, 19.
MacLeod, Roy, and Philip F Rehbock, editors
   1988   *Nature in its Greatest Extent: Western Science in the Pacific.* Honolulu: Univer-
          sity of Hawai'i Press.
Maguire, Daniel C
   2004   Sex and the Sacred. *Cross Currents* 54 (3). Available online at http://www.
          crosscurrents.org/Maguire0304.htm [accessed 23 March 2007]
   2008   *Whose Church? A Concise Guide to Progressive Catholicism.* New York: The New
          Press.

MARC, Micronesian Area Research Center
    1985   The Cause of Beatification: San Vitores Materials Now Available at MARC.
            Press Release, 5 September.
Maruchi, Orazio
    1908   Archeology of the Cross and Crucifix. *The Catholic Encyclopedia* 4. New York:
            Robert Appleton Company. Available online at http://www.newadvent.
            org/cathen/04517a.htm [accessed 3 August 2007]
Marvin, Garry
    1984   The Cockfight in Andalusia, Spain: Images of the Truly Male. *Anthropologi-
            cal Quarterly* 57 (2): 60–70.
Matson, Ernest A
    1991   Water Chemistry and Hydrology of the "Blood of Sanvitores": A Microne-
            sian Red Tide. *Micronesica* 24 (1): 95–108.
Mayo, Larry
    1984   Occupations and Chamorro Social Status: A Study of Urbanization in
            Guam. PhD dissertation, University of California, Berkeley.
McGrath, Thomas
    1972   A Man Determined. *Guam Recorder* 2 (2–3): 43–45.
    1985   *Blessed Diego of the Marianas (Be'atu Diego di Marianas: I Nubena Para Si).*
            Agaña: Guam Atlas Publications.
McGregor, Davianna Pōmaika'i
    2007   *Nā Kua'āina: Living Hawaiian Culture.* Honolulu: University of Hawai'i Press.
Meagher, P K
    1967   Novena. *New Catholic Encyclopedia* 10:543–544.
Memmi, Albert
    1965   *The Colonizer and the Colonized.* Boston: Beacon Press.
Mesa, Maria "Tita" Pangelinan Leon Guerrero
    1992   Audiotaped interview with author. Tumon, Guam, 10 February.
Micklethwait, John, and Adrian Wooldridge
    2004   *The Right Nation: Conservative Power in America.* New York: Penguin.
Molinari, Paulo
    1967   Canonization of Saints: History and Procedure. *New Catholic Encyclopedia*
            3:55–59.
Monnig, Laurel
    2007   Proving Chamorro: Indigenous Narratives of Race, Identity, and Decol-
            onization on Guam. PhD dissertation, University of Illinois, Urbana-
            Champaign.
Moraga, Cherríe
    1983   *A Long Line of Vendidas: Loving in the War Years.* Boston: South End Press.
Moraga, Cherríe, and Gloria Anzaldúa, editors
    1981   *This Bridge Called My Back: Writings by Radical Women of Color.* New York:
            Kitchen Table, Women of Color Press.
Morley, David, and Kuan-Hsin Chen, editors
    1996   *Stuart Hall: Critical Dialogues in Cultural Studies.* London: Routledge.
Munoz, Faye Untalan
    1977   Family Life Patterns of Pacific Islanders. In *Women of Guam,* edited by
            Cecilia Bamba, Laura Souder, and Judy Tompkins, 27–32. Agaña: The
            Guam Women's Conference.

Murphy, Joseph
    1988   *Santería: An African Religion in America*. Boston: Beacon Press.
Murphy, F X
    1967   Martyr. *New Catholic Encyclopedia* 9:312–314.
Nā Maka o ka 'Āina
    1993   *Act of War: The Overthrow of the Hawaiian Nation*. VHS Color, 59 minutes. Honolulu: Nā Maka o ka 'Āina Productions.
Najita, Susan
    2006   *Decolonizing Cultures in the Pacific*. New York: Routledge.
Navy News
    1946   Guam Vicariate Shifted to US. *Navy News*, 11 January, 17.
Neill, Stephen
    1986   *A History of Christian Missions*. Revised edition. London: Penguin Books.
Nelson, Cary, and Lawrence Grossberg, editors
    1988   *Marxism and the Interpretation of Culture*. Chicago: University of Illinois.
Olano, Miguel Ángel de
    1949   *Diary of a Bishop*. Manila: University of Santo Tomas Press.
Olive y García, Francisco
    1984   *The Mariana Islands 1884–1887: Random Notes concerning Them*. Translated from the Spanish and annotated by Marjorie G Driver. Mangilao, Guam: Micronesian Area Research Center, University of Guam.
Oliver, Douglas
    1979   *The Pacific Islands*. Honolulu: University of Hawai'i Press.
O'Neill, C
    1967   Saint. *New Catholic Encyclopedia* 12:852–853.
Osorio, Jonathan Kamakawiwo'ole
    1992   Songs of Our Natural Selves: The Enduring Voice of Nature in Hawaiian Music. In *Pacific History: Papers from the Eighth Pacific History Association Conference*, edited by Donald Rubinstein, 429–432. Mangilao: University of Guam Press and Micronesian Area Research Center.
    2001   "What Kine Hawaiian Are You?" A Mo'olelo about Nationhood, Race, History, and the Contemporary Sovereignty Movement in Hawai'i. *The Contemporary Pacific* 13:359–379.
    2002   *Dismembering Lāhui: A History of the Hawaiian Nation to 1887*. Honolulu: University of Hawai'i Press.
Pacific Voice
    1974a   Bishop on Rome: "I came away with a completely different impression." *Pacific Voice*, 11 August, 1.
    1974b   Interview with Pablo Molinari. *Pacific Voice*, 18 August, 1, 3.
    1985a   Decree, Sacred Congregation for the Causes of Saints. *Pacific Voice*, 31 March, 1, 3.
    1985b   A Great Way to Help San Vitores Fund. Advertisement. *Pacific Voice*, 30 June, 1.
    1985c   Knights of Columbus Donate for Sanvitores Statue. *Pacific Voice*, 24 March, 1.
    1985d   Knights Spearhead Fund Drive. *Pacific Voice*, 10 February, 1.
    1985e   US Stamp Honoring San Vitores Proposed. *Pacific Voice*, 13 October, 1.

References

Pagels, Elaine
1987   *Adam, Eve, and the Serpent.* New York: Random House.
Palomo, Benigno
2000   Women Have Always Held a Special Place in Traditional Chamorro Culture. *Pacific Daily News,* 5 May.
Palomo, Tony
1984   *An Island in Agony.* Agaña: T Palomo.
PDN, Pacific Daily News
1985a   Biba, Sanvitores, Biba! Special supplement, 56 pages. *Pacific Daily News,* 10 November.
1985b   The Blessed One. Biba, Sanvitores, Biba! *Pacific Daily News,* 10 November, 13–14; 41–55.
1985c   Chamorros Make History. Biba, Sanvitores, Biba! *Pacific Daily News,* 10 November, 33–34.
1985d   Elderly Priest Wins Pilgrims' Hearts: Jesuit Recognizes Hymns' Tunes. Biba, Sanvitores, Biba! *Pacific Daily News,* 10 November, 27.
1985e   Five Hundred Islanders to Travel to Vatican. Biba, Sanvitores, Biba! *Pacific Daily News,* 10 November, 19.
1985f   Notes from a Participant Observer. Biba, Sanvitores, Biba! *Pacific Daily News,* 10 November, 2.
1985g   One Step From Sainthood. Biba, Sanvitores, Biba! *Pacific Daily News,* 10 November, 20.
1985h   Pope Addresses Marianas Pilgrims. *Pacific Daily News,* 9 October, 3.
1985i   San Vitores Fund Gets Carnival Profits. Biba, Sanvitores, Biba! *Pacific Daily News,* 10 November, 18.
1985j   Statue to be Unveiled: Blessed Be Sanvitores. Biba, Sanvitores, Biba! *Pacific Daily News,* 10 November, 32.
Perez, Cecilia T
1996   A Chamorro Retelling of "Liberation." In *Kinalamten Pulitikåt: Siñenten I Chamorro (Issues in Guam's Political Development: The Chamorro Perspective),* 70–77. Agaña: Guam Political Status Education Coordination Commission.
1997   Signs of Being: A Chamoru Spiritual Being. MA Plan B paper, University of Hawai'i, Mānoa.
Perez, Ginger
1985   Spanish Martyr the Saving Grace for the Marianas. *Pacific Daily News,* 11 November, 1, 4.
Perez, Michael P
1997   The Dialectic of Indigenous Identity in the Wake of Colonialism: The Case of Chamorros of Guam. PhD dissertation. University of California, Riverside.
2005   Chamorro Resistance and Prospects for Sovereignty in Guam. In *Sovereignty Matters: Locations of Contestation and Possibility in Indigenous Struggles for Self-Determination,* edited by Joanne Barker, 169–190. Lincoln: University of Nebraska Press.
Perez, Remedios L G, and Alice W Wygant
1951   *Guam Past and Present.* Agaña: Guam Department of Education.

Perez-Howard, Chris
  1993   Thoughts and Confession of a Chamorro Advocate. In *Hinasso': Tinige'
         Put Chamorro (Insights: The Chamorro Perspective)*, 154–161. Hale'-ta Series.
         Agaña: Political Status Education Coordination Commission.
Pesch, William
  2002   Praying Against the Tide: Challenges Facing the Early Protestant Mission-
         aries to Guam, 1900–1910. MA thesis, University of Guam, Mangilao.
Pigafetta, Antonio
  1969   *Magellan's Voyage: A Narrative Account of the First Circumnavigation.*
         Volume 1, translated and edited by R A Skelton. New Haven: Yale
         University.
Plaza, Felicia, MMB
  1972   Companions of San Vitores. *Guam Recorder* 2 (2–3): 46–48.
  1980   *Sanvitores in the Marianas.* MARC Working Paper 22. Mangilao: Microne-
         sian Area Research Center.
Poehlman, Joanne
  1979   Culture Change and Identity Among Chamorro Women. PhD disserta-
         tion, University of Minnesota, Minneapolis.
Positio [Positio Super Vita et Martyrio Ex Officio Concinnaia]
  1981a Authentic Information that Was Made in the Mariana Islands on the
         Glorious Death for Christ of the Apostle of Those Islands the Venerable
         Father Diego Luis de San Vitores. A copy. In *Positio* 1981b, 474–484.
  1981b *The Cause of the Beatification of Ven Diego Luis de Sanvitores, Apostle of the
         Marianas. Deposition on the Life and Martyrdom,* compiled and translated by
         Fr Juan Ledesma, SJ. Rome: The Sacred Congregation for the Causes of
         Saints, Historical Section 94.
Priest, Robert J
  2001   Missionary Positions: Christian, Modernist, Postmodernist. *Current Anthro-
         pology* 42 (1): 29–68.
PSECC, Political Status Education Coordinating Commission
  1993a *Hale'-ta: Hestorian Taotao Tano' (History of the Chamorro People).* Hale'-
         ta Series. Agaña: Guam Political Status Education Coordinating
         Commission.
  1993b *Hinasso': Tinige' Put Chamorro (Insights: The Chamorro Identity).* Hale'-ta Series.
         Agaña: Guam Political Status Education Coordinating Commission.
  1994   *I Ma Gubetna-ña Guam (Governing Guam: Before and After the Wars).*
         Hale'-ta Series. Agaña: Guam Political Status Education Coordinating
         Commission.
  1995   *I Manfâyi (Who's Who in Chamorro History).* Volume 1. Hale'-ta Series.
         Agaña: Guam Political Status Education Coordinating Commission.
  1996a *Inafa'maolek: Chamorro Tradition and Values.* Hale'-ta Series. Agaña: Guam
         Political Status Education Coordinating Commission.
  1996b *Kinalamten Pulitikåt: Siñenten I Chamorro (Issues in Guam's Political Devel-
         opment: The Chamorro Perspective).* Hale'-ta Series. Agaña: Guam Political
         Status Education Coordinating Commission.
Quitugua, David C
  1995   The Vicar Apostolic in the 1983 Code of Canon Law. PhD dissertation,
         Pontifical University of Saint Thomas Aquinas, Rome.

240 References

Radao, Florentino
2005 Monsignor Olano, a Bishop in World War II. *Micronesian Journal of the Humanities and Social Sciences* 4 (2): 85–101.
Rafael, Vicente
1989 Imagination and Imagery: Philippine Nationalism in the Nineteenth Century. *Inscriptions* 5:25–48.
1993 *Contracting Colonialism: Translation and Christian Conversion in Tagalog Society Under Early Spanish Rule.* Durham, NC: Duke University Press.
Ranke-Heinemann, Uta
1990 *Eunuchs for the Kingdom of Heaven: Women, Sexuality, and the Catholic Church.* New York: Doubleday.
Riding, Alan
1989 Vatican "Saint Factory": Is It Working Too Hard? *New York Times*, 15 April, 5.
Risco, Alberto
1935 *En Las Islas de los Ladrones: El Apóstol de las Marianas, Diego Luis de San Vitores de la Compañia de Jesús.* Bilbao: Cultura Misional.
Rivera, Ron F
1992 Organization of People for Indigenous Rights. Statement to the Special Committee on Decolonization, Papua New Guinea, 28 July.
Rogers, Robert F
1995 *Destiny's Landfall: A History of Guam.* Honolulu: University of Hawai'i.
Rosaldo, Renato
1989 *Culture and Truth: The Remaking of Social Analysis.* Boston: Beacon Press.
Ross, N Crumrine
1982 Praying and Feasting: Modern Guamanian Fiestas. *Anthropos* 77:89–112.
Russell, Scott
1998 *Tiempon I Manmofo'na: Ancient Chamorro Culture and History of the Northern Mariana Islands.* Saipan: CNMI Division of Historic Preservation.
Sablan, David
1983 *The Book of My Life.* Agaña: Guam Publications.
Sablan, Joaquin Flores
1990 *My Mental Odyssey: Memoirs of the First Guamanian Protestant Missionary.* Poplar Bluff, MS: Stinson Press.
Safford, William E
1903–1905 The Chamorro Language of Guam. *American Anthropologist* 5, 6 and 7.
1905 *The Useful Plants of the Island of Guam with an Introductory Account of the Physical Features and Natural History of the Island, of the Character and History of its People, and of their Agriculture.* Volume 9. Washington, DC: Bulletin of the US National Museum (Smithsonian Institution).
1911 *Guam.* Reprint of a Lecture to the Society of the Sons of the American Revolution, Washington, DC.
Sanchez, Adrian
1990 *The Chamorro Brown Steward.* Tamuning, Guam: Star Press.
Sanchez, Pedro C
1979 *Uncle Sam, Please Come Back to Guam.* Tamuning, Guam: Sanchez Publishing.

1989   *Guahan/Guam: The History of Our Island*. Agaña: Sanchez Publishing House.

Sandoval, Chela
2000   *Methodology of the Oppressed*. Minneapolis: University of Minnesota.

Santos, Angel
1991a   Transfer of Chamoru Land from One Thief to Another. *The Guam Tribune*, 5 October, 14.
1991b   US Return Was Reoccupation, Not Liberation. *Pacific Daily News*, 21 July, 20, 22.
1991c   What Happened to Chamorro Land Trust Act? *The Guam Tribune*, 26 October, 14.

Santos, Elaine
1991   Speaking Words of Wisdom. *Hafa Magazine*, April, 8–12.

San Vitores, Diego Luis de
1981   Motives for Not Delaying Longer the Settlement and Christianization of the Islands of the Ladrones, Manila, May 1665. In *Positio* 1981b, 267–273.

Sardar, Ziauddin, and Borin Van Loon
1998   *Introducing Cultural Studies*. New York: Totem Books.

Scott, James
1985   *Weapons of the Weak*. New Haven: Yale University Press.

Searles, Paul J, and Ruth Searles
1937   *A School History of Guam*. Agaña: Guam Department of Education.

Siguenza, Eduardo
1992   Interview with author. Tumon, Guam, 10 February.

Silva, Noenoe K
2004   *Aloha Betrayed: Native Hawaiian Resistance to American Colonialism*. Durham, NC: Duke University Press.

Sizemore, Margaret
1985   Faithful Observe Martyrdom Mass of Sanvitores. *Pacific Daily News*, 3 April, 3

Skinner, Carlton
1997   *After Three Centuries: Representative Democracy and Civilian Government for Guam*. San Francisco: McDuff Press.

Smith, Andrea
2005   *Conquest: Sexual Violence and American Indian Genocide*. Cambridge, MA: South End Press.
2008   *Native Americans and the Christian Right: The Gendered Politics of Unlikely Alliances*. Durham: Duke University Press.

Solano, Francisco
1981   Letter of Father Francisco Solano, Superior of the Mission of the Ladrones, Guam, April 26, 1672. In *Positio* 1981b, 441– 450.

Souder, Laura Marie Torres
1987   *Daughters of the Island: Contemporary Chamorro Women Organizers on Guam*. Agaña: Micronesian Area Research Center.
1989   Psyche Under Siege: Uncle Sam, Look What You've Done to Us. Paper presented at the Ninth Annual Guam Association of Social Workers Conference, Guam, 30 March.

1991   A Tale of Two Anthems. Paper presented at the 17th Pacific Science Congress, Honolulu, Hawai'i, 31 May.

1992   *Daughters of the Island: Contemporary Chamorro Women Organizers on Guam.* Second edition. Lanham, MD: University Press of America.

Souder, Laura M T, and Robert A Underwood, editors

1987   *Chamorro Self-Determination (I Direchon y Taotao).* Agaña: The Chamorro Studies Association and Micronesian Area Research Center.

Spivak, Gayatri C

1988   Can the Subaltern Speak? In *Marxism and the Interpretation of Culture,* edited by Cary Nelson and Lawrence Grossberg, 271–313. Chicago: University of Illinois.

Stade, Ronald

1998   *Pacific Passages: World Culture and Local Politics in Guam.* Stockholm: Stockholm University.

Stevenson, Thomas B

2006   *Sons of the Church: The Witnessing of Gay Catholic Men.* Binghamton, NY: Haworth Press.

Stillman, Amy Ku'uleialoha

2001   Re-membering the History of Hawaiian Hula. In *Cultural Memory: Re-Configuring History and Identity in the Pacific,* edited by Jeannette Marie Mageo, 187–204. Honolulu: University of Hawai'i Press.

2003   Passed from the Past: Women and the Perpetuation of Hawaiian Music and Hula. In *Asian/Pacific Islander American Women: An Historical Anthology,* edited by Shirley Hune and Gail M Nomura, 205–218. New York: New York University Press.

2004   Pacific-ing Asian Pacific American History. *Journal of Asian American Studies* 7 (3): 241–270.

Story, John

1996   *What is Cultural Studies?* London: Edward Arnold.

Sturken, Marita, and Lisa Cartwright

2001   *Practices of Looking: An Introduction to Visual Culture.* London: Oxford.

Sullivan, Julius

1957   *The Phoenix Rises: A Mission History of Guam.* New York: Seraphic Mass Association.

Superior Court of Guam

1989a   Complaint for Injunctive Relief. CV 0-165-89. Agaña: Superior Court of Guam.

1989b   Ex Parte Motion for Temporary Restraining Order. CV 0165-891989. Agaña: Superior Court of Guam.

1989c   Settlement Agreement. CV 0165-89. Agaña: The Superior Court of Guam.

Tadiar, Neferti Xina

1993   Sexual Economies in the Asia-Pacific Community. In *What's in a Rim? Critical Perspectives on the Pacific Region Idea,* edited by Arif Dirlik, 183–210. Boulder, CO: Westview Press.

Taussig, Michael

1987   *Shamanism, Colonialism, and the Wild Man: A Study in Terror and Healing.* Chicago: University of Chicago Press.

Teaiwa, Teresia
  1997 Yaqona/Yagona: Roots and Routes of a Displaced Native. In *Dreadlocks in Oceania*, edited by S Mishra and E Guy, 7–13. Suva: Department of Literature and Language, University of the South Pacific.
  2000 bikinis and other s/pacific n/oceans. In *Voyaging Through the Contemporary Pacific*, edited by David Hanlon and Geoff White, 91–112. Lanham, MD: Rowman & Littlefield. First published in *The Contemporary Pacific* 6:87–109 (1994).
  2001a L(o)osing the Edge. *The Contemporary Pacific* 13:343–357.
  2001b Militarism, Tourism and the Native: Articulations in Oceania. PhD dissertation, University of California at Santa Cruz, Santa Cruz.
Te Awekotuku, Ngahuia
  1991 *Mana Wahine Maori: Collected Writings on Maori Women's Art, Culture, and Politics*. Auckland: New Women's Press.
Tengan, Ty Kāwika
  2008 *Native Men Remade: Gender and Nation in Contemporary Hawai'i*. Durham, NC: Duke University Press.
Teves, Oliver
  1998 Catholic Church Apologizes. *Pacific Daily News,* 19 March, 13.
Thompson, Laura
  1941 *Guam and Its People*. Studies of the Pacific 8. San Francisco: American Council Institute of Pacific Relations.
Thurston, Herbert
  1912 Devotion to the Blessed Virgin Mary. In *The Catholic Encyclopedia*. Volume 15. New York: Robert Appleton Company. Available online at http://www.newadvent.org/cathen/15459a.htm.
Tobin, Jeffrey
  1994 Cultural Construction and Native Nationalism: Report from the Hawaiian Front. In *Asia/Pacific as Space of Cultural Production,* edited by Rob Wilson and Arif Dirlik. Special issue of *Boundary* 2:111–133.
Topping, Donald, Pedro M Ogo, and Bernadita Dungca
  1975 *Chamorro-English Dictionary*. Honolulu: University of Hawai'i Press.
Trask, Haunani-Kay
  1991 Natives and Anthropologists: The Colonial Struggle. *The Contemporary Pacific* 3:159–167.
  1999 *From a Native Daughter: Colonialism and Sovereignty in Hawai'i*. Revised edition. Honolulu: University of Hawai'i Press and the Center for Hawaiian Studies.
Trompf, G W, editor
  1987 *The Gospel is Not Western: Black Theologies from the Southwest Pacific*. Maryknoll, NY: Orbis Books.
Tueller, James
  2000 Local Religion in Early Modern Guam: Chamorros, Spaniards and Others in the Marianas. Paper presented at the Society for Spanish and Portuguese Historical Studies, New York City, 30 April.
Umatuna Si Yuus
  1970 Soutane Worn by Fr San Vitores when He Suffered Martyrdom. *Umatuna Si Yuus* [*Praised Be the Lord,* Agaña diocesan newsletter], 14 June, 4.

Underwood, Jane H
  1973   Population History of Guam: Context of Microevolution. *Micronesica* 9
          (1): 11–44.
  1976   The Native Origins of the Neo-Chamorros of the Mariana Islands. *Micro-*
          nesica 12 (2): 203–209.
Underwood, Robert A
  1977   Red, Whitewash and Blue: Painting Over the Chamorro Experience.
          Islander Magazine, Pacific Daily News, 17 July, 6–8.
  1984   On Self Determination. *Guam Tribune,* 19 May.
  1985   Excursions into Inauthenticity: The Chamorros of Guam. In *Mobility and*
          Identity in the Island Pacific, edited by Murray Chapman. Special issue of
          Pacific Viewpoint 26 (1): 160–184.
  1987   American Education and the Acculturation of the Chamorros of Guam.
          PhD dissertation, University of Southern California, Los Angeles.
  1990   The Consciousness of Guam and the Maladjusted People. *Pacific Ties* 13
          (4): 9, 18.
  1997   Teaching Guam History in Guam High Schools. In *Guam History: Per-*
          spectives, edited by Lee D Carter, William L Wuerch, and Rosa Roberto
          Carter, 1:1–10. Mangilao: Richard F Taitano Micronesian Area Research
          Center.
  2001   Afterword. In *A Campaign for Political Rights on the Island of Guam, 1899–*
          1950, by Penelope Bordallo Hofschneider, 201–213. Saipan: CNMI Divi-
          sion of Historic Preservation.
United States Navy
  1951   *US Navy Report on Guam, 1898–1950.* Washington, DC: US Government
          Printing Office.
Van Meijl, Toon, and Paul van der Grijp
  1993   Introduction: Politics, Tradition and Social Change in the Pacific. *BKI*
          Bijdragen tot de Taal-, Land- en Volkenkunde 149:635–647.
Van Peenen, Mavis Warner
  1974   *Chamorro Legends on the Island of Guam.* Mangilao: Micronesian Area
          Research Center.
Velarde, Pedro Murillo, SJ [Society of Jesus]
  1987   *The "Reduccion" of the Islands of the Ladrones, the Discovery of the Islands of the*
          Palaos, and Other Happenings. Translated by Felicia Plaza, MMB. MARC
          Working Paper 51. Mangilao: Micronesian Area Research Center.
von Kotzebue, Otto
  1821   *A Voyage of Discovery into the South Sea and Bering's Straits.* Translated by H E
          Lloyd. London: Longman, Hurst, Rees, Orme, and Brown.
Walter, Richard
  1928   *Anson's Voyage Round the World.* London: Martin Hopkinson Ltd.
White, Geoffrey M
  1991   *Identity Through History: Living Stories in a Solomon Islands Society.* Cam-
          bridge, UK: Cambridge University Press.
White, Geoffrey M, and Lamont Lindstrom
  1998   *Chiefs Today: Traditional Pacific Leadership and the Postcolonial State.* Palo
          Alto, CA: Stanford University Press.

White, Geoffrey M, and Ty Kāwika Tengan
    2001   Disappearing Worlds: Anthropology and Cultural Studies in Hawai'i and the Pacific. *The Contemporary Pacific* 13:381–416.

White, Hayden
    1973   *Metahistory: The Historical Imagination in Nineteenth-Century Europe.* Baltimore, MD: Johns Hopkins University Press.
    1978   *Tropics of Discourse: Essays in Cultural Criticism.* Baltimore, MD: Johns Hopkins University Press.
    1981   The Narrativization of Real Events. *Critical Inquiry* 7 (4): 793–798.
    1987   *The Content of the Form: Narrative Discourse and Historical Representation.* Baltimore, MD: Johns Hopkins University Press.

Wood, Houston
    2003   Cultural Studies for Oceania. *The Contemporary Pacific* 15:340–374.

Woodward, Kenneth L
    1990   *Making Saints: How the Catholic Church Determines Who Becomes a Saint, Who Doesn't, and Why.* New York: Simon & Shuster.

Yaoch, Felix
    1985   A Homily of Priestly Reflections. Biba, Sanvitores, Biba! *Pacific Daily News,* 10 November, 35, 39.

Young, Kanalu G
    1998   *Rethinking the Native Hawaiian Past.* New York: Garland Publishing.

Young, Robert
    2001   *Postcolonialism: An Historical Introduction.* Oxford: Blackwell Publishers.

Index

About the Author

Vicente "Vince" Diaz is Pohnpeian and Filipino from Guam. He attended the University of Guam and transferred to the University of Hawai'i at Mānoa, where he earned his bachelor's and master's degrees in political science in the early to mid 1980s. While at Mānoa Diaz also earned a graduate certificate in urban and regional planning, worked with the Pacific Basin Development Council in Honolulu, and later, served as a graduate researcher at the East-West Center's Institute of Culture and Communication. In 1992 he received his doctorate degree from the History of Consciousness program at the University of California at Santa Cruz, and returned to the University of Guam where he taught Pacific history and Micronesian studies. Diaz moved to the University of Michigan in 2001 where he helped create the Asian/Pacific Islander American Studies unit in the Program in American Culture

A student and practitioner of traditional Carolinian seafaring, Diaz served as the coordinator of the Micronesian Seafaring Society, and helped found the Guam Traditional Seafaring Society and its canoehouse, Sahyan Tasi Fachemwaan, which enjoys close relations with the *utt*s (canoe houses) Wenemai and Wenebuku, from Polowat Atoll in the Central Caroline Islands. Diaz wrote and directed the 1997 documentary *Sacred Vessels: Navigating Tradition and Identity in Micronesia.*

Production Notes for Diaz / Repositioning the Missionary

Designed by UH Press Design & Production Department
with text in New Baskerville and display in Palatino

Printing and binding by The Maple-Vail Book Manufacturing Group